International Labour Law

International Labour Law

Fifth Edition

Jean-Michel Servais

This book was originally published as a monograph in the International Encyclopaedia of Laws/Labour Law and Industrial Relations.

Founding Editor: Roger Blanpain
General Editor: Frank Hendrickx

Wolters Kluwer

Published by:
Kluwer Law International B.V.
PO Box 316
2400 AH Alphen aan den Rijn
The Netherlands
Website: www.wolterskluwerlr.com

Sold and distributed in North, Central and South America by:
Wolters Kluwer Legal & Regulatory U.S.
7201 McKinney Circle
Frederick, MD 21704
United States of America
Email: customer.service@wolterskluwer.com

Sold and distributed in all other countries by:
Quadrant
Rockwood House
Haywards Heath
West Sussex
RH16 3DH
United Kingdom
Email: international-customerservice@wolterskluwer.com

ISBN 97890-411-8909-7

e-Book: ISBN 97890-411-8938-7
web-PDF: ISBN 97890-411-8979-0

This title is available on www.kluwerlawonline.com

The Author

Professor Jean-Michel Servais (born 23 June 1945) studied at the University of Liège, in Belgium. He obtained a first degree in philosophy and literature in 1965, and a doctorate of law in 1968. The same year he was appointed barrister-at-law in Liège and also research assistant at the Faculty of Law of the University of Liège. He was awarded *Doctor honoris causa* from the University Attila J'zsef (Szeged, Hungary) in 1997.

He joined the International Labour Office in Geneva on an external competition in 1972. He was in particular Deputy Regional Director of the ILO for Asia and the Pacific in Bangkok (Thailand), Research Coordinator at the International Institute for Labour Studies, and Director of Operations of the ILO Regional Office for Arab States, in Beirut (Lebanon). He retired from the ILO in 2005.

He was elected Secretary-General (1988–2001) and later Honorary President of the International Society for Labour Law and Social Security. He is a member of the International Industrial Relations Association, and a non-national member of the Russian Association of Labour Law and Social Security. Visiting professor at the Faculty of Law of the University of Liège (1993–2015) and Gerona (Spain), since 2006, he has given courses and lectures in various universities and other institutions in a number of countries. He is an Associate Member of COMPTRASEC (Centre of Comparative Labour and Social Security Law, University Montesquieu Bordeaux IV), a member of various academic associations and of the scientific committee of several reviews. He is the author of numerous books and articles in the field of international and comparative labour law and industrial relations. They have been published in French, English, Spanish, Bulgarian, German, Portuguese, Japanese, Russian and Greek.

They include: *The International Labour Organization*, in R. Blanpain (ed.), *International Encyclopaedia of Laws* (Deventer), Kluwer, 3rd edn, 2011; *Droits en synergie sur le travail. Eléments de droits international et comparé du travail*, Brussels, Bruylant, 1997; Portuguese version: São Paulo, LTr, 2001; *Droit international du travail*, Brussels, Larcier, 2015; *Droit social de l'Union européenne*, 2nd edn, Brussels, Bruylant, 2011.

The Author

Table of Contents

Table of Contents

List of Abbreviations

ANN	*Annuaire Français de droit international*
BYBIL	*The British Year Book of International Law*
CEACR	Committee of Experts for the Application of Conventions and Recommendations
Comp. Labour Law	*Comparative Labour Law and Policy Journal & Pol. Journal*
CFA	ILO Governing Body Freedom of Association Committee
CJEU	Court of Justice of the European Union
Dr. Soc.	*Droit Social*
ECOSOC	United Nations Economic and Social Council
EBRD	European Bank for Reconstruction and Development
ELLJ	*European Labour Law Journal*
EU	European Union
FAO	Food and Agriculture Organization of the United Nations
GATT	General Agreement on Trade and Tariffs
GB	Governing Body of the International Labour Office
IBRD	International Bank for Reconstruction and Development
ICAO	International Civil Aviation Organization
ICEM	Inter-governmental Committee for European Migration
ICFTU	International Confederation of Free Trade Unions
ICJ	International Court of Justice
ICM	Inter-governmental Committee for Migration
ICSC	International Civil Service Commission
IILS	International Institute for Labour Studies

List of Abbreviations

IJCLLIR	*International Journal of Comparative Labour Law and Industrial Relations*
ILC	International Labour Conference
ILO	International Labour Organization/International Labour Office
ILR	*International Labour Review*
IMF	International Monetary Fund
IOE	International Organization of Employers
IPEC	International Programme on the Elimination of Child Labour
ISSA	International Social Security Association
ITS	International Trade Secretariats
L. of N.	League of Nations
MERCOSUR	Common Market of the Southern Cone
MLC	Maritime Labour Convention
NAFTA	North American Free Trade Agreement
NGO	Non-governmental organization
OAS	Organization of American States
OAU	Organization of African Unity (African Unity (AU) from 2001)
OB	Official Bulletin of the International Labour Organization
OECD	Organisation for Economic Cooperation and Development
PCIJ	Permanent Court of International Justice (from 1922 to 1946)
PIACT	International Programme for the Improvement of Working Conditions and Environment
RCADI	*Recueil des Cours de l'Académie de Droit international*
Rev. Dr. Int.	*Revue de Droit international et de Législation comparée et Lég. Comp.*
Rev. fr. aff. soc.	*Revue Française des affaires sociales*
RGDIP	*Revue générale de Droit international public*
RP	Record of Proceedings of the ILC
RTDeur	*Revue trimestrielle de droit européen*
SMEs	Small- and medium-sized enterprises
SPF	Social Protection Floor

STEP	Strategies and Tools against Social Exclusion and Poverty
UN	United Nations
UNDP	United Nations Development Programme
UNESCO	United Nations Educational, Scientific and Cultural Organization
UNFPA	United Nations Population Fund
UNHCR	Office of the United Nations High Commissioner for Refugees
WCL	World Confederation of Labour
WFP	World Food Programme
WHO	World Health Organization
WTO	World Trade Organization

Preface

1. The subject of this monograph is international labour law. The book discusses legal rules, although the reader will occasionally be reminded that not all of the texts adopted have the force of law. It considers a branch of law that is international, and more specifically universal, in origin; it does not deal with regional instruments directly because they address a wide range of issues. The question of what law applies, of where jurisdiction lies in situations with a foreign component, is also distinct; it is a matter for private international labour law. The concept of labour, for its part, is used in the broad sense that also covers social security. One final terminological note: the vocabulary employed here was chosen with an eye to the readers for whom these pages were written, namely researchers and practitioners who are familiar with the law. It does not necessarily correspond to the language routinely used in international institutions.

2. There are many reasons for lawyers, political and other social scientists to acquaint themselves with or to look in greater depth at this branch of the law. One obvious aim is to familiarize oneself with the legal instruments in force and with the scope of States' obligations. Ratifications by the States play a key role in this respect, hence, as we shall see, the measures taken by the International Labour Organization (ILO) to promote them. But that is not the only reason. Even in the absence of ratification, legislators base their texts, the government its social policy, employers' organizations and trade unions their collective bargaining positions, companies their codes of conduct, and the judiciary[1] its rulings, on the international labour conventions and recommendations. The value of the latter therefore far exceeds their intrinsic legal force. Lastly, international labour standards are invaluable benchmarks in comparative law. Indeed, when texts from several countries are compared, especially when those countries are dissimilar in nature, international labour standards are both useful instruments of analysis and excellent yardsticks for identifying common denominators. They even serve to gauge the degree to which a given body of law conforms to universally accepted general principles.[2]

1. M. Brassey, 'Something new, something borrowed … : comparative labour law in South Africa', in R. Blanpain and M. Weiss (eds.), *The Changing Face of Labour Law and Industrial Relation: Liber amicorum Clyde W. Summers*, Baden-Baden, Nomos Verlagsgesellschaft, 1993, pp. 139–140.
2. J.-M. Servais, *Droits en synergie sur le travail. Eléments de droits international et comparé du travail*, Brussels, Bruylant, p. 25 *et seq.*

3. The monograph's outline is simple. The general introduction puts international labour law in perspective. It analyses the reasons for its inception and its relevance in a world that has changed beyond recognition. It considers in particular the long-standing – but still topical – question of the relationship between international law and economic competition and situates international labour standards within the constitutional framework of ILO, which has issued most of them. Part I inquires into the sources of this branch of the law. Part II examines the content of international labour legislation and Part III, its implementation.

General Introduction

Chapter 1. The Founding Principles of the ILO and their Relevance Today

§1. The Founding Principles of International Labour Legislation

4. The basic intention of the founders of ILO was to create a standard-producing institution, for several reasons. Chief among them was the plight of workers – men, women and children – in the countries industrializing in the 19th century. The first to be concerned were not only thinkers (the economist Jérôme-Adolphe Blanqui), politicians and leaders of the emerging labour and socialist movements, they were also civil servants (the Belgian Edouard Ducpétiaux, General Inspector of Prisons and Benevolent Establishments), and medical doctors like Louis-René Villermé (whose celebrated *Tableau de l'état physique et moral des ouvriers employés dans les manufactures de coton, de laine et de soie* was published in Paris in 1840). They were also humanistic employers such as Robert Owen and Charles Hindley in Great Britain and Daniel le Grand in France.

5. In the case of employers and politicians, however, the charitable urge to impose constraints on *laissez-faire* conditions of labour was set against a preoccupation that was economic in nature:[3] the firms introducing improvements in employment conditions could find themselves penalized *vis-à-vis* their direct competitors in that their production costs rose as a result. The leaders of those firms consequently sought to obtain generalized minimum guarantees for wage earners and regulations that were applicable to everyone.[4] National parliaments were prompted to act out of the same concern. In 1802, the British Parliament adopted a statute prohibiting children from working longer than twelve hours per day. In actual fact, however, the statute applied only to those – no matter what their age – placed as apprentices by parishes in new factories; it was apparently not effectively

3. Concerns of this kind can even be found in the writings of the Swiss Financier and Minister of State under the French King Louis XVI, particularly in a passage of his book *De l'importance des opinions religieuses* (Liège), C. Plomteux, 1788, pp. 203–211, devoted to the 'day of rest'.
4. *See* J.-J. Oechslin, 'Les employeurs et les normes internationales du travail', in R.J. Dupuy (ed.), *Mélanges en l'honneur de Nicolas Valticos*, Droit et Justice, Paris, Pedone, 1999, p. 586. This reason differs from the questionable argument that relies solely on market failures to justify international labour standards: *see* G. Davidov, 'Comment on Alan Hyde: The Perils of Economic Justifications for International Labor Standards', *Law and Ethics of Human Rights*, Vol. 3(2), 2009, Article 3.

implemented, at least not immediately.[5] Prussia enacted legislation on the matter in 1839, France in 1841.[6] Other statutes and other countries followed.

6. Another reason for enacting legislation was related to the deteriorating physical strength of a large swathe of the population. It is a little known fact that many young working class men were declared unfit for military service, a sign that their health was rapidly deteriorating because of the conditions in which they worked and lived. The toiling masses were in part becoming so physically worn out that their condition could affect the productive and even strategic capacities of the countries concerned. Yet another factor was concern to safeguard industrial harmony and political peace. Indeed, the so-called 'social question' risked undermining the unity of the State.

7. The movement sought to consolidate its accomplishments by having them adopted internationally, for the same reasons. Robert Owen set the example in his own workshops and worked to spread his ideas for reform. He travelled to Germany, France and Switzerland, and presented two *mémoires* in 1818: the first in Frankfurt, to the German Diet for all governments, the first and second to the plenipotentiaries of the Conference of European Powers meeting in Aix-la-Chapelle. It would seem, however, that the idea of international labour treaties was first expressed by another industrialist, Charles Hindley, a member of the British Parliament. It surfaced again some little time later in France, in the words of L.R. Villermé and J.-A. Blanqui, and above all in the letters of Daniel le Grand. All were concerned that stiff economic competition between manufacturers and countries should be no obstacle to the introduction of the necessary changes.[7] Nevertheless, the first national labour laws were adopted before the first international rules.

8. The desire to ease the plight of workers, compounded by the fear – challenged by some – that any easing of employment conditions would work in favour of foreign competitors, led to a multitude of efforts for international legislation. The International Benevolent Conference, behind which E. Ducpétiaux was one of the driving forces, worked to that end during successive sessions in Brussels and Frankfort. International legislation was also discussed in Germany, France, Austria and Belgium, in particular in academic circles and among industrialists. The French Parliament followed in their footsteps, as did the Swiss. Indeed, the latter were the first to give the idea a more official form. On 30 April 1881, the Helvetic Confederation invited the Federal Council to consult with other industrialized States about the adoption of such legislation. This first initiative was not very favourably received in

5. *See for example* E. Mahaim, *Le droit international ouvrier,* Paris, Librairie de la Société du Recueil Sirey, 1913, pp. 7–8; J.W. Follows, *Antecedents of the International Labour Organization*, Oxford, Clarendon Press, 1951, p. 179.
6. With the exception of an Imperial Decree of 1813 that prohibited underground work of children under 10.
7. *See in particular* G. Scelle, *L'Organisation internationale du Travail et le BIT,* Paris, Rivière, 1930, p. 19 *et seq.*; Follows, *op. cit.*, pp. 1–57; N. Valticos, *Droit international du travail*, Paris, Dalloz, 2nd edn, 1983, para. 3 *et seq.*; V.Y. Ghebali, *L'Organisation internationale du Travail (OIT)*, Geneva, Georg, 1987, p. 21 *et seq.*

the countries contacted. From that moment on, however, there was growing pressure for international rules and, most importantly, international legislation won the support of socialist and trade union congresses, which until then had been dominated by the partisans of purely revolutionary action.[8]

9. We know more about what happened next.[9] The German Kaiser, Wilhelm II, took up the Swiss proposal to convene an international conference on working conditions. The resulting conference was held in Berlin, in March 1890, and was attended by Germany, Austro-Hungary, Belgium, Denmark, France, Great Britain, Italy, Luxembourg, the Netherlands, Portugal, Sweden, Norway and Switzerland. The outcome fell short of expectations. The following year, however, Pope Leon XIII published his famous encyclical, *Rerum Novarum*, calling on the public authorities to take 'the necessary measures to safeguard the health and interests of the working class'. Following the conference, two other international conferences were held in 1897: one of workers in Zurich, which was attended by the representatives of socialist and social Christian workers' organizations, the other in Brussels, which was attended by numerous academics and representatives of business, administrative and diplomatic circles (in particular delegates to the Berlin Conference). Both conferences proposed the establishment of an international association for the legal protection of workers. The concept had been set in motion. It took tangible form in 1900 in Paris, during an international conference on labour legislation.

10. Under the terms of its statutes, the purpose of the International Association for the Legal Protection of Workers[10] was to serve as a link between those in industrialized countries who considered legislation to protect workers a necessity. It was given the task of organizing, an essential step in the history of the establishment of ILO, an international labour agency whose mission was to publish (in German, English and French) a periodic review of national labour legislation. The Association was also charged with promoting examination of concordance between laws protecting workers and to prompt the convening of international conferences on labour legislation. Although it was private, the Association had the support of many quarters in European governments and received assistance from some of them. The Swiss authorities provided the newly established office with headquarters in Basle. The International Committee heading the Association was made up of delegates from the national sections and of government representatives. The constituent

---

8. A more detailed analysis of the development in the concept of an international labour legislation during that period may be found in Follows, *op. cit.*, p. 43 *et seq.*; Valticos, *op. cit.*, para. 12 *et seq.*; Mahaim, *op. cit.*, p. 196 *et seq.*

9. *See* J.-M. Servais, 'International Labour Organization' (ILO) in R. Blanpain (ed.) *International Encyclopaedia of Laws*, The Hague, Kluwer, 3rd edn, 2011; J.T. Shotwell (ed.), *The Origins of International Labor Organization,* New York, Columbia University Press, Vol. 1, 1934; E. Mahaim, 'L'Organisation Permanente du Travail', *RCADI* (Brussels), 1924, Vol. III, p. 69 *et seq.*

10. *See in particular* E. Mahaim, 'L'Association internationale pour la protection légale des travailleurs. Son histoire. Son but. Son oeuvre', *Revue économique intenationale* (Brussels), October 1904, p. 3 *et seq.*; L.E. Troclet, *Législation sociale internationale,* Brussels, Librairie Encyclopédique, 1952, I, pp. 213–218.

assembly was held in Basle, in September 1901, and was attended by delegates from Germany, Austria, Belgium, France, Italy, the Netherlands and Switzerland. Other countries, including the United States, joined later.

11. The delegates meeting in Basel identified the issues to be dealt with first: the prohibition of night work for women and regulation of the use of two especially toxic products, white phosphorus and lead. The Cologne Assembly, held the following year, decided not to follow up on the latter issue. Preparatory work got under way on the other, and the results were submitted to two successive conferences organized in Bern, a technical conference held in 1905 and a diplomatic conference held in 1906, that adopted two international labour conventions. Although bilateral treaties already existed (one example being the Franco-Italian Treaty of 15 April 1904), these were the first truly international labour conventions. They stipulated that the governments would inform each other of the laws and regulations they adopted on the subject-matter dealt with and would produce periodic reports on implementation. This marked the starting point of the system by which international labour standards are drawn up and monitored. The Association was in the process of drafting other instruments when war broke out in 1914.

§2. The First World War and the Founding of the ILO

12. The First World War considerably changed the general, political and social context in which these initial attempts at international regulation took place. All the belligerents, including those on the side of Germany, acknowledged the suffering and sacrifices of workers during this period and the debt of gratitude they were owed by their countries. The workers, for their part, were represented by powerful political organizations and trade unions that were markedly international in character. Some of these movements – those that triumphed in Russia – were revolutionary in nature, others were reformist and believed in thorough but peaceful change.[11] Fear of the former undoubtedly acted as a powerful stimulus for politicians like Clemenceau and Lloyd George, the French and British Prime Ministers, and caused them to cast a very favourable eye on proposals to include labour clauses in the peace treaties. Indeed, the workers had been promised that their conditions would be improved once the hostilities had ended. At the same time, the future of millions of demobilized soldiers was becoming a matter of urgent concern.

13. Part XIII of the Peace Treaty signed on 29 June 1919 in the Hall of Mirrors at the Chateau of Versailles was devoted to labour and the establishment of a permanent labour organization. It laid the foundation for the ILO Constitution and for the new institution's tripartite character, i.e. the participation in its governing bodies, in particular the annual Conference and the Governing Body, of employers' and workers' representatives alongside government delegates. The Preamble speaks of

---

11. An in-depth analysis of the workers' organizations at the time where the ILO was created may be found in A. Berenstein, *Les organisations ouvrières. Leur compétence et leur rôle dans la Société des Nations et notamment dans l'Organisation internationale du Travail,* Paris, Pédone, 1936.

the links between universal peace and social justice, and states that 'conditions of labour exist involving such injustice, hardship, and privation to large numbers of people as to produce unrest so great that the peace and harmony of the world are imperilled'. Part XIII ends with Article 427, which lists the methods and principles for regulating labour conditions which all industrial communities should endeavour to apply, so far as their special circumstances permit. It provides a non-exhaustive list of nine such methods and principles:

> First. … labour should not be regarded merely as a commodity or article of commerce.
>
> Second. The right of association for all lawful purposes by the employed as well as by the employers.
>
> Third. The payment to the employed of a wage adequate to maintain a reasonable standard of life as this is understood in their time and country.
>
> Fourth. The adoption of an eight hours day or a forty-eight hours week as the standard to be aimed at where it has not already been attained.
>
> Fifth. The adoption of a weekly rest of at least twenty-four hours, which should include Sunday wherever practicable.
>
> Sixth. The abolition of child labour and the imposition of such limitations on the labour of young persons as shall permit the continuation of their education and assure their proper physical development.
>
> Seventh. The principle that men and women should receive equal remuneration for work of equal value.
>
> Eighth. The standard set by law in each country with respect to the conditions of labour should have due regard to the equitable economic treatment of all workers lawfully resident therein.
>
> Ninth. Each State should make provision for a system of inspection in which women should take part, in order to ensure the enforcement of the laws and regulations for the protection of the employed.

The article goes on to state that, without claiming that these methods and principles are either complete or final, 'the High Contracting Parties are of [the] opinion that they are well fitted to guide the policy of the League of Nations; and that, if adopted by the industrial communities who are members of the League, and safeguarded in practice by an adequate system of such inspection, they will confer lasting benefits upon the wage-earners of the world'.

14. Article 396 defines the functions of the Organization's secretariat, the International Labour Office. Those functions include the collection and distribution of information 'relating to the international adjustment of conditions of industrial life and labour', in particular the examination of subjects to be brought to the attention of the annual International Labour Conference, 'with a view to the conclusion of international conventions, and the conduct of such special investigations as may be ordered by the Conference'. Numerous other articles deal with the procedures for preparing and monitoring international labour standards, an area in which ILO obviously played a pioneering role. The matter is discussed in detail later in this monograph.

15. The idea of establishing treaty-based labour regulations was thus founded on the fundamental principles already underlined and summed up in the Preamble to Part XIII of the Treaty of Versailles. The first was obviously the pursuit of social justice and the eradication of unacceptable working conditions. Tackling the problem internationally would serve to produce joint realistic and coherent solutions to complex issues pertaining to industrial relations; this approach also made it easier to solve conflicts of law when the labour relationship had a foreign component, in that it implied the harmonization of national legislation and limited the number of contradictions between bilateral treaties (in particular in the case of migrants). The ILO's standards naturally served as a reference for national lawmakers, and their ratification strengthened the national laws enacted, since the latter could no longer be amended in a way that was less favourable than the convention to the workers.[12]

16. The Preamble expressly links social justice with the desire for lasting peace: peace, and harmony in the world, would be imperilled by miserable working conditions, with serious unrest the result. The text clearly refers to internal as much as to international harmony; as we have seen, the communist revolution worried more than one statesman.

17. The Preamble ends with the famous whereas clause that 'the failure of any nation to adopt humane conditions of labour is an obstacle in the way of other nations which desire to improve the conditions in their own countries'. This can be interpreted to refer to two things[13] that are far from being mutually exclusive: one is the danger of contamination by a 'poor example', the other is the risk that firms and countries will use labour costs to obtain a competitive edge. In the latter interpretation, international labour standards are said to work as a firewall against those who seek to profit, in a context of stiff international competition, from mediocre or exploitive working conditions. This argument, as we can see, is intended more to dissipate a fear than to stimulate the preparation of an international labour code, and indeed it is shot through with ambiguity. How easy it is to demonstrate the potential for confusion between the individual interests of the manufacturers and the general interest of the national economy, not to mention the impossibility of putting a figure on what proportion of an item's production cost is eaten up by obviously limited social costs; how easy to protest the argument's overuse for protectionist purposes, and to point out that it is relatively flimsy in that the States retain the sovereign right to ratify any conventions adopted, which, moreover, contain no truly coercive measures. What is more, in many cases national lawmakers had not waited for the vote on international instruments to provide workers with guarantees, and industry did not suffer as a result, quite the contrary. All this being said it must nevertheless be added that ILO has always promoted, including in its standards, a harmonious balance between social progress and economic development. Indeed, Article 427 of the Treaty of Versailles provides that 'differences of climate, habits, and customs, of

12. Article 405, last paragraph already provided that 'in no case shall any Member be asked or required, as a result of the adoption of any recommendation or draft convention by the Conference, to lessen the protection afforded by its existing legislation to the workers concerned'.
13. *See for example* Shotwell, *op. cit.*, p. 15.

economic opportunity and industrial tradition, make strict uniformity in the conditions of labour difficult of immediate attainment'.

§3. The Inter-war Period and the Consolidation of the System

18. The provisions of the Treaty of Versailles that led to the establishment of ILO gave the Organization broad authority in a number of areas. It is hardly surprising that their exact reach soon gave rise to controversy. Nor is it surprising that the controversy broke out at a time when the economic crisis that appeared on the heels of the First World War was fostering a tendency to retrench the generous plans for labour drawn up when the hostilities ended. Between 1922 and 1932, the Permanent Court of International Justice handed down four opinions in which it spoke of the very broad terms in which ILO's constitutional texts had been drafted. It considered in particular that the Organization's mandate extended to the regulation of the working conditions of people employed in agriculture, of employers who toiled alongside their workers (on a subsidiary basis and in order to protect certain wage earners) and to non-manual labourers (a propos of the applicability of Convention No. 4 on the night work of women, 1919, to women who held positions of supervision and management and were not ordinarily engaged in manual work). In the fourth case – relating to agricultural production – the Court considered that ILO could not be prevented from deliberating matters that had been entrusted to it on the pretext that such deliberation implied the examination of certain aspects of the means and methods of production, or the effect of the measures proposed on production.[14]

19. The inter-war period also saw the first of the Organization's technical assistance missions. These constituted an indispensable supplement to the standard-setting work undertaken since ILO's inception, and concerned specifically labour legislation in general (Venezuela, 1936), subjects dealt with in international labour conventions and recommendations or related thereto (social insurance: Greece and Romania, 1930; United States, 1936; Canada and Venezuela, 1938; Ecuador, United Kingdom, Turkey, 1939; migration: Venezuela, 1938; occupational health and safety: Egypt, 1939; labour inspection and administration: China, 1931; Egypt, 1932; Cuba, 1934; Venezuela, 1936) and other subjects (cooperatives: France, 1937).[15]

---

14. *See* advisory opinions No. 2 of 12 August 1922, No. 3 of the same date, No. 13 of 26 July 1926 and the one dated 15 November 1932 respectively in the *Official Bulletin* of 6 September 1922, Vol. VI, No. 10, pp. 339–351; 13 September 1922, Vol. VI, No. 11, pp. 377–382; 30 September 1926 (revised edition), Vol. XI, No. 5, pp. 302–316; and 15 December 1932, Vol. XVII, No. 5, pp. 179–197; *see also* C.W. Jenks, 'La compétence de l'Organisation internationale du Travail. Examen de quatre avis consultatifs rendus par la Cour permanente de Justice internationale', *Rev. Dr. Int. et Lég. Comp.* (Brussels), No. 1, 1937, pp. 156–183, No. 3, pp. 586–623; Valticos, *op. cit.*, paras 114 and 232–236; L. Chaudouart, *Le rôle de l'Organisation internationale du Travail dans l'activité économique*, Paris, Domat-Montchrestien, 1933, p. 16 *et seq.*
15. *See* ILO, *First Report of the International Labour Organization to the United Nations* (Geneva), ILO, 1947, p. 123 *et seq.*; *see also* on this point A. Aboughanem, *Etude sur les relations entre les*

§4. THE CONSEQUENCES OF THE 1939–1945 WAR: FIRM PRIORITIES

20. During the Second World War, the Organization – which had moved to Montreal, Canada – sought to maintain its routine activities in spite of the easily imagined obstacles, most of them budgetary, it encountered. It continued to conduct technical assistance projects relating to international labour standards, namely on labour legislation (Bolivia, French Provisional Government, Haiti), social insurance (Bolivia, Chile, United Kingdom, Canada, Haiti, Venezuela), labour statistics (Argentina, Brazil, Canada, Chile, Uruguay)[16] and industrial relations (Canada).

21. In the meantime, on 14 August 1941 the President of the United States, Franklin Roosevelt, and the British Prime Minister, Winston Churchill, issued a joint declaration from the *Potomac*, 'somewhere in the Atlantic Ocean', containing a set of principles that laid the groundwork for the future peace.[17] The Atlantic Charter emphasized freedom from fear – respect for human rights – and freedom from want – the fight against poverty. It clearly was a source of inspiration for the authors of the declaration adopted in Philadelphia on 10 May 1944 by the International Labour Conference to update the Organization's objectives and underscore its priorities. That Declaration was solemnly appended to the ILO Constitution.

22. The Declaration spells out four fundamental principles. First, labour is not a commodity; this, the principle of protection of the worker's person, is a fundamental principle of labour legislation. Secondly, two human rights, freedom of expression and of association, are of vital importance (without them, there can be no independent workers' or employers' associations). Third is the war on poverty (poverty 'anywhere constitutes a danger to prosperity everywhere') and want ('to be carried on with unrelenting vigour within each nation, and by continuous and concerted international effort'). Fourth is the principle of tripartism (the international effort must involve 'the representatives of workers and employers, enjoying equal status with those of governments' and participating 'in free discussion and democratic decision with a view to the promotion of the common welfare'). The Declaration also recalls that lasting peace is based on social justice, which must constitute the central aim of any national or international policy: 'all human beings, irrespective of race, creed or sex, have the right to pursue both their material well-being and their spiritual development in conditions of freedom and dignity, of economic security and equal opportunity'.

---

normes internationales du travail et la coopération technique (Geneva, ILO), 1985, (limited distribution), p. 13; A. Alcock, *History of the International Labour Organization*, London, Macmillan, 1971, pp. 134–148. From 1925 to 1929, the League's High Commissioner for Refugees had even requested the ILO's collaboration in employment programmes for refugees. *See* ILC, 12th session (Geneva, 1929), Vol. II: *Report of the Director presented to the Conference*, Geneva, ILO, 1929, pp. 32 and 215–217.

16. ILO, *First Report of the International Labour Organization*, *op. cit.*
17. Servais, *op. cit.*, para. 30 *et seq.*

23. The Declaration casts a fresh light on the role of economic and social policies in attaining social goals.[18] It sets out a ten-point programme of action:

(a) full employment and the raising of standards of living;
(b) the employment of workers in the occupations in which they can have the satisfaction of giving the fullest measure of their skill and attainments and make their greatest contribution to the common well-being;
(c) the provision, as a means to the attainment of this end and under adequate guarantees for all concerned, of facilities for training and the transfer of labour, including migration for employment and settlement;
(d) policies in regard to wages and earnings, hours and other conditions of work calculated to ensure a just share of the fruits of progress to all, and a minimum living wage to all employed and in need of such protection;
(e) the effective recognition of the right of collective bargaining, the cooperation of management and labour in the continuous improvement of productive efficiency, and the collaboration of workers and employers in the preparation and application of social and economic measures;
(f) the extension of social security measures to provide a basic income to all in need of such protection and comprehensive medical care;
(g) adequate protection for the life and health of workers in all occupations;
(h) provision for child welfare and maternity protection;
(i) the provision of adequate nutrition, housing and facilities for recreation and culture;
(j) the assurance of equality of educational and vocational opportunity.

24. The Declaration is applicable 'to all peoples everywhere'. Although it states that due regard must be given to the stage of social and economic development reached by each people, its progressive application to all 'is a matter of concern to the whole civilized world'.

25. ILO was prompted by the programme's focus on full employment to give top priority to the matter: it adopted new instruments that were programmatic in nature rather than containing specific legal obligations (Employment Policy Convention (No. 122), 1964, and Human Resources Development Convention (No. 142), 1975, in particular, as well as several recommendations); it conducted employment-related technical cooperation activities; and in 1969, on the occasion of the Organization's fiftieth anniversary, it launched a world employment programme.[19]

26. The Philadelphia Declaration also placed special emphasis on human rights, in particular freedom of association (and of expression) and equality of opportunity and treatment. Those issues have been at the heart of the Organization's work ever

18. *See* E. Lee, 'The Declaration of Philadelphia: Retrospect and Prospect', *ILR*, Vol. 133, No. 4, 1994, pp. 470–472; also C.W. Jenks, 'The Declaration of Philadelphia after twenty-five years', in *Social Policy in a Changing World: The ILO Response: Selected Speeches*, Geneva, ILO, 1976, p. 60.
19. C.W. Jenks, *Social Policy in a Changing World: The ILO Response: Selected Speeches*, Geneva, ILO, 1976, p. 29; Lee, *op. cit.*, p. 527.

since. They were on occasion fiercely debated in connection with the struggle for decolonization (and against apartheid) and democratization (thus, the countries of communist Europe were frequently denounced for infringements of freedom of association, for forced labour and employment discrimination). Of course, ILO had not waited until 1944 to take up the human rights cause, but it did enter the fray with renewed vigour after the Second World War. For example, in 1948 and 1949 it adopted the two conventions that are to this day the cornerstones of freedom of association: Convention No. 87 on freedom of association and protection of the right to organize and Convention No. 98 on the right to organize and collective bargaining. In 1957 it adopted the Abolition of Forced Labour Convention (No. 105, which followed on the 1930 Convention, No. 29, on forced labour) and the following year the Discrimination (Employment and Occupation) Convention (No. 111); earlier, in 1951, it had adopted Convention No. 100 on equal remuneration. Other instruments were to follow.[20]

27. Alongside the procedures specifically set down in its Constitution, in 1951 ILO established, in agreement with the United Nations Economic and Social Council (ECOSOC), a special mechanism to examine complaints about violations of freedom of association. It conducted inquiries and special studies in the fields of forced labour, freedom of association and discrimination in specific situations. In 1951, together with the United Nations, it created the Ad Hoc Committee on Forced Labour, whose work was monitored by an ILO committee until 1959. In 1955 it asked a committee – the so-called McNair Committee, named after its chairman – to examine the independence of employers' and workers' organizations. The Governing Body subsequently asked the International Labour Office to conduct a series of inquiries into the trade union situation in national practice; these were carried out between 1958 and 1963 in the United States, the United Kingdom, the Soviet Union, Sweden, Malaysia and Burma, at the invitation of the governments of those countries. Other studies were carried out in Franco's Spain (1967), when numerous complaints about violations of the right to organize were filed against that country, and in Hungary, Norway, post-Franco Spain, Yugoslavia and Austria between 1982 and 1984, pursuant to resolutions adopted by the European Regional Conference. Investigations into equality of opportunity and treatment conducted annually since 1978 in Israel and the occupied Arab territories have considered various aspects of the issue. Follow-up was also given to the Declaration concerning the Policy of Apartheid of the Republic of South Africa, which was adopted in 1964 and amended on several occasions (in order, for example, to extend its scope to Namibia).

28. These human rights issues were one of the principal battlegrounds between East and West during the Cold War, specifically between the USSR (which returned to ILO in 1954) and the United States of America (which, as we will see, was briefly absent from 1977 to 1980).[21] Although the matter is now essentially of historical interest, some aspects are nevertheless worth examining here.

---

20. For more information, *see* Valticos, *op. cit.*, para. 293 *et seq.*; L. Betten, *International Labour Law: Selected Issues*, Deventer, Boston, Kluwer, 1993, p. 65 *et seq.*
21. For more details, *see* Alcock, *op. cit.*, p. 252 *et seq.*; Tortora, *op. cit.*, p. 357 *et seq.*

29. The difficulties that had arisen when the Soviet Union first joined ILO in 1934 were even more strongly felt on its return because the number of States belonging to the 'communist bloc' had grown in the meantime. Tripartism, one of ILO's fundamental principles, was basically precluded by the ideology and practice of those countries. Private companies were in principle banished, and the heads of public corporations were mere civil servants answering to the ministry concerned. Any trade unions that existed – affiliation was indeed even strongly encouraged in a number of ways – were subordinate (usually on the basis of a constitutional text) to the communist party in power. Relations between the latter, the government and the trade union movement were regularly examined by ILO's supervisory bodies, which clearly concluded on more than one occasion that allegiance to the party and a trade union monopoly were violations of Convention No. 87 on freedom of association and protection of the right to organize. They also issued observations on the manner in which those countries complied with Conventions No. 29 (1930) on forced labour and No. 111 (1958) on discrimination (employment and occupation).[22] The result was a heated debate in which the delegates of the Soviet Union in particular questioned the impartiality of the supervisory bodies and even, in the case of the Committee on Freedom of Association, its fundamental principles. In so doing, they of course won the sympathy of many developing States that, although not of Marxist-Leninist persuasion, had similar structures and were therefore subject to the same criticisms on the part of ILO's supervisory bodies. A majority cobbled together for the circumstances even resulted more than once[23] in the International Labour Conference failing to adopt the report of its Committee of Experts on the Application of Conventions and Recommendations.

30. By thus disputing the Organization's fundamental principles, those States stirred serious concern among other delegations, notably employers' representatives and the United States, whose criticism that tripartism was being undermined was compounded by the fear that a majority of States could impose on ILO a selective attitude – a double standard – in terms of fundamental rights. They were also concerned about excessive politicization, notably during the discussion and adoption of resolutions (which they felt in some instances circumvented legal procedures). In the 1975 letter[24] in which the United States gave notice of its withdrawal from the Organization, Secretary of State Henry Kissinger stressed, in addition to the above points, that: 'questions involving relations between States and proclamations of economic principles should be left to the United Nations and other international agencies where their consideration is more relevant to those organizations' responsibilities'. From the latter point of view, the United States considered that ILO had interpreted its terms of reference too broadly. To this was added, obviously, the traditional hostility of the more conservative circles, among the partisans of *laissez-faire* economics, towards an institution that insisted that the States needed

22. *See* on this point J.-M. Servais, 'Evolution en Europe centrale et orientale et droit du travail', *Dr. soc.*, No. 5, May 1990, pp. 393–398.
23. Specifically in 1974, 1977 and 1982.
24. Letter communicated on 6 November 1975 to the Director-General Francis Blanchard by Ambassador Francis L. Dale; *see* GB, 198th session (Geneva, Nov. 1975), Document GB.198/22/11.

to adopt provisions to protect the employment conditions of workers, whether as individuals or organized in the form of a trade union.[25] The United States nevertheless returned to ILO in 1980 after a series of reform measures had been implemented in response to the criticisms formulated.

§5. ILO Standards and Globalization

31. The founding principles of international labour law, whose roots are to be found in the Industrial Revolution, have acquired a new dimension with the emergence of situations that are usually referred to generically as 'globalization'. More specifically, the disappearance of the communist bloc, the concomitant consolidation of the market economy, the emergence of newly industrialized countries, and the sweeping changes in production and communication technologies and hence in the composition of the work force, wrought obvious changes worldwide in the 1980s and 1990s. Their impact was also felt on employment levels and labour law. Some aspects of national law are no longer suited for practices that reach beyond a country's borders. For example, the capacity to conclude collective work agreements is often beyond the scope of local players. By the same token, the rules on redundancies in force in Europe and Japan, for instance (assessment of the economic reasons, obligation to seek other jobs for the workers affected) can become irrelevant when activities are transferred within multinational groups. The French Court of Cassation has had times ago occasion to rule on this point.[26] Some people fear that if the States lose some of their regulatory authority, the result will be a downward levelling of employment conditions and real social breakdown in countries that have traditionally been protective of workers' rights but are subject to stiffer competition.

32. These developments highlight the need for economic change to be accompanied by labour regulations, the fruit if possible of ILO cooperation with international economic, financial and trade institutions. It is no easy matter to devise those regulations. A fierce debate followed – and feelings of unease – about the future of international labour standards.

33. The need for international labour regulations is at all times apparent. There are both longstanding and freshly minted forms of inequality between States and within States. Technical innovations have widened the gap, disrupting the international division of labour, modifying its nature and doing away with existing jobs without necessarily creating enough new ones. The result is a situation of unemployment, underemployment and precarious employment that spares almost no country, a steadily growing number of human rights violations in the workplace and living conditions that are still all too often inhuman. The reasons for the creation of ILO remain valid; the Organization's labour goals are as pertinent as ever. The

25. *See* Alcock, *op. cit.*, p. 213.
26. *See* G. Lyon-Caen, 'Sur le transfert des emplois dans les groupes multinationaux', *Dr. soc.*, No. 5, May 1995, pp. 489–494.

obstacles to attaining those goals, though, are as numerous as ever. Tension subsists between economic imperatives and social concern, between countries of differing levels of economic development. There has also been a marked return, within the Organization, to the natural conflict of interests between employers' and workers' representatives.

34. We shall return to these developments, and in particular to the 'Decent Work' strategy adopted to try to overcome those difficulties,[27] but not before we have drawn a more complete picture of that policy. Let us start by taking another look at the dilemma posed by the cost of labour standards.

27. *See* ILC, *Decent Work*, Report of the Director-General to the 87th session (1999) of the International Labour Conference (Geneva), ILO, 1999; ILC, *Working out of Poverty*, Report of the Director-General to the 91st session (2003) of the International Labour Conference (Geneva), ILO, 2003, as well as the Declaration on Social Justice for a Fair Globalization, adopted by the ILC on 10 June 2008.

Chapter 2. The Social Clause Dilemma

§1. A Dilemma That Straddles the Borderline between Law and Economics

35. The idea of supplementing international trade treaties with what is known as a social clause imposing minimum or equitable labour standards is based on apparently simple reasoning: if a country allows its companies to employ their workers in deplorable working conditions and for miserable wages – two concepts that have to be defined – it will be able to export its products at a lower price and thus obtain an unfair advantage over its competitors. Hence the proposal to oblige that country to guarantee minimum rights for its workers within the framework of international economic regulations.

36. 'Protectionism', say those who see this as a backhanded but effective means of raising customs barriers to the import of merchandise produced at competitive costs, essentially by developing States. 'Not at all', retort the supporters of the social clause, since it merely tends to correct poor practices and offers the dual advantage of improving the lives of workers in exporting countries and protecting industries in importing countries from competition based on exploitation. A social clause could prevent the closure of companies and loss of jobs in importing countries, for the great benefit of the workers concerned. But will the workers in the hypothetically poorer countries exporting cheap goods not in turn lose their jobs if obstacles are put in the way of the sale of those goods abroad? In other words, is it not best to make allowances for widely varying levels of economic development and to reflect on the role of international technical cooperation? The question arises in connection with the problems of arranging international economic relations and reconciling economic and social development goals.

§2. A Brief Look at the Past

37. The concern to connect international trade and labour standards has been around for a long time, probably as long as the standards themselves. Jacques Necker, a minister of State and banker, wrote as early as 1788 that a country that did away with the weekly day of rest would undoubtedly obtain an advantage, but only if it was the only one to do so: the situation would revert to the *status quo ante* if other countries followed suit.[28]

38. These preoccupations, as we have seen, were present when ILO was founded. We have also seen that at the outset, the Organization devoted most of its

28. For more historical background on this question, *see for example*, L. Dubin, *La protection des normes sociales dans les échanges internationaux*, Aix-en-Provence, Presses Universitaires d'Aix-Marseille, 2003; ILO, *World of Work Report 2009. The Global Crisis and Beyond*, Geneva, 2009; F. Maupain, *Entre persuasion et régulation, quel avenir pour l'OIT face à la mondialisation financière et son déficit de dimension sociale?* Genève, BIT, 2012, p. 143 *et seq.*

efforts to the adoption of international labour legislation whose purpose was to bring about greater harmony in the rules of labour protection and thus reduce the differences between countries in the social cost of production. This explains why some States ratified international labour conventions only on the express condition that those same instruments were ratified by their main competitors, who were expressly named. Their reservations faded with time, or were no longer given the same importance, probably because of the doubts expressed about the true cost of social protection. After all, does not the production cost of any item depend on countless other factors?

39. The question of the connection between labour standards and international trade resurfaced in places where the conditions of competition changed. This was the case when the European Common Market was established: the disappearance of customs and tax barriers provoked fear that the social component would figure more largely in the calculation of a product's final cost. Article 68(2) of the treaty establishing the European Coal and Steel Community (1951) contained a social clause that considered the hypothesis of undertakings charging abnormally low prices because they were paying abnormally low wages compared with the wage level in the same area.

40. The social aspects of European economic integration were analysed and discussed as of 1955, notably at ILO. The same concerns were expressed.[29] The treaty on the functioning of the European Union contains, like its previous versions, social provisions (Articles 136–145). The Union and the States members should have as one of their objectives improved living and working conditions, so as to make possible their harmonization while the improvement is being maintained. The discussions that took place each time the European Union expanded reflected the fear expressed in more than one quarter that a few countries might obtain a competitive edge because of the lower social cost of their products. Clearly, economic considerations and social motivations were closely interwoven in the efforts made with a view to harmonizing working conditions in European States.

41. Although the idea of introducing a social clause into a global economic agreement is not new, the political and economic context in which it exists has changed. The discussions referred to above concerned the possible effects of labour standards on the production price of merchandise in countries whose development levels were more or less on a par with each other. The first international labour conventions, moreover, contained derogations to the rules for expressly designated countries, such as India and Japan, whose economic development was considered at the time to be less advanced. Today, it is the developing countries, at least some of them, who are suspected of seeking to obtain a decisive advantage for the sale of

29. ILO, *Social aspects of European economic cooperation*, Report by a Group of Experts (Geneva, 1956); Comité intergouvernemental créé par la conférence de Messine, *Rapport des chefs de délégation aux ministres des Affaires étrangères* (Spaak Report), Brussels, 21 April 1956, p. 63 *et seq.*

their goods by adopting a *laissez-faire* attitude in social matters, and of financing their economic take-off by limiting the rights of their workers.

42. The comparison of development levels between competing States is clearly a key element to be borne in mind when seeking a solution to this nettlesome dilemma. Developing country spokesmen have fiercely opposed the social clauses proposed, initially at GATT and later at the World Trade Organization (WTO), considering that concern for social considerations was a smokescreen for protectionism. Nor did they fail to point out that many ILO conventions had not been ratified by the developed States and that their content could therefore hardly be included in the social clauses of the trade agreements concluded with them. They also stressed the practical impediments to implementing the clauses. The partisans of social clauses retorted that, far from having a protectionist effect, the introduction, at national level, of minimum labour standards would lead to trade liberalization (or, as some held, would prevent the establishment of customs barriers) between the North and the South while enabling workers throughout the world to benefit from the increase in trade and financial exchanges.

43. Several commodity agreements now contain articles stipulating respect for equitable working conditions with a view to improving the standard of living of the workers concerned. There is some doubt, however, about the practical effect of such provisions, which seem to be statements of intent rather than true legal undertakings. Much depends on the balance of power between the forces concerned and on the real possibilities for the more powerful to demand that the provisions be implemented.

44. The debate on the social clause in trade agreements, in particular in the context of GATT and the founding acts of WTO, was reignited at a time when emphasis was being placed on the need to make labour legislation more flexible. Although the proponents of one or the other view were usually different, in some industrialized countries they joined forces to demand deregulation at home and improved guarantees elsewhere. There was a real risk that labour legislation would be reduced to the lowest common denominator.

45. The aim of inserting minimum labour standards into economic agreements is to strengthen the protection afforded by ILO standards and procedures. It is based on two observations. The first is that nothing obliges a State to ratify an ILO convention (and therefore to undertake specifically to respect certain labour standards); at the very most there is an exception for fundamental conventions.[30] The second concerns the non-binding nature of the conclusions adopted by ILO's supervisory bodies, which involve no sanctions for violations of the rules of the kind imposed by labour law. This shows how interesting it would be to give renewed consideration to sanctions in international public law.

30. *See* paras 50 and 67 *below*.

§3. The Technical Difficulties

46. This is the context in which closer links between equitable labour standards and international trade are debated. The question, really, is whether the social clauses inserted into international treaties can be supplemented with effective, for the most part economic, sanctions to penalize violations. The answer requires us to take a closer look at the technical problems associated with the implementation of a social clause.

47. A first problem is the concept of minimum or equitable labour standards. Does it or does it not cover all the standards contained in ILO conventions and recommendations, or at least those which the Governing Body considers are still relevant to its consideration of the Organization's standard-setting activities? If yes, it might be wise nevertheless to provide for arrangements whereby those standards exist alongside or are even replaced by less demanding ILO instruments that are better adapted to the situation of the countries concerned.

48. One wonders whether it might in any event not be more realistic to exempt some of the standards and recommendations. To facilitate reflection on this point, we shall use a three-category classification of the standards to which we shall refer again later.[31] The first category covers programmatic instruments. These are drafted in general terms and take full account, in principle, of the special situation of developing countries. They constitute, for example, the basis for ILO policy in the fields of employment and vocational training. There seems to be little point in applying a social clause to such standards, which set general objectives to be met via an ongoing programme of action, rather than formulating specific, immediately applicable rules that a State undertakes to respect through its ratification.

49. Most of the conventions fall within the second group and have a more specific technical content. They deal with matters such as working conditions and social security, industrial relations and labour administration. It does not seem very realistic to advocate the incorporation of all of these standards into a social clause, nor would be easy to establish the criteria for choosing which ones to include.

50. Many people therefore consider that it would be best to limit the social clause to those standards concerning fundamental workers' rights, which can be either technical or programmatic in nature but all of which embody essential principles drawn, in many cases, from ILO's Constitution. The States therefore agreed to respect them when they joined the Organization. Moreover, the Organization has decided to promote their application as a priority, as its activities in the past half century and longer have patently demonstrated. The Declaration adopted in 1998 on fundamental principles and rights at work clearly confirms this. It lists those rights: freedom of association and the right to collective bargaining; the elimination of forced labour and the abolition of child labour; the elimination of discrimination in the workplace. Some people would like to add other provisions on occupational

31. *See* para. 1164 *et seq. below*.

health (in the name of the right to life) and labour inspection (when the United States insisted on adding a social annex to the North American Free Trade Agreement (NAFTA) was it not chiefly concerned to ensure effective compliance with existing labour legislation, in Mexico in particular?).

51. A second problem is whether the social clause should be limited to referring to ILO standards or whether it should set new standards. In the first case, should it refer to the conventions or to the principles they contain?

52. In addition, should the same rules be applied to all States or should distinctions be made on the basis of their degree of development? More specifically, should the poorest States be placed in one category and what are considered to be newly industrialized States in another? By the same token, should the standards concerned apply to all sectors of the national economy or only to those involved in international trade (free export zones, modern export sectors, etc.)? This means thinking about the field of application of labour standards. ILO has always defended the position that the rules it adopts should be universal in nature. However, various clauses and flexible wording have been included in many conventions in order to take account of economic disparities. They serve temporarily to waive those instruments in respect of certain sectors of activity or occupational categories. Should they be included here as well?

53. A third problem is the form of the commitment made by the signatory States. Usually States formally undertake the obligation to respect an international convention in the form of a ratification or some other written instrument. A social clause would therefore have to be ratified with the treaty containing it. It should be remembered, however, that ILO procedures do not all require the States concerned to ratify the relevant instruments. A case in point is the complaints submitted to the Committee on Freedom of Association. Other approaches have been suggested, such as a modification of the WTO procedures, or the adoption of a convention on this subject specifically. There are also less binding procedures, such as the adoption of codes of conduct for multinational companies operating in countries where labour protection is limited. Compliance with such codes can allow the company to put a social 'label' on its product, although it remains to be seen how the code's application is evaluated. The Tripartite Declaration of Principles concerning Multinational Enterprises and Social Policy, adopted by the ILO Governing Body in 1977, has the same approach. Purely voluntary in nature, it makes no provision for a supervisory mechanism as such, but rather for mechanisms of interpretation access to which is limited by conditions of admissibility that are hard to meet without a consensus.

54. Other methods can be encouraged, such as the preparation of plans of action in specific fields. If the States were required by a social clause to prepare such plans and to implement them, the obligation would usually be of programmatic value.

55. A fourth problem resides in the way in which violations are ascertained. Here, too, various possibilities come to mind. The first is international or national judicial proceedings, with, if necessary, a court of appeal. Another idea put forward concerns a mechanism based on the right of the parties to the international agreement to look jointly into the facts – if necessary with the assistance of ILO – and to draw conclusions. And there is no reason, as has been pointed out, not to fall back on ILO's traditional supervisory bodies[32] or to adopt a format similar to the *ad hoc* fact-finding and conciliation missions, or missions of good services ILO has conducted on countless occasions in the past.

56. Other questions remain to be answered, such as how to determine who can launch the procedure. Another State? Should that State be required to be bound by the standards invoked? Employers' associations and trade unions? All of them, or only those directly concerned by the matter? Would it be best – and if so, why – to draw the limit at those with ILO consultative status? Could the body designated to check whether national legislation and practice were in conformity with the provisions cited act ex officio, examine any difficulties on the basis of complaints or periodic reports?

57. The sources of funding for the mechanisms selected remain to be identified, as do the means of making the conclusions of any monitoring bodies as effective as possible. This, in turn, raises the problem of sanctions. As we shall see, in the framework of traditional ILO procedures the methods used to incite the States to comply with the standards and to follow the conclusions of the supervisory bodies are essentially moral in order (published reports and public debate, 'mobilization of shame'). One significant point: Article 28 of the ILO Constitution at one time provided for the possibility of economic sanctions after the complaint had been considered by a commission of inquiry. That provision disappeared when the Constitution was amended after the Second World War. Although there is nothing to prevent the Organization's policy-making bodies from taking really dissuasive measures in respect of a recalcitrant State,[33] it can find it politically inadvisable to do so. There is nothing to make us believe that things would be different for a social clause.

58. The decision to apply sanctions implies a decision to determine who applies them and if they are limited to the most serious cases. It has been argued that once the violation has been ascertained, each State should be free to raise dissuasive customs tariffs or to adopt other economic sanctions against the violating country. The decision to apply sanctions could also be left to an independent body. Whatever the case may be, legal experts will have to consider whether it is advisable to require a link of cause and effect between the violation and the proven injury suffered by the protesting State. Should the sanction penalize the country as a whole, the sector of activity concerned or the company that violated the standard, and should it be conceived and implemented at national or international level?

59. As we can see, even from the technical point of view the introduction of a social clauses poses a dilemma. They have nevertheless been introduced in the

32. *See* para. 1028 *et seq. below*.
33. Based on Article 33 of the Constitution. *See* para. 1068 *below*.

national trade legislation of some countries as well as in a number of international trade agreements. Their very existence and the pressure they imply on concerned States may objectively help the ILO to implement its standards, even if the Organization is not part of the arrangement. The same may be said of the social provisions introduced in the codes of conduct of many enterprises.

§4. Other Possible Solutions

I. Unilateral Procedures

60. Political resistance and technical problems have prompted countries like the United States to take unilateral initiatives. American statutes contain specific provisions subordinating the economic advantages granted to other countries to compliance on their part with minimum workers' rights. Examples include the Generalized System of Preferences (GSP), as modified, and existing trade legislation. The EU Regulation No. 978/2012 also applies a scheme of generalized tariff preferences. The preferential arrangements may be withdrawn for serious and systematic violation of principles laid down, *inter alia*, in the ILO fundamental. The text however takes also a more positive approach, granting additional tariff preferences 'to those developing countries which, due to a lack of diversification and insufficient integration within the international trading system, are vulnerable, in order to help them assume the special burdens and responsibilities resulting from the ratification of core international conventions on human and labour rights', including the ones considered as fundamental by the ILO.[34]

61. The objections raised to this type of legislation stem from its unilateral character, from the fact that it allows the State to issue its own definitions of what equitable labour standards are, to be the only one to assess their application in other countries, to make compliance with them a factor of the economic or customs advantages it grants and to impose sanctions if they are violated. Many find it preferable, and in the interests of all the parties, to draw up universal instruments able to avert both the dangers of protectionism and the risk of multiple unilateral decisions or conventions by which only a few are bound. The absence of universal instruments could set off, they say, a kind of labour-related race to the lowest common denominator and foster situations of exploitation and even the rollback of existing national measures of labour protection. We hardly need add that poor labour practices are sometimes the work of foreign investors that would not act in the same way at home. What is more, although unilateral provisions are often based on what are considered fundamental ILO standards, the Organization cannot help implement the rules adopted by one State for the conduct of its trade relations with other countries. There is nothing, however, to prevent a government that has determined, in the light of ILO instruments, a number of minimum workers' rights and that is examining whether or not they are respected from looking to the comments made by ILO supervisory bodies on the conventions – or standards – used as a reference.

34. *See* the 11th consideration of the Regulation, its Articles 9, 19 and Annex VIII.

62. The private sector regularly, and on a purely voluntary basis, makes unilateral social commitments. There are various forms of such self-regulation. The most frequently encountered are the codes of conduct proclaiming a company's labour policy or principles, social labels that provide information on the conditions of labour in which a product was manufactured or a service provided, and so-called 'ethical' investments that seek to reconcile social change and economic yield. These practices are obviously useful and just as obviously have shortcomings.[35]

II. Non-universal Trade Agreements with a Social Component

63. A growing number of the bilateral trade cooperation agreements being signed, in particular by Canada, the United States and the European Union, contain social provisions. Examples are Canada's agreements with Chile and Costa Rica, American agreements with Cambodia, Chile, Jordan and Singapore, and European Union agreements with South Korea[36] or India. The number of multilateral trade agreements is also growing. Treaties relative to the construction of Europe, which go much further in the process of integration than mere free trade agreements, are a separate case. However, the North American Free Trade Agreement (NAFTA) is a classic example; negotiations with a view its expansion to a free trade area of the Americas (FTAA), have failed up to now. The United States has also signed the Dominican Republic-Central America-United States Free Trade Agreement (CAFTA-DR) with five Central American countries (Costa Rica, El Salvador, Guatemala, Honduras, and Nicaragua) and the Dominican Republic.[37]

64. Agreements have periodically been concluded between the European Union and a group of developing countries in Africa, the Caribbean and the Pacific. They have recognized, as an essential component of the preferential trade relation established between Europe and its former colonies, respect for human rights and fundamental freedoms, including basic labour rights, and for democracy based on the rule of law. The present Cotonou agreement refers expressly to the labour standards ILO considers to be fundamental: freedom of association and the right to collective bargaining, the elimination of forced labour and the abolition of the worst forms of child labour, and non-discrimination in employment.

65. Much has been said about the geographical and also substantive limitations to these agreements. It is true, even in the case of NAFTA, that the provisions they contain are relatively general. Their purpose also differs sharply from that of international labour conventions; they are above all economic in scope and the argument relating to competition used to justify the inclusion of social provisions is readily

35. *See below*, para. 225 *et seq.*

36. *See* A. Perulli, 'Fundamental Social Rights, Market Regulation and EU External Action', *IJCLLIR*, Vol. 30(1), March 2014, pp. 27–47.

37. The ILO website contains a list of such agreements under 'Free Trade agreements and labour Rights'. See also the Foreign Trade Information System of the Organization of American States (dealing with free trade agreements which are already entered into force, signed, or still being negotiated) on http://www.sice.oas.org/tpd_e.asp.

discernible in more than one declaration on them. Nevertheless, the fact that they aim to mitigate the negative social repercussions of trade liberalization also brings them closer to ILO concerns. One example was the trade agreement concluded on 20 January 1999 between Cambodia and the United States on the textile sector.[38] It contained a social clause implemented in association with ILO, at the request of both parties. A technical assistance project had been set up that comprised a procedure for evaluating compliance with Cambodian labour legislation and ILO conventions, and measures to remedy any shortcomings observed. If this example were to be repeated, it would mark the beginning of a new role for the ILO that of a third party charged with examining the social provisions introduced in non-universal treaties.

§5. The Road Taken by the ILO

66. The ILO is no stranger to these differences of opinion, these bones of contention. Little by little, however, some clarity has been obtained and lessons have been learned about the technical difficulties of implementing a social clause and the political resistance to its adoption. The discussion has moved from wondering about whether it is advisable or even possible to impose a minimum of social protection for all workers to consideration of what conditions would enable workers to benefit fairly from international trade liberalization by participating in the establishment of labour regulations suited to national conditions. The World Summit for Social Development, held in 1995 in Copenhagen, marked a major step forwards in that direction. The following year, the WTO ministerial meeting in Singapore reaffirmed the ILO's role as the body competent to set essential labour standards and to monitor their application.

67. At almost the same time, the International Labour Conference adopted, in June 1998, the Declaration on Fundamental Principles and Rights at Work and its Follow-up, which seeks to associate social justice with economic growth.[39] In it, all ILO Member States undertake to respect, to promote and to realize, in good faith, the principles and rights concerning freedom of association and collective bargaining, the elimination of forced labour and the abolition of child labour, and the elimination of discrimination in respect of employment and occupation. The Declaration acknowledges that ILO Member States, even if they have not ratified the relevant conventions, are obliged to respect, 'in good faith and in accordance with the Constitution', the principles relating to the fundamental rights set forth in those conventions. The annex on follow-up invokes Article 19 of the ILO Constitution and

38. D. Wells, 'Best Practices in the Regulation of International Labor Standards, Lessons from Cambodia Textile Agreement', *Comp. Labor Law & Policy Journal*, Vol. 27(3), 2006, pp. 357–376; D. Brown, R. Deheja and R. Robertson, 'Regulations, Monitoring and Working Conditions. Evidence from Better Factories Cambodia and Better Work Vietnam' and Ch. Oka, 'Evaluating a Promising Model of Non-State Labour Regulation: The Case of Cambodia's Apparel Sector', in D. McCann, S. Lee *et al.*, *Creative Labour Regulation: Indeterminacy and Protection in an Uncertain World*, Geneva, ILO, Basingstoke, Palgrave MacMillan, 2014, pp. 259–279 and 185–203.

39. *See* paras 203–212 *below*.

requires States that have not ratified those fundamental conventions to submit annual reports on the progress made towards implementing the principles they enshrine. Lastly, the ILO undertakes to mobilize its budgetary resources and to exercise its influence to help the Members meet those objectives. The new Declaration on Social Justice for a Fair Globalization adopted in 2008 confirms the emphasis put on the instruments classified as core labour standards, while underlining the importance of those regarded as most significant from the viewpoint of governance covering tripartism, employment policy and labour inspection.[40]

68. The programme carried out by ILO to that end has a threefold purpose: to raise awareness of the 1998 Declaration within countries and regions as well as at the international level; to deepen understanding of how these fundamental principles and rights reinforce development, democracy and equity and help empower all women and men; to promote policies that implement these principles and rights in practice in the development conditions of each country. The programme implies:[41]

- *media and educational campaigns*, targeted at various cultural and economic contexts;
- *research*, investigating how each of the rights and principles relates to economic growth, employment creation, poverty reduction and gender equity;
- *social reviews*, responding to countries' requests to examine what is hindering or facilitating implementation of the Declaration;
- *policy advice*, advising on job creation and social protection underpinned by respect for the fundamental principles and rights;
- *legal support*, strengthening the capacity of lawmakers and labour administrations to enforce laws that give expression to the fundamental rights and principles;
- *widening involvement*, working with employers' organizations, trade unions and other civil society groups and regional and international organizations to make use of the Declaration; and
- *permeating the ILO*, refining the ways in which respect for these principles and rights can be woven into ILO work across the board.

40. *See* para. 1164 *below.*
41. ILC, Report of the Director General, *Decent Work*, 87th Session, ILO, Geneva, 1999, p. 15.

Chapter 3. The Institutional Framework

§1. ILO's Mandate and Structures

69. The ILO Constitution tasks the Organization with working to achieve the objects set forth in the Preamble and in the Philadelphia Declaration. We have already examined the content of the latter,[42] but it is useful to cite the Preamble *in extenso* for it sets the framework for the ILO's law-making activities.

70.

> Whereas universal and lasting peace can be established only if it is based upon social justice;
>
> And whereas conditions of labour exist involving such injustice hardship and privation to large numbers of people as to produce unrest so great that the peace and harmony of the world are imperilled; and an improvement of those conditions is urgently required; as, for example, by the regulation of the hours of work including the establishment of a maximum working day and week, the regulation of the labour supply, the prevention of unemployment, the provision of an adequate living wage, the protection of the worker against sickness, disease and injury arising out of his employment, the protection of children, young persons and women, provision for old age and injury, protection of the interests of workers when employed in countries other than their own, recognition of the principle of equal remuneration for work of equal value, recognition of the principle of freedom of association, the organization of vocational and technical education and other measures;
>
> Whereas also the failure of any nation to adopt humane conditions of labour is an obstacle in the way of other nations which desire to improve the conditions in their own countries;
>
> The High Contracting Parties, moved by sentiments of justice and humanity as well as by the desire to secure the permanent peace of the world, and with a view to attaining the objectives set forth in this Preamble, agree to the following Constitution of the International Labour Organization: … .

71. The mandate is not defined more specifically. The sole purpose of the authors of the Peace Treaties in drawing up this non-exhaustive list was 'to give the Organization some lines of action and an initial impulse by drawing its attention to certain reforms which seemed particularly urgent'. 'Definition always implies to some extent limitation. The authors of the Peace Treaties wished to avoid any formula which, being inspired by the circumstances of the moment, might impede the future progress of the Organization by preventing it from taking such action as later circumstances might require.'[43]

42. *See* para. 22 *et seq. above*.
43. ILO, *The International Labour Organization: The First Decade*, Geneva, 1931, pp. 96–97.

72. We shall not return to the tripartite composition of ILO, having already said that employers' and workers' representatives are members of the Organization's different bodies, in particular its annual conference and its Governing Body.

§2. The Adoption and Termination of ILO Standards

I. The Process of Preparation

73. ILO's founders basically expected the Organization to adopt international labour conventions and recommendations and to promote and monitor their application. The conventions are binding on the States upon ratification, i.e. after a voluntary act by which the States undertake to apply them. The recommendations are not mandatory: they contain reference standards to which the States are encouraged to refer for their laws and practice.

74. The Governing Body settles the agenda for all meetings of the Conference.[44] It is up to it to submit subjects for the preparation of new standards. Once it has selected such a subject for discussion at the Conference, the International Labour Office prepares a report on the law and practices of different countries in respect of that subject. That report is in itself a valuable source of comparative law. The Office also draws up a questionnaire to which the governments must reply after having consulted with the most representative employers' and workers' organizations. The Office then drafts a fresh report on the basis of the replies received and forwards it to the governments. The texts submitted are the subject of a first and usually also a second discussion at a Conference committee before being adopted in plenary by a qualified two-thirds majority. This procedure is instead of the traditional signing of treaties by the contracting parties.

75. The conventions and recommendations cover all, or almost all, fields pertaining to labour and social security, and were therefore grouped, shortly before the Second World War, in a methodical collection known as the International Labour Code.[45] The Code also contains numerous explanations of and references to the preparatory work. The term 'code' should not be misconstrued: the provisions of the Code are the outcome of texts voted separately by the ILO Conference since 1919. The term also has a different meaning in the consolidated Maritime Labour Convention (MLC[46]) n° 186, the terminology of which harks back to the codes of conduct appended to certain Anglo-Saxon laws. This being said, the fact that the conventions and recommendations adopted on maritime labour are consolidated in a single convention undoubtedly makes the latter akin – in its field – to a code in the meaning of the term in continental Europe.

44. Article 14 of the Constitution. The Conference may also decide, by two-thirds of the votes, to include any subject in the agenda for the following session (Article 16). *See also* para. 95 *below*.
45. ILO, *The International Labour Code*, 1951 (Geneva, 1952), 2 volumes.
46. The ILO only refers to the Convention by its acronym.

76. The length of the process for adopting conventions and recommendations, and hence its slowness, may be surprising. The entire mechanism, however, consisting as it does of successive rounds of consultation and negotiation by a Conference committee, is aimed at obtaining the broadest possible support with a view to widespread ratification and unrestricted implementation. The facts that social justice is viewed in many ways and that economic development takes many forms make this no easy task. The negotiated character of the preparatory process therefore implies, if ILO standards are to have a genuine and universal impact, the active participation of all delegations.

II. The Choice of Subjects

77. The way in which the Governing Body chooses the subjects for new standards was recently a topic of protracted debate.[47] One tendency has been towards rationalization of the selection process. Thus the Conference has introduced the scheme of recurrent discussions on the four strategic objectives of the Organization, i.e. employment, fundamental principles and rights at work, social protection and social dialogue. Another point of debate has been how best to integrate the different instruments with each other and with the Organization's other possibilities for action, in particular technical cooperation.

78. These efforts to enhance coordination are aimed first at the process by which conventions and recommendations are prepared. ILO therefore conducts more in-depth studies of the subjects to be dealt with, including their general context. The Conference can, if it so decides, launch an initial discussion of a given subject for the purpose, not of producing standards, but rather of setting a programme of action, of identifying possibilities for adopting new texts, of clearly defining their goals and the form they may take, or of suggesting that existing instruments be reviewed. The second aim of this 'integrated' approach is to bolster the impact of the standards adopted with better coordinated and more systematic promotion and evaluation operations. This question is discussed in the last part.

79. Called on to draft new legal rules on labour, the international lawmaker is inevitably confronted with contradictory objectives, with tensions between the divergent interests of employers and workers, and between governments of the North and South, for example. Choices must be made, the fruit of negotiation and reciprocal concessions, in order to obtain the minimum consensus that will allow the standard to be observed in fact. This is no simple task, and the efforts at systematization mentioned above are obviously insufficient.

47. *See* ILC, 'Strengthening the ILO's capacity to assist its Members'efforts to reach its objectives in the context of globalization (general discussion)', Report of the Conference's Committee, Provisional Record No. 23, 96th Session, ILO, Geneva, 2007, p. 23/66, para. 7; GB document 319/INS/2, Geneva, ILO, October 2013.

80. Agreement is easier to reach in fields like occupational health and security. Employers and trade unions share the same broad concerns, arising in good part from technical changes, although they diverge on practical implementation measures and the pace of reform. A consensus is much more difficult to obtain on subjects over which the partisans of a rigorous approach and the defenders of flexibility conflict. Working time is a case in point: ILO has not yet been able to update the old instruments on hours of work. How best to adapt them to technical constraints and new social aspirations remains a matter of vigorous debate. A compromise formula has yet to be found.

81. Such controversy is part of the natural process by which standards are produced. It would be surprising were it otherwise. A formula acceptable to all the parties usually ends up seeing the light of day, but finding it can take time. Impasses are not the result of red tape or of an inflexible system: they arise from the difficulty of reconciling divergent and varied interests on complex and important subjects. For many years, for example, the labour world was divided on the elimination of the prohibition of night work for women in industry. Proposals presented by ILO finally resulted in instruments that were more in keeping with present day reality. The workers' group agreed to have the prohibition raised, but in principle on the basis of a collective work agreement; in exchange, it obtained the adoption of a convention and a recommendation on improved conditions for night work, for men as well as women.

82. The difficulty consists in striking a balance, in obtaining the requisite flexibility to take account of various situations, while not divesting the standards of their substance. The standards must be paid more than lip service, they must have real and lasting significance.

83. International labour law is without doubt imperfect, as is the community of States, but it is also undoubtedly less imperfect than the law of other universal or regional institutions. It draws its strength not only from the support provided by the Member States, but also from the backing of employers' and workers' associations. That backing makes it all the more cogent and relevant.

III. The Termination of ILO Conventions and Recommendations

84. International treaties are usually terminated when they are abrogated, denounced or reviewed. Since 1929, international labour conventions have contained a final provision authorizing the Conference to close them to any new ratification by the adoption of a revising convention. The States can also denounce a convention under the terms set forth in its final articles. Neither procedure puts an end, however, to the effects of the instrument concerned for the States that have ratified it. The ILO Constitution did not specify the conditions for abrogation. The stopgap measures considered, such as making the convention 'dormant' or putting it on 'standby', were unsatisfactory for lack of clarity.[48] The Conference therefore adopted an amendment to the Constitution enabling it to abrogate outdated conventions in accordance with the *acte contraire* procedure, i.e. the mode of terminating the convention must be the same as the mode of concluding it; the amendment has entered into force on 8 October 2015.[49] It is not deemed necessary for conventions that have not entered into force (or for recommendations) that impose no legal obligation on other Member States or the Organization itself;[50] there is nothing to prevent these from being terminated by the *acte contraire* procedure.

§3. Labour Standards in Other International Institutions

85. The ILO is still today the main source of international labour law. States however have always adopted labour provisions in their bi- or multilateral relations. International labour standards have also been produced by universal (as the United Nations) or regional institutions (such as the EU, the Council of Europe or American and Arab institutions).[51] Let it be already said that ILO often cooperates with these institutions on the preparation of their respective texts so as to avoid conflicts.

86. The treaties adopted by the United Nations and its specialized agencies, such as the United Nations Educational, Scientific and Cultural Organization (UNESCO), are not directly related to issues of labour and social security since those fields are the special preserve of ILO within the UN structure. General instruments, such as the International Covenants on Human Rights, nevertheless cover all or some of the fundamental labour freedoms and social rights. We shall analyse them only as far as they deal with labour and employment matters. Furthermore some instruments are the outcome of conferences organized jointly by two international organizations. The ILO, for example, cooperated with UNESCO on the preparation and helps monitor the application of the International Convention for the Protection of Performers, Producers of Phonograms and Broadcasting Organizations (Rome, 26 October 1961) and the recommendation (adopted in Paris on 5 October 1966) concerning the status of teaching personnel.

87. Nor will this monograph consider the numerous bilateral and multilateral treaties concluded in the field of labour and social security. Those treaties deal first of all with migration, equality and the transfer of social security entitlements. They are too diverse to be analysed here. Mention should be made however of some international legal instruments prepared with the assistance of the ILO, by a special

48. *See below* paras 102 *et seq*. *See also* F. Maupain, 'Une révolution tranquille dans le droit des traités: l'abrogation des conventions internationales du travail obsolètes', *Annuaire français de droit international*, XLII, 1996, pp. 629–635.
49. Article 19 §9 of the Constitution. See also Article 45*bis* of the The Standing Orders of the International Labour Conference.
50. In addition, as will be seen, to submit the Convention to competent authorities: *see* Document GB.267/LILS/WP/ PRS/1 of the ILO Governing Body, paras 5–7.
51. J.M. Thouvenin and A. Trebilcock (eds.), *Droit international social* (2 volumes), Brussels, Bruylant, 2013.

conference convened to discuss a topic of interest to only a limited number of States; they concern in particular European countries. They resulted for example in the 1950 agreements concerning Rhine Boatmen and the 1956 European Convention Concerning the Social Security of Workers Engaged in International Transport. These instruments were subsequently revised or supplemented.[52]

88. Furthermore, we have just mentioned private provisions that also complete the *corpus iuris*.

52. N. Valticos and G. von Potobsky, *International Labour Law*, 2nd edn, The Hague, Kluwer, 1995, para. 132.

Part I. The Sources of International Labour Law

89. In the main, the following pages focus on ILO instruments while occasionally referring to other provisions of direct interest for international and national labour law. The following chapters consider in succession the Organization's Constitution, its conventions, other standard-setting instruments and the relations between these different kinds of provisions.

Chapter 1. The ILO Constitution

90. The Preamble to the ILO Constitution and the Philadelphia Declaration appended thereto contain[53] basic precepts to which the States are presumed to adhere when they join the Organization. These precepts include in particular the protection of children, freedom of association and equality of opportunity and treatment. They are the general principles underpinning the law of the Organization. They also lay the foundation for the mechanisms for complaining about violations of freedom of association and for following up the Declaration on Fundamental Principles and Rights at Work; the States therefore need not have ratified the relevant conventions nor even given their consent in the case at hand.[54]

91. It is nevertheless a fact that the intensity of the Organization's activities depends on whether or not the States have ratified the convention(s) on the subject. If not, the Organization focuses even more strongly on promotion of the principles and, in the event of a conflict, on conciliation and mediation. All the arrangements relating to proceedings before the Committee on Freedom of Association have been made with those specific aims in mind.

92. The Philadelphia Declaration recalls that the Organization must strike a fair balance between economic and social considerations in all of its activities. This vision must underpin the entire process by which ILO standards are implemented. The Declaration affirms the Organization's right to examine economic policies and problems in terms of the fundamental objective that 'all human beings, irrespective of race, creed or sex, have the right to pursue both their material well-being and their spiritual development in conditions of freedom and dignity, of economic security and equal opportunity'. 'All national and international policies and measures, in particular those of an economic and financial character, should be judged in this light and accepted only in so far as they may be held to promote and not to hinder the achievement of this fundamental objective'; 'in discharging the tasks entrusted to it the International Labour Organization, having considered all relevant economic and financial factors, may include in its decisions and recommendations any provisions which it considers appropriate'. ILO remains vitally concerned to strike the best possible balance between economic progress and social justice.

53. *See* paras 26 and 27 *above*.
54. Except for the setting up of a Fact-Finding and Conciliation Commission. On those procedures, *see* paras 208–210 and 1046 *et seq. below*.

Chapter 2. The International Labour Conventions

93. In the General Introduction, we looked at some of the main aspects of ILO conventions, the basic instruments of international labour law. In Part I, we shall examine the conventions in greater detail, considering by turn their adoption, revision, termination and withdrawal (1), their characteristics (2), the nature of the rights and obligations they contain (3), and their interpretation (4). The supervisory and possible appeal procedures are analysed in Part III.

§1. Preparation, Revision and Termination of ILO Conventions

I. Preparation

94. It is usually the ILO Governing Body that sets the agenda for the Conference. To that end it considers any proposal submitted by a government, an organization representing employers or workers or even an organization of international public law. It falls to the Governing Body to ensure that the preparatory technical and political work is conducted to a high standard. If, on the one hand, the matter at hand implies knowledge of the national laws in force, the International Labour Office must place before the Governing Body a concise report of existing laws and practices; the Governing Body can also convene a preparatory technical conference, whose composition is in principle tripartite. Discussions are guided by a desire for consensus and by the objective of universal applicability; the elaboration of the instrument may therefore be preceded by an informal tripartite meeting (as for the Worst Forms of Child Labour Convention, 1999 No. 182) or a general discussion, i.e. not leading immediately to the drafting of an instrument, at the Conference (as for the Promotional Framework for Occupational Safety and Health Convention, 2006, No. 187); the Maritime Labour Convention, 2006 No. 186 was the product of five years of preparation involving numerous consultations and meetings.[55]

95. Any government of a Member State can object to the inclusion of one (or more than one) item on the Conference agenda. The Conference can go ahead with that item only if two-thirds of the delegates present so agree. The Conference can also, by the same majority, decide to table an item for its next session. Furthermore, the Governing Body has been known to decide to include a controversial or complex item on the Conference agenda simply for general discussion (i.e. not for the purpose of immediately adopting a convention); an initial debate of this kind serves to clarify the situation and to facilitate the decision whether or not to take normative action.

96. Draft instruments are in principle subject to the double-discussion procedure by the Conference before they are adopted. The Governing Body can, in special

55. GB Document 298/LILS/4, 298th session, Geneva March 2007, paras 11–12.

instances (for example, in an emergency), opt for the simplified, single-discussion procedure.[56]

97. The double-discussion procedure starts with a report in which the International Labour Office provides detailed information on national legislation and practice and any other useful information. The Office also draws up a questionnaire to which the governments are invited to respond – giving reasons for their replies – after having consulted their most representatives employers' and workers' associations. These documents must reach the governments at least 18 months before the opening of the Conference session, and the governments have in principle seven months in which to react. The Office uses the replies to draw up a further report indicating the main elements requiring consideration and submits it to the Conference, where the matter is usually considered by one of the technical committees. If the committee and subsequently the Conference in full sitting decide that the matter is suitable to form the subject of a convention (or, as we shall see, of a recommendation), they adopt the appropriate conclusions. The Conference reserves that item for its next session.[57]

98. On the basis of the first discussion by the Conference and of the replies received to the questionnaire, the Office prepares one or more draft conventions or recommendations and communicates them to the governments, which must state within three months, after consulting the most representative organizations of employers and workers, whether they have any amendments to suggest or comments to make. The Office then drafts a final report with the text, amended as required, of the convention(s) and recommendation(s) and transmits it to the governments, in principle 'so as to reach them not less than three months before the opening of the session of the Conference at which the question is to be discussed'.[58] At the same time as it asks the governments for their comments on the draft instrument, the Office should also consult the United Nations and its specialized agencies about any provision affecting their activities; their comments are also brought before the Conference.[59]

99. The procedure for the second round of discussion is the same as that for the first. A Conference technical committee usually examines the report and decides whether it will use the text prepared by the Office as a basis for discussion.[60] The drafts adopted in committee are discussed in full Conference article by article. A drafting committee then prepares the final text of the convention or recommendation for adoption by the Conference by a two-thirds majority of the delegates present. If the convention obtains only a simple majority on the final vote, the Conference immediately decides whether or not to refer it to the drafting committee for

56. Article 38 of the ILC Standing Orders describes in details the various stages of the procedure.
57. The Conference may also request the Governing Body to include the item at a following session: *see* Article 38 of the ILR Standing Orders. On the deadlines, *see* Article 39.
58. Article 39, paras 7 and 8 of the ILC Standing Orders.
59. *Ibid.*, Article 39*bis*.
60. For further details, *see ibid.*, Article 40.

drafting as a recommendation. The draft can also be the object of a special convention between Member States wishing to adopt it.[61]

100. Two copies of the convention or recommendation are signed by the President of the Conference and by the Director-General, and by them alone: the ILO Constitution makes no provision for the traditional formality of State signatures. One of the copies is sent to the Organization's archives and the other is forwarded to the United Nations Secretary-General. The ILO Director-General sends a certified copy to each of the Member States.

101. The Conference's official languages are French and English. The texts are authentic in both those languages. ILO also translates all documents into Spanish,[62] including conventions (and recommendations). Translations into other languages, such as German, Arabic, Chinese and Russian, are provided by special arrangement and documents in those languages are not authentic.[63]

II. Revision, Withdrawal, Abrogation

102. Procedures similar to those for the double-discussion adoption of instruments apply to their revision.[64] The final clauses of the conventions usually provide that the Governing Body reports, whenever it considers it necessary to do so, on the application of the original convention and examines whether or not its revision in whole or in part should be placed on the agenda of the Conference.

103. In the event of a revision, the Conference adopts an entirely new convention that contains both new or amended provisions and others from the original convention. The earlier convention continues to be binding on the States that ratified it, but the final clauses of each convention specify the effect of any revision. The standard clauses adopted since 1929 (and supplemented in 1933) provide that the States ratifying the revising convention are considered as denouncing the earlier convention (unless the Conference decides otherwise); in addition, the original convention is closed to any further ratification as of the date of entry into force of the revising convention (again, unless the Conference decides otherwise).[65] In some cases a new instrument is adopted to supplement an existing one without revising it in the technical sense of the word.

104. The Conference has also adopted protocols to existing conventions. It did so for the first time in 1982, in respect of Convention No. 110 on plantations. Protocols have also been adopted to Convention No. 81 on labour inspection (1995 Protocol), Convention No. 89 on night work by women in industry (1990 Protocol),

61. Articles 21 of the Constitution and 41 of the ILC Standing Orders.
62. Articles 24 and 58 of the ILC Standing Orders.
63. *Ibid.*, Article 42.
64. Article 44 of the ILC Standing Orders.
65. *See* Valticos, *op. cit.*, paras 127–131 and 284–285.

Convention No. 147 on merchant shipping (1996 Protocol) and Convention No. 155 on occupational safety and health (2002 Protocol). This procedure is of practical use when the aim is to amend but a few provisions, because it obviates the need to adopt an entirely new convention. It does not, of course, close the original convention to ratification, but in every other respect it has the same effects as a revising convention. It is analysed from the legal point of view as a form of con-vention, is adopted in the same way and has the same effects.

105. The ILO Constitution and the Conference Standing Orders contain no express provisions relating to the amendment of conventions (or protocols). Some instruments do, however, stipulate a specific procedure for that purpose and contain detailed arrangements. They may do so in respect of their annexes[66] or in respect of special provisions that are applicable to certain countries.[67] The consolidated maritime labour convention applies the amendment technique more widely to all of its provisions. It nevertheless operates a distinction among them, and only provisions in the appended 'Code' can be amended through a tacit acceptance procedure. Amendments differ from routine revisions essentially in that the amended text is intended to replace the original text. Unlike a protocol, it contains neither preamble nor final provisions. The base convention provides certain details; thus, only the amended text is open for new ratifications either as soon as the amendment has been adopted or when it enters into force as anticipated. By the same token the amendment is submitted for either ratification or acceptance to the parties to the original convention. The amendment technique has the advantage of simplicity at all stages in the process. It nevertheless introduces a dual system that is less visible than the adoption of a protocol or of a revising convention (if the earlier convention is not denounced).[68]

106. The procedures for withdrawal and abrogation are the same as those for adoption by virtue of the *acte contraire* principle.[69]

§2. The Effects of International Labour Conventions

I. The 'Objective' Entry into Force of the Conventions

107. The final provisions of ILO conventions usually provide that they enter into force twelve months after the ratifications of two Member States have been

66. The Labour Standards (Non-Metropolitan Territories) Convention, 1947 (No. 83); the Migration for Employment Convention (Revised), 1949 (No. 97); the Employment Injury Benefits Convention, 1964 (No. 121); the Seafarers' Identity Documents Convention (revised), 2003, (No. 185); the Work in Fishing Convention, 2007 (No. 188).
67. The Minimum Age (Revised) Conventions, 1937 (Nos. 59 and 60); the Medical Examination of Young Persons (Industry) Convention, 1946 (No. 77); the Night Work Conventions (Young Persons, Women), 1946 and 1948 (Nos. 79, 89 and 90).
68. *See* Governing Body Document GB.276/LILS/WP/PRS/2 and GB.286/LILS/1/2.
69. *See* Article 45*bis* of the ILC Standing Orders and para. 84 *above*.

registered by the Director-General. Once that objective condition has been met, ratification makes the convention binding on the individual State, either immediately if it is one of the two States that ratified it, or at some point in the future after its subsequent ratification. The standard final clause specifies the two elements needed for entry into force: a specific number of ratifications (two) and a timeframe (twelve months after the registration of the second ratification); a third element concerning the status of the Member States from whom ratification is required is sometimes also stipulated.[70]

108. The entry into force of ILO conventions after the registration of two ratifications is borne out by consistent practice. There have been few exceptions,[71] one being maritime labour, where the number of ratifications needed is 30 for the MLC Convention, 2006 (No. 186).

109. At present, the standard final provisions set the timeframe between the registration of the last ratification required and the entry into force of the instruments at twelve months. The first ILO conventions set no deadline after the registration of the final ratification needed: they entered into force immediately. In 1927, a deadline of 90 days was introduced in order to inform States that had already ratified the instrument in advance. That timeframe was extended to 12 months in 1928. This lapse of time figures in the final clauses of all the conventions adopted since then, with few exceptions, such as the maritime conventions.[72]

110. A number of conventions also require that specific Member States ratify the convention. Thus Conventions Nos. 31 and 46 (hours of work in coal mines), Convention No. 110 (plantations) and a dozen conventions on maritime labour stipulate that the ratifications needed for entry into force must come from members figuring among the countries listed.[73] The Maritime Labour Convention, 2006 (No. 186) requires the ratification by at least 30 countries with a total share in the world gross tonnage of ships of 33 per cent.

II. Bringing the Conventions before the Competent Authorities

111. When a convention (or recommendation) is adopted, the ILO endeavours immediately to promote its application using methods that go far beyond classic international law. While it is true that the principal obligations of a State in respect of an instrument arise from its ratification, the State must nevertheless assume some obligations as soon as the International Labour Conference has voted. More specifically, Article 19(5) of the Constitution provides that:

---

70. For more details, *see* the Governing Body Document GB.286/LILS/1/2 para. 12 and *et seq.*
71. The Unemployment Convention, 1919 (No. 2) requires three ratifications.
72. *See* Document GB.286/LILS/1/2, para. 121.
73. Convention (No. 31) requires for example the ratification of two Member States included in a list of seven countries, Convention (No. 109), the ratification of nine countries included in a list of 27 and Convention (No. 110), the ratification of two countries included in a list of 40. *See* GB Document GB.286/LILS/1/2, paras 19–20.

(a) the Convention will be communicated to all Members for ratification;
(b) each of the Members undertakes that it will, within the period of one year at most from the closing of the session of the Conference, or if it is impossible owing to exceptional circumstances to do so within the period of one year, then at the earliest practicable moment and in no case later than 18 months from the closing of the session of the Conference, bring the Convention before the authority or authorities within whose competence the matter lies, for the enactment of legislation or other action;
(c) Members shall inform the Director-General of the International Labour Office of the measures taken in accordance with this article to bring the Convention before the said competent authority or authorities, with particulars of the authority or authorities regarded as competent, and of the action taken by them;
(d) if the Member obtains the consent of the authority or authorities within whose competence the matter lies, it will communicate the formal ratification of the Convention to the Director-General and will take such action as may be necessary to make effective the provisions of such Convention;
(e) if the Member does not obtain the consent of the authority or authorities within whose competence the matter lies, no further obligation shall rest upon the Member except that it shall report to the Director-General of the International Labour Office, at appropriate intervals as requested by the Governing Body, the position of its law and practice in regard to the matters dealt with in the Convention, showing the extent to which effect has been given, or is proposed to be given, to any of the provisions of the Convention by legislation, administrative action, collective agreement or otherwise and stating the difficulties which prevent or delay the ratification of such Convention.

112. This is a way for ILO to promote ratification of its instruments. The States remain free to ratify or not, but the decision to do so does not lie with the Executive alone, even if the latter is the treaty-making power: it must bring the convention before the authority within whose competence the matter lies, within a short period of time. That authority examines the convention and decides either to turn it into law or to take 'other measures'. The procedure should also enable trade organizations, and concerned public opinion, to be informed of the convention's existence. At the time, the fact that States were obliged to implement a procedure that could culminate in ratification revolutionized legal thinking and practice in international law. Modern authors still speak of the measure's originality, even though an institution like UNESCO has introduced a similar provision in its Constitution.

113. In the course of the negotiations on the Treaty of Versailles, the expression 'authority or authorities within whose competence the matter lies' replaced 'legislature', which was used in the British draft that served as a basis for Part XIII. It was specified that the change was aimed at cases in which competence on a matter belonged to the states making up a federation, not to the federal authorities. It was also intended to cover countries which had no parliamentary institutions.[74] Consistent practice considers that the authority in question is the legislative branch, an

74. Valticos, *op. cit.*, para. 696, footnote 2.

interpretation that clearly arises from the constitutional text. That authority, at least in democratic States, is the parliament.

114. What are the respective roles of the European Union and its member countries when it comes to the submission and ratification of ILO conventions? Referred to by the European Commission, on 19 March 1993 the Court of Justice handed down an opinion specifically on the ratification of Convention No. 170 (1990) on chemicals. The Court ruled that the European Union could not, in the present state of international law, itself ratify an ILO convention, and that it could only do so through the intermediary of the Member States. It concluded that the States and the Union had shared competence and consequently needed to cooperate closely if they wanted to ratify the convention.[75] The European Union today applies that case-law for the ratification of all ILO conventions covered by so-called joint competence. This practice has had the effect of limiting the possibilities for ratification by some European States that were traditionally active in this field. In practice, the Commission has even established a procedure of authorization for the ratification of such instruments, as exemplified by the Council Decision No. 2007/431 of 7 June 2007 with regard to the MLC, 2006.[76]

115. Since the aim is to allow parliaments to decide on the follow-up to be given to the conventions, the ILO bodies consider that governments have to provide explicit proposals when submitting a convention for ratification, and that they must do so in all cases, not just when they think ratification is possible. This does not prevent them from nevertheless formulating negative recommendations. The aim is to stimulate debate with a view to a decision. New Member States do not have a retroactive obligation to submit to their legislative authorities all the conventions (and recommendations) adopted before they joined the Organization.[77]

116. The Members also have an obligation to report to ILO on the submissions made and the consequent decisions of the legislative authorities. ILO's supervisory bodies can thus verify that the States are complying with their obligations in this respect. They have often observed that complete compliance is problematic. The difficulties are sometimes very real, as in the case of federal States. This is why the ILO Constitution has a provision specifically on them.[78] Briefly, federal States have the same obligations as other States for conventions that are of federal competence. For others, the government must:

(a) make arrangements with the federated States for a reference to either the federal legislative authorities or those of the federated States;
(b) arrange consultations with the latter with a view to promoting coordinated action to give effect to ILO instruments;
(c) inform ILO of the measures taken to that effect.

75. *See* Documents GB.256/SC/1/3 and GB.259/LILS/4/7 of the Governing Body.
76. *JO* L 161 of 22 June 2007, pp. 63–64. *See also* S. Robin-Olivier, 'Politique sociale de l'Union européenne. Chronique 2013', *RTDeur.*, April–June 2013, pp. 387–393.
77. For further details, *see* Valticos, *op. cit.*, paras 706–710 and 714.
78. Article 19, para. 7.

117. Another way of encouraging ratification is to oblige the State, whether federal or unitary, to report on any conventions (and recommendations) that were not in the end ratified, at the request of the ILO Governing Body. The reports must indicate the impediments to ratification, the difficulties encountered in the implementation of the instruments, the measures already taken and those planned to that effect. These reports are also examined by ILO's supervisory bodies.[79]

III. The 'Subjective' Entry into Force of the Conventions: Ratification

A. Concept and Conditions

118. Ratification is a purely voluntary and sovereign act whereby a State undertakes to implement the provisions of an international instrument, in this case an ILO convention. Under the terms of Article 19(5)d. of the Constitution, 'if the Member obtains the consent of the authority or authorities within whose competence the matter lies, it will communicate the formal ratification of the Convention to the Director-General and will take such action as may be necessary to make effective the provisions of such Convention'. No special form is required. The ratifying State undertakes not only to apply the convention but also to send periodic reports on how it does so (Articles 22 and 23) and to cooperate with the supervisory mechanisms provided for in the ILO conventions (Articles 24 *et seq.*).

119. In the case of some conventions, ratification can or must be accompanied by a declaration. Sometimes the State must specify which option it has chosen. This is the case in particular of instruments allowing some flexibility for countries with a limited level of economic development: those countries are asked to indicate what level of the standard they undertake to observe (for example, the minimum age of employment under Convention No. 138 of 1973). Sometimes a State may have to make a declaration if it wishes to benefit from a derogation (for example, employment injury benefits, Articles 2 and 3 of Convention No. 121 of 1964). Lastly, the State must indicate whether it meets the conditions for ratification, such as the ratification of previous conventions with regard to the Merchant Shipping (Minimum Standards) Convention, 1976 (No. 147).[80]

120. The Member States are also bound, by their ratification of a convention, to communicate to the Director-General a declaration stating to what extent they will apply it to the non-metropolitan territories for whose international relations they are responsible. The principle established in Article 35 of the ILO Constitution is clearly an extension of application *per se* to such territories; exceptions are made in cases where the convention is inapplicable owing to local conditions or if modifications are needed to adapt to those conditions. Any State can update its declaration

79. *See* para. 1030 *below*.
80. For further details, *see* Article 5.

if the situation changes. When the subject matter of the convention is within the self-governing powers of the authorities of the territory, the Member State's declaration is made in full coordination with those authorities.[81] In any event, reports are required on the situation in respect of the convention, even in the absence of a declaration extending application. This procedure has undoubtedly played a significant role in the past, in particular when former colonies were becoming independent. It still applies today to a limited number of territories.

121. ILO has always refused to accept ratifications accompanied by reservations made because of the involvement of employers' and workers' organizations in the process of adopting the conventions and in their implementation mechanisms. Such reservations are also deemed to be incompatible with the purpose of the conventions, namely the establishment of standardized employment conditions.[82]

122. On the other hand, the Organization has accepted the ratification of a convention that is contingent on ratification by other States. This, it has been said,[83] is a purely political question; any difficulty that could arise from this condition is non-legal in nature. It in no way signifies that the ratification cannot be registered. Indeed, what is reflected here is concern to avoid unfair competition on the part of States that did not make the same commitments in order to obtain an economic advantage. Such conditional ratifications are rare. As we have seen, however, some conventions expressly require ratification by certain States before they can enter into force.

B. *Effects of Ratification*

123. The action necessary to make effective the provisions of the convention depends on what kind of standards the convention contains.[84] Most standards have a specific technical content and often require an adaptation of domestic legislation and/or administrative arrangements (for example, when it comes to labour inspection). Others are programmatic in nature and tend to require that the State adopt a genuine policy in a given field rather than laws and rules. Such is the case for employment and human resources development. These standards are flexibly and generally worded, and their aim is chiefly to prompt action; they set goals to be attained. Their implementation therefore implies various kinds of measures, some related to the law, others to economics, training, information, and frequently relies on technical cooperation. ILO fundamental standards, lastly, can require simply that a State refrain from acting in a certain way. More often, they impose some form of positive action to promote freedom of association and the right to collective

81. For further details, *see* Article 35.
82. ILO, *The International Labour Code*, 1951, *op. cit.*, pp. xcix–civ.
83. *See* ILO, *ibid.*, p. ciii.
84. *See* para. 1164 and *et seq. below*.

bargaining, the elimination of forced labour and the abolition of child labour, and equality of opportunity and treatment; that action is legal or not, as the case may be.

124. Must legislative steps be taken when the provisions of the convention are incorporated into domestic legislation by virtue of the existing constitutional system? In what are known as monistic systems, a treaty's ratification (or its promulgation and/or publication) automatically makes it an integral part of the domestic legal order. In dualistic systems, however, ratification implies the adoption of legal measures in all cases for which legislative arrangements are required. For ratification to have this effect in a monistic system, the terms of the convention must allow for its immediate application under domestic law, in other words they must be self-executing. If this is not the case, additional national provisions have to be adopted. What is more, the constitutional provision on its own may be insufficient: the ratifying State undertakes to apply the provisions of the convention in practice, which it cannot do if the standards, even if theoretically incorporated into internal law, are not known in the country. The State would have to take other, perhaps even legislative, measures to comply with its international undertakings. Indeed, some conventions make express reference to the means of implementation, including additions to domestic legislation.

125. Another question is whether collective agreements can constitute the measures required for the implementation of ILO instruments.[85] Some instruments make express provision for this: for obvious reasons, this is the case of certain programmatic conventions (such as Convention No. 100 of 1951 on equal remuneration) or those concerning a specific sector (such as Convention No. 101 of 1952 on holidays with pay in the agricultural sector and various maritime conventions). However, every lawyer familiar with labour law knows the limits to this method of implementing ILO standards. They relate to the scope of application of collective agreements (even if they have been extended), to their lifespan and even, as in Great Britain, to the extent to which they are binding in nature. This is why ILO conventions (such as No. 158 of 1982 on termination of employment) provide that they shall be given effect by laws or regulations if they cannot be made effective by means of collective agreements.[86]

126. Article 19 of the Constitution goes on to say (in paragraph 8) that in no case shall the adoption of a convention (or recommendation) or its ratification by a State 'be deemed to affect any law, award, custom or agreement which ensures more favourable conditions to the workers concerned … '. Thus, ILO standards are minimum rules from which derogations are allowed if they are favourable to the workers. This approach is traditional in labour law, and is viewed in some quarters as a

85. *See* C.W. Jenks, 'The Application of International Labour Conventions by means of Collective Agreements', *Zeitschrift für Ausländisches Öffentliches Recht und Völkerrecht*, 19, 1958 (Kohlhammer), pp. 197–224.

86. Article 1 of Convention No. 158 also refers to arbitration awards and Court decisions. *See also* for example Article 12 of the Maternity Protection Convention, 2000 (No. 183) that still adds 'or in any other manner consistent with national practice'.

general principle of that branch of the law.[87] It is now laid open to question in the name of the balance that must of necessity be struck between the employer and the wage-earner, a new vision reflected in recent ILO instruments expressly authorizing derogations that are not necessarily favourable to the workers. The 1990 Protocol to Convention No. 89 on the night work of women, for example, allows collective agreements to include exemptions to the prohibition of night work.[88]

127. A convention that has been incorporated into the domestic legal order and whose provisions are directly applicable may be in contradiction with national legal rules. International treaty law contains the solution to this kind of conflict. If the national constitutional system places the treaty concerned on an equal footing with domestic legislation, the treaty abrogates earlier legislation but is itself abrogated by subsequent legislation. If the treaty has primacy, as is the case in France, it pre-empts existing and subsequent law.[89] In the first hypothesis in particular, measures must be taken in all cases: in the event, obviously, that a later law alters the effects of the convention in the country concerned, but also in the event that the convention implicitly abrogates earlier law. This has led to uncertainty among practitioners about which standard to apply. It is considered that only an express abrogation or other measures announcing the exact status of the law are indispensable to ensure satisfactory execution of the convention standards.[90]

128. The ratification of an ILO convention gives rise to the obligation not only to respect the provisions thereof but also to cooperate in overseeing their application. That obligation takes two forms.

129. Every Member State is obliged to submit periodic reports[91] on the measures it has taken to make the conventions it has ratified effective. The ILO Governing Body establishes the form of the report and what information the government must provide. In practice, the Governing Body approves a questionnaire on each convention in force. The governments must communicate a copy of their reports to their employers' and workers' organizations; the quality and meaningfulness of the reports is enhanced by the fact that such organizations can comment on them.

130. The States must also cooperate in the supervisory mechanisms, which are based on the filing of complaints, and in particular respond to allegations that they

87. See, however, J. Pélissier, 'Existe-t-il un principe de faveur en droit du travail?', in *Mélanges dédiés au Président Michel Despax*, Toulouse, Presses Université des sciences sociales de Toulouse, 2002, pp. 389–398.
88. Or, in some cases, after consultation: *see* Article 1 of the Protocol.
89. G. and A. Lyon-Caen, *Droit social international*, Paris, Dalloz (Précis), 8th edn, 1993, paras 8–9.
90. *See* Valticos, *op. cit.*, paras 229 and 763.
91. Article 22 requires Member States to make annual reports. The increase however in the number of conventions (adopted and ratified) and consequently in the volume of documents to be dealt with leads to spread out the periodicity of the reports when no major problem arises.

have violated a convention.[92] If they have ratified an instrument, they can also file a complaint against another State for non-compliance.

131. ILO's original and sophisticated mechanism for monitoring application of its conventions and recommendations is discussed in Part Four.

IV. The Cessation of Effects

132. The hypothesis of a convention being terminated has already been examined.[93] Conventions also cease to have effects in other cases as well, either in respect of a given State or more generally.

A. Denunciation

133. A Member State may definitively free itself of its undertakings under a convention it has ratified, including its constitutional obligations in respect of that convention, by means of a denunciation. There are two types of denunciation: first, those resulting automatically from the ratification of a convention revising an earlier convention, in accordance with the current standard final provisions; and second, denunciations pure and simple which are communicated to the ILO Director-General. The provision now in use is usually worded:

1. A Member which has ratified this Convention may denounce it after the expiration of [ten] years from the date on which the Convention first comes into force, by an act communicated to the Director-General of the International Labour Office for registration. Such denunciation shall not take effect until [one year] after the date on which it is registered.
2. Each Member which has ratified this Convention and which does not, within the year following the expiration of the period of [ten] years mentioned in the preceding paragraph, exercise the right of denunciation provided for in this Article will be bound for another period of [ten] years and, thereafter, may denounce this Convention at the expiration of each period of [ten] years under the terms provided for in this Article.

134. The article provides for a number of time periods:

- a period of validity of the convention – usually ten years, exceptionally five years – reckoned from the date on which it first enters into force;
- the period during which it may be denounced: usually one year;

92. Articles 24, 25, 26 *et seq.* of the Constitution. In the event of the reference of a complaint to a Commission of Inquiry, every Member State has the obligation, whether or not they have ratified the convention concerned, to place at the disposal of the Commission all the information in their possession which bears upon the subject matter of the complaint (Article 27).
93. *See* para. 84 *above*.

- a further period of validity if the convention has not been denounced: in most cases, a further ten years;
- a period of notice between the date on which denunciation is registered and the date on which it takes effect; this has always been one year.[94]

It therefore follows that a State that has ratified a given convention cannot denounce it if the convention has not obtained the number of ratifications required for its entry into force. In certain conditions, the State can then have the registration of its ratification cancelled.[95]

B. Withdrawal from the Organization

135. Article 1(5) of the ILO Constitution provides that a State's withdrawal from the Organization does not affect the continued validity for the period provided for in the convention of all obligations arising there under or relating thereto. This provision reflects earlier practice.[96]

C. Succession of States

136. The principle of the succession of States has been widely applied to ILO conventions. Newly independent countries in particular have almost unanimously acknowledged that they are bound by the instruments ratified in their name. The same has usually applied in cases in which States have merged or split, in particular when the former Soviet Union and the former Yugoslavia split into two series of separate States; there have nevertheless been several exceptions.[97]

D. War and Radical and Unforeseeable Changes in Circumstances

137. Some ILO conventions provide that their application shall be suspended in the event of war or of a threat to national security, in a case of *force majeure* or in the public interest in especially grave circumstances. This can be found in several instruments on hours of work. The Organization's supervisory bodies have always interpreted such provisions narrowly and required detailed information on any derogations decided by virtue thereof.[98] In the absence of a clause to that effect, the principles of international public law have usually been applied. In respect of multilateral conventions, war leads only to the suspension of their effects between belligerents of opposing camps. A change of circumstances, for its part, can usually

94. *See* Governing Body Document GB.286/LILS/1/2, Geneva, March 2003.
95. Valticos, *op. cit.*, p. 561.
96. ILO, *The International Labour Code, 1951, op. cit.*, pp. xcvii and xcviii.
97. Valticos and von Potobsky, *op. cit.*, para. 631; ILO, *op. cit.*, p. xcviii; D. Marchand, 'Les conventions internationales du travail et les Etats nouveaux d'Europe', *Droit social*, January 1993, pp. 3–9.
98. Valticos, *op. cit.*, para. 737.

only be invoked if it results in the denunciation or revision of an instrument in accordance with existing procedures.[99]

138. Both the ILO and the Council of Europe have been requested to examine the consequences on their labour standards of the restrictive social policy imposed to countries unable to pay their debts. In the case of Greece, the European Committee of Social Rights[100] has pointed out various violations of the European Social Charter. While less critical, the ILO High Level Mission to Greece of September 2011[101] has also underlined the risks of discrepancies with its conventions on freedom of association and collective bargaining, on wages, social security, labour administration and inspection and employment policies. The CEAC has endorsed the report and the ILO supervisory bodies have followed it up, with special consideration given to social dialogue, labour administration and social security.[102]

§3. The Interpretation of ILO Conventions

139. International labour conventions are interpreted not only by various international bodies but also at national level (practitioners may debate the meaning of an instrument when its provisions are incorporated into domestic law). In monist-type constitutional systems, national courts may refuse to apply, or even declare invalid, a provision that would contradict an international norm. More frequently however they aim at reconciling both standards. In many cases, they refer to international labour standards, not to substitute, but rather to strengthen a solution based on national law, when, for instance, no legislation exists on an issue covered by an ILO instrument.[103] Still more revealing are the sentences, in common law systems in particular, where courts used even non-binding international labour standards (as

---

99. *See* ILO, *op. cit.*, pp. xcvi and xcvii, as well as note 35 under Article 197, p. 152; Valticos, *op. cit.*, paras 737–738; Ch. Rousseau, *Droit international public*, Paris, Dalloz (Précis), 7th edn, 1973, para. 71 *et seq.*
100. S. Laulom, 'Les droits sociaux fondamentaux, rempart contre les déconstructions des droits du travail', *Revue de droit du travail*, No. 6, June 2013, pp. 410–412; M. Schmitt, 'Europe sociale et crise économique', *Journal de droit européen*, May 2013, No. 199, pp. 182–183; Ch Deliyanni-Dimitrakou, 'La Charte sociale européenne et les mesures d'austérité grecques: à propos des décisions Nos. 65 et 66/2012 du Comité européen des droits sociaux', *Revue de droit du travail* No. 7/8, July–August 2013, pp. 457–470. *See also* the decision of the European Committee of Social Rights dated 7 December 2012, complaint No. 76/2012 of the Federation of Employed Pensioners of Greece.
101. *Report of the Committee of Experts on the Application of Conventions and Recommendations*, Report III (Part 1A) 101tst Session, 2012, ILO, Geneva, 2012, observation concerning Greece.
102. *Report of the Committee of Experts on the Application of Conventions and Recommendations*, Report III (Part 1A) 103rd Session, 2014, ILO, Geneva, 2014, pp. 111–112, 375–378, 516–518.
103. C. Thomas, M. Oelz and X. Beaudonnet, 'The use of international law in domestic courts: Theory, recent jurisprudence, and practical implications', in J.C. Javillier and B. Gernigon (eds.), *Les normes internationales du travail. Un patrimoine pour l'avenir. Mélanges en l'honneur de Nicolas Valticos*, Geneva, BIT, 2004, p. 268; F. Villanueva, 'La définition du niveau de négociation collective au pérou: un processus singulier d'appropriation des décisions du Comité de la liberté syndicale de l'OIT par le Tribunal constitutionnel', *Revue de droit comparé du travail et de la sécurité sociale*, 2016/1, pp. 70-83.

unratified conventions or recommendations) with a view to interpreting national provisions or identifying new general principles of law. The trend seems even on the increase.[104]

140. This implies the risk that the decision of the national court would be objected to by international institutions, as they may do for legislative provisions which contradict their own rulings. The French *Conseil d'État* had, for instance considered 'of reasonable duration' under Article 2, 2(b) of the Termination of Employment Convention, 1982, No. 158, a national provision that required a period of two years before certain categories of workers could enjoy the protection of the instrument, in particular the obligation to justify dismissal. The ILO supervisory bodies have considered such a period as too long and asked France to modify the relevant legislation.[105] It must be added that in evaluating the reasonable character of the period, the ILO organs should refer only to the preparatory work of the Convention and to other relevant international elements. To use arguments based on French law is allowable with a view of assessing the situation *vis-à-vis* the Convention, not interpreting an international instrument. Otherwise, the country concerned would be seen as both judge and party in the same case; the principle of the autonomy of the different legal orders would not be respected. The risk would then exist of interpreting the provisions differently depending on the country involved and contradicting the equality of Member States and the objective of convergence that inspires the ILO standards.

141. The principles outlined above apply to traditional international instruments. The control of compatibility between legal orders however, arises in different terms in the law of the European Union.[106] Following the EU Treaties, the national courts of the Member States may in particular refer a case in which the respect of the EU regulation is doubtful, to the European Court of Justice for preliminary ruling.

142. We shall focus now on the main international interpreters of the law, with a view to considering the legal value of the conclusions reached by the Organization's supervisory bodies. There is a distinction between the modes of interpretation established by the ILO Constitution and other less formal modes that are so often used in ILO practice that recourse to the former has almost never been the case. We shall conclude with a discussion of a number of methodological problems inherent in ILO instruments.

---

104. See X. Beaudonnet (ed.), *International Labour Law and Domestic Law: A Training Manual for Judges, Lawyers and Legal Educators*, ILO, Turin, 2010. G. von Potobsky, 'Eficacia jurídica de los convenios de la Oit en el plano nacional', in J.C. Javillier and B. Gernigon, *op. cit.*, pp. 287–305; A. Fiorentino *et al.*, 'La Jurisprudence Sociale et le Droit International: Complémentarité ou Hostilité?', *Revue de droit comparé du travail et de la sécurité sociale*, 2016/1, pp. 93 *et seq. See also* the site of the International Training Centre of the ILO (ITCILO) http://compendium.itcilo.org.
105. ILO Governing Body, document GB.300/20/6, 300th session, Geneva, November 2007, para. 71.
106. *See also* Valticos and von Potobsky, *op. cit.*, para. 654.

I. Principal Interpreters[107]

A. *Constitutional Bodies*

143. Article 37 of the Constitution provides that:

1. Any question or dispute relating to the interpretation of this Constitution or of any subsequent Convention concluded by the Members in pursuance of the provisions of this Constitution shall be referred for decision to the International Court of Justice.
2. Notwithstanding the provisions of paragraph 1 of this article the Governing Body may make and submit to the Conference for approval rules providing for the appointment of a tribunal for the expeditious determination of any dispute or question relating to the interpretation of a Convention which may be referred thereto by the Governing Body or in accordance with the terms of the Convention. Any applicable judgment or advisory opinion of the International Court of Justice shall be binding upon any tribunal established in virtue of this paragraph. Any award made by such a tribunal shall be circulated to the Members of the Organization and any observations which they may make thereon shall be brought before the Conference.

144. Much has been written about the jurisdiction of the International Court of Justice and its predecessor, the Permanent Court of International Justice, in respect of ILO instruments. The latter was asked on only one occasion to rule in relation to a convention. The case concerned Convention No. 4 of 1919 on the night work of women; the majority of the Court ruled in an advisory opinion that the text applied also to women holding positions of supervision or management and not ordinarily engaged in manual work.[108]

145. In 1945 it was deemed desirable, for reasons that were essentially practical, to grant the ILO Governing Body authority to establish an ad hoc tribunal able rapidly to resolve any question or difficulty arising from the interpretation of a convention. The following year the Conference therefore adopted a constitutional amendment adding a second paragraph to Article 37 of the Constitution. That paragraph has never been used.

B. *Interpretation by the Organization's Secretariat*

146. It is quite common, however, for governments that have doubts about the meaning of a convention to ask the International Labour Office for its opinion. The

---

107. *See* Governing Body Document GB.256/SC/2/2 and F. Maupain, 'L'interprétation des conventions internationales du travail', in R.-J. Dupuy (ed.), *Mélanges en l'honneur de Nicolas Valticos. Droit et justice*, Paris, Pedone, 1999, pp. 567–583.
108. For further details, *see* ILO, *op. cit.*, pp. 368–372. In other cases, the Permanent Court of International Justice as interpreted constitutional provisions: *see* para. 18 *above* and para. 581 *et seq. below*.

Office has always responded positively to such requests, nevertheless pointing out that it has no special authority in the matter. When they are of more general interest, the Office's opinions are submitted to the Governing Body and published in the ILO *Official Bulletin*. Although they are by no means authoritative, the fact of publishing these opinions undoubtedly lends them weight and enhances their value.[109] They are supplemented by the numerous documents and memoranda issued by the Office on a wide range of issues, many of which relate to international labour standards.[110]

C. Interpretation by the ILO's Supervisory Bodies

147. Without entering into the details of the supervisory procedures contained in ILO conventions (and recommendations) – they are discussed later in this monograph – we will nevertheless say that they have recourse to both tripartite representative bodies (the Conference or the Governing Body or a committee established by them) and to other bodies made up of independent individuals chosen for their expertise and impartiality. Both, by the nature of their work, are called on to indicate the meaning they give to international labour standards and consequently to provide interpretations that are not, however, authoritative.[111] This is especially true of the expert committees, usually made up of lawyers, whose weight comes from the moral and professional authority of their members. Their conclusions have resulted in a kind of case-law, or more precisely a collection of recommendations that is available to States seeking to introduce a given instrument into their law and practice.

148. The above observations prompt two comments: first, the conclusions of the experts or representative bodies, no matter what the quality of the individuals involved, are of undoubted moral value but do not have the legal authority of a court judgement; and second, for the supervisory system to be credible, the conformity of national situations with ILO standards must be evaluated in accordance with a strictly legal method.

149. Indeed, while it is important for ILO conventions to be flexibly worded in order to take account of the wide range of national situations, the supervisory bodies, for their part, interpret them narrowly when ascertaining the existence of major discrepancies between a given instrument and the legislation or practice of a State that has undertaken to respect it by virtue of an absolutely voluntary, sovereign and express act. This provides the requisite guarantee that the same verification methods are applicable to all and that no room is made for a subjective appraisal of factors that are not provided for in the convention. Even though the means of overcoming the difficulties encountered are not all taken from the arsenal of the law

109. *See* ILO, *op. cit.*, p. cix.
110. Valticos and von Potobsky, *op. cit.*, para. 127.
111. ILC (102nd session, 2013), *Report of the Committee of Experts for the Application of Conventions and Recommendations*, General report, Geneva, ILO, 2013, paras 33–35.

but are in some cases based on cooperation and technical assistance, the process by which such discrepancies are ascertained suffers no compromise.

150. The Committee of Experts on the Application of Conventions and Recommendations, the linchpin of the ILO supervisory system, says this in its reports: its function is to determine whether the requirements of a given convention have been met, no matter what the economic and social conditions prevailing in a given country, subject only to any derogations expressly authorized in the convention itself. It also says that it is guided in its task only by the rules set forth in the convention: these are international standards, and the way in which their degree of application is evaluated must be the same for all, without regard for the concepts drawn from a particular economic or social system.[112]

II. Matters Relating to Method

151. The interpretation of ILO standards has given rise to controversy. It could hardly have been otherwise: such is the risk of all legal interpretations, especially when they involve powerful interests. What is undoubtedly most surprising is the very low number of controversies. We shall not look at all of them here, but only at those which, alongside other points less open to dispute, raised serious questions of method.[113]

A. Consideration of Economic and Social Conditions

152. A good comparative analysis of international standards and national law cannot consider the texts alone. It must bear in mind the specificities of the countries concerned, their history and culture, the respective power of their main social players (employers' associations and trade unions as they relate to the State's senior administrative authorities), the political and philosophical context, the economic substratum, the role of the law in social organization, etc.[114] A clear distinction must nevertheless be made between legal arguments and those that are purely socio-economic. The latter must not be allowed to serve as a pretext for defending the indefensible and affirming that two laws provide the same solutions when the differences are legally self-evident. The example below illustrates this well. It is taken from the implementation of fundamental rights at work in the former socialist regimes with planned economies in Eastern and Central Europe.

---

112. ILC (73rd session, 1987), *Report of the Committee of Experts for the Application of Conventions and Recommendations*, General report, para. 20; Governing Body Document GB.256/SC/2/2, para. 19 *et seq.*

113. The ILO competence to deal with certain topics is a different matter: *see* para. 18 *above*.

114. *See* for example with regard to the USA: S. McCune Lindsay, 'The problem of American cooperation', in J.T. Shotwell (ed.), *The Origins of the International Labour Organization*, Vol. 1, New York, Columbia University Press, 1934; *see also* J. Bauer and D.A. Bell (eds.), *The East Asian Challenge for Human Rights*, Cambridge University Press, 1999.

153. Certain civil liberties are essential if trade unions and employers' organizations are to exercise their activities as usual: in addition to freedom of association, these are guaranteed personal safety, freedom of assembly, freedom of opinion and expression, protection from arbitrary interference in the private sphere, etc. As a rule, the constitutions of the countries in question recognized a fair number of these freedoms and their legislation provided for their comprehensive protection in specific texts such as the civil or penal code. Those same provisions nevertheless set conditions for the exercise of those freedoms, for fear that they would be used to thwart the established political, economic and social system. Those restrictions allowed the authorities to refuse, for example, the creation of organizations the purpose of which did not correspond to the objectives of building a socialist society.

154. But who could decide if an activity was or was not in keeping with the interests and promotion of a socialist system? The answer to that question led to queries about the extent of the powers of the Interior Ministry in the absence of jurisdictions in charge of checking the lawfulness and operations of administrations. It also raised questions about the independence of the judiciary, especially since the legal formulas set forth, for example, in the penal code, were general and therefore liable to differing interpretations. In short, what were the limits, if any, to the administration's discretionary power? That power risked being exercised in a particularly discretionary fashion when the administration feared that the existing social order would be disrupted. The authorities in countries concerned played an essential role in the interpretation and application of the legal texts on these basic freedoms, and this inevitably led to paralysis and frequent abuse of authority.[115]

155. Ultimately, in the countries of Eastern and Central Europe the law was considered a means to a certain end, namely the consolidation and development of a socialist society. Legal texts were construed using a teleological method. Indeed, countless legal scholars in those countries stressed that the recognized rights did not have an abstract content, and that they were to be fulfilled in a real society, that they depended on the economic and social system.[116] This obviously did not shield the interpreter from subjectivism.

156. The question resulted in a long controversy about the observation by the USSR and other communist countries of the ILO conventions on the fundamental rights of workers (freedom to form employers' and workers' associations, absence of forced labour, equality of opportunity and treatment in employment).

157. The governments of those countries long held that the existing economic and social conditions or systems were a factor in the evaluation of the conventions on those rights. They expressed reservations about the opinions of the Committee

---

115. J.-M. Servais, 'Evolution en Europe centrale et orientale et droit du travail', *Droit social*, No. 5, May 1990, pp. 393–398.
116. *See also* S.A. Ivanov, 'Sur les études comparatives en droit du travail', *Revue internationale de droit comparé*, No. 2, April–June 1985, especially p. 383 *et seq.*

of Experts on the Application of Conventions and Recommendations on the implementation in their countries of those instruments and reiterated that the real conditions had to be taken into account when examining their application. They held that it was impossible to obtain a clear picture of the organization, functions and rights of trade unions without taking into consideration the economic, political, social and legal structure of the socialist State.

158. In short, they believed that the international labour conventions, which were universal by nature, slotted into differing social realities which could all be in conformity with ILO standards. The methods by which those instruments were made effective in capitalist countries, and the results of their implementation, were not the only ones that were in conformity with the conventions. Opposing views, which they denounced, were in their eyes incompatible with the fundamental principles of international law, which were based on peaceful co-existence.

159. The majority of the members of ILO's supervisory bodies rejected those arguments. The Committee of Experts on the Application of Conventions and Recommendations, in particular, conceded that differing social realities prevailing in different social and political systems could be in harmony with a given ILO convention and, conversely, that discrepancies between national law or practice and a ratified instrument could clearly arise in countries belonging to one or the other system. It nevertheless emphasized the following point: in assessing national legislation and practice in respect of ILO conventions, its role is to ascertain whether the provisions of a given convention are being applied, no matter what the economic and social conditions in the country concerned. The requirements of that instrument are constant and uniform for all States, subject only to any derogations that the convention itself expressly authorized. In performing its task, the Committee is guided solely by the standards contained in the conventions, although it never loses sight of the fact that the arrangements for their implementation may differ from one State to another. These are international standards, and the way in which their application is evaluated must be uniform and not affected by concepts derived from a specific social or economic system.[117]

160. In the final analysis, this is a question of interpretation that arises in respect of national law, comparative law and international law: nothing allows a distinction to be made if the standard to be applied does not make that distinction. Of course, the judge in a criminal case, for example, makes allowances for attenuating circumstances; he does this, however, on the basis of the legal texts authorizing him to do so. The same holds true for all branches of the law. In the case at hand, the majority opinion of the Committee of Experts seems to have won over most of ILO's experts and delegates.

117. *See in particular* ILC (73rd session, 1987): *Report of the Committee of Expert for the Application of Conventions and Recommendations*, report III (Part 4A) (Geneva, ILO), 1987, para. 20; *see also* paras 22–24, 50–52.

161. The above observations call for additional comment. A national or international piece of legislation may expressly or indirectly authorize derogations to a common rule in the light of economic and social conditions. This is the case for the 'flexibility' clauses and devices inserted in ILO conventions to enable above all developing States to make the convention effective gradually and in time with their economic progress. Consideration of these factors is in those cases a function of the texts analysed. It would be preferable for those texts to stipulate clearly who can assess the circumstances, to what extent and with what effect.

162. More and more frequently, national legislation and international instruments take express account of these conditions in the choice of means of application. Indeed, the consideration of conformity covers not only the letter of the texts but also the way in which they are implemented. This may seem obvious, but the exercise is a perilous one. What is more, economic and social factors are a necessary part of the strategy devised to surmount the difficulties encountered in applying the conventions that have been ratified. Whether or not these instruments have any true impact depends to a large extent on whether or not they are part of a genuine social policy.

163. Several developing countries, notably in Asia, have recently insisted that the implementation of the conventions must be evaluated flexibly and the socioeconomic context taken into account. ILO's supervisory bodies and a majority of delegations in its governing bodies have refused to see things this way. They acknowledge the dictates of economic progress and the struggle to eliminate poverty, but they also maintain that the austerity policies inevitably adopted had to respect the principles of equity and not oblige the most deprived to bear the burden of development. They further consider that international labour standards are not just admirable but somewhat unrealistic moral concerns, especially in times of crisis. The standards have a meaning, they have a real impact in promoting dynamic and harmonious economic growth. They are also precise legal rules that the States are obliged to respect when they have made the commitment to do so. Hard times are therefore no argument for relaxing their application: although ILO standards are drafted in sufficiently flexible terms that they can be adapted to different levels of development and to different legal, economic or social systems, the same flexibility does not apply when it comes to ascertaining the degree to which a convention is applied in a given country.

164. The Conference has not been indifferent to the numerous obstacles faced by developing countries striving to reach the level set by ILO standards, obstacles arising from the crisis, their modest resources, at times also the inadequacy of their officials, technicians and administrators. The overwhelming majority of States has asked that a much more substantial effort be made for these countries, in particular through technical cooperation programmes.[118]

---

118. *See* J.-M. Servais, 'Normes internationales du travail et disparités économiques et sociales', in *Liberté, égalité, fraternité. Actualités en droit social*, Bordeaux, Editions LCF, 1990, pp. 233–244.

B. Interpreting the Conventions Separately or as Part of a Legal Corpus

165. The specificity of the adoption and implementation procedures have led some people to infer, somewhat hastily, as we have seen,[119] that ILO standards are parts of an integrated legal corpus rather than a series of distinct treaties. In a word, they hold that the legislative nature of the conventions has won out over their synallagmatic character. According to this analysis, in case of doubt the conventions are to be construed in terms of each other; they constitute an articulated whole, as evidenced by the fact that in the preparatory work the authors strove to ensure that successive texts did not contradict each other.

166. The question arose concretely in an early case submitted to the ILO Governing Body's Committee on Freedom of Association.[120] In January 1984 the British Government adopted measures whose effect was to oblige agents under civilian contract to the Government Communications Headquarters (GCHQ) in Cheltenham to renounce their affiliation with the trade union of which they were members. The authorities said those measures were warranted by the interests of national security. They further said that Convention No. 151 of 1978 on labour relations in the public service made an exception for workers whose responsibilities were highly confidential in nature. The Committee on Freedom of Association rejected that argument. It affirmed that Convention No. 87 of 1948 on freedom of association and protection of the right to organize guaranteed that all workers 'without distinction whatsoever' were entitled to establish organizations of their choosing and to become members of them. Convention No. 151, which was adopted to supplement Convention No. 98 of 1949 on the right to organize and collective bargaining, can neither overrule nor limit that fundamental right: the exclusion of certain categories of workers by these two instruments cannot be construed as affecting or limiting in any way the right to organize granted to all workers by Convention No. 87. There is nothing in Conventions Nos. 98 and 151, the Committee continued, to indicate that the intention was to limit the scope of Convention No. 87; quite the contrary, both the terms of the two conventions and the work done preparatory to the adoption of Convention No. 98 bespeak the opposite intention. In addition, Article 1(1) of Convention No. 151 provides that the convention applies to all persons employed by public authorities 'to the extent that more favourable provisions in other international labour Conventions are not applicable to them'. If Convention No. 98 leaves the rights guaranteed to civil servants in Convention No. 87 intact, then logically Convention No. 151 does not limit them.

167. Although the particular nature of ILO instruments has certain effects, there is nothing to authorize, except an express indication, anyone to go beyond the law governing classic treaties and to interpret each convention independently.

---

119. *See* para. 76 *above*.
120. *See* case No. 1261, 234th report of the Committee on Freedom of Association, *Official Bulletin* (ILO), Vol. LXVII, 1984, series B, No. 2, paras 343–371; *see also* Wood, *op. cit.*

C. The Programmatic Conventions

168. Some conventions, as we have already said,[121] are programmatic in nature, in that they tend to require States to implement a true policy in a given field (employment, vocational training, etc.) rather than to adopt laws and regulations. This approach modifies the scope of the legal rule and hence its interpretation. The provisions of these instruments do not as a rule place immediate obligations on the States, but rather obligations of means: to implement certain policies, prepare or approve specific programmes and, more basically, justify their activities in the field under review. Monitoring the application of standards of this kind gives rise to specific problems in that it is the often of a non-legal character means used rather than the results ultimately obtained that must be examined.

169. The form for the preparation of the periodic reports on the application of Convention No. 122 of 1964 on employment policy, for example, comprises questions on the relations between the policy's objectives and other economic and social objectives. It refers expressly to general and sector development policies and to the measures adopted, for instance, in terms of investment, fiscal and monetary policy, trade, prices, income, wages and regional development. It also refers to education and training policies and to labour market policies.

170. By the same token, the provisions of Convention No. 142 of 1975 on human resources development are essentially incentive: they set goals to be attained. The comments made by the ILO CEACR therefore focus on general points such as the vocational training-job relationship, vocational guidance and effective cooperation – which the convention does not require in any specific form – with employers' and workers' organizations.

171. The interpreter can therefore not limit his role to that of legal expertise. In order to give these instruments their full meaning, he must have a minimum knowledge of the issues concerned, in this case labour economics, and call on recognized experts and specialists in the relevant fields (in the above examples, in industry, finance and trade). That is the price to pay if the instruments are to have an impact.

§4. The Characteristics of ILO Conventions

172. ILO conventions are shaped by the institutional framework and are thus distinct from classic international treaties. They are not drawn up during a diplomatic conference but rather by an assembly composed of government, employer and trade union delegates. They are adopted and revised by a two-thirds majority rather than unanimously. The formalities of signature and registration are reduced to a bare minimum. Application in non-metropolitan territories is covered by the specific provisions of Article 35 of the ILO Constitution.

121. *See* paras. 48 and 123 *above* and, for more details paras 1171–1183 *below*.

173. The mere fact of a convention's adoption gives rise to obligations for the Member States, even before they ratify it. As we have seen,[122] the ILO endeavours to promote application using methods that also go far beyond classic international law. Naturally, the main obligations of the State stem from ratification, the voluntary commitment to apply the convention and to provide periodic reports on the conformity of national legislation and practice with it. As soon as the Conference votes on a convention, however, the Member States must submit it to the competent national authorities 'for the enactment of legislation or other action' and report on that point.[123] They must also report on conventions they have not ratified, at the request of the ILO Governing Body. The reports must discuss the difficulties encountered in making the conventions effective, on the measures already taken to that end, etc. It is even held that the ILO Constitution contains certain standards, certain fundamental principles to which the States accede when they join the Organization and that they are bound to honour even if they have not ratified the conventions on those issues specifically. One example is the procedure for filing complaints about violations of the right to organize, which does not require ratification of the relevant conventions. Moreover, reservations to ratifications are not accepted.[124] Even if the State withdraws from the Organization it remains bound by the conventions it has ratified.[125] The monitoring system, lastly, serves to follow up and correct the implementation of these standards much more systematically than the traditional international treaties (or even the instruments of many other international institutions). Authoritative interpretation of the latter and of the conventions is the remit of the International Court of Justice,[126] and not of the States party.

174. The peculiar nature of the mechanism for establishing these standards and others relating to promotion and supervision[127] has given rise to protracted debate about the nature of ILO conventions especially during the first years of the Organization's existence.[128] At the time, legal scholars were less accustomed to instruments being adopted by an international institution. In many respects, they have the appearance of international legislative texts, voted by a kind of international labour

122. *See* para. 111 *et seq. above*.
123. Article 19, para. 5 of the Constitution.
124. *See* para. 121 *above*.
125. As provided in Article 1, para. 5 of the Constitution.
126. Article 37 of the Constitution. It also provides that an *ad hoc* tribunal may be established for the purpose.
127. *See* paras 165–167 *above* and J. Wood, 'International Labour Organization Conventions – Labour Code or Treaties?' *International and Comparative Law Quarterly*, Vol. 40(3), July 1991, pp. 649–657; Valticos, 'Contrat – Convention – Traité – Loi? Les conventions internationales du travail', *op. cit.*; P. Reuter, *Institutions internationales*, Paris, PUF (Thémis), 7th edn, 1972, p. 98.
128. For more details, *see* Valticos and von Potobsky, *op. cit.*, para. 76 *et seq.*; Scelle, *op. cit.*, pp. 181–185; J. Morellet, 'Un type original de traités: les conventions internationales du travail', *Revue critique de droit international privé*, No. 1, January–March 1938, pp. 1–219; Valticos, 'Contrat – Convention – Traité – Loi? Les conventions internationales du travail', *Revue des sciences morales et politiques*, 1996, pp. 403–413; J. Wood, 'International Labour Organization Conventions – Labour Code or Treaties?', *International and Comparative Law Quarterly*, Vol. 40, Part 3, July 1991, pp. 649–657; P. Reuter, *Institutions internationales*, Paris, PUF (Thémis), 7th edn, 1972, p. 98.

parliament attended by employers' and workers' delegates and submitted – persistently, as we shall see – for ratification to the Member States. The fact that the Organization aims at creating a minimum legal threshold amongst Member States only serves to heighten the latter's legislative character. This peculiarity has resulted in reservations to ratification being refused.[129] Although it does have certain effects, it would be hasty to conclude that ILO instruments have lost their contractual character. The presence of employers' and workers' delegates at the International Labour Conference adopting them does not alter their contractual nature, quite the contrary.These instruments are not a mere exchange of good intentions between States: they are negotiated with the representatives of employers and workers. To punctuate the point, the International Labour Conference Standing Orders requested governments to consult the most representative organizations of employers and workers before finalizing their replies to the preparatory questionnaires and their observations on draft instruments.[130] ILO instruments thus appear to be tripartite agreements or covenants of international public law.

---

129. ILO, The International Labour Code, 1951, *op. cit.*, pp. xcix–civ.
130. In the same manner, summaries of the employers' and workers' organizations replies and observations must be included in the ILO reports on the matters, when they are no part of the governments' replies, but are submitted separately. For further details on the question, *see* Articles 38 and 39 of the ILC Standing Orders, as amended.

Chapter 3. The Other Standard-setting Instruments

175. ILO conventions have been repeatedly, especially in recent years, and harshly criticized for their lack of realism and their failure to have any real impact on national legislation and practice. Most criticism has focused on precarious forms of employment in their most extreme manifestation, in the informal sector of developing countries. It may therefore be useful to reflect on the application of the conventions to precarious workers as an introduction to consideration of the other modes of regulation used by the Organization in its endeavours to tackle these shortcomings.

§1. Precarious Work and ILO Standards

176. To what extent can worker protection be extended to precarious activities, which remain – in a way by definition in the case of what are known as informal economies – relatively impervious to the influence of national or international legal rules?[131]

177. Many conventions apply only to wage-earners, whereas precarious employment is also if not mainly to be found among the self-employed. Indeed, the exceptions and flexibility clauses the conventions contain frequently exempt from their field of application all or some of the workers, whether wage-earners or not, in sectors of activity in which precarious employment is the rule. This is the case for workers employed in family businesses and on small farms. Convention No. 138 of 1973 on minimum age is a very characteristic example of an instrument whose scope can in practice be limited to mainstream activities.

178. Some standards, on the other hand, cover all workers and sometimes even contain provisions that refer expressly to the informal sector. Convention No. 78 of 1946 on medical examination of young persons (industry) provides[132] that 'national laws or regulations shall determine (…) the measures of identification to be adopted for ensuring the application of the system of medical examination for fitness for employment to children and young persons engaged either on their own account or on account of their parents in itinerant trading or in any other occupation carried on in the streets or in places to which the public have access'. In monitoring of this instrument, the CEACR was pleased to note the promulgation of legislation expressly protecting these young workers. Admittedly, however, compliance with such provisions is especially difficult to impose and verify, be it in international or national law.

131. ILC, *Transitioning from the Informal to the Formal Economy*, Report V(1), Geneva, ILO, 2014, paras 42 *et seq*.
132. Article 7(2).

179. The informal sector in developing countries is not a monolithic whole. It comprises traditional activities performed within the family circle, usually agricultural work in the broad sense. It also comprises undeclared odd jobs and small, one-man operations run by carpenters, mechanics, repairmen of all kinds, etc. It also includes small businesses that are known to the authorities and registered by them but that find it relatively difficult to apply all administrative, tax or social legislation.

180. How is labour legislation applied to these activities? Agricultural labour is excluded from most African labour codes. Nor is it really possible to apply specific labour rules to urban odd-job men, and even if it were, it would be impossible to monitor compliance. Rather than including these activities theoretically in a labour code, it would be more useful to look to the fundamental rules of private or even customary law for ways of avoiding exploitation, to identify essential safeguards in the mechanisms of civil law or in the enhanced protection of a service contract. African researchers have suggested that provisions on civil liability, unjust enrichment or agency of necessity be used to that effect.

181. Small businesses that have at least partially integrated into the formal sector find themselves in an intermediate situation in terms of standards on conditions of work in particular, better able to apply some – which must be identified – than others.

182. The dilemma is there. Precarious workers, more than others, need clear and protective legislation, since their shaky position renders them more vulnerable. The weak, more than the strong, need to be able to bank on the certainty of written texts, Jean-Jacques Dupeyroux wrote about 'atypical' work. Henri Lacordaire, writing in more general terms, said that 'between the weak and the strong, between the rich and the poor, between the lord and the slave, it is freedom which oppresses and the law which sets free'.[133] We are back at the origins of labour law. The arguments advanced in favour of the application of national and international labour and social security law to these special categories of workers are therefore very solid. The workers are thus ensured, at least on paper, of protection on a par with that of other workers; equality of treatment is respected; there are no second-class citizens.

183. And yet the current tendency to encourage employment of this kind reflects a specific concern: to promote the recruitment of extra workers by reducing the company's social costs, to push employers reluctant to take on staff on traditional contracts to hire anyway. The employers might, on the other hand, be perfectly willing to hire people when there is work, i.e. when and only for as long as the orders come in.

133. J.-J. Dupeyroux: 'Et maintenant?', *Droit social*, special issue, July–August 1981, p. 487; Henri-Dominique Lacordaire, 'Du double travail de l'homme' , 52nd conférence de Notre-Dame, 16 April 1848, reproduced in *Œuvres du R. P. Henri-Dominique Lacordaire*, vol. IV, Paris, Poussièlgue Frères, 1872, pp. 471–495.

184. This is particularly true of small and medium-sized businesses, which are highly sensitive to the vicissitudes of the economy. And for the unemployed, an 'odd job' is undoubtedly better than no job at all. But this reasoning, and concern for greater flexibility in the applicable rules and in the type of labour relations chosen, precludes the assimilation of precarious with traditional workers, who are said to cost more: the source of jobs would dry up. Conversely, insisting that such workers be treated on an equal footing with the others is consequently tantamount, objectively speaking, to trying to limit recourse to such forms of employment.

185. Nor, from the technical point of view, is it easy simply to extend the Labour Code to people such as home or temporary workers, not to mention self-employed tradesmen. The Code would need numerous adjustments and adaptations to take account of these workers' specific needs.

186. The level of protection from which precarious workers benefit is ultimately a balancing act, performed differently depending on the context and the actual conditions in each country, between conflicting requirements: equality of treatment, minimum guarantees for the life, health and well being of these workers and their families, the company's economic imperatives, and the need to preserve job possibilities.

187. The wording of each convention serves to determine whether or not it applies to all or some of these workers. To put it in a nutshell, the ILO standards establishing fundamental labour rights in principle cover all employment situations. Admittedly, however, they are difficult to implement when it comes to freedom to organize, equality of opportunity and treatment and the abolition of child labour. The standards on the promotion of employment and vocational training do not distinguish between workers either. Since they are programmatic in nature and place no very detailed and specific legal burden on the States, they are relatively easy to apply in the short term. In terms of the policies to adopt, however, they refer to measures that are favourable to workers in unstable situations.

188. On many other subjects – industrial relations, working conditions, labour inspection – and no matter what the scope of the texts establishing the field of application, the instruments adopted were not conceived for certain kinds of work. It therefore does not suffice theoretically to extend the provisions in question to precarious workers, and even if it did, it would, as we have said, be extremely awkward to monitor application of the rules. The persons concerned could fall through the cracks, as the saying goes, of the social security systems promoted by Convention No. 102 and more recent ILO instruments.

189. In such conditions, should specific standards be adopted? Conventions have in fact been adopted on temporary work (regulating private employment agencies), on home work and on part-time work. Positive results have also been obtained by adapting general rules to the specific constraints faced by these workers, as suggested in recent instruments on occupational health and safety.

190. Beyond that, many delegates to the Governing Body and the International Labour Conference have insisted that consideration also be given to other modes of regulating labour that are less binding but better suited to people living in poverty. The ILO for example has adopted in June 2015 a recommendation on transitioning from the informal to the formal economy.[134] The ILO is preparing for example a recommendation on transitioning from the informal to the formal economy; it should be adopted in June 2015.[135] These standards of a different kind complement rather than replace those we have just examined. This may constitute a first step towards protection when the conditions do not allow a State to ratify a convention. Instruments of this kind may also not exist because it was considered that the time was not ripe for regulatory action.

§2. The Other ILO Standard-setting Instruments

I. Recommendations

191. International labour recommendations form the first category of other standard-setting instruments. The ILO Constitution contains numerous provisions on them that are very similar to those on the conventions (and indeed often deals with them in the same articles). There is, however, a crucial difference: the measures they put forward do not become obligatory on ratification but rather constitute mere reference standards on which countries are encouraged to base their labour policies, legislation and practice. The recommendations nevertheless place specific obligations on ILO Member States.[136]

192. The procedure for preparing recommendations is the same as for preparing conventions. Suffice it to refer to the latter.[137] The decision to adopt a recommendation on a given subject instead of or as a complement to a convention is taken by the Conference in full meeting on the proposal of the competent committee. The suggestion can obviously have been made beforehand. It should be recalled that if a draft convention does not obtain the required two-thirds majority at the final vote, the Conference can decide to refer it to the Drafting Committee to be drafted in the form of a recommendation. The recommendation must be voted before the end of the session.[138]

---

134. ILC, *Transitioning from the Informal to the Formal Economy*, Report V(1), Geneva, ILO, 2014; ILC (104th Session, 2015), *Provisional Record no. 10-1*, Geneva, ILO, 2015.
135. ILC, *Transitioning from the Informal to the Formal Economy*, Report V(1), Geneva, ILO, 2014; ILC (103rd Session, 2014), Provisional Record No. 11, Geneva, ILO, 2014.
136. On the historical background of recommendations, *see* G.P. Politakis and K. Markow, 'Les recommandations internationales du travail: instruments mal exploités ou maillon faible du système normatif', in J.-C. Javillier, B. Gernigon (eds.), and G.P. Politakis (coordinator), *Les normes internationales du travail. Un patrimoine pour l'avenir. Mélanges en l'honneur de Nicolas Valticos*, ILO, Geneva, 2004, pp. 500–502.
137. *See* paras 94 *et seq. above*.
138. Article 41 of the ILC Standing Orders.

193. The Conference adopts recommendations, as it does conventions, by a two-thirds majority of the delegates present. Two copies are signed, in this case as well, by the President of the Conference and by the Director-General: one is deposited in the ILO archives, the other is dispatched to the United Nations Secretary-General. The Director-General communicates a certified copy to each Member State 'with a view to effect being given to it by national legislation or otherwise'.[139]

194. The recommendations give rise for the Member States to effects that are similar to those of conventions:[140]

(a) The governments undertake to bring the recommendation before the authority or authorities within whose competence the matter lies for the enactment of legislation or other action; they have one year, in exceptional cases 18 months, from the end of the Conference session to do so.
(b) They inform the Director-General of the measures taken to that end, providing any information required.
(c) They report to the Director-General, as requested by the Governing Body, on the position of the law and practice in their country in regard to the matters dealt with in the recommendation, showing the extent to which effect has been given, or is proposed to be given, to the provisions of the recommendation and any modifications thereof as have been found or may be found necessary to make in adopting or applying them.

195. Article 19(6) of the Constitution stipulates that the Member States are under no other obligation in respect of recommendations. Paragraph 8 adds that, as in the case of conventions, their adoption does not affect 'any law, award, custom or agreement which ensures more favourable conditions to the workers concerned'.

196. The rules for revising and withdrawing from recommendations correspond *mutatis mutandis* to those discussed earlier for conventions.[141] Here, too, the new procedure for abrogation, which has been adopted but has not yet entered into force, was not deemed indispensable for recommendations, which contain no legal obligations other than those we have just mentioned.

II. Declarations and Resolutions

197. The terms 'declarations' and 'resolutions'[142] cover social policy instruments of widely varying origins – and hence of respective weight – and content. Both are adopted by the Conference itself, by the Governing Body or by other ILO

139. Article 19 of the Constitution.
140. *See* F. Maupain, 'International Labor Organization: Recommendations and Similar Instruments', in D. Shelton, *Commitment and Compliance: The Role of Non-Binding Norms in the International legal System*, Oxford University Press, 2000, pp. 372–393.
141. *See* paras 102 *et seq.*
142. Not to mention the 'conclusions' of ILO meetings: A Wisskirchen and Ch. Hess, *Employers' Handbook on ILO Standards-related Activities*, Geneva, ILO, 2001, pp. 45–46.

bodies. The word 'declaration' emphasizes both the importance of the content and the consequent desire to express that content with some solemnity; it is usually used for reference texts issued by the Conference or Governing Body. The content of both declarations and resolutions also varies considerably depending on whether they proclaim fundamental principles, the Organization's essential aims, or whether they contain more or less general technical standards.

198. Some ILO declarations have had a peculiar past. One example is the declaration adopted by the Conference in Philadelphia in 1944, towards the end of the Second World War. It brought the Organization's goals and objectives up to date while underscoring certain fundamental principles.[143] The delegations preferred to adopt a declaration than to amend the Constitution directly, for reasons dictated by the circumstances: a constitutional amendment would have taken time to enter into force whereas the text had to be rapidly updated so that ILO could make its voice heard in the new United Nations system. This being said, the 1945–1946 revision of the Constitution legitimized the declaration: Article 1 as amended refers to it expressly and announces that the text of the declaration is appended. Let us examine more in details other declarations.

A. *The Tripartite Declaration of Principles concerning Multinational Enterprises and Social Policy*

199. The growth of multinational enterprises in the 1960s and 1970s provoked intense debate in international forums. At ILO, the discussions centred on the impact those enterprises could have on the social situation of the countries in which they were established. For some, their presence in the host countries represented advantages in terms of modernizing the economy, employment and well-being; others expressed concern about the excessive concentration of economic power, the abuse that concentration could lead to and the conflicting nature of the enterprises' objectives and national policy goals. The difficulty of reconciling these points of view precluded the possibility of drafting an international labour convention on the subject. The Governing Board opted instead for a declaration, a non-binding instrument.

200. The Tripartite Declaration of Principles concerning Multinational Enterprises and Social Policy, adopted by the Governing Body on 16 November 1977, as amended, starts with several explanatory and general policy paragraphs. It then turns in succession to questions of employment (employment promotion; equality of opportunity and treatment; security of employment), training, conditions of work and life (*inter alia*, wages, benefits, minimum age; health and safety) and industrial relations (the right to organize, collective bargaining, consultation, examination of grievances and settlement of industrial disputes). The Annex contains a list of the

143. *See* paras 22 *et seq. above*.

conventions and recommendations to which the Declaration refers; the list includes all the instruments on fundamental workers' rights.[144]

201. The aim of the Declaration is to encourage the positive contribution which multinational enterprises can make to economic and social progress and to minimize and resolve the difficulties to which their operations may give rise. The text emphasizes that governments and professional organizations are recommended to observe the principles enshrined in the Declaration on a voluntary basis. One reporting procedure was established to monitor follow-up to the Declaration, another to consider disputes over its application.

202. The issue has since evolved. Sensitive to the criticisms – whether well founded or not – of which they are the target and to their image among consumers, large businesses have adopted codes of conduct and other social initiatives that are discussed below. Today the debate is not so much about multinationals as about the general process of globalization and its social repercussions. In 1998, the ILO adopted another declaration in response to those concerns.

B. The Declaration on Fundamental Principles and Rights at Work

203. The quickening pace of globalization gave rise to hopes for sweeping economic progress and fears of the effect the process would have on the underprivileged. Calls were made for the process to be social as well as economic and intense debate broke out at the ILO on how best to regulate it. The discussions centred on the cost of labour standards and again whether or not to include a social clause in trade agreements.[145]

204. A World Summit for Social Development held in Copenhagen in 1995 laid the groundwork for an agreement on a number of basic principles. The Heads of State and of government who attended the Summit made several pledges and agreed a programme of action to defend and promote the fundamental rights of workers. The following year, at the WTO Ministerial Conference in Singapore, the States parties renewed their pledge to observe internationally recognized fundamental labour standards, confirmed that ILO was competent to establish those standards and reaffirmed their support for ILO activities to promote them and make them effective. It

144. *See* ILO, *Tripartite Declaration of Principles concerning Multinational Enterprises and Social Policy*, Geneva, 2006; ILO Governing Body, Document GB.313/POL/9 (Rev.), Geneva, ILO, February 2012; F. Morgenstern, 'Déclaration de principes tripartite de l'OIT sur les enterprises multinationales et la politique sociale. Nouveaux problèmes, nouvelles méthodes', *Journal du Droit international* (Clunet), 1983, No. 1, pp. 61–75.

145. *See* paras 35–59 *above*. For an extensive discussion on the relationship between international trade and employment, *see* M. Jansen and E. Lee, *Trade and Employment: Challenges for Policy Research*, Geneva, ILO/WTO, 2007, and the comments on this book in 'Liberalisation du commerce et justice sociale: lectures croisées d'une étude menée conjointement par le BIT et l'OMC', *Revue de droit du travail*, no. 10, October 2007, pp. 608–615. *See also*, on the legal dimension, I. Daugareilh (ed.), *Mondialisation, travail et droits fondamentaux*, Brussels, LGDJ, Paris, 2005.

was in this political framework that the Declaration on Fundamental Principles and Rights at Work was adopted.[146] Briefly, the aim is to maintain the link between economic growth and social progress in a situation of growing economic interdependency. In this context the guarantee of fundamental principles and rights at work is particularly important and significant in that it enables the persons concerned to claim freely and on the basis of equality of opportunity their fair share of the wealth they helped create and to achieve fully their human potential.[147]

205. The Declaration stresses that labour standards should not be used for protectionist trade purposes, and that nothing in its wording and its follow-up may be invoked or used for such purposes; the comparative advantage of any country should in no way be called into question by the Declaration and its follow-up.

206. The Declaration presents itself as a 'promotional' instrument[148] serving to translate the ILO's values into integrated development programmes. It recalls the obligations inherent in membership of the ILO,[149] independently of the ratification of the conventions on fundamental rights at work, and calls for a strong political commitment to ensure respect for those rights, their promotion in economic and social practice and reports on those points. Efficient follow-up should be a decisive factor in reducing the political tension that emerged with globalization.[150]

207. The Declaration thus recalls that by the very fact of their membership in the Organization the Members agreed to the principles and rights enshrined in the ILO Constitution and appended Philadelphia Declaration; they undertook to work to achieve the Organization's overall objectives 'to the best of their resources and fully in line with their specific circumstances'. Those principles and rights 'have been expressed and developed in the form of specific rights and obligations in Conventions recognized as fundamental both inside and outside the Organization'. Even if they have not ratified the conventions, the Members States thus have an obligation to respect, promote and realize, in good faith, the following fundamental principles:

(a) freedom of association and the effective recognition of the right to collective bargaining;

146. *See* H. Kellerson, 'The ILO Declaration of 1998 on fundamental principles and rights: A challenge for the future', *ILR*, Vol. 132, No. 2, 1998, p. 223 *et seq.*; F. Maupain, 'L'OIT, la justice sociale et la mondialisation', *RCADI*, Vol. 278, 1999, p. 262 *et seq.*; J. Bellace, 'The ILO Declaration of Fundamental Principles and Rights at work', *International Journal of Comparative Labour Law and Industrial Relations*, Vol. 17(3), fall 2001, pp. 269–287; S. Charnovitz, *Trade Law and Global Governance*, London, Cameron, May 2002, p. 273 *et seq.*; A. Trebilcock, 'The ILO Declaration on Fundamental Principles and Rights at work and its Follow-up', in ILO, *International Labour Standards: A Global Approach*, Geneva, 2001, pp. 16–25; I. Duplessis, 'La déclaration de l'OIT relative aux droits fondamentaux au travail. Une nouvelle forme de régulation efficace?', *Relations industrielles/Industrial Relations*, Vol. 59, No. 1, pp. 52–72.
147. *See* the considerations of the document.
148. *See* operative paragraph 4.
149. *See* para. 90 *above*.
150. ILC, Report of the Director General, *Decent Work*, 87th Session, ILO, Geneva, 1999, p. 8.

(b) the elimination of all forms of forced or compulsory labour;
(c) the effective abolition of child labour; and
(d) the elimination of discrimination in respect of employment and occupation.

208. It is incumbent on the Organization to help the States meet those objectives and to mobilize for that purpose all 'its constitutional, operational and budgetary resources'; the Declaration specifically mentions external resources and support from other international organizations. It provides for a follow-up mechanism to be implemented as specified in the annex; that mechanism, it goes without saying, is not a substitute for established supervisory mechanisms nor is it intended to impede their work.[151]

209. The first component of the follow-up is the annual review of reports submitted by the Member States on the fundamental conventions they have not yet ratified.[152] These reports – which are requested under Article 19(5) of the Constitution – are compiled and archived by the ILO. That presentation is followed by a Governing Body debate. The second component is a global report that the ILO Director-General submits every year for discussion to the Conference on one of the four above-mentioned categories of fundamental principles and rights. The report presents a dynamic global picture of each category of fundamental principles and rights during a four-year period, and serves as a basis for assessing the effectiveness of ILO assistance and for determining the technical cooperation priorities for the following period. It covers both countries that have ratified the relevant conventions and those that have not.

210. An assessment made several years after the Declaration's adoption was positive. The Declaration attracted contributions from donors, notably the United States, eager to encourage its implementation. These resources financed important ILO programmes. The Declaration has also been a factor in the success of the campaign for ratification of the ILO fundamental conventions, and beyond that for the dissemination of the rights and principles they enshrine.[153] What is more, in a significant development, today's bilateral or multilateral cooperation treaties often contain a clause on respect for the principles and rights set forth in the Declaration,

151. Paragraph 2 of the annex.
152. At the time of the adoption of the Declaration, seven Conventions were considered fundamental: the Freedom of Association and Protection of the Right to Organize Convention, 1948 (No. 87), the Right to Organize and Collective Bargaining Convention, 1949 (No. 98), the Forced Labour Convention, 1930 (No. 29), the Abolition of Forced Labour Convention, 1957 (No. 105), the Minimum Age Convention, 1973 (No. 138), the Equal Remuneration Convention, 1951 (No. 100), and the Discrimination (Employment and Occupation) Convention, 1958 (No. 111). To these has been added the Worst Forms of Child Labour Convention, 1999 (No. 182), which was adopted unanimously in June of that year and entered into force on 17 November 2000.
153. Trebilcock, *op. cit.*, pp. 22–23; G. von Potobsky, 'El devenir de las normas internacionales del trabajo', *Revista de Derecho Social – Latinoamérica*, No. 3 – 2007; U. Muckenberger, 'Hybrid Global Labour Law', in R. Blanpain and F. Hendricks (eds.), *Labour Law between Change and Tradition. In Honour A. Jacobs,* The Hague, Kluwer, 2011.

giving it special legal value. The adoption of the Declaration has led to an acute controversy concerning its effects on the ILO standards-setting activities as a whole. Some[154] have underlined its non-binding character and the risk of focusing only on the so-called core labour standards, while forgetting the others whose importance should not be underestimated on the life, health and well-being of the workers. Doubts are also raised about the actual implementation of those basic principles when most populated countries like China, India or the USA have not yet ratified such a fundamental convention as the one on freedom of association.[155] Other writers[156] have rather insisted on the present need for flexibility in the labour market, and on the capacity of the Declaration to respond to the constraints of the enterprises. Those views, clearly of a political as much as of a technical nature, represent two different visions of the future of labour protection: the first is more concerned with the necessary guarantees for the workers, the second, with the economic development of the enterprises whose return normally benefits to its staff.

C. The Declaration on Social Justice for a Fair Globalization

211. The International Labour Conference unanimously adopted a Declaration on Social Justice for a Fair Globalization on 10 June 2008.[157] It builds on the Philadelphia Declaration of 1944 and the Declaration on Fundamental Principles and Rights at Work of 1998. The 2008 Declaration reaffirms and adjusts the ILO's mandate in the era of globalization. It recalls the values of the Organization, emphasizes its four 'strategic' objectives of employment creation, social protection development, social dialogue promotion, and fundamental rights at work – what is called in the ILO terminology 'the Decent Work Agenda' – and stresses a holistic and integrated approach by underlining that they are 'inseparable, interrelated and mutually supportive' and by ensuring the role of international labour standards as a means of achieving all of them.

212. At the same time, the Organization is asked to 'review and adapt its institutional practices to enhance governance and capacity building in order to make the best use of its human and financial resources and of the unique advantage of its tripartite structure and standards system'. The Organization and its Members must

154. P. Alston, Core Labour Standards and the Transformation of the International Labour Rights Regime', *European Journal of International Law*, Vol. 15, No. 3, 2004, pp. 457–521; *ibid.* 'Facing up the complexities of the ILO's core labour standards agenda', *European Journal of International Law*, Vol. 16, No. 3, 2005, pp. 467–480.

155. Von Potobsky, *op. cit.*; Thouvenin and Trebilcock (eds.), *op. cit.*, Vol. 1, p. 177.

156. F. Maupain, 'Revitalization, not retreat: the real potential of the 1998 ILO Declaration for the unversal protection of workers' rights', *European Journal of International Law*, Vol. 16, No. 3, 2005, pp. 452–454; B. Langille, 'Core labour rights – the true story (reply to Alston)', *European Journal of International Law*, Vol. 16, No. 3, 2005, pp. 409–437.

157. *See* http://www.ilo.org/global/ What_we_do/Officialmeetings/ilc/ILCSessions/97thSession/pr/lang–en/docName – WCMS_094042/index.htm.

mobilize all available means of action, both nationally and internationally, to promote the goals of the Declaration and implement its commitments in the most effective and efficient way. The document contributes to policy coherence for sustainable development in national policies, among international organizations and in development cooperation, bringing together social, economic and environmental objectives. It highlights that international and regional organizations with mandates in closely related fields can play a role in the implementation of the integrated approach required. It finally calls for developing new partnerships with non-state entities and economic actors, such as multinational enterprises and trade unions operating at the global sector level, in order to enhance the effectiveness of ILO operational programmes and activities.[158]

III. Model Codes and Codes of Practice

213. There is a tendency, in the field of occupational health in particular, to take preventive rather than curative action, to limit the amount of legislative or regulatory text and to encourage the establishment by the public authorities and/or occupational organizations of standards and practical guidelines that do not as a rule have force of law but that can be rapidly adapted to technological developments. This tendency has been observed both nationally and internationally. In the past, ILO drafted model codes on occupational health and safety. More recently, it has published codes of practice that compile all that is known and has been experienced on a given subject in terms of possible conflicts, real problems and suggested policy solutions. Codes (or 'guidelines') have been adopted for specific sectors of activity (construction, opencast mines, coal mines, iron and steel industries, non-ferrous metals industries, agriculture, shipbuilding and ship repairing, forestry for example), on protecting workers against certain hazards (such as radiation, lasers, visual display units, chemicals, asbestos, airborne substances), and on certain safety and health measures (e.g. occupational safety and health management systems; ethical guidelines for workers' health surveillance; recording and notification of occupational accidents and diseases; protection of workers' personal data; safety, health and working conditions in the transfer of technology to developing countries).

214. These codes of practice supplement the conventions and recommendations and contain detailed practical guidelines without creating legal obligations. They can also, as in the case of the protection of personal data, be preferred to more formal instruments when the subject matter is not, or not yet, suitable for sophisticated standard-setting action. They are drafted in a process of in-depth consultation with the governments and employers' and workers' organizations, and following examination by a technical meeting of experts and/or representatives of the occupation. Their publication is subject to approval by the Governing Body. In addition, meetings of experts convened by ILO can adopt technical guidelines.

158. J. Somavía, Preface to the published text of the instrument, Geneva, ILO, 2008.

§3. CODES OF CONDUCT AND SIMILAR INITIATIVES

215. A code, as we know, is a set of rules, precepts or instructions that may (a penal code, a general tax code) or may not (a code of good taste or of honour) be obligatory under the law. The same holds true of codes of conduct, in many ways a redundant term now customarily used in particular to refer to the written document by which a company pledges to follow a certain policy or certain principles.

216. This section discusses the latter kind of code and other initiatives that put the accent on the social responsibility of multinational companies in particular.[159] They obviously have a place in this monograph, whether they are the work of the company or of an international institution; in this respect, we will take a special look at the guidelines of the Organization for Economic Co-operation and Development (OECD) for multinational enterprises. Another example is the Global Compact launched by the United Nations in July 2000 together with several other international institutions, including ILO. A purely voluntary initiative, the Global Compact aims to promote corporate civic responsibility and sets out nine principles that are the object of a universal consensus, four of them drawn directly from the 1998 Declaration on Fundamental Principles and Rights at Work.[160]

217. Mention should also be made of the Guiding Principles for the Implementation of the UN 'Protect, Respect and Remedy' Framework endorsed by the United Nations Human Rights Council on 16 June 2011.[161] They clarify the meaning of the corporate responsibility to respect human rights and provide an authoritative global standard for preventing and addressing the risk of adverse impacts on human rights linked to business activity. Paragraph 31 underlines that non-judicial grievance mechanisms, both State based and non-State based, should be: legitimate (enabling trust from the stakeholder groups for whose use they are intended, and being accountable for the fair conduct of grievance processes), accessible (being known to all stakeholder groups for whose use they are intended, and providing adequate assistance for those who may face particular barriers to access); predictable (providing a clear and known procedure with an indicative timeframe for each stage, and clarity on the types of process and outcome available and means of monitoring implementation) equitable (seeking to ensure that aggrieved parties have reasonable access to sources of information, advice and expertise necessary to engage in a grievance process on fair, informed and respectful terms) transparent (keeping parties to a grievance informed about its progress, and providing sufficient information about the mechanism's performance to build confidence in its effectiveness and meet any public interest at stake), rights-compatible (ensuring that outcomes and

159. On codes of conduct, *see* the Governing Body Document GB.273/WP/SDL/1, paras 26 *et seq.*

160. *See* www.unglobalcompact.org. *See* also L. Boisson de Chazournes and E. Mazuyer (ed.), *Le Pacte mondial des Nations-Unies 10 ans après*, Brussels Bruylant, 2011. The present publication is about international law and will not deal with purely national initiatives.

161. UN, *Guiding Principles on Business and Human Right. Implementing the United Nations 'Protect, Respect and Remedy' Framework,* New York and Geneva, 2011; P. Alston and R. Goodman, *International Human Rights*, Oxford University Press, 2013.

remedies accord with internationally recognized human rights) a source of continuous learning (drawing on relevant measures to identify lessons for improving the mechanism and preventing future grievances and harms). Operational-level mechanisms should also be based on engagement and dialogue: consulting the stakeholder groups for whose use they are intended on their design and performance and focusing on dialogue as the means to address and resolve grievances.

I. OECD Guidelines for Multinational Enterprises

218. In 1976 the OECD Council of Ministers adopted the Declaration on International Investment and Multinational Enterprises. The Declaration is a policy commitment by adhering governments to provide an open and transparent environment for international investment and to encourage the positive contribution multinational enterprises can make to economic and social progress. The Declaration and the Decisions that followed are periodically reviewed. The Declaration also comprises Guidelines for Multinational Enterprises that are in fact recommendations compliance with which is voluntary and the application of which is encouraged and facilitated by national contact points in the member countries.[162]

219. The Guidelines are voluntary standards, non-binding recommendations addressed to the multinationals by the adhering governments; they aim to encourage these enterprises to operate in harmony with national policies and social expectations. They cover the entire range of multinational activities and are based on implementation procedures in the OECD countries and in several non-OECD countries that have adhered to the Declaration (let us mention Argentina, Brazil, Colombia, Costa Rica, Peru, Lithuania, Romania, Egypt, Jordan, Morocco and Tunisia). They are supplemented with explanatory commentaries and clarifications on interpretation pursuant to the deliberations of the Committee on International Investment and Multinational Enterprises.

220. The Guidelines open with concepts and general policies, the latter including:[163]

> 2. Respect the internationally recognised human rights of those affected by their activities.
>
> 4. Encourage human capital formation, in particular by creating employment opportunities and facilitating training opportunities for employees.
>
> 5. Refrain from seeking or accepting exemptions not contemplated in the statutory or regulatory framework related to human rights, environmental, health, safety, labour, taxation, financial incentives, or other issues. […]

162. *See* the OECD website: www.oecd.org/daf/investment/guidelines/mnetextf; *see also* R. Blanpain (ed.), *Multinational Enterprises and the Social Challenges of the Century*, The Hague, Kluwer, 2001; I. Daugareilh, 'La dimension sociale des principes fondateurs de l'OCDE à l'intention des entreprises multinationales', in *Revue générale de droit international public*, 2008, No. 3, pp. 567–599.

163. http://mneguidelines.oecd.org/oecddeclarationanddecisions.htm.

8. Promote awareness of and compliance by workers employed by multinational enterprises with respect to company policies through appropriate dissemination of these policies, including through training programmes.

9. Refrain from discriminatory or disciplinary action against workers who make *bona fide* reports to management or, as appropriate, to the competent public authorities, on practices that contravene the law, the *Guidelines* or the enterprise's policies.

13. In addition to addressing adverse impacts in relation to matters covered by the *Guidelines*, encourage, where practicable, business partners, including suppliers and sub-contractors, to apply principles of corporate conduct compatible with the *Guidelines*.

221. The Guidelines continue with recommendations pertaining to numerous fields: disclosure of information, human rights, employment and industrial relations, environment, combating bribery, bribes solicitation, extortion, consumer interests, science and technology, competition and taxation. The approach is very broad.

222. The text on employment and industrial relations is worded as follows:

Enterprises should, within the framework of applicable law, regulations and prevailing labour relations and employment practices and applicable international labour standards:

1. a) Respect the right of workers employed by the multinational enterprise to establish or join trade unions and representative organisations of their own choosing.

   b) Respect the right of workers employed by the multinational enterprise to have trade unions and representative organisations of their own choosing recognised for the purpose of collective bargaining, and engage in constructive negotiations, either individually or through employers' associations, with such representatives with a view to reaching agreements on terms and conditions of employment.

   c) Contribute to the effective abolition of child labour, and take immediate and effective measures to secure the prohibition and elimination of the worst forms of child labour as a matter of urgency.

   d) Contribute to the elimination of all forms of forced or compulsory labour and take adequate steps to ensure that forced or compulsory labour does not exist in their operations.

   e) Be guided throughout their operations by the principle of equality of opportunity and treatment in employment and not discriminate against their workers with respect to employment or occupation on such grounds as race, colour, sex, religion, political opinion, national extraction or social origin, or other status, unless selectivity concerning worker characteristics furthers established governmental policies which specifically promote greater equality of employment opportunity or relates to the inherent requirements of a job.

2. a) Provide such facilities to workers' representatives as may be necessary to assist in the development of effective collective agreements.
   b) Provide information to workers' representatives which is needed for meaningful negotiations on conditions of employment.
   c) Provide information to workers and their representatives which enables them to obtain a true and fair view of the performance of the entity or, where appropriate, the enterprise as a whole.
3. Promote consultation and co-operation between employers and workers and their representatives on matters of mutual concern.
4. a) Observe standards of employment and industrial relations not less favourable than those observed by comparable employers in the host country.
   b) When multinational enterprises operate in developing countries, where comparable employers may not exist, provide the best possible wages, benefits and conditions of work, within the framework of government policies. These should be related to the economic position of the enterprise, but should be at least adequate to satisfy the basic needs of the workers and their families.
   c) Take adequate steps to ensure occupational health and safety in their operations.
5. In their operations, to the greatest extent practicable, employ local workers and provide training with a view to improving skill levels, in co-operation with worker representatives and, where appropriate, relevant governmental authorities.
6. In considering changes in their operations which would have major employment effects, in particular in the case of the closure of an entity involving collective lay-offs or dismissals, provide reasonable notice of such changes to representatives of the workers in their employment and their organisations, and, where appropriate, to the relevant governmental authorities, and co-operate with the worker representatives and appropriate governmental authorities so as to mitigate to the maximum extent practicable adverse effects. In light of the specific circumstances of each case, it would be appropriate if management were able to give such notice prior to the final decision being taken. Other means may also be employed to provide meaningful co-operation to mitigate the effects of such decisions.
7. In the context of bona fide negotiations with workers' representatives on conditions of employment, or while workers are exercising a right to organise, not threaten to transfer the whole or part of an operating unit from the country concerned nor transfer workers from the enterprises' component entities in other countries in order to influence unfairly those negotiations or to hinder the exercise of a right to organise.
8. Enable authorised representatives of the workers in their employment to negotiate on collective bargaining or labour-management relations issues

and allow the parties to consult on matters of mutual concern with representatives of management who are authorised to take decisions on these matters.

223. As we can see, the Guidelines refer to the fundamental principles and rights at work enshrined in the 1998 ILO Declaration. The commentaries accompanying the text refer specifically to the Declaration and to the ILO Tripartite Declaration on Multinational Enterprises and Social Policy. They specify that the OECD Guidelines have a role in promoting observation of the principles and rights of the 1998 Declaration by multinational enterprises. Both the Guidelines and the ILO Declaration on Multinational Enterprises, they say, deal with how enterprises are expected to conduct themselves; they 'are intended to parallel and not conflict with each other'. The ILO Tripartite Declaration is 'of use in understanding the *Guidelines* to the extent that it is of a greater degree of elaboration', even though the follow-up procedures are institutionally separate.

224. The commentaries also mention various ILO instruments, especially on the abolition of child labour (Conventions Nos. 182 and 138; Recommendation No. 146), the elimination of forced labour (Conventions Nos. 29 and 105), non-discrimination in employment and occupation (Convention No. 111 in particular, but also the Maternity Protection Convention No 183 of 2000, Employment (Disabled Persons) Convention No159 of 1983, the Older Workers Recommendation No162 of 1980 and the HIV and AIDS at Work Recommendation No 200 of 2010) and consultation and cooperation between employers and workers at the level of the undertaking (Recommendation No. 94). The ILO List of Occupational Diseases Recommendation No. 194 of 2002, Human Resources Development Recommendation No195 of 2004 and Recommendation No. 198 on Employment Relationship of 2006 are also referred to.

II. Social Initiatives by Private Companies

225. The agreements reached by international institutions are not the only means of regulating, at supra-national level, labour and employment conditions. In this area, as in others, it is useful to have a look at 'field' experiences, in particular those of enterprises with activities in more than one country. In addition, the quickened pace of globalization is blurring the respective roles of the States and the large multinational corporations.[164] Their concern to respect the fundamental labour rules stems first and foremost from a sensibility to social issues in the broad sense. They also often consider that good conditions of employment stimulate productivity. And

164. *See also* B. Hepple, 'A race to the top? International investment guidelines and corporate codes of conduct', *Comparative Labor Law and Policy Journal*, 1999, Vol. 20, pp. 347–363; O. Boiral, 'The certification of corporate conduct: Issues and prospects', *ILR*, Vol. 42 (No. 3), 2003, pp. 317–340; A. Sobczac, *Réseaux de sociétés et codes de conduite. Un nouveau modèle de régulation des relations de travail pour les entreprises européennes*, Paris, LGDJ, 2002.

finally, they wish to have a brand image that is not tarnished by reprehensible working methods. Such methods can even, as experience has shown, provoke press campaigns and boycotts instigated by trade unions, consumer associations and non-governmental organizations (NGOs). In brief, more and more firms consider that they have a social or societal corporate responsibility.

226. Certain firms have pledged to meet minimum labour standards in the private contracts concluded with their suppliers, subcontractors, licencees and customers. More often – but one does not exclude the other – they do this within the company or the group in documents added to their own working rules. The measures have often gone by the generic term of 'codes of conduct'. Enterprises have also taken other kinds of initiatives.

A. *Codes of Conduct*

227. Codes of conduct set out the company's voluntary undertakings, i.e. without being legally bound to do so. In the case of multinationals, such commitments are analysed in the light of the applicable law, either private international labour law or European law. They can take the form of collective agreements signed with trade unions or of contracts concluded with NGOs.[165] If they are unilateral commitments, domestic law may recognize such acts as unilateral undertakings with legal effects, implicit clauses introduced in the employment contract or additions to the company work rules, or public declarations leading to civil liability in case of false statement. The legal value of those codes remains difficult to prove.

228. Whether elaborated by national and international enterprises, these codes are either 'operational' or called 'model codes' when they are published by associations of enterprises, trade unions, NGOs and States, either jointly or separately. The latter are not applicable *per se*, but help enterprises to draw up their own codes. ISO standards constitute a well-known example of the model codes;[166] in spite of serious difficulties,[167] the ILO collaborates with the standards elaborated in the field of labour.

229. It seems, but complete information is rather difficult to collect, that codes and similar corporate documents contain few references to fundamental international labour standards (non-discrimination in employment; the prohibition of forced labour and child labour; freedom of association and the right to collective bargaining). They tend to relate, in the field we are concerned with, to matters of occupational health and the calculation of wages (on the basis, as the case may be,

165. Several international framework agreements lay the foundation for building up a structure to deal with grievances: usually, rather than stipulating a system of mediation (ombudsperson), a chain of grievance resolution is laid out: *see* http://www.eurofound.europa.eu/publications/htmlfiles/ef0810 2.htmhttp://www.eurofound.europa.eu/publications/htmlfiles/ef08102.htm, *European and international framework agreements: Practical experiences and strategic approaches*, 2008.
166. www.iso.org.
167. ILO Governing Body, document GB.325/INS/11, Geneva, ILO, 2015.

of national legislation, standards for the sector of activity or a *sui generis* formula). When, however, the code is the work of several stakeholders (trade unions, NGOs, corporate or industrial associations), more frequent reference is made to fundamental standards.[168]

230. A question often raised is whether these commitments can really be monitored. The codes usually contain provisions on supervision in the form of internal mechanisms or inspection by a third party (the latter in some cases complementing the former). Effective verification that the commitments made are being upheld depends not only on how technically competent and independent the supervisory bodies are, but also on how clearly the pertinent clauses are worded.

231. The codes therefore appear to be useful guarantees in the workplace. Their value nevertheless varies considerably depending on their content, the extent to which they can be enforced and the quality of any audits. They can further, to the extent we have just said, the implementation of international labour standards. Need we say, however, that the application of these standards cannot be limited to such codes.[169]

B. Other Social Initiatives

232. 'Social labelling' has been widely reported on in the media. It is used to communicate information on the social conditions in which a product was manufactured or a service provided. It can be placed on the product itself or on its packaging, or be carried by the seller. What we have said about codes of conduct applies *mutatis mutandis* to labels.

233. Investors have taken different kinds of ethical initiatives. Shareholders sometimes try to influence corporate social policy, officially (during annual general meetings) or in informal contacts. In some cases the choice of indexed shares included in investment portfolios is based on the social performance of the company (or, conversely, some shares are excluded on that basis). Socially responsible investment encompasses the establishment of indexes, ratings and investment.

---

168. J.C. Javillier (ed.), *Governance, international law and corporate social responsability*, IILS, Geneva, 2008; I. Daugareilh (ed.), *Responsabilité social de l'entreprise et globalisation*, Brussels, Bruylant, 2010; E Mazuyer (ed.), *Regards croisés sur la responsabilité sociale de l'entreprise*, Paris, La documentation française, 2010; J.M. Servais, 'Normes internationales du travail et responsabilité sociale des entreprises', in Ph. Auvergnon (ed.), *Quelle responsabilité sociale pour l'entreprise? Approches juridiques nationales et comparatives*, Bordeaux, University Montesquieu-Bordeaux IV, (Comptrasec), 2005, pp. 37–58; M.A. Moreau, 'Travail forcé, RSE et sous-traitance dans l'industrie textile en Asie: réflexion sur l'action de l'OIT', *Droit social*, no. 5, May 2014, pp. 413–422.
169. M. Dumas, 'Three Misunderstanding about Consumocratic Labor Law', *Comp. Labour Law & Pol. Journal*, Vol. 35(1), fall 2013, pp. 67–91; R. Locke, *The Promise and Limits of Private Power: Promoting Labor Standards in the Global Economy*, Ithaca, Cornell University Press, 2013; R.J. Flanagan and W.B. Gould IV, *International Labor Standards. Globalization: Trade and Public Policy*, Stanford (California), Stanford University Press, 2003, p. 10.

234. It would be remiss of us not to mention social accreditation or certification systems and corporate social reports. All these initiatives presuppose, if they are to be meaningful, the existence of criteria to evaluate social policies and hence of standards of conduct of the kind we have just mentioned.

Chapter 4. Provisions from Other Sources and Conflicts between Standards

235. The UN 1966 International Covenants on Civil and Political Rights, and more, the one on Economic, Social and Cultural Rights constitute today the basis for a number of ILO Conventions and Recommendations; they will be mentioned whenever necessary. UN Conventions have also completed ILO standard-setting, especially with regard to discrimination and migration; we will also refer to them. Mention has already be made that the ILO has collaborated with the UNESCO in the drafting, adoption and supervision of international instruments, as in the teaching sector, and with the Council of Europe in the field of social rights in general, including social security. The Organisation has maintained close contacts with the EU and with ISO for the elaboration of the relevant standards.

236. As the number of international bilateral, multilateral, regional and universal instruments grows, conflicts are bound to arise with international labour standards.[170] It should be added that the oversight mechanisms for their application are markedly different from those of ILO, although this dissimilarity is no bar to cooperation on matters of common interest. More often, however, tension has been observed between the policies implemented by international institutions (at one time, for example, between ILO and the international financial organizations) than real contradictions between their standards. It is true that these institutions have endeavoured to avoid such contradictions by effectively coordinating the preparation and supervision of their standard-setting instruments. Arrangements to that effect exist between ILO and United Nations or European bodies, in particular the Council of Europe. They have often inserted compatibility clauses in their instruments, as in the case of the United Nations Covenants on Human Rights in respect of ILO Convention No. 87.[171] In some cases (as for the Council of Europe), the organizations exchange observers who sit in on certain meetings of the other institution's supervisory bodies, in order to ensure that the decisions taken by those bodies are as coherent as possible. The problem is different if the conflict is between an ILO convention and another source of ILO law. In that case there are two possible solutions. The first consists in inquiring into whether the other source is legally binding or not, and in respect of whom; the second, in recognizing a clear hierarchy between standards, with the Constitution having primacy and the conventions preempting all others.

170. J. Bellace, 'Human Rights at Work: the Need for Definitional Coherence in the Global Governance System', *Comp. Labour Law & Pol. Journal*, Vol. 30(2), 2014, pp. 175–198.

171. Article 8, para. 3 of the International Covenant on Economic, Social and Cultural Rights, adopted in 1966 by the United Nations, provides for example that 'nothing in this article shall authorize States Parties to the International Labour Organization Convention of 1948 concerning Freedom of Association and Protection of the Right to Organize to take legislative measures which would prejudice, or apply the law in such a manner as would prejudice, the guarantees provided for in that Convention'. A similar provision exists in Article 22, para. 22 of the International Covenant on Civil and Political Rights (also adopted by the United Nations in 1966).

237. Otherwise, when two provisions appear to contradict each other a check must be made of whether they are truly incompatible. Only in rare cases has a State ratified contradictory standards by which it is bound. It may also happen that international supervisory bodies interpret differently relatively similar rules.[172] The problem has been given no definitive answer because there is no hierarchical order to international instruments. The emergence of a law of international organizations alongside the classical law of treaties has made the question more complex. International labour law long worked on the principle of the interpretation that was most favourable to the worker, which was enshrined in many acts of domestic legislation. Domestic legislation often casts doubt on that principle today. One can therefore wonder about its validity should a conflict arise between ILO conventions and other international standards, even if relations between ILO-made law and domestic law are governed by that principle as a constitutional rule.[173]

238. The conformity of domestic law and practice with ILO standards concern Member States rather than regional organization such as the EU, although the latter may be indirectly obliged to manage the political consequences of the discrepancies. Oppositions between International and European law are not frequent. Let us point out that the EU concept of 'flexicurity' has much in common with the ILO notion of 'decent work'. Conflicts exist however, in particular in the case law of the Court of Justice of the EU[174] that will be mentioned in the relevant paragraphs. They concern the civil liability of the trade unions in case of strike and its compatibility with the ILO freedom of association conventions (Case *Laval un Partneri* of 18 December 2007), the consequences of the *Rüffert* case (of 3 April 2008) on the application of the ILO Labour Clauses (Public Contracts) Convention, 1949 (No. 94) as well as the implementation of restrictive social policy imposed to countries, like Greece, unable to pay their debts. In the same manner, the European Court of Human Rights and the CJEU have decided that the freedom of association also covers the right not to join a trade union. The competence of the EU in social matters also means, as we have seen, that the European authorities have their say when their Member States intend to ratify an ILO Convention.

172. *See for example* J. Malmberg, 'Enforcement of Labour Law', in B. Hepple and B. Veneziani (eds.), *The Transformation of Labour Law in Europe: A Comparative Study of 15 Countries 1945–2009*, Oxford and Portland, Oregon, Hart Publishing, 2009, p. 282.
173. *See* para. 126 *above*; *comp.* Valticos, *op. cit.*, para. 224 *et seq.*
174. A. Bronstein, *Derecho internacional del trabajo*, Buenos Aires, Astrea, 2013, pp. 147–161.

Part II. The Content of International Labour Standards

239. Part II looks at three major themes:

- freedom of association and social dialogue;
- labour and employment;
- social security.

240. Any separation – whether for educational or academic purposes – is relative. Care must be taken not to consider each theme as separate from the others. Indeed, it is the link between them that gives international labour law its dynamism.

Chapter 1. Freedom of Association and Social Dialogue

241. ILO conventions and recommendations emphasize the importance of the individual and collective freedoms of workers and employers, and of harmonious relations between them for good corporate management. These are fundamental rights.

242. The International Covenant on Civil and Political Rights, adopted by the United Nations General Assembly on 16 December 1966, states[175] that everyone has the right to freedom of association with others, including the right to form and join trade unions for the protection of their interests. The International Covenant on Economic, Social and Cultural Rights, adopted the same day, is more specific:

> Article 8
>
> 1. The States Parties to the present Covenant undertake to ensure:
>   (a) The right of everyone to form trade unions and join the trade union of his choice, subject only to the rules of the organization concerned, for the promotion and protection of his economic and social interests. No restrictions may be placed on the exercise of this right other than those prescribed by law and which are necessary in a democratic society in the interests of national security or public order or for the protection of the rights and freedoms of others;
>   (b) the right of trade unions to establish national federations of confederations and the right of the latter to form or join international trade-union organizations;
>   (c) the right of trade unions to function freely subject to no limitations other than those prescribed by law and which are necessary in a democratic society in the interests of national security or public order or for the protection of the rights and freedoms of others;
>   (d) the right to strike, provided that it is exercised in conformity with the laws of the particular country.
> 2. This article shall not prevent the imposition of lawful restrictions on the exercise of these rights by members of the armed forces or of the police or of the administration of the State.
> 3. Nothing in this article shall authorize States Parties to the International Labour Organization Convention of 1948 concerning Freedom of Association and Protection of the Right to Organize to take legislative measures which would prejudice, or apply the law in such a manner as would prejudice, the guarantees provided for in the Convention.

243. This provision basically reiterates the standards set forth in ILO Convention No. 87 on freedom of association and protection of the right to organize, and adds an express reference to the right to strike. On the other hand, it authorizes broader exceptions to the rights granted to public servants, and in the interests of

175. Article 22.

national security, public order or the protection of the rights and freedoms of others. Paragraph 3 nevertheless expressly safeguards the obligations arising from the Convention in respect of the States party thereto.

244. The Covenants and, for that matter, ILO conventions use very general terms so that they can serve as a basis for various systems of industrial relations. International labour standards do not seek to impose a specific system. Since every domestic legal order has to integrate countless political, economic, social and cultural factors, including a historical component, it would be unrealistic to put forward more than minimum rules, basic principles that can be transplanted into most if not all national systems. ILO law therefore aims to reconcile defence of the general principles of freedom with respect for the individual characteristics of each country when it comes to the technical means of incorporating those principles into domestic legislation.

245. Collective labour relations are naturally a major topic of analysis, reflection and discussion at ILO, a tripartite organization, and in international labour law. As we have seen, the Declaration on Fundamental Principles and Rights at Work has included freedom of association and effective recognition of the right to collective bargaining among those principles and rights.[176]

246. Collective relations take form between employers (individually or as a group), workers organized in trade unions or otherwise represented, and, in some instances, the public authorities. In particular, employers' associations and trade unions play an intermediary role and help the State regulate collective relations and strike the best possible balance between everyone's interests.

247. Paragraph 1 below starts by examining the freedom these private players have to form their own groups and the conditions required for the development of their associations, usually a legal framework establishing the organizations' independence and ensuring they are able to act. It also considers the bipartite and tripartite relations – depending on whether or not the public authorities are involved – between the players. International law proposes channels of communication, procedures for dialogue, and requires that the players operate on a truly equal footing.

248. Social dialogue can take place at different levels: the firm or enterprise, the region or municipality, the sector or sub-sector of activity, at national – or federal – inter-occupational level, supranationally (European, multinational or global dialogue). Paragraph 2 reviews the specific international standards that govern relations within the undertaking and underscore the particular nature of what constitutes the production site. In some sectors of activity industrial relations can be difficult to develop. More recent ILO standards contain positive measures for overcoming the obstacles encountered; these are briefly discussed in paragraph 3 on freedom of association and social rights.

176. *See* para. 207 *above*.

§1. General Standards on Freedom of Association and Collective Bargaining

249. ILO has adopted two basic instruments we have already mentioned: Convention No. 87 on freedom of association and protection of the right to organize (1948), and Convention No. 98 on the right to organize and collective bargaining (1949). The first deals more with the relations of employers, workers and their organizations with the public authorities, the second with relations between employers, wage earners and their respective associations. The standards set down in these instruments are supplemented by the conclusions of ILO's supervisory bodies which, while not binding,[177] nevertheless provide useful guidelines for translating the provisions of the conventions into national reality. Other international labour conventions and recommendations contain more detailed provisions on the application of these general standards in specific fields.

I. Freedom of Association for Workers and Employers

A. *The Freedom to Create and Join an Association*

250. Few States still question the existence of trade unions.[178] A look at the relevant legal texts and at national reality nevertheless shows that numerous restrictions continue to be placed on the very freedom to constitute and join workers' organizations. There are basically three kinds of restrictions: limits to the right to organize for certain categories of workers; the requirement of prior authorization by the public authorities; denial of the right to choose a trade union.

251. Article 2 of Convention No. 87 stipulates that all workers, no matter what their sector of activity (with the sole possible exception of the armed forces and the police), political opinion, sex, nationality, race, etc., have the right to establish trade unions. Certain countries, for example, deny the express or indirect recognition of this right to all personnel in the service of the State, or draw distinctions as to the rights of the various categories of public servants. Other categories of workers, such as agricultural and domestic workers, are regularly denied the right to establish trade unions.[179] The Convention further stipulates that trade unions do not require the approval of the administrative authorities, either direct or indirect, i.e. through formalities amounting to approval (registration or approval of statutes, for example, as a condition for the trade union to exist in law or in fact); the provisions on the acquisition of legal personality can also be a form of indirect approval.

177. *See* paras 147–148 *above*.
178. Trade union rights are still not recognized however in countries such as Saudi Arabia or Oman.
179. ILC (101st Session, 2012), *Giving Globalization a Human Face*, Report III (Part 1B), Geneva, ILO, 2012, paras 64 *et seq*.; ILC (104th session, 2015), *Giving a Voice to Rural Workers*, Report III (Part 1 B), Geneva, ILO, 2015, paras 325–327.

252. The workers must be free to choose their trade union at the level of the undertaking and at other levels, a right that is restricted in many, at times subtle, ways. Different forms of pressure (discriminatory declarations or acts) may be exerted on the workers to keep them from joining a specific trade union. Regulations may be introduced that, in law or in practice, preclude the establishment of more than one trade union representing the firm's workers (by setting a high number of minimum members or other conditions that are too severe). The law can impose a unified trade union system running from the firm up to the national and inter-occupational levels.

253. The various systems of trade union monopoly imposed on workers are at variance with the principle of free choice. The latter does not presuppose the existence of several workers' organizations; it merely establishes the right for any group of workers to set up an organization outside the existing structure if it considers this to be the best means of defending its material or moral interests. In short, while it is usually to the workers' advantage to avoid the existence of multiple trade unions, the unity of the trade union movement must be agreed and not imposed by the State.[180]

254. ILO's supervisory bodies have accepted the distinctions the laws and regulations of several countries make between trade unions depending on their degree of representativity. The system generally ensures, with a view to preventing abuse, that the criteria used to assess representativity – in principle, usually the number of members – are objective, pre-determined and brook no argument, and that minority organizations are sufficiently protected so that they can pursue and develop their trade union activities. Although the principle of a difference between workers' organizations is thus acknowledged in many countries, in particular to facilitate the harmonious development of industrial relations, it remains to be seen whether the priority or exclusive status granted to some organizations when it comes to representation is not of a kind substantially to limit the activities of minority trade unions and hence to influence the workers when it comes to choosing an organization. To that end, the advantages given to some trade unions should not go further than priority in representation, especially for the purposes of collective bargaining. The representativity of workers' organizations is usually (in Spain and in France) gauged at different levels: an organization that is in the minority at the national and inter-occupational level but representative either in a sector of activity or of a specific group of workers is just as capable as large nation-wide trade union movements of adequately defending the specific interests of its members, of negotiating their employment conditions and of concluding collective agreements.[181]

180. *See* ILO: *Freedom of Association. Digest of decisions and principles of the Freedom of Association Committee of the Governing Body of the ILO*, 5th (revised) edition, Geneva, 2006, para. 318 *et seq.*
181. *See* ILO, *Freedom of Association. Digest of decisions*, *op. cit.*, para. 346 *et seq.*; ILC, *op. cit.*, paras 224 *et seq.*

B. *The Right to Form Federations and Confederations and to Join International Employers' and Workers' Organizations*

255. The formation of occupational federations or confederations raises few specific problems, and any difficulties that do arise are usually the same as those experienced by the base organizations. On the other hand, more than one government has expressed reluctance about membership of major international confederations and some have even prohibited it. Many others have made relations between confederations and their national members difficult or even impossible: they prohibit the national delegate from attending meetings of the international trade union or the latter's representative from entering the country, do not authorize the international trade union to organize meetings in the country or to provide financial support for the national federation, restrict the exchange of publications, etc.[182]

C. *The Protection of Trade Unions from Administrative Suspension or Dissolution*

256. Trade unions cannot act with impunity, be it towards the employer, a public authority, their members or non-unionized workers. It is best, however, not to allow assessment of the fault or of the penalty to be imposed in such cases to the discretion of the public authorities. Article 4 of Convention No. 87 stipulates that workers' organizations are not liable to be suspended or dissolved by administrative authority. The suspension or dissolution can be indirect: withdrawal of legal personality or cancellation of registration. The mere threat of an administrative dissolution can very well, in practice, constitute an infringement of the trade union's rights when the pressure thus exercised risks influencing the workers' choice of organization.

257. According to the Committee on Freedom of Association, the only means of guaranteeing the rights of the defence are judicial proceedings. The Committee has further indicated, in specific cases, that the criminal liability incurred by trade union leaders for individual offences they are alleged to have committed should not result in any measures depriving the trade union itself or the rest of its leaders of their possibilities for action.

D. *Rights and Guarantees of Trade Union Activity*

258. There are four main aspects to trade union activity: the free election of representatives, the planning and implementation of trade union operations, the preparation of statutes and regulations, and the organization of management. They have

182. For further details, *see* J.-M. Servais, 'Labour Law and Cross-Border Cooperation among Unions', in M.E. Gordon and L. Turner (eds.), *Transnational Cooperation among Labor Unions*, Ithaca (NY), ILR Press, 2000, pp. 44–59.

one principle in common, set down in Convention No. 87, namely that the authorities are asked to refrain from any interference that would restrict those activities or impede the lawful exercise thereof; the trade unions, for their part, must abide by the law of the land (insofar, of course, as that law does not infringe on the guarantees in question).

259. In practice, the degree to which these guarantees are infringed varies widely. Among the most serious problems encountered are those in which a government prohibits a trade union – or trade unions in general – from carrying out any activities, and those in which the public authorities take over one or several workers' organizations (removing elected leaders from office, appointing a provisional administrator, freezing trade union funds and occupying the premises).

260. In other, more frequently encountered situations, the infringements relate more specifically to one of the four guarantees mentioned above.

261. The possibility for its members freely to choose their representatives is undoubtedly a fundamental guarantee for a trade union. Comparative law nevertheless reveals that this guarantee is often and in many ways restricted. In some cases, the law simply appears to be excessively detailed, setting conditions of eligibility or outlining the electoral procedure; in others, the public authorities seem to want to shape the union representative as they see fit or, at the least, exclude certain groups. They have also removed a trade union leader or eliminated a candidate by means of restrictive legal or regulatory provisions on eligibility, or by invoking their authority to take certain administrative decisions (approve the results of the elections, for example); they have also be known to take action, to exert pressure.

262. Again, trade union leaders cannot act with impunity. But it is usually up to the union's members and, in some cases, the courts to invalidate an election or remove an official.

263. A workers' organization must be able to act freely, i.e. to define and implement its objectives and programme in absolute independence. This raises the question of the line between trade unions and political action, a complex issue at the level of both the country as a whole and the undertaking[183]. Trade union leaders are often the target of measures, such as arrest, that keep them from performing their duties.

264. State interference in the drafting of trade union statutes and regulations comes in two main forms. In some cases the law obliges the trade union to submit the statutes to administrative control. This poses a problem, as we have seen, above all when the law makes the trade union's legal existence dependent on the approval of its statutes. Sometimes the law requires the inclusion of specific clauses. This second kind of interference poses no difficulties in terms of freedom of association

183. *See* ILO, *Freedom of Association. Digest of decisions, op. cit.*, paras 497–507; ILC, *op. cit,* paras 115–116.

when the law simply obliges workers' organizations to cover certain matters in their statutes, without instructing them how to regulate them; the same holds true when the labour ministry issues non-binding model statutes.

265. Other legal provisions concern the internal management of trade unions, in particular rules of procedure for trade union meetings, their frequency, voting procedures, etc. The legal obligation to obtain certain kinds of majorities on subjects of crucial importance to the life of the trade union and the rights of its members does not really constitute interference on the part of the public authorities, on condition that it does not seriously hinder the union's work in the circumstances and does not to all intents and purposes make it impossible to adopt decisions.

266. Another essential aspect of an association's independence, namely control of its assets, has been the subject of countless grievances to the Committee on Freedom of Association. There have been many cases in which the national authorities have somehow attacked the assets of a trade union with which they were in open conflict.[184]

267. The cases considered by the Committee concerned mainly funds (trade union finances, in particular the establishment of dues; financial management; seizure, freezing, confiscation of funds) or trade union premises (occupation and searches). There is little reason, however, to draw too fine a line between the problems raised by one or the other kind of case, for they all concern the material means the trade union needs to perform its tasks and are therefore closely related. Public interference in the trade union's accounts can take the form of an obligation to communicate the books and records to the administration, or of a police raid on the union's premises. The acquisition of premises usually presupposes the existence of funds, a seizure can concern a trade union building and sums of money, and if the organization is wound up, the disposal of its real assets raises the same questions as that of other assets. Here, too, the Committee on Freedom of Association considered that any control should be performed by the courts.

E. Freedom of Association, Civil and Political Rights

268. The right to form trade unions is set down, as we have seen, in the two United Nations Covenants on human rights, one on civil and political rights, the other on economic, social and cultural rights. This underscores the interconnection between the two categories of rights and, in this case, that freedom of association can only truly be exercised in a general climate of respect for the major civil liberties.[185]

184. *See* E. Gravel, I. Duplessis and B. Gernigon, *The Committee on Freedom of Association: Its Impact over 50 Years*, Geneva, ILO, 2001, pp. 50–51.
185. *See* for example the Labour Relations (Public Service) Convention, 1978 (No. 151), Article 9.

269. Those liberties include guarantees against summary execution, ill-treatment and arbitrary arrest as well as equal access to courts and tribunals. The Committee on Freedom of Association has received an astounding number of grievances about arrests. Its view is that while trade unionists cannot claim any form of immunity from legal proceedings, they nevertheless have to be tried promptly, in accordance with ordinary court proceedings, and should not be troubled in connection with routine trade union activities.

270. The enjoyment of other civil liberties – freedom of expression (freedom of the trade union press and freedom of speech), the right of assembly (public and private), the inviolability of trade union premises (except for searches authorized by the law and carried out with a search warrant) and of trade union correspondence and conversations (on the telephone, via e-mail and elsewhere) – is particularly important for the exercise of trade union rights.

271. One final point: traditionally, civil liberties are considered to provide guarantees against excessive control by the State authorities, who have essentially a negative obligation, namely not to do anything in contradiction of those rights and freedoms. Here, however, the State has a positive obligation: the public authorities must, if necessary, take concrete action to ensure that these liberties can indeed be exercised. A compelling example is to be found on plantations, where the workers live on the employer's land, in housing provided by him. Some employers have invoked their rights as landowners to bar entry to trade union representatives or to prohibit public or private trade union meetings on the grounds of the plantation. In such situations, ILO's supervisory bodies have urged the government concerned to adopt the legal and administrative provisions required to enable trade union leaders to have effective access to the plantations and to give the workers concerned the full benefit of the right of assembly. Indeed, Convention No. 87 and Convention No. 110 (1958) on plantations require the States to take all necessary and appropriate measures to ensure that workers may exercise freely the right to organize. By the same token, Convention No. 141 (1975) on rural workers' organizations requests governments to adopt and carry out a policy of active encouragement to these organizations, particularly with a view to ensuring that national laws and practices do not inhibit the establishment and growth of rural workers' organizations.

II. Collective Relations between Social Players

A. The Promotion of Collective Bargaining

272. The rights and guarantees just mentioned are sine qua non conditions for a trade union to be able to play its role of promoting and defending the interests of its members. Collective bargaining is a fundamental means of attaining that objective. The law and practice of a vast majority of States recognize the principle of collective bargaining, but national legislation has widely varying approaches to its implementation. Some in particular deprive important categories of workers of this right. The CEACR has had to recall that this should also cover organizations representing the workers in religious or charity organizations (Ethiopia), and migrant workers (Bangladesh, China/Macau, Eritrea, Kuwait). These restrictions are in addition to two trends. The first is the tendency for the legislature in several countries to give precedence to individual rights over collective rights in employment matters, while the Collective Agreements Recommendation, 1951 (No. 91) recalls the need for collective agreements to bear binding effects, and their primacy over individual contracts of employment (with the exception of provisions which are more favourable to the workers). Secondly direct agreements between employers and non-unionized workers are, in certain countries, more numerous than the collective agreements concluded with the representative organizations of workers.[186]

273. ILO Convention No. 98, and Convention No. 154 and Recommendation No. 163 on the promotion of collective bargaining (1981), call on the States to take positive measures to that end, in particular to enable all employers and all categories of workers to negotiate at all levels. Convention No. 98 nevertheless allows exceptions not only in the case of the armed and police forces but also in that of public servants (i.e. those engaged in the administration of the State). The aim is also to extend bargaining to all questions pertaining to the establishment of conditions of work and employment, the regulation of employer-worker relations and the regulation of relations between employers or their organizations with one or several workers' organizations.

274. The ILO conventions that govern collective bargaining thus call on the States to do far more than abstain from an activity: not only should the States not unduly limit the independence of the parties (for example, by imposing a prior authorization for the entry into force of an agreement), it is incumbent on them to promote social dialogue. This being said, the Committee on Freedom of Association has agreed that restrictions can be placed on collective bargaining in time of crisis, if they are limited in time and subject-matter (essentially wages).[187]

275. One effective means of doing this is undoubtedly to establish mechanisms – bodies or procedures – able to facilitate collective bargaining. Some countries, such as Belgium, provide for the establishment of joint committees (at the undertaking, regional, sector or inter-occupational level) that can or must conclude collective agreements. In other countries – Ireland and Italy, for instance – it is the task of specialized institutions to promote this kind of dialogue between social partners. Procedures for extending collective agreements exist in Belgium, France and Germany; they aim to make their 'standard-setting' provisions binding, even on employers and workers who are not represented by the signatories.

276. In some countries – France, Japan, Sweden, the United States – there exists a genuine obligation to bargain. Obviously, the attitude of one of the parties towards the other's claims (conciliatory or intransigent) is a matter for discussion between the two; the public authorities must nevertheless ensure that both employers and

186. *See* ILC, *op. cit.*, para. 199 *et seq.*
187. *See* ILO, *Freedom of Association. Digest of decisions, op. cit.*, paras 1004, 1021, 1023–1029.

workers negotiate in good faith and strive to reach an agreement. Recommendation No. 163 calls for the parties to have access to the information they need for meaningful negotiations, and the laws and regulations of several countries make provision for this.

B. Social Dialogue

277. The outcome of collective bargaining is not necessarily a proper legal agreement. If the bargaining is tripartite, it involves the public authorities at the sector and national level in a dialogue that may cover far more than wages and employment conditions.

278. At the international level, social dialogue is dealt with in ILO Recommendation No. 113 on consultation at the industrial and national levels, which stipulates that cooperation should serve to promote joint consideration of matters of mutual concern with a view to arriving, to the fullest possible extent, at agreed solutions. In addition, the public authorities should seek 'the views, advice and assistance' of employers' and workers' organizations in respect of matters such as:

(i) the preparation and implementation of laws and regulations affecting their interests;
(ii) the establishment and functioning of national bodies, such as those responsible for organization of employment, vocational training and retraining, labour protection, industrial health and safety, productivity, social security and welfare; and
(iii) the elaboration and implementation of plans of economic and social development.

279. Social dialogue on these points grew considerably in most Western European countries in the late 1960s and 1970s. In many, it remains a basic component of social policy, even if the discussions have often faltered in the face of unemployment-related concerns.

C. Strikes

280. In any society, there are those who are more inclined to get into a conflict – no matter how or when – and those who are not. The laws governing industrial disputes depend on the political system and vary considerably throughout the world. Quite often collective conflict between employers and wage earners is seriously restricted and even unlawful. Strikes can have a revolutionary flavour and work against social and production relations; this is anathema to the authorities, even if they are not totalitarian. Trade union leaders and democratic lawmakers have sought to incorporate, the former into their strategy, the latter into their laws, the form of direct action known as a strike, which more often than not expresses an irritation, a spontaneous revolt against what are deemed to be unacceptable employment conditions.

281. Strikes therefore come in many forms, depending on the country and the times. They are a freedom in some common law countries (in that this form of work stoppage does not result in criminal penalties, a fine or prison, but leaves the question of contractual responsibility intact). More often than not they are now a right (and therefore, except in certain circumstances, the employer cannot invoke a fault to break off the employment relationship nor take other punitive measures). Strikes may be a means of action only trade unions are authorized to take (Sweden) or recognized for individual workers (France). In some instances they are an exceptional measure the workers can invoke when the employer does not fulfil its obligations. They may be allowed only in the classic form or extended to cover work slowdowns, rotating strikes, work-to-rule, boycotts and other kinds of direct action.

282. The ILO has counted 93 countries in which the right to strike is now constitutionally guaranteed.[188] Whereas however the International Covenant on Economic, Social and Cultural Rights, the European Social Charter and the Charter of the Fundamental Rights of the EU include provisions on strikes, Conventions Nos. 87 and 98 do not.[189] Fear of restricting the freedom of relations between employers' and workers' organizations, and fear of restricting the possibility of direct action, would seem to be one of the main reasons why so few ILO standards have been adopted on the settlement of industrial disputes. While the preparatory work of Convention No 87 do not contain definitive argument in favour or against, the ILO's supervisory bodies have considered that the right collectively to stop work necessarily arises from the articles of Convention No. 87 entitling trade unions to formulate their programmes and organize their activities.[190] Employers have contested that approach, above all the extension given to the right to strike, mentioning in particular labour conflicts in essential services.[191] The CEACR had maintained its position in its reports to the ILC in 2013 and 2014.[192] An agreement has finally been reached at the March 2015 session of Governing Body confirming workers' and employers' right to take industrial action in support of their legitimate industrial

188. ILC, *op. cit.,* paras. 8 and 123.

189. Some ILO instruments refer however to labour conflicts: *see* the Unemployment Provision Convention, 1934 (No. 44), Article 10; the Voluntary Conciliation and Arbitration Recommendation, 1951 (No. 92), paras 4, 6 and 7; the Social Security (Minimum Standards) Convention, 1952 (No. 102), Article 69; the Abolition of Forced Labour Convention, 1957 (No. 105), Article 1.

190. *See* J.-M. Servais, 'ILO Law and the Right to Strike', *The Canadian Labour and Employment Law Journal*, Vol. 15, No. 2, 2010 pp. 147–163.

191. ILC (101st session, 2012), *op. cit.*, para. 117 *et seq. See* J. Bellace, 'The ILO and the right to strike', *ILR*, Vol. 153(1), 2014, pp. 29-70.

192. ILC (102nd Session, 2013), *Report of the Committee of Experts on the Application of Conventions and Recommendations*, Report III (Part 1A), ILO, Geneva, 2013, paras 31 and 102; ILC (103rd Session, 2014) *Report of the Committee of Experts. ..*, Report III (Part 1A), ILO, Geneva, 2014, para. 25. *See also* K.D. Ewing, 'Myth and Reality of the Right to Strike as a "Fundamental Labour Right"', *IJCLLIR*, Vol. 29(2), June 2013, pp. 145–165.

interests. The conditions required to go on strike are examined on a case by case basis.[193]

283. In the *Viking* and *Laval*[194] cases, the Court of Justice of the EU has recognized the right to collective action, including strike. It has however considered that this right should be conciliate with the free movement of establishment and of services enshrined in the European Treaties, giving the preference to the latter especially in the second case. In view of these sentences, the CEACR has stressed the need to ensure fuller protection of the right of workers to exercise legitimate industrial action in practice and considers that adequate safeguards and immunities from civil liability are necessary to ensure respect for this fundamental right. The Committee has further raised the concern that the omnipresent threat of an action for damages that could bankrupt the union, possible in the light of the Viking and Laval judgments, created a situation jeopardizing the exercise of the rights under the Convention No. 87.[195]

284. Once they had decided that the Convention included the right to strike, the ILO's supervisory bodies were faced with the need to determine what the acceptable restrictions were, rather than leaving it as an absolute right. They did this on a case-by-case basis over the years. They have allowed, subject to further discussions within the ILO decision bodies, the restrictions to collective labour stoppages that figure in a variety of ways in many national law and regulations: for reasons of security in companies, while voluntary procedures of conciliation and arbitration are ongoing, or while a collective agreement is still valid (social peace obligation); they have also accepted that purely political strikes may be prohibited, or that the right to strike can be suspended during an acute, in particular economic, national crisis. It has also allowed that strikes may be prohibited in what are considered to be essential services and in the public service; such a measure must be accompanied by compensating guarantees in the form of impartial, rapid and effective procedures for conciliation and arbitration with the participation of those concerned.[196] In some cases, the Committee on Freedom of Association has suggested that a minimum service be required in the workplace, as certain national laws have done, rather than prohibiting strikes.

285. Making the right to call a stoppage of work the sole preserve of trade union organizations is compatible with Convention 87. A demand for recognition of a union is nevertheless a legitimate interest, in support of which collective action may

193. Document GB.323 INS 5 and its annexes; ILO GB. 323rd Session, March 2015 *Decisions and other outcomes*; ILC (104th session, 2015), *Provisional Record*, no. 14, Geneva, ILO, 2015, §39.

194. *International Federation of transport workers and Finnish Union of seafarers* (*Viking*), 11 December 2007, Case C-438/05, http://eur-lex.europa.eu (case law 2007); *Laval un Partneri,* 18 December 2007, case C-341/0, http://eur-lex.europa.eu (case law, 2007).

195. *Report of the Committee of Experts on the Application of Conventions and Recommendations*, Report III (Part 1A) 102nd Session, 2013, ILO, Geneva, 2013, pp. 176–180 (Sweden) and 196 (United Kingdom).

196. ILO, *Freedom of Association. Digest of Decisions, op. cit.*, paras 595 *et seq.*; *see* also para. 288 *below.*

be used. The same is true of collective action in support of multi-employer contracts. The CFA has stated that the denial of various forms of collective action (demonstration, wild-cat strikes, tools-down, go-slow, working to rule and sit-down strikes) may be justified only if the action ceases to be peaceful. Employees should be able to launch a sympathy strike if it is in support of a strike that is itself lawful. The CEACR has noted that such strikes are becoming increasingly frequent because of the move toward the concentration of enterprises, the globalization of the economy and the delocalization of work centres. A general prohibition on this kind of collective action could lead to abuse.[197]

286. The CFA has also admitted, at least indirectly, the validity of the lock-out, i.e. the withholding of work from employees or closing down of a workplace by an employer during a labor dispute.[198] The last-mentioned agreement reached within the ILO Governing Body confirmed this interpretation.[199]

D. Voluntary Conciliation and Arbitration

287. At ILO there is basically just one (brief) recommendation (No. 92) on voluntary conciliation and arbitration (1951) and it is limited to general principles. What is more, the matter is left to the discretion of the parties concerned. The final paragraph of the Recommendation states, as though it needed to be said, that none of its provisions may be interpreted as 'limiting, in any way whatsoever, the right to strike'. The Recommendation provides for the establishment of voluntary conciliation machinery to assist in the prevention and settlement of industrial disputes. It proposes that the procedure should be free of charge and expeditious and set in motion either by one of the parties or by the voluntary conciliation authority. If a dispute has been submitted to the conciliation procedure with the consent of all the parties concerned, the latter should be encouraged to abstain from strikes and lock-outs while conciliation is in progress. The same holds true if they have agreed to arbitration for final settlement; they should also be encouraged to accept the arbitration award.

288. The ILO's supervisory bodies have considered as essential in order to gain and retain the parties' confidence that all the members of the conciliation, mediation and arbitration institutions should not only be impartial, but, if the confidence of both sides, on which the successful outcome even of arbitration really depends, is to be gained and maintained, they should also appear to be impartial both to the employers and to the workers concerned. Any arbitration system in particular should be truly independent and the outcomes should not be predetermined by legislative criteria.[200]

197. ILO, *Freedom of Association, Digest of Decisions, op. cit.*, paras 524, 534–535, 545, 534; ILC (101st Session, 2012), *Giving Globalization a Human Face*, *op. cit.*, para. 125.
198. ILO, *Freedom of Association. Digest of Decisions, op. cit.*, paras 600 and 853.
199. *See* para. 282 *above*.
200. Servais, *op. cit.*

E. The Elimination of Anti-Trade Union Employment Practices

289. An employer who dismisses, lays off, transfers or demotes a unionized worker, refuses to pay him a bonus, give him a promotion or penalizes him in some other way, or does not hire him, cannot obviously be reproached for discrimination. Likewise, a dynamic policy encouraging productivity and staff participation in the decision-making process can lead to a decline in the trade union's presence in the undertaking, for which the employer cannot be criticized. It would be otherwise if he acted out of anti-union motives, i.e. if his decision were explained by the worker's union membership or activities within a union (steps taken to establish a union or obtain its recognition; opinions expressed during trade union meetings; claims made, trade union action, strikes, etc.) or his policy was aimed at weakening the unions.

290. The main difficulty here is proving the anti-union or discriminatory nature of the decision made: proof must be obtained not of a fact but of an intention, namely to violate freedom of association in employment. Although in some cases the employer's attitude or conduct manifestly betrays a malicious intent (for example, if he grants an advantage on condition that all union activities cease), the problem is often more delicate. This is why ILO Recommendation No. 143 on workers' representatives[201] suggests that one of the measures the States can take to fight such practices is to reverse the burden of proof, i.e. to make it incumbent on the employer to prove that the measure was truly justified.

291. More generally speaking, ILO Convention No. 98 and several more recent instruments[202] require that national laws and regulations provide workers with adequate protection against acts of discrimination based on union membership or trade union activities. The practice of 'blacklists' of trade union activists used in the context of hiring procedures is particularly incompatible with the Convention.[203]

292. Reversing the burden of proof, as in Slovenia, is by no means a measure the State is obliged to take, but rather one of the guarantees protecting workers' representatives in the undertaking put forward in Recommendation No. 143, an instrument that is not open for ratification. Workers' representatives are more exposed to anti-union practices, as the many cases dealt with by the Committee on Freedom of Association confirm. The Recommendation also suggests other measures for providing effective protection: a detailed and precise definition of the reasons for the termination of employment; a requirement of consultation with, an advisory opinion from, or agreement of an independent or joint body, before the dismissal; a special recourse procedure (in the event of unjustifiable termination, a change in

201. Para. 6. *See also* Article 9 of the Termination of Employment Convention, 1982 (No. 158).

202. Convention No. 98, Article 1. *See also* the Workers' Representative Convention, 1973 (No. 135) and Recommendation (No. 143), Article 5 and para. 6(2) respectively; the Labour Relations (Public Service) Convention, 1978 (No. 151), Article 4, and the Termination of Employment Convention, 1982 (No. 158), Article 5.

203. ILC (101st Session, 2012), *Giving Globalization a Human Face*, *op. cit.*, paras 122 and 178.

conditions of employment or unfair treatment); reinstatement, if the dismissal was unjustified, with payment of unpaid wages and maintenance of acquired rights; priority with regard to retention in employment if the workforce is reduced.

293. Although trade union leaders are not entitled to claim any form of immunity from criminal prosecution, they must also be protected, in particular in view of their vulnerable position as well as the fact that the decisions taken against them may also damage the activities of the trade unions they represent. One of the means of ensuring such protection is to provide, as France does, that they cannot be dismissed either in the exercise of their duties or for a certain period after the end of their term of office, except, obviously, if they have engaged in serious misconduct. Preventive judicial or administrative procedures of prior authorization and the reinstatement of a worker dismissed with retroactive constitutes the most effective remedy. In any case, compensation and fines, should be higher than that prescribed for other kinds of dismissal, be adapted in accordance with the size of the enterprises concerned (the CEACR has considered that compensation of up to six months' wages may be a deterrent for small and medium-sized enterprises, but is not necessarily the case for highly productive and large enterprises), and the amount be reviewed periodically.[204]

294. The existence of legal provisions prohibiting acts of anti-union discrimination is not enough if they are not accompanied by effective and rapid procedures to ensure their application in practice. The methods used to combat such discriminatory practices nevertheless also depend, in each State, on the historical, social and legal context in which trade unionism developed, on the power of occupational organizations, the experience of their leaders, the respective role of legislation and collective agreements in the system under review, the quality of the bodies to which appeals can be made and the trust they inspire, etc.

295. Cases of interference in trade union affairs on the part of individual employers or employers' associations (such as promoting a 'yellow dog union') have rarely been raised at ILO. The problem is nevertheless considered in Conventions Nos. 98 and 151, which call for protection as needed.

296. The ILO's supervisory bodies have also been called on to consider situations in which non-unionized workers or workers who were not members of a specific union had suffered what are known as union security practices or agreements, which serve to limit employment in some companies or give other benefits to the members of a given union. They refused to consider those allegations, citing the preparatory work for Conventions Nos. 87 and 98, from which it is clear that the standards contained in those conventions must not be construed as authorizing or prohibiting such clauses and practices; the situation would be different, and incompatible with the standards in those conventions, were trade union security not to be based on an agreement, even tacit, between the parties but imposed by regulations. Contrary to the ILO, both the Council of Europe and the Court of Justice of the EU

204. *Ibid.*, paras 182–185.

consider that the freedom of association include the right not to join a trade union.[205] National legislation usually prohibits, to varying degrees, clauses and practices limiting the 'negative' freedom not to unionize.

§2. SPECIFIC STANDARDS ON INDUSTRIAL RELATIONS WITHIN THE UNDERTAKING

I. The Protection of Workers' Representatives

297. The above-mentioned standards and principles are given effect in many forms in relations between employers and workers' delegates at undertaking level. ILO Convention No. 135 and Recommendation No. 143 deal specifically with workers' representation at that level.

298. Contrary to what is the case in many domestic laws and regulations, neither the Convention nor the Recommendation distinguishes small and medium-sized enterprises from large corporations, even though the former are in many ways in a special situation. The principles contained in both the Convention and the Recommendation are much too generally worded for any differences to be noted. Trade unions nevertheless find it difficult to organize the staff of SMEs. The obstacles they encounter stem from the fact that the work places are dispersed over a large area, from the practical problems of establishing relatively heavy representative structures in small establishments, and from the more personal nature of the relations between the employer and the workers, who constitute, even if they are united, a lesser force in the face of management.

299. Both the Convention and the Recommendation leave States free to choose the most adequate form of dialogue between management and staff. They also provide for the two traditional formulas: either trade union representatives (appointed or elected by the unions or their members), or representatives freely elected by the undertaking's workers. Many countries, in Europe and Asia in particular, recognize forms of staff participation at undertaking level that are different in status and function from trade union representation and collective bargaining. Among these mechanisms, a special place is reserved for works committees, including those today set up at European level.

300. The cohabitation of such committees with trade union delegations is no problem when, as is the case in Germany and Belgium, their respective fields of authority are clearly defined and well accepted. It is also true that in those two

205. *See* the decision of 15 May 2003 of the European Committee of Social Rights (Complaint No. 12/2002, *Confederation of Swedish enterprises against Sweden*), the cases Nos. 52562/99 and 52620/99 of the European Court of Human Rights, *Sørensen & Rasmussen* v. *Denmark*, 11 January 2006, especially paras 54–58 recording previous case law; *see also* for the public sector the sentence *Enerji Yapi-Yol Sen* v. *Turkey of* 21 April 2009 (Case No. 68959/01). *See* Court of Justice of the EU, case *Werhof* of 9 March 2006.

countries, established trade unions play a preponderant role in the committees' functioning.

301. Many legislative acts, and the above-mentioned ILO Convention and Recommendation, specifically protect these representatives from the harmful measures that may be taken against them because of their duties or activities as trade union representatives. Often, those guarantees are extended to candidates for posts of worker representatives and to those who are no longer delegates, for a specific period; at the end of their term of office, representatives who performed their functions within the undertaking in which they were employed and who return to their jobs maintain or recover, in principle, all their entitlements, including those relating to the nature of the job, their salary and their seniority.

302. The Convention and the Recommendation establish another important principle: these representatives must benefit within the undertaking from facilities enabling them to carry out their functions promptly and efficiently. In this connection, however, account should be taken of the characteristics of the national industrial relations system and the needs, size and capabilities of the undertaking concerned: the granting of such facilities should not impair the undertaking's efficient operation.

303. Examples of such facilities are to be found in the Recommendation and in some national laws (France) and collective agreements: representatives must be given the necessary time off from work for carrying out representation functions and for attending union meetings and training courses, access to all workplaces and to management, authorization to collect trade union dues, to post trade union notices and to distribute trade union publications, material facilities, and the possibility to receive any information needed for the exercise of their functions. The Recommendation specifies that trade union representatives who are not employed in the undertaking but whose trade union has members employed by it should be granted access to the undertaking.

II. Participative Management

304. There is an alternative to autocratic staff management that gives workers a greater say in the decision-making process. The interest of such policies has often been emphasized, even in terms of profit.

305. They have been referred to in several early ILO instruments that only contain a few basic provisions, further elaboration being left to the parties concerned.

306. Recommendation No. 129, adopted in 1967, deals with communications between management and workers in the undertaking. It lays the groundwork for the rapid dissemination and exchange of information and for consultation. Significantly, it insists that these methods of communication should in no way derogate from freedom of association: the methods chosen should in no way cause prejudice to freely chosen workers' representatives or to their organizations or curtail the functions of bodies representative of the workers.

307. Recommendation No. 94 of 1952 goes further, but without being very specific. It seeks to promote true cooperation between employers and workers at the level of the undertaking, 'on matters of mutual concern not within the scope of collective bargaining machinery, or not normally dealt with by other machinery concerned with the determination of terms and conditions of employment'.

308. Other ILO instruments reiterate, in connection with specific issues – occupational health and safety, dismissal[206] – the obligation employers have to inform the workers and their representatives, to consult and even cooperate with them.

309. In national legislation and practice, these provisions often take the form of works committees. There are different concepts of such committees. In some cases they comprise management members (Belgium, France), in others not (Germany, the Netherlands). In some countries, they have only limited powers (essentially to be informed and consulted). The election of their members nevertheless serves to gauge, above and beyond the unionization rate, the real authority of the workers' organizations fielding candidates. It also serves to assess the importance of non-unionized members who are elected. In other European countries, works committees have been given more substantial powers to negotiate (Spain) or take decisions (Belgium), depending on whether they represent only the workers or are bipartite.

310. In Japan, consultation committees are set up in undertakings (especially small and medium-sized businesses) in which the unions are not really present. Where the unions have a significant presence, they constitute the driving force on those committees. A similar system exists in the Republic of Korea, where, contrary to Japan, the law makes provision for such committees. Elsewhere in Asia, works committees often exist in law but have very little impact in practice.

311. In the United States, successive proposals to establish works committees, in the face in particular of the unions' waning influence, have not been followed up.

312. Works committees play, in Germany, a significant part. The unions have a leading role in them. The tasks have been clearly distributed: collective bargaining for trade union organizations, active participation in the life of the undertaking (including cases of dismissal) for the committees. The latter have even acquired unique authority, with the appearance of new forms of worker management and human resources development. The German approach usually prefers 'participative' management, which is not regarded as a threat to the unions. This also seems

206. *See* for example the Occupational Safety and Health Convention (No. 155) and Recommendation (No. 164), 1981, Articles 19 and 20 and para. 12 respectively; the Occupational Health Services Convention (No. 161) and Recommendation (No. 171), 1985, Article 13 and para. 22 respectively; the Termination of Employment Convention (No. 158) and Recommendation (No. 166), 1982, Article 13 and para. 20 respectively.

to be true in Japan. Elsewhere (in the United States, in various Latin American countries), the trade unions take on, directly or as a function of their position in the undertaking, some or all of the tasks performed by these committees.

III. Grievances

313. Another ILO recommendation, adopted in 1967, deals specifically with consideration of grievances within the undertaking with a view to settling them. This recommendation, No. 130, provides that any worker, acting individually or jointly with other workers, should have the right to submit grievances without suffering any prejudice whatsoever as a result and to have such grievances examined pursuant to an appropriate procedure.

314. In some industrial relations systems, in particular in Scandinavia, a distinction is implicitly made between conflicts of rights and conflicts of interests. The Recommendation specifies that its provisions are not applicable to collective claims aimed at the modification of terms and conditions of employment. The grounds for a grievance may be any measure or situation which concerns the relations between employer and worker or which affects or may affect the conditions of employment of one or several workers in the undertaking when that measure or situation appears contrary to the provisions of an applicable collective agreement or of an individual contract of employment, to works rules, to national laws or to the custom or usage of the occupation, branch of economic activity or country, 'regard being had to principles of good faith'.

315. This distinction, which is traditionally made in opposition to that operated between individual and collective disputes, ultimately corresponds to a concept of the judicial system that limits the jurisdiction of the courts to pure application of the law. Even in those instances, however, cases have arisen in which it is hard to distinguish between what is a right and what is an interest (even if it is only the case of an attorney cloaking a conflict of interests in a conflict of rights). How, for example, to separate the two in the implementation of the German principle of proportional strikes? It is nevertheless true that in such judicial systems, the distinction has the advantage, in most cases, of greater clarity.

316. The Recommendation takes the precaution of adding that when procedures for the examination of grievances are established through collective agreements, the parties to the agreement should be encouraged to include in it a provision renouncing direct action: they should undertake, during the period of validity of the agreement, to promote settlement of grievances under the procedures provided and to abstain 'from any action which might impede the effective functioning of these procedures'. This enshrines the obligation of social peace provided for by the law or established by the case-law of many States. That obligation may, as we know, be relative or absolute.

317. The CFA has accepted that strikes be prohibited while a collective agreement is in force. It has asked that the restriction be compensated for by the right to have recourse to impartial and rapid mechanisms, within which individual or collective complaints about the interpretation or application of collective agreements can be examined. This type of mechanism not only allows the inevitable difficulties which may occur in this respect to be resolved while the agreements are in force, but also has the advantage of preparing the ground for future rounds of negotiations, given that it allows problems which have arisen during the period of validity of the document to be identified.[207] We also find such a mechanism in the works rules or in the codes of conduct of major national and multinational enterprises. It corresponds to the spirit of the OECD Guidelines for Multinational enterprises whose provisions are no more specific.

318. The Recommendation states that, as far as possible, grievances should be settled within the undertaking itself according to effective procedures which are adapted to the conditions of the country, branch of economic activity and undertaking concerned and which give the parties concerned every assurance of objectivity. Where all efforts to settle the grievance within the undertaking have failed, there should be a possibility for final settlement through one or more of the following procedures:

(a) procedures provided for by collective agreement, such as joint examination of the case by the employers' and workers' organizations concerned or voluntary arbitration by a person or persons designated with the agreement of the employer and worker concerned or their respective organizations;
(b) conciliation or arbitration by the competent public authorities;
(c) recourse to a labour court or other judicial authority;
(d) any other procedure which may be appropriate under national conditions.

319. No provision of the Recommendation restricts the worker's right to apply directly to the competent labour authority, to a labour court or to another judicial authority. The solution of a legal conflict as a result of a difference in interpretation of a legal text should be left to the competent courts. The CFA has considered that a prohibition of strikes in such a situation does not constitute a breach of freedom of association.[208]

§3. Freedom of Association and Social Rights

320. These, briefly, are the rights and principles arising from freedom of association as conceived by ILO. Not only are they proclaimed, not only are they defended in the supervisory body conclusions for which they are the basis, they are driven by one essential idea: the constant concern to enable employers, workers and

207. ILO, *Freedom of Association: Digest of Decisions, op. cit.*, §533.
208. *Ibid.*, §532.

their organizations to establish relations on an equal footing, to enable them to consult, discuss, negotiate 'on equal terms', in short, to promote the common search for solutions to the employment and labour problems that inevitably arise and that economic difficulties only serve to exacerbate. This joint dialogue is more fraught in some sectors than in others, in particular the public service and agriculture. The International Labour Conference has therefore voted specific rules for those branches: Convention No. 141 and supplementary Recommendation No. 149 on rural workers' organizations, 1975; Convention No. 151 and supplementary Recommendation No. 159 on labour relations in the public service, 1978. Later on, the Domestic Workers Convention, (No. 189) and Recommendation (No 201), 2011, have asked States to take measures to promote and realize freedom of association and the right to bargain collectively.

321. The difficulties that arise in the public service sector are essentially due to an old concept of the State that continues to be held in several Latin American countries in particular: the State is the personification of sovereignty, and can but treat its employees well; its representatives are emanations of public authority and are therefore not able to negotiate with private individuals. More than one country refuses – at least officially – to recognize groups of its agents. No matter what the case, industrial relations must be conducted in forms better adapted to the sector's characteristics.

322. Trade unionism emerged from and developed in industry and in services. It followed only later in agriculture, where it is still not always accepted. Hence the need, here too, for standards that are better adapted to the specific circumstances of the branch of activity. Difficulties for domestic workers to enjoy these rights are very well known.

323. The standards set down in the above instruments reflect a broad and dynamic vision of human rights. The concept that emerged in the 18th century, as for example in the USA Declaration of Independence, 1776 and the French Declaration on the Rights of Man and Citizen, 1789, refers essentially to what are today known as 'civil and political rights'. That concept subsequently evolved. The 19th century was confronted with the labour issue and realized that it was not enough to recognize political rights relating to democracy and freedoms (of assembly, expression and thought, education, security of the person, the inviolability of the home, of correspondence, etc.), which, although essential, basically imposed on the State an obligation to refrain from rather than to take action.

324. It became clear that all dimensions of the human being had to be protected and account taken of the socio-economic conditions in which people live and work. The Industrial Revolution created a new situation; it had to be taken into consideration, and the corresponding rights and freedoms established. Thinkers, political leaders gradually sculpted the notions we know today as economic and social rights. These were enshrined in 20th-century constitutions and by the United Nations in 1966 in the covenant mentioned earlier. In short, and to quote Winston Churchill and Franklin Roosevelt in the joint declaration they signed 'somewhere in the Atlantic in 1941', the aim was to free men and women not only from fear, but also from want.[209]

325. Although social rights were the last to appear at the national level, they were the first to be properly established internationally:[210] the Treaty of Versailles and the ILO Constitution (even the international labour conventions adopted several years earlier) contained provisions to that effect, including the affirmation of the principle of freedom of association. Increasingly today, the content of collective agreements expand beyond wage issues and include new content: protection of fundamental rights and individual privacy, dignity at work, gender and parity issues, anti-harassment measures, protection of the workplace, family responsibilities, maternity, prevention of occupational risks, etc. Moreover, it is observed that in some countries, beyond the regulation of employment conditions, collective bargaining is increasingly used, especially in times of crisis, as a means of achieving greater efficiency and better management of the enterprise or public institution.[211]

326. The social rights required that the States not just refrain from action but also take positive measures to guarantee those rights, more precisely to respect them, to abstain from any contradictory measure, to protect the beneficiary workers and to promote the realization of these rights by all appropriate means.[212] The implementation of social rights called not only for legal measures, i.e. the adoption of protective legislation, judicial (and other) remedies and sanctions, but also the definition and adoption of effective economic policies and programmes. It does not suffice, for example, to authorize agricultural trade unionism in the law; a favourable environment must be fostered for the development of workers' associations able to defend their interests efficiently. It does not suffice to proclaim that such associations are entitled to be consulted about social matters, they must be part of the institutions in charge of employment, occupational training and labour protection. This paved the way for the entire range of programmatic standards.[213]

327. Convention No. 141 confirms the right of all rural workers, whether wage earners or self-employed, to form associations of their choosing. It adds that one objective of national policy concerning rural development should be to facilitate the establishment and growth, on a voluntary basis, of strong and independent organizations of rural workers as an effective means of ensuring the participation of rural

209. *See* W. Arnold-Foster, *Charters of the Peace: A Commentary on the Atlantic Charter and the Declarations of Moscow, Cairo and Teheran*, London, Victor Gollancz, 1944, pp. 9–10 and 136. *See also* A.F. Frangulis (ed.), *Dictionnaire diplomatique*, Paris, Académie diplomatique internationale, Vol. IV, n.d., p. 118.
210. C.W. Jenks, *Human Rights, Social Justice and Peace: The Broader Significance of the ILO Experience*, Norwegian Nobel Institute, Symposium of the International Protection of Human Rights (25–27 September 1967), pp. 2–3.
211. ILC (102nd Session, 2013), *Collective Bargaining in the Public Service: A Way Forward*, Report of the Committee of Experts on the Application of Conventions and Recommendations Report III (Part 1B), Geneva, ILO, 2013, paras 318–320.
212. Thouvenin and Trebilcock, *op. cit.*, vol. II, pp. 854 *et seq.*
213. *See* Part III, chapter 2, §4 *below*.

workers, without discrimination, in economic and social development and in the benefits resulting there from. This obligation to take action contains both a negative (eliminate legislative and administrative barriers to the activities of such organizations) and a positive dimension that Recommendation No. 149 expresses more explicitly. It suggests measures relating to education and training, good public information and, if necessary, financial and material assistance 'in a manner which fully respects their independence and interests and those of their members'. It further proposes that the public authorities ensure that there is effective consultation and dialogue with rural workers' organizations on matters relating to conditions of work and life in rural areas.

328. Convention No. 151 covers not only the right to organize in the public service but also the procedures for determining the terms and conditions of employment. It aims to adapt the general principles of freedom of association to the conditions inherent in the public service. The States are invited to establish institutions of protection and negotiation in accordance with a relatively detailed scheme. This instrument is less programmatic in nature. Recommendation No. 159 provides that the procedures for recognition of public employees' organizations should be based on objective and pre-established criteria; they should not encourage the proliferation of such organizations.

329. The Convention allows exceptions for high-level employees, or employees whose duties are of a highly confidential nature. It contains a compatibility clause with other international labour conventions that applies, for example, to Convention No. 98. Other provisions cover protection of the right to organize and the facilities to be afforded to public employees' organizations and reiterate the principles already mentioned in more general terms. Article 7 deals with the full development and utilization of machinery for negotiation of terms and conditions of employment between the public authorities concerned and public employees' organizations; it nevertheless allows for the possibility of using other methods enabling representatives of public employees to participate in the determination of those conditions. Article 8 indicates that disputes should be settled through negotiation, or through independent and impartial machinery such as mediation, conciliation and arbitration, established in such a manner as to ensure the confidence of the parties involved. Article 9 refers to public employees' civil and political rights, 'subject only to the obligations arising from their status and the nature of their functions'.

330. In taking measures to ensure that domestic workers enjoy freedom of association and the right to collective bargaining, States should, in accordance Recommendation No 201, give consideration to taking or supporting measures to strengthen the capacity of workers' and employers' organizations, to promote effectively the interests of their members, provided that the independence and autonomy, within the law, of such organizations are protected.

Chapter 2. Labour and Employment

331. Concern to protect labour lies at the roots of labour legislation and ILO; job creation is an obsessive preoccupation for all modern States. The two are inseparably intertwined. More than ever before, the best means must be found of synthesizing the guarantees given to workers, the fight against unemployment, the ability of undertakings to compete and the consequences of global competition between them. In other words, the means must be found of enabling every man and woman to obtain 'decent and productive work, in conditions of freedom, equity, security and human dignity'.[214]

332. ILO standards are at the conflux of several social philosophies: one is laissez-faire and individualistic, and seeks to render the State more performing, less centralized and more streamlined, in the eyes of its partisans an indispensable condition for generating jobs; another is third world, or at least centred on development problems, and gives priority to employment, as a means of combating poverty, and to such basic objectives as access to safe water; a third is interventionist and emphasizes values of equality and solidarity, calling for specific labour regulations. So delicate is the link between the standard-setting independence of the social partners and active State policy that the result can be contradictions in legal logic.[215] ILO documents often underline the importance of dialogue between the two.

333. The first two paragraphs of this chapter deal with fundamental principles and rights in the work place: the abolition of forced labour and child labour, on the one hand, and equality of opportunity and treatment, on the other. The third deals with the promotion of employment. Subsequent paragraph focus successively on labour administration, hours of work, salary, occupational health and safety, special labour conditions, and the situation of migrants and other specific categories of workers.

§1. Forced Labour and Child Labour

334. For labour not to be a commodity, for it to be carried out in decent conditions, presupposes first and foremost that it be chosen without constraint: freedom of work is a fundamental aspect of democratic life. The International Covenant on Civil and Political Rights declares that no one shall be held in slavery or servitude, or required to perform forced or compulsory labour.[216] The Covenant on Economic, Social and Cultural Rights, which recognizes the right to work, stipulates that this includes the right of everyone to the opportunity to gain his living by work which

214. ILC, Report of the Director General, *Decent Work*, 87th Session, ILO, Geneva, 1999 p. 3.
215. *See* J.-C. Javillier, *Droit du travail*, 7th edn, Paris, LGDJ (Manuel), 1999, para. 98.
216. Article 8. Forced compulsory labour may be authorized for a person under detention in consequence of a lawful order of a court, as a service of a military character, as part of normal civil obligations, etc.

he freely chooses or accepts.[217] Both Covenants echo longstanding principles set forth in many national laws which, like the Napoleonic Code, provide that a person's services can only be engaged for a determined time or undertaking.[218]

335. The Declaration on Fundamental Principles and Rights at Work, adopted by ILO in 1998, also stipulates that the Member States, even if they have not ratified the conventions in question, have an obligation arising from the very fact of their membership in the Organization to respect, to promote and to realize the principles contained in certain basic conventions, including those that require the abolition of all forms of forced or compulsory labour.

336. The Declaration also refers to the conventions on the effective abolition of child labour. And indeed, who would argue that children are free to choose when they want to work? In fact, it is a traditional principle of labour law that children do not have full capacity to contract.[219] The reasons their parents are not opposed to sending them out to work are discussed below.

337. The International Covenant on Economic, Social and Cultural Rights also requires that special measures of protection and assistance be taken on behalf of all children and young persons, 'without any discrimination for reasons of parentage or other conditions'. Children and young persons are to be protected from economic and social exploitation; their employment in work harmful to their morals or health or dangerous to life or likely to hamper their normal development should be punishable by law. States should also set age limits below which the paid employment of child labour is prohibited.[220] The issue of children and young people at work therefore boils down to two matters that international law and most national laws and regulations have on the whole dealt with in the same way. The first is to confirm what is not allowed: to make children work; the second, to stipulate what must be done: protect young people at work or who are seeking employment. This is also the approach of the Convention on the Rights of the Child, which was adopted by the United Nations in 1989 and which deals, in general terms, with all the guarantees children require.

338. Section I below therefore covers forced labour and the standards adopted to abolish it, section II the prohibition of child labour, and section III the guarantees needed to help young people find a job and to protect them in that job.

I. Forced Labour

339. Two ILO conventions, Convention No. 29 of 1930 and Convention No. 105 of 1957, are aimed at excluding and condemning forced labour. They cover any

217. Article 6. On the right to work, *see* paras 439–442 *below*.
218. Article 1780.
219. Even if a number of legislations specify a minimum age for admission to employment below the civil majority.
220. Article 10, para. 3.

work or service which is exacted from any person under the menace of any penalty and for which that person has not offered himself voluntarily.[221] The CEACR has considered the prohibition of forced or compulsory labour in all its forms as a peremptory norm of international law on human rights; it is of an absolutely binding nature from which no exception is permitted. [222]

340. It should be borne in mind, in this respect, that freedom of work can be limited externally or indirectly by practices such as retaining the identity papers of a migrant worker.[223] The prohibition extends to prohibiting workers from leaving their jobs.[224] Thus, enrolment in the armed forces in exchange for higher training (as a doctor, pilot, etc.) cannot deprive the individual concerned of the right to leave the service in time of peace within a reasonable timeframe, either at specific intervals or on prior notice, subject to the routine conditions required to ensure continuity of service. In determining that period, account can be taken of the length of obligatory military service. In addition, consideration can be given to having the individuals concerned reimburse their training costs on a pro rata basis.

341. Convention No. 29 calls on the States to suppress the use of forced or compulsory labour in all its forms within the shortest possible period.[225] The State is therefore bound both not to do something and to do something: it must refrain from imposing such labour and it must not allow the people it administers to impose it. It must in particular abrogate any legislative or regulatory provision under which recourse may be had to forced labour.[226] The Convention allowed recourse to forced or compulsory labour during a transitional period, for public purposes only and as an exceptional measure. The elimination of those derogations, which date from 1930, has been confirmed with the adoption, in 2014, of a protocol to Convention n°29 and a complementary recommendation.[227] The new instruments detail the measures of prevention, protection, enforcement and international cooperation that should be taken.

342. Exceptions concern the following activities:[228]

(a) 'Any work or service exacted in virtue of compulsory military service laws for work of a purely military character'. It is therefore prohibited to employ conscripts on public works.[229]

---

221. Article 2, para. 1 of the Forced Labour Convention, 1930 (No. 29); *see* ILC (96th session, 2007), *Eradication of Forced Labour*, Report III (part 1B), Geneva, ILO, para. 35 *et seq.*
222. ILC (101st Session, 2012), *Giving Globalization a Human Face*, *op. cit.*
223. M. Kern and C. Sottas, 'The abolition of forced or compulsory labour', in ILO, *Fundamental Rights at Work and International Labour Standards*, Geneva, 2003, p. 36.
224. ILC, *op. cit.*, paras 40 and 96–97.
225. Article 1. Article 25 states that the illegal exaction of forced labour shall be punishable as a penal offence; penalties must be 'really adequate' and 'strictly enforced'.
226. Kern and Sottas, *op. cit.*, p. 34.
227. Valticos, *op. cit.*, para. 531; Kern and Sottas, *op. cit.*, p. 69.
228. Article 2 of the Convention.
229. ILC, *op. cit.*, para. 44.

(b) 'Any work or service which forms part of the normal civic obligations of the citizens of a fully self-governing country.'
(c) 'Any work or service exacted from any person as a consequence of a conviction in a court of law, provided that the said work or service is carried out under the supervision and control of a public authority and that the said person is not hired to or placed at the disposal of private individuals, companies or associations'. Thus, detainees who have not been convicted (and prisoners awaiting trial) cannot be obliged to work;'[230] they can only be obliged to work once they have been found guilty of a crime; in the absence of such a judgement, even a court decision cannot impose labour.
(d) 'Any work or service exacted in cases of emergency, that is to say, in the event of war or of a calamity or threatened calamity, such as fire, flood, famine, earthquake, violent epidemic or epizootic diseases, invasion by animal, insect or vegetable pests, and in general any circumstance that would endanger the existence or the well-being of the whole or part of the population.'
(e) 'Minor communal services of a kind which, being performed by the members of the community in the direct interest of the said community, can therefore be considered as normal civic obligations incumbent upon the members of the community, provided that the members of the community or their direct representatives shall have the right to be consulted in regard to the need for such services.'

343. Whether in its earlier or present-day forms, from slavery and bonded labour to human trafficking, forced labour remains one of the thorniest issues facing many communities, States and the international community.[231] Two other ILO instruments endeavour to combat the specific conditions of compulsory labour.

344. The International Labour Conference supplemented Convention No. 29 with Recommendation No. 35, which is a statement of the principles that appear best able to guide the Member States in endeavouring to avoid any indirect compulsion of labour which would lay too heavy a burden on the population. The Recommendation states that the amount of labour available, the capacities for labour of the population, and the evil effects which too sudden changes in the habits of life and labour may have on the social conditions of the population, are factors which should be taken into consideration in deciding questions connected with the economic development of territories in a primitive stage of development, in particular when deciding on:

(a) increases in the number and extent of industrial, mining and agricultural undertakings in such territories;
(b) the non-indigenous settlement, if any, which is to be permitted;

230. *Ibid.*, para. 51.
231. ILO, *Stopping Forced Labour* (Geneva), 2001; *ibid.*, *Profits and Poverty: The Economics of Forced Labour*, Geneva, 2014.

(c) the granting of forest or other concessions, with or without the character of monopolies.[232]

The Recommendation goes on to say that it is desirable to avoid indirect means of artificially increasing the economic pressure upon populations to seek wage-earning employment, and specifically cites measures such as:

(a) imposing such taxation upon populations as would have the effect of compelling them to seek wage-earning employment with private undertakings;
(b) imposing such restrictions on the possession, occupation, or use of land as would have the effect of rendering difficult the gaining of a living by independent cultivation;
(c) extending abusively the generally accepted meaning of vagrancy;
(d) adopting such pass laws as would have the effect of placing workers in the service of others in a position of advantage as compared with that of other workers.[233]

345. It also recommends that no restrictions be placed on the voluntary flow of labour (from one form of employment to another or from one district to another) which might compel workers to take employment in particular industries or districts.[234] The history of Europe is replete with cases in which severe limits were placed on the voluntary flow of people, even within the borders of a country. The laws on vagrancy in particular were used to that end.[235] The International Labour Conference sought to prevent these abuses from reoccurring. The question nevertheless arose again with the duty to work imposed by the constitutions of certain States. The CEACR indicated that the duty to work did not violate the forced labour conventions when it was simply a moral obligation and failure to observe it was not penalized.[236] The laws and regulations of some countries went further, however, and obliged able citizens who were not receiving instruction to have a lucrative activity under threat of being forced to do a specific job or of being penalized. This situation runs counter to ILO standards, as do certain national laws that define vagrancy very broadly and therefore have the same result.

346. Contrary to Convention No. 29, Convention No. 105 focuses on the prohibition of specific situations of forced or compulsory labour.[237] It discusses all forms of forced labour:

---

232. The Forced Labour (Indirect Compulsion) Recommendation, 1930 (No. 35).
233. Para. 2.
234. Except, adds para. 3, where such restrictions are considered necessary in the interest of the population or of the workers concerned.
235. R. Castel, *Les métamorphoses de la question sociale. Une chronique du salariat*, Paris, Fayard, 1995.
236. ILC (65th session, 1979), *Abolition of Forced Labour*, Report III (Part 4B), Geneva, ILO, para. 45 *et seq.*
237. Article 1.

(a) as a means of political coercion or education or as a punishment for holding or expressing political views or views ideologically opposed to the established political, social or economic system;
(b) as a method of mobilizing and using labour for purposes of economic development;
(c) as a means of labour discipline;
(d) as a punishment for having participated in strikes;
(e) as a means of racial, social, national or religious discrimination.

The reports of the Conference committee that discussed the draft convention acknowledge that in some circumstances, penalties can be imposed for participation in unlawful strikes and that those penalties can comprise routine prison work; those penalties ensue, in many national laws and regulations, from provisions prohibiting strikes in certain sectors, during conciliation procedures or on the basis of collective agreements. In considering the compatibility of these provisions with the Convention, the supervisory bodies applied the principles relating to freedom of association.[238]

II. The Prohibition of Child Labour

347. The prohibition of child labour is one of the first measures adopted by industrialized States to counteract the excesses of the Industrial Revolution. The first to react were national lawmakers, but the International Labour Conference, at its first session in 1919, adopted Convention No. 5 on minimum age, which prohibits the employment of children under the age of fourteen in industrial undertakings. Shortly thereafter, several other instruments established an equivalent minimum age for other branches of activity. The standard was subsequently raised to fifteen, and even higher for difficult work. In 1973, ILO codified, as it were, the earlier rules in a general convention, No. 138, and a supplementary recommendation, No. 146.[239]

348. Convention No. 138 rephrases the provisions contained in the earlier instruments. It starts with a programmatic obligation: the States undertake to pursue a policy designed to ensure the effective abolition of child labour and to raise progressively the minimum age for admission to employment 'to a level consistent with the fullest physical and mental development of young persons'.[240]

---

238. ILC (101st Session, 2012), *Giving Globalization a Human Face*, *op. cit.*, para. 313. With regard to the principles of freedom of association, *see* title I, Chapter 1 *above*.

239. *See also* the Private Employment Agencies Convention, 1997 (No. 181), Article 9 and the Home Work Recommendation, 1996 (No. 184), para. 10.

240. Article 1. Recommendation No. 146 suggests a number of measures; they include full-time attendance at school or participation in approved vocational orientation or training programmes. *See* paras 1–5. The minimum age for admission to employment will apply within the territory of the ratifying state as well as on means of transport registered in its territory: Article 2, para. 1 of the Convention.

349. This framework having been established, the Convention does not give a specific age: it asks the States to specify a minimum age in a declaration appended to their ratification. The minimum age thus specified must not be less than the age at which compulsory schooling ends and, in any case, not less than 15 years. A logical link is therefore drawn between the end of a person's schooling and the start of his working life. Experience has shown that where no such link exists, the risk is greater that young people with no defined activity will engage in unreported work. Article 2 allows countries 'whose economy and educational facilities are insufficiently developed' initially to authorize young people to work as of the age of 14. The declaration to that effect can, obviously, be followed by others raising the minimum age. Recommendation No. 146 stipulates, moreover, that the objective is to gradually raise the age to 16.[241]

350. In addition, any State 'whose economy and administrative facilities are insufficiently developed' can start by indicating which branches of economic activity or types of undertaking do not fall within the scope of Convention No. 138. The States are granted yet another facility, which can be combined with the previous ones: they can exclude certain categories of activity in respect of which the Convention's application would meet with special and sizeable obstacles.[242] The Convention does not list the categories (which may include employment in family businesses[243] or work in the home); the national authorities therefore have great latitude for adapting the relevant provisions to the country's situation.

351. The Convention requires[244] a minimum age of 18 for admission to employment which, by its nature or the circumstances in which it is carried out, is likely to jeopardize the health, safety or morals of young persons; that age may be lowered to 16 years, after consultation with the organizations of employers and workers concerned, on condition that the health, safety and morals of the young persons concerned are fully protected and that they have received adequate specific instruction or vocational training. Neither the Convention nor the Recommendation defines the work in question. The Recommendation nevertheless requires that account be taken

241. Para. 7.
242. Articles 4 and 5. Article 5 requires that the Convention be applicable as a minimum to the following: 'mining and quarrying; manufacturing; construction; electricity; gas and water; sanitary services; transport; storage and communication; and plantations and other agricultural undertakings mainly producing for commercial purposes, but excluding family and small-scale holdings producing for local consumption and not regularly employing hired workers'. Recommendation No. 146, para. 11, adds that were a minimum age is not immediately fixed, in accordance with the article mentioned *above*, 'appropriate minimum age provisions should be made applicable therein to types of employment or work presenting hazards for young persons'.
243. Recommendation (No. 52), 1937, suggests that State Members apply their legislation relating to the minimum age of admission to all industrial undertakings, including family undertakings.
244. The Minimum Age (Non-Industrial Employment) Recommendation, 1932 (No. 41) provides for a specific protection in cases of light work and employment in public entertainments on the one hand, of dangerous employments, on the other; it also states that persons who have been condemned for certain serious offences or who are notorious drunkards should be prohibited from employing children other than their own.

of relevant international labour standards, such as those concerning dangerous substances, agents or processes (including ionizing radiations), the transport of heavy loads and underground work.[245]

352. On the other hand, children under the age of 13 or even 12 can do light work if it is not harmful to their health or development nor prejudicial to their attendance at school or their participation in vocational orientation or training programmes,[246] and the Convention does not apply to work performed as part of a course of education or training.[247] Further exceptions are allowed for participation in activities such as artistic endeavours.[248]

353. The authorities are required to stipulate the length (in hours) and conditions in which the light work is performed. The Recommendation draws attention in particular to the following points in respect of young people under the age of 18:

(a) the provision of fair remuneration and its protection, bearing in mind the principle of equal pay for equal work;
(b) the strict limitation of the hours spent at work in a day and in a week, and the prohibition of overtime, so as to allow enough time for education and training (including the time needed for homework related thereto), for rest during the day and for leisure activities;
(c) the granting, without possibility of exception save in genuine emergency, of a minimum consecutive period of 12 hours' night rest, and of customary weekly rest days;
(d) the granting of an annual holiday with pay of at least four weeks and, in any case, not shorter than that granted to adults;
(e) coverage by social security schemes, including employment injury, medical care and sickness benefit schemes, whatever the conditions of employment or work may be;
(f) the maintenance of satisfactory standards of safety and health and appropriate instruction and supervision.[249]

354. Although it is flexibly worded, Convention No. 138 has given rise to considerable implementing difficulties, especially in many developing countries. The children are employed, not in light work but in activities that border on exploitation. Some young people have to put in long hours in poor or even dangerous conditions. In any case, they often lose years of essential schooling. Poverty is the main cause of their plight (the children help their parents earn a living because the family income is not sufficient for the bare necessities); this is compounded by shortcomings in the educational system, the perpetuation of social inequalities, including in

245. Para. 10.
246. Article 7 which adds that such light work should not be such as to prejudice their capacity to benefit from the instruction received.
247. Article 6 details the conditions in which the exception applies.
248. *See* Article 8.
249. Para. 13.

respect of women, and the forces inherent in any informal economy. Even though the global number of child labourers seems to go down, millions of children find themselves in practice in a position that eludes any oversight.[250]

355. There are also children who work in the textile industry, in agriculture, in bars, hotels and restaurants, and in the sales and distribution sectors of industrialized countries. These activities are usually clandestine and carried out in small undertakings or family businesses, after or instead of school. Occupational accidents are common.[251]

356. It is therefore good to recall, even in industrialized countries, the importance of the enforcement measures required by the Convention and the Recommendation. These consist, in the first place, of providing for and imposing truly dissuasive sanctions, which in turn implies effective labour inspection. Employers should keep registers or other documents indicating the names and ages or dates of birth of workers under the age of 18.[252]

357. Everyone agrees that effective means of fighting child labour are to combat pockets of poverty in rich countries as well, and to make school attendance compulsory up to a reasonable age (that at which young people can be admitted to employment). Many European countries confronted with rising unemployment have raised the age limit for compulsory schooling. In these countries, a sophisticated social security system also serves, in principle, to ensure that young people do not need to work; shouldering the cost of children is the natural corollary to the rule setting a minimum age for admission to work. As we saw, Recommendation No. 146 makes that suggestion explicitly.

358. Likewise, the United Nations Convention on the Rights of the Child obliges the States parties[253] to set minimum age for admission to employment; it asks them to provide child care services for the children of working parents; it stipulates the principle that every child has the right to benefit from social security and medical services and from special measures if he is physically or mentally impaired; it underscores the need to reunite the families of migrant workers. The Convention also calls on the States to protect children from any work endangering their health, education or development, and to regulate employment conditions; it provides that all children must have access to information and educational and occupational orientation.

250. ILO, *Marking Progress against Child Labour: Global Estimates and trends 2000–2012*, Geneva, ILO, 2013.

251. ILC (90th session, 2002), *A Future without Child Labour* (Geneva), ILO, 2002, p. 21 *et seq*. Andras Szalay, *Child Labour in the Developed Countries*, Tilburg Law School, 2010; electronic copy available at http://ssrn.com/abstract=1869170.

252. Convention No. 138, Article 9 and Recommendation No. 146, paras 14–16.

253. The Convention has been ratified by almost all countries. For the purposes of this instrument, the term 'child' applies to all persons under the age of 18, except if the majority is fixed before in accordance with the law in force.

359. Intolerable situations nevertheless exist. Many men, women and also children continue to be forced to work in all kinds of activities, and are sometimes drawn under false pretences into occupations they then cannot leave. Many girls and boys find themselves in situations of bonded labour because of a debt that neither they nor their parents can pay off. The debt grows and the servitude is handed down from generation to generation. Some of these children work in appalling conditions; they often suffer from respiratory difficulties or skin disease and are harassed and beaten.

360. In 1992, for the specific purpose of eliminating this scourge, ILO launched a far-reaching programme known by the acronym IPEC.[254] In 1999, for the same reason, it adopted a convention, No. 182, and a recommendation, No. 190 that focus on the worst forms of child labour. The term 'child' is used in these instruments to refer to anyone under the age of 18. The States must take immediate and effective measures to eliminate such practices, to wit:

(a) all forms of slavery or practices similar to slavery, such as the sale and trafficking of children, debt bondage and serfdom and forced or compulsory labour, including forced or compulsory recruitment of children for use in armed conflict;
(b) the use, procuring or offering of a child for prostitution, for the production of pornography or for pornographic performances;
(c) the use, procuring or offering of a child for illicit activities, in particular for the production and trafficking of drugs as defined in the relevant international treaties;
(d) work which, by its nature or the circumstances in which it is carried out, is likely to harm the health, safety or morals of children.[255]

Recommendation No. 190 stipulates that the types of work referred to in (d) above can be authorized as from the age of 16 in the same conditions as the equivalent provision in Convention No. 138, namely: (a) consultation with workers' and employers' organizations, (b) on condition that the health, safety and morals of the children concerned are fully protected, and (c) that the children have received adequate specific instruction or vocational training.[256]

361. The Recommendation also provides further information on the elements to take into account when determining what constitutes prohibited activities and in identifying where they exist. Those elements include:

(a) work which exposes children to physical, psychological or sexual abuse;
(b) work underground, under water, at dangerous heights or in confined spaces;

---

254. *See* para. 1120 *below*.
255. Article 3. Article 4 indicates how to determine the types of work, to identify where they exist, and to periodically examine and, as necessary, revise their list.
256. Para. 4.

(c) work with dangerous machinery, equipment and tools, or which involves the manual handling or transport of heavy loads;
(d) work in an unhealthy environment which may, for example, expose children to hazardous substances, agents or processes, or to temperatures, noise levels, or vibrations damaging to their health;
(e) work under particularly difficult conditions such as work for long hours or during the night or work where the child is unreasonably confined to the premises of the employer.[257]

362. It does not suffice to make the political decision to eliminate such practices or even to draw up the programmes of action that go with it; both have to be implemented. This is when the most daunting problems arise, especially given that the prohibited activities tend to be clandestine. Hence the difficulty, for instance, in collecting the necessary data and compiling reliable statistics. Supervision is awkward, for the same reasons. Convention No. 182 and Recommendation No. 190 contain several provisions on these matters,[258] which are compelling examples of the problems posed by the fulfilment of the obligations laid down in the ILO instruments we will turn to in the last chapter. The United Nations Convention on the Rights of the Child, what is more, embodies the recent tendency of family and social security law to recognize that children have rights that are specific to them. Indeed, some parents need to be relieved of the conviction that their offspring belong to them. The Convention is intended to bring about a change in attitudes and strengthen the parents' reluctance to have their children perform unacceptable tasks.

III. The Protection of Young People at Work

363. The special attention paid to the occupational integration of adolescents is the natural corollary to the prohibition of child labour. Young people should be helped to find a suitable activity, a suitable job, especially since almost everywhere the unemployment rate among young people is high[259] and we know the human and social cost of prolonged inactivity at the beginning of a person's working life. Appropriate vocational training and occupational guidance are therefore of crucial importance. The standards on this point, and others on the promotion of employment and on placement services, are considered in §§3 and 4 of this chapter. What is basically at stake is every individual's ability successfully to manoeuvre the passage from childhood to adulthood, from the school to the workshop or office. In fact, the reasoning underlying the new kinds of apprenticeships in which young people alternate between classroom learning and company internships as they approach the end of their vocational training period is to facilitate their entry into the world of work. The tendency is to integrate the two, to bridge the gap between training and

257. Para. 3.
258. For more details, *see* R. Hernandez-Pulido and T. Caron, 'Protection of children and young persons', in *Fundamental Rights at Work and International Labour Standards, op. cit.*, p. 110 *et seq.*
259. ILC (101st Session, 2012), *The Youth Employment Crisis: Time for Action,* Report V, Geneva, 2012.

employment, to start work before the training is over and to continue training after work has started.

364. Concern to facilitate employment for young people goes hand-in-hand with the desire to protect them in that they are more vulnerable than adults. As we just saw, 1973 Recommendation No. 146 provides guarantees for young workers under the age of 18. Other ILO instruments, backed up by national laws and regulations, contain guarantees for workers: medical examinations, working hour arrangements, prohibition of certain activities or restrictions on their performance, special facilities.[260]

A. Medical Examinations

365. Three conventions require a medical examination of the fitness of young people for work in industrial undertakings (Convention No. 77 of 1946), and in particular for underground work in mines and quarries (Convention No. 124 of 1965) and in non-industrial occupations (Convention No. 78 of 1946). The latter term covers 'all occupations other than those recognized by the competent authority as industrial, agricultural and maritime occupations'.[261] Recommendation No. 79, which was also adopted in 1946, contains a list of such establishments and activities.[262]

366. As we will see later,[263] employers has been encouraged to plan a systemic action against occupational hazards, i.e. to identify, assess, prevent any risk, and to inform and train the staff, in particular the representatives they have elected to this end. The approach is reflected in the international standards on young workers' health. The principle is that young people cannot be admitted to employment or an industrial occupation unless they have been found fit by a thorough medical examination carried out by a qualified physician. Their fitness is certified either by a medical certificate or by an endorsement on the work permit or in the workbook, which can stipulate specific conditions of employment. The young people concerned must be subject to medical examinations at intervals of not more than one year until they reach the age of 18; in some cases, additional examinations can be required.[264]

367. In occupations which involve high health risks (the case for underground work in mines and quarries) medical examinations and re-examinations must be carried out until at least 21 years of age.[265]

---

260. *See also* the Promotional Framework for Occupational Safety and Health Recommendation, 2006 (No. 197), paragraph 3.
261. Article 1 of Convention No. 78.
262. Para. 1; *see also* para. 2.
263. *See* §7 on health and security at work.
264. Articles 2 and 3 of Convention No. 77 and Articles 2 and 3 of Convention No. 78.
265. Convention No. 77, Article 4 and Convention No. 78, Article 4; Convention No. 124, Articles 1 and 2; the latter permits alternative arrangements for medical supervision of young persons working underground in mines and quarries after medical advice and agreement of the most representative organizations of employers and workers concerned.

368. The medical examinations must not involve the child or young person, or his parents, in any expense.[266] Recommendation No. 79 describes how the medical examinations are to be organized. Convention No. 124 stipulates that an X-ray film of the lungs is required at the initial medical examination and, if necessary, at subsequent re-examinations.[267]

369. Children and young people found to be unsuited to certain types of work or to have physical handicaps or limitations must receive vocational guidance and physical and vocational rehabilitation. Recommendation No. 79 makes specific suggestions on this point.[268]

370. Recommendation No. 125 underscores the usefulness of practical and theoretical instruction in the health and safety hazards to which workers in mines and quarries are exposed. It requires that adequate information be provided on protective measures and on facilities for the workers' welfare (sports and other recreational activities, changing rooms and showers, diet).

371. In order to help labour inspectors do their job, the employer must file and keep available for them either the medical certificate or another document showing that there are no medical objections to the employment.[269]

B. Arrangement of Working Time

372. According to Recommendation No. 125, young persons under 18 years of age working underground in mines and quarries should be entitled to an uninterrupted weekly rest of at least 36 hours, and if possible 48 hours; this should include the day of the week established as a day of rest by local traditions or customs and there should be no exceptions.[270] Recommendation No. 103 (1957) adds that young persons employed in commerce or offices should be granted an uninterrupted weekly rest of two days with no partial or total temporary exemptions.[271] In more general terms, as we have seen, Recommendation No. 146 provides that all young people under the age of 18 are entitled to customary weekly rest days, 'without possibility of exception save in genuine emergency'.[272]

373. ILO's standards also stipulate that young persons under the age of 18 are entitled to annual paid leave. That leave must amount to at least 24 working days

266. Articles 5 of Convention No. 77 and 5 of Convention No. 75; Article 3, para. 3 of Convention No. 124.
267. Article 3, para. 2.
268. Articles 6 of Convention No. 77 and 6 of Convention No. 78; paras 9 and 10 of Recommendation No. 79.
269. Articles 7 of Convention No. 77 and 7 of Convention No. 78. *See also* paras 11 to 14 of Recommendation No. 79. Article 4 of Convention No. 124.
270. Paras 9 and 10.
271. The Weekly Rest (Commerce and Offices) Recommendation, 1957 (No. 103), para. 4.
272. Para. 13(i), *see also* para. 353 *above*.

(corresponding to four weeks of work) per 12-month period of service if they work underground in mines or quarries.[273] For all other workers under the age of 18 it must be longer (the exact period is not stated) than the minimum two weeks per 12-month period of service provided for in Recommendation No. 98 (1954) on holidays with pay.[274] Recommendation No. 146 extends that period to four weeks at least.[275]

374. Recommendation No. 116 (1962) on reduction of hours of work states that due consideration should be given to the special circumstances of young persons under 18 years of age when arranging overtime.[276] Recommendation No. 146 is more radical: it prohibits overtime and strictly limits the length of the work day and week.[277] In more general terms, Recommendation No. 116 provides that when carrying out measures for progressively reducing hours of work, priority should be given to industries and occupations which involve a particularly heavy physical or mental strain or health risks for the workers concerned, particularly where these consist mainly of young persons (and women).[278]

375. Recommendation No. 146 establishes the principle that young persons under the age of 18 are not to work at night: it invites the States to guarantee, 'without possibility of exception save in genuine emergency', a minimum consecutive period of 12 hours' night rest.[279] Earlier conventions and recommendations contain more flexible and detailed rules pertaining to industry,[280] agriculture[281] and non-industrial occupations;[282] these standards, which ILO's managing bodies have not placed in the list of up to date instruments,[283] define the period of night (both its length and the interval at which it occurs) and authorize exceptions as of a certain age, for certain sectors or in exceptional circumstances.

C. Dangerous Work

376. We have just seen that Recommendation No. 125 imposes certain conditions in respect of the work of young people in underground facilities in mines and quarries. Several other ILO instruments limit the exercise of certain activities by

---

273. *See* paras 11 and 12 of Recommendation No. 125.
274. Para. 10; *see also* para. 3 which excludes from its scope seafarers, agricultural workers and family undertakings.
275. Para. 13(i) which adds 'and, in any case, not shorter than that granted to adults'. *See also* para. 353 *above*.
276. Para. 18.
277. Para. 13(i); *see also* para. 353 *above*.
278. Para. 9.
279. Para. 13(i); *see also* para. 353 *above*.
280. The Night Work of Young Persons (Industry) Convention, 1919 (No. 6); the Night Work of Young Persons (Industry) Convention (Revised), 1948 (No. 90).
281. The Night Work of Children and Young Persons (Agriculture) Recommendation, 1921 (No. 14).
282. The Night Work of Young Persons (Non-Industrial Occupations) Convention (No. 79) and Recommendation (No. 80), 1946.
283. *See* para. 1087 *below*.

young people (generally speaking until the age of 18) or ban them outright. Some examples are occupations that result in lead poisoning,[284] use white lead in industrial painting,[285] or involve exposure to radiation,[286] the manual transport of loads[287] or exposure to benzene.[288]

D. Facilities

377. Recommendation No. 125 puts forward measures aimed at maintaining the health of young people working underground in mines and quarries and at promoting their normal physical development. It refers specifically to sports and other recreational activities, to changing rooms and showers, if possible separate from those for adults, and to a diet suitable to their stage of development, if circumstances so require.[289] Recommendation No. 102 (1956) on welfare facilities, for its part, suggests that young people be provided with seats if, in the course of their work, there are 'opportunities for sitting without detriment to their work'.[290]

* * *

378. ILO's general conventions and recommendations apply in principle to young men and women under the age of 18. There also exist specific standards that meet concerns relating to the physical and mental development of young people. While these standards are useful, they may also discourage an employer from hiring young people under the impression – right or wrong – that they will add to his production costs. This is a thorny issue that comes up every time a specific category of wage earners benefits from additional guarantees and that is particularly nettlesome in view of the fact that unemployment among young people is a source of constant concern everywhere. In order to make the right decision, or rather to strike the best possible balance between these at times contradictory objectives, we have to come back to the reasoning behind these rules: if adolescence is considered as a transition period, then there are solid grounds for having rules that protect the first few years in a given occupation. After all, is this not an effective means of ensuring a smooth transition to the working life and proper integration into society?

§2. EQUALITY OF OPPORTUNITY AND TREATMENT

379. Historically, constitutional and legislative texts established the principle of equality before the law as a means of abolishing the immunities and privileges

284. The Lead Poisoning (Women and Children) Recommendation, 1919 (No. 4).
285. The White Lead (Painting) Convention, 1921 (No. 13).
286. The Radiation Protection Convention, 1960 (No. 115), Article 7 and complementary Recommendation (No. 114), para. 4.
287. The Maximum Weight Convention, 1967 (No. 127), Article 7 and complementary Recommendation (No. 128), paras 19–23.
288. The Benzene Convention, 1971 (No. 136), Article 11, para. 2 and complementary Recommendation (No. 144), para. 20.
289. Para. 6.
290. Para. 16.

accorded to some people or classes by the former monarchies. The States were asked to respect a simple obligation of abstention: not to give preferential treatment to certain citizens. To discriminate implies to focus on one or more characteristics of the person concerned, while forgetting the others, to separate him or her from the group, and treat him or her less well. The principle of non-discrimination, for its part, consists in rejecting the criteria for differentiation cited in the positive law: race, religion, political opinion, social origin, etc.[291]

380. Those texts undoubtedly gave greater weight to equality of treatment than to initial disparities. At least they authorized distinctions where situations differed, and made it possible to provide special protection for categories of people considered to be more vulnerable, such as children, women (until recently), and even more generally wage earners, who were viewed as the weaker party in the labour relationship. In short, national lawmakers gradually took into account the socioeconomic substratum in order to move towards more genuine equality. Many labour laws and regulations are based on this approach.

381. The notion of equality has gradually become both broader and more positive in scope, in particular under the influence of Anglo-Saxon thinking. The State must no longer simply refrain from doing something, it must encourage equality by taking tangible action, by giving greater effect to equality and narrowing natural or social divides. The question that then arises – whether measures favouring certain categories (priority hiring and promotion, for example) are not in turn discriminatory – recently came up in connection with women workers. It could be asked every time a specific group is given an advantage. The response, in law, is given by the legislative branch, which decides whether or not it accepts such 'positive discrimination', and up to what point. In all events, however, the determination to introduce greater equality takes the material form of a policy, of projects and decisions. The standard is often programmatic, and the action taken as much practical as it is legal.

382. Equality between human beings is a fundamental right in the workplace. What is more, it is an essential component of other rights, in that recognition of those rights is meaningful only if they are granted to all.[292] We made the same point about freedom of association.

383. Equality of opportunity and of treatment before the law is set down in the laws and regulations of most States, usually in the constitutional text.[293] It is

291. K.J. Partsch, 'Fundamental principles of human rights: self-determination, equality and non-discrimination', in K. Vasak (ed.), *The International Dimension of Human Rights*, Vol. 1 (Paris), UNESCO, 1982, p. 61 *et seq.*; A. Supiot, 'Principi di eguaglianza é limiti della razionalitá giuridica', *Lavoro e diritto*, VI(2), Spring 1992, pp. 211–221; G. Borenfreund and I. Bacarie, *Le droit social, l'égalité et les discriminations*, Paris, Dalloz, 2013.

292. *See* in this regard T. Ramm, 'Discrimination: International Development and remarks of legal theory', in F. Schmidt (ed.), *Discrimination in Employment*, Stockholm, Almqvist and Winksell, 1978, p. 508; *see also* Partsch *op. cit.*, p. 61.

293. *See* R. Blanpain, H. Nakakubo and T.Araki (eds.), 'New developments in discrimination employment law', *Bulletin of Comparative Labour Relations*, Kluwer, The Hague, No. 68, 2008.

expressed in general terms, however, that leave a great deal of scope for interpretation, with the attendant risks. At the world level, numerous treaties, conventions and recommendations establish the principle of equality. A number of regional instruments also refer to the equality of opportunities and treatment.
Suffice it to mention, because they deal with the field of employment.

- the two 1966 United Nations covenants on human rights;
- the International Convention on the Elimination of All Forms of Racial Discrimination (United Nations, 1965);
- the Convention on the Elimination of All Forms of Discrimination Against Women (United Nations, 1979);
- the International Convention on the Protection of the Rights of Migrant Workers and Members of Their Families (United Nations, 1990);
- the Convention on the Rights of People with Disabilities (United Nations, 2006)
- the Convention (and recommendation) against Discrimination in Education (UNESCO, 1960).

384. This section nevertheless focuses on ILO standards, which are the most detailed in terms of employment. The principle of 'equal pay for equal work' is set forth in the Preamble to the ILO Constitution, that of general equality in the Philadelphia Declaration appended to the Constitution and in the 1998 Declaration on Fundamental Principles and Rights at Work. The general principle of equality is reiterated in many instruments. Convention No. 111 (supplemented by Recommendation No. 111) of 1958 on discrimination in employment and occupation contains the basic standards. There are also Convention No. 100 (and Recommendation No. 90) of 1951 on equal remuneration, Convention No. 156 (and Recommendation No. 165) of 1981 on workers with family responsibilities, and Convention No. 118 of 1962 concerning equality of treatment of nationals and non-nationals in social security; the latter is examined in Chapter 3 hereafter.

385. Section I below looks at the promotion of occupational equality in general, Section II at discrimination between men and women.

I. The Promotion of Occupational Equality

386. Under ILO Convention No. 111, discrimination includes 'any distinction, exclusion or preference made on the basis of race, colour, sex, religion, political opinion, national extraction or social origin, which has the effect of nullifying or impairing equality of opportunity or treatment in employment or occupation'. The States can obviously add other causes of discrimination. If they do so, the Convention says, they must first consult with representative employers' and workers' organizations, where such exist, and with other appropriate bodies.

387. The text below considers the causes of discrimination, protected areas, discriminatory acts or situations, the scope of the standards and their implementation.

A. The Causes of Discrimination

388. Convention No. 111 mentions several causes of discrimination. Let us point out that a person may be subjected simultaneously or successively to multiple discrimination, i.e. discrimination on more than one ground.[294]

389. Race or skin colour are well-known criteria for discrimination that have led to segregation and apartheid. Negative conduct strikes in particular at sizeable minorities, less at groups who are fewer in number.[295] In fact, it is not so much the race, colour or ethnic origin of the person targeted that gives rise to discrimination as the negative values the discriminator considers the victim to embody.[296] In some countries migrants and Roma workers face serious race discrimination. The CEACR considers that the term 'race' includes any discrimination against linguistic communities or minority groups whose identity is based on religious or cultural characteristics, or national or ethnic origin.[297]

390. Convention No. 111 also cites national extraction. It thus targets the distinctions made in respect of naturalized foreigners, or citizens from different national communities and cultures within the same country. It does not concern nationality; foreigners are covered by other ILO standards, in particular Convention No. 143 (and supplementary Recommendation No. 151) of 1975 on migrations in abusive conditions and equality of opportunity and treatment of migrant workers.

391. Differences in treatment based on sex are the focus of most debates on unacceptable discrimination versus legitimate distinctions. Unacceptable discrimination includes the spinsterhood imposed on some women if they want to keep their jobs (air hostesses are one example). The criteria for differentiation are not just marital status: a specific requirement (not to marry) is imposed on the members of one sex alone. It also covers the question of how to achieve true equality of remuneration for the same function (or for an equivalent task). Legitimate distinctions, on the other hand, relate to discussion of whether the special protection of women in the workplace is compatible with the principle of equality. We shall return to these two questions.

392. Other causes of discrimination are political and religious convictions, and relate to freedom of opinion and expression and their limits in the employment relationship. Here, too, the interpreter will in each case have to exercise his judgement

294. D. Schiek and Anna Lawson (eds.), *European Union Non-discrimination Law and Intersectionality: Investigating the Triangle of Racial, Gender and Disability Discrimination*, Ashgate, Farnham, 2011; C. Deliyanni-Dimitrakou, 'Egalité multidimensionnelle et discriminations multiples en droit comparé', *Revue internationale de droit comparé*, July–September 2013, pp. 681–718.

295. *See also* B. Aaron, 'Discrimination based on race, color, ethnicity and national origin', in F. Schmidt (ed.), *Discrimination in Employment*, Stockholm, Almqvist and Winksell, 1978, p. 51 *et seq.*

296. *See* ILC (83rd session, 1996), *Equality in Employment and Occupation* (Geneva), ILO, 1996, para. 32.

297. 302. See ILC (101st Session, 2012), *Giving Globalization a Human Face, op. cit.*, para. 762.

in drawing the line between what is admissible and what is not: to what extent can the freedom of opinion and expression of those occupying certain posts be limited; can a specific belief be required to perform a specific function (in a religious institution, for example); is religion enough to exempt the worker from the standard rules on leave or dress (for example, the obligation to wear a helmet); can religions be observed at the workplace, or influence what the job entails? The international texts, which were drafted in general terms, provide no specific answers to these complex questions.

392bis. The CEACR has raised issues of mandatory dress codes for women, or the prohibition of the wearing of religious signs, including head coverings in cases regarding Denmark, France, Turkey and the United Kingdom. With regard to legislation prohibiting the wearing in public schools of any conspicuous religious signs or apparel on pain of disciplinary measures, including expulsion, the Committee has found it important that measures be taken to ensure that the application of such legislation does not have the effect of reducing the opportunities of girls to find employment in the future (France). Similarly, laws or regulations prohibiting all forms of head coverings applying to men and women on university premises may have a discriminatory effect on women with regard to their access to university education, and subsequent employment (Turkey). In other cases, the Committee has considered that regulations imposing a mandatory dress code for women in the public sector, or rules imposing observance of the Islamic veil for students in universities and higher education institutions, could have a negative impact on the employment of women in the sector or their access to education (Iran). Some positive steps have been noted in the area of 'religious appearance or dress', for example in Australia (South Australia) where legislation explicitly prohibits discrimination on this ground.

392ter. Discrimination on the basis of actual or perceived religion, combined with exclusions and distinctions based on other grounds such as race, national extraction or nationality has acquired greater significance, especially in the context of increasing global movements of people looking for better opportunities, and concerns about countering and preventing terrorism.

393. The CEACR, on the other hand, has pointed out that the legal provisions of some countries grant clearly illegitimate preferences to people on the basis of their social origin or the (political) merits of their parents to obtain access to a job or a training course; the same provisions also allow exclusions from employment or training on the basis of the same criteria. Discrimination based on political opinion are primarily related, but not confined to the public service. The Committee has continued to monitor employment restrictions in the public service affecting persons linked to former political systems, for example, in Central and Eastern Europe.[298]

---

298. ILC (101st Session, 2012), *Giving Globalization a Human Face*, *op. cit.*, paras 799, 801, 800 and 805.

In addition, the application of Convention No. 111 is hampered when the national society is divided into clear classes or castes.

394. Several ILO instruments mention factors of discrimination that are not expressly cited in Convention No. 111: trade union membership or action (Convention No. 98 of 1949 on the right to organize and collective bargaining), the activity of staff representatives (Convention No. 135 and Recommendation No. 143 of 1971 on workers' representatives), the family situation (Convention No. 156 and Recommendation No. 165 of 1981 on workers with family responsibilities), marital status, pregnancy and family responsibilities (Convention No. 158 of 1981 on termination of employment), HIV and AIDS (Recommendation No. 200 of 2010). Other instruments deal with the elimination of discrimination against specific categories of workers, such as migrants, the disabled (Convention No. 159 and Recommendation No. 168 of 1983 on the vocational rehabilitation and employment of disabled persons) and older workers (Recommendation No. 162 of 1980). This last text tackles the issue of whether setting a mandatory retirement age constitutes age-based discrimination: it suggests that the provisions making the termination of employment mandatory at a specified age be re-examined, states that retirement should be voluntary and encourages countries to make the qualifying age for an old-age pension flexible. The HIV and AIDS Recommendation, 2010 (No. 200) ask Governments to afford protection to prevent discrimination based on real or perceived HIV status. As well as the Private Employment Agencies Recommendation, 1997 (No. 188), the instrument include a provision to prevent discrimination based on sexual orientation.

395. Other reasons for discrimination did not result in the adoption of specific international standards: language, private life, illnesses other than AIDS, legal prosecution or criminal conviction. National legislation often goes by the rule that distinctions are permitted only where the elements on which they are based have an influence on the performance of the task. This national criterion corresponds to the provision of Convention No. 111 that authorizes distinctions, exclusions and preferences in respect of a particular job based on the inherent requirements thereof.[299] Whether or not discrimination has occurred is always hard to gauge, however, because of the difficulty of being completely objective.

B. The Areas Protected

396. Convention No. 111 refers to employment and occupation. It specifies that these terms cover access to vocational training, access to employment and to different occupations and the conditions of employment. It applies to self-employed workers. Providing to everyone, free from considerations based on stereotypes or prejudices, vocational guidance and access to education and training, appears especially important when unemployment is high.[300]

299. *See* para. 402 *below*.
300. ILC (101st Session, 2012), *Giving Globalization a Human Face*, *op. cit.*, para. 750.

397. Recommendation No. 111, for its part, lists the areas to be protected:

access to vocational guidance and placement services;

- access to training and employment of their own choice on the basis of individual suitability for such training or employment;
- advancement in accordance with their individual character, experience, ability and diligence;
- security of tenure of employment;
- remuneration for work of equal value;
- conditions of work including hours of work, rest periods, annual holidays with pay, occupational safety and occupational health measures, as well as social security measures and welfare facilities and benefits provided in connection with employment.

It adds that employers should not practice or countenance discrimination in engaging or training any person for employment, in advancing or retaining that person in employment, or in fixing the terms and conditions of employment. The same holds true for employers' and workers' organizations in respect of admission, retention of membership or participation in their affairs.

398. Equality of remuneration between men and women is the subject of Convention No. 100 and Recommendation No. 90, and equality of treatment of nationals and foreigners in social security, of Convention No. 118. These points are discussed later in this monograph.

C. Discriminatory Acts and Situations

399. Discrimination can stem from the law itself. More often, it results from actual circumstances. Convention No. 111 refers to any distinction, exclusion or preference that has the effect of nullifying or impairing equality of opportunity or treatment. This wording does not limit discrimination to deliberate acts, negative conduct or even simple preference: it also covers the objective consequences of certain apparently neutral distinctions.

400. The Convention deals with both direct and indirect discrimination. Examples of indirect discrimination are legislation making admission to certain occupations contingent on possession of diplomas from specific institutions or special conditions, or work stoppages relating to pregnancy and maternity that are not calculated for the purposes of seniority when seniority is a decisive factor for promotion or in the period of notice for dismissal. Indirect discrimination also occurs when collective dismissals for economic reasons enable the employer selectively to get rid of workers for the reasons given in the Convention. The text covers all discrimination irrespective of the intention of the author of a discriminatory act. Legal provisions do not always cover indirect discrimination, or are ambiguous in this regard. The CEACR has observed that the concept is well understood and recognized everywhere. It is, however, imperative to identify and address situations in which certain treatment is extended equally to everybody, but leads to discriminatory results for one particular group protected by the Convention, such as ethnic and religious groups. Such discrimination is subtle and less visible, making it even more important to ensure there is a clear framework for addressing it, and proactive measures are required to eliminate it. [301]

401. Discrimination can be difficult to prove in these instances, a matter we discuss below. Equally clear is the extent to which the principle of equality can be at odds with the contractual freedom granted, in particular by private law, to the employer. The latter nevertheless usually has the right to hire whom he wants and to decide what vocational qualifications[302] are needed to hire, transfer or promote someone.

402. Convention No. 111 does not define as discrimination distinctions, exclusions or preferences based on the inherent requirements of a particular job, measures to safeguard security and special measures of protection and assistance for specific groups of persons. These exceptions are hard to work with and the risk of abuse obvious.

403. The qualifications required for certain jobs, to start, must correspond to the objective characteristics of those jobs and be in proportion to those specific characteristics. The CEACR has accepted restrictions for a narrow range of jobs associated with particular religious institutions or non-profit organizations and organizations specifically promoting the well-being of an ethnic group. The Commission has added that criteria such as national extraction and religion may be taken into account as inherent requirements of certain posts involving special responsibilities. However, the inherent requirements of the particular job must still be evaluated in the light of the actual bearing of the tasks performed on the institution's or organization's objective. The question arose in a case concerning Norway and inquiries into the Christian faith of those applying for jobs – even menial positions – in religious institutions. According to the competent ILO body, the real requirements for each post considered and their incidence on the objectives of the employing institution had to be carefully examined. Applicants for certain positions (cleaner, cook, gardener, etc.) could not be obliged to belong to a specific religion: it all depended on the nature of the post to be filled.[303]

404. The same principles apply to political opinions. In public administration, for example, political opinion should influence admission only to certain senior positions that imply special trust or greater discretion.

---

301. *Ibid.*, paras 745 and 746.
302. *See* already P. Horion, 'Les discriminations en matière d'emploi en Belgique', *Revue internationale de droit comparé*, No. 1, 1968, paras 69 and 72.
303. ILC (101st Session, 2012), *Giving Globalization a Human Face, op. cit.,* para. 831. Governing Body Document GB.222/18/23 (Geneva), ILO, 1983.

405. The following point is closely related to the requirements of State security or, as the Convention puts it, to 'measures affecting an individual who is justifiably suspected of, or engaged in, activities prejudicial to the security of the State'. The Convention refuses to consider these measures as discriminatory, provided that the individual concerned has the right to appeal to a competent body established in accordance with national practice.

406. The CEACR stated the conditions in which the Convention does not consider such measures to be discriminatory.[304] The Convention refers first to the activities of the person, not to his belonging to a group or to a specific association. By the same token, simply stating one's opinions or beliefs is not tantamount to an activity that is prejudicial to State security. This was the case, for example, of the Czechoslovak workers' support for the manifesto of the Charter 77 movement.[305] Finally, measures aimed at ensuring State security must be sufficiently well defined and delimited not to give rise to discrimination based on political opinions or religion, which would nullify the very principle of equality of opportunity and treatment. The application of such measures must be analysed in the light of the effects a given activity could have on the effective performance of job, function or occupation of the person concerned.[306] Provisions couched in broad terms, such as 'lack of loyalty', 'the public interest' or 'anti-democratic behaviour' or 'harm to society' must be analysed in the light of the effects a given activity could have on the effective performance of job, function or occupation of the person concerned.[307]

407. Convention No. 111 adds to these conditions of substance a procedural guarantee: the right to appeal to a competent body. The ILO's supervisory bodies have specified that judicial oversight does not suffice if the provisions to be applied do not respect the basic conditions sought. They have also said that the appeal body must be other than the administrative or governmental authorities, that it has to afford guarantees of objectivity and independence and that it has to enable the appellant to present a complete defence. An ILO commission of inquiry had occasion to recall this in time of the military dictatorship in Chile.[308]

408. Convention No. 111 does not deem as discriminatory the special measures of protection or assistance provided in other ILO conventions and

304. *See* ILC (83rd Session, 1996), *Equality in Employment Occupation*, Report III (Part 4B), Geneva, ILO, Geneva, 1996, para. 124 *et seq.;* ILC (101st Session, 2012), *Giving Globalization a Human Face*, *op. cit.*, paras 833–835.

305. *See* Official Bulletin (ILO), Supplement, Vol. LXI, 1978, Series A, No. 3, para. 21 in a case concerning the application of Convention No. 111 by Czechoslovakia.

306. *See* Report of a Commission of Inquiry concerning the application of Convention No. 111 by Germany, *ibid.*, Supplement 1, Vol. LXX, 1987, Series B, para. 576 *et seq.*

307. *See* Report of a Commission of Inquiry concerning the application of Convention No. 111 by Germany, *ILO Official Bulletin,* Supplement 1, Vol. LXX, 1987, Series B, para. 576 *et seq.*; ILC (101st Session, 2012), *Giving Globalization a Human Face, op. cit.,* paras 834 and 833.

308. *Report of the Commission appointed under Article 26 of the Constitution to examine the observance by Chile of the Hours of Work (Industry) Convention, 1919,* No. 1 and the Discrimination (Employment and Occupation) Convention, 1958, No. 111, Geneva, ILO, 1975, in particular paras 174 and 175.

recommendations. The same holds true for the special measures a country may adopt to meet the particular requirements of persons who, for reasons such as sex, age, disablement, family responsibilities or social or cultural status, or because of their trade union function or role as a staff representative, are generally recognized to require special protection or assistance.

409. The issue of protection as opposed to equality arose above all, as we have said, in connection with women workers, although specific provisions exist for several other categories of workers as well. Although these provisions can undoubtedly discourage employers looking to recruit staff, the same employers may hesitate even in the absence of a protective text: they assume liability if they give a pregnant woman (or one who may be pregnant) work that exposes her health or that of her child to risks. These points were also made earlier in connection with positive discrimination aimed at promoting true equality.

D. The Scope and Implementation of the Standards on Equality

410. Convention No. 111 is one of those programmatic conventions[309] that obliges the States to implement a specific policy, to set goals and endeavour to meet them by taking various legal, economic and administrative measures. Any country ratifying the Convention is obliged to justify any action it takes before the ILO bodies. The States are also bound, however, to abrogate immediately any law or regulation and cease any activity that is counter to the stated policy.

411. This dual point of view can be discerned in the comments made by the ILO's supervisory bodies, which do not limit themselves to following up policies and programmes aimed at implementing the Convention's standards. They have often specifically asked the government to amend a law or change a practice that was clearly incompatible.

412. An active policy of equality of opportunity and treatment presupposes a coordinated series of actions: information campaigns, education (in particular of employers and workers) and other promotional activities; the adoption of new laws and the revision of existing legislation; the establishment of appeal bodies and other institutions whose task is to follow up these issues or to prescribe the damages that are due in the event of proven discrimination, etc.[310] The CEACR has pointed out that specialized bodies are increasingly dealing with an expanded range of discrimination issues. Some equality bodies dealing with specific grounds have in recent years been merged to address a wider range of grounds of discrimination that are often difficult to disentangle, thus addressing systemic and multiple discrimination. For example, the Equality and Anti-Discrimination Ombud of Norway was established through the merging of the Equality Ombud, the Equality Centre and the Centre against Ethnic Discrimination, and the Office of the Equality Ombudsman in

309. *See* para. 87 *above* and paras 1181–1188 *below*.
310. *See* the measures suggested by para. 2 *et seq.* of Recommendation (No. 111).

Sweden was formed through the merger of four previous anti-discrimination bodies into a single body. The Equality and Human Rights Commission in the United Kingdom brings together the mandates of three previous equality commissions, with the new Commission addressing discrimination based on age, disability, gender including gender reassignment, race, religion and belief, and sexual orientation.[311]

413. It would be a mistake to believe, however, that damages or a sum of money can compensate for the wrong that has been done. They have little impact on the continuing consequences of a past discriminatory act. Indeed, an unscrupulous employer will see them as a kind of tax he occasionally has to pay in order to act as he pleases. Annulment of the discriminatory measure is in many cases the most effective step to take. Fear of victimization may lead workers to refrain from lodging complaints or bring cases. A worker or a witness who has filed an appeal or a staff member who refuses to follow discriminatory instructions must also be protected from reprisals.

414. No matter what the legal remedy, much depends on the historical, cultural, political, economic and social factors inherent in each civil society, and on the conviction with which the forces in a country, starting with the social partners if they are powerful enough, can fight all forms of discrimination, even the most twisted and insidious.

415. This being said, victims seeking compensation face a huge legal hurdle: proving that discrimination has occurred. In some cases, notably those involving anti-trade union practices, the proof must be about a deliberate element, a motive, hostility to membership or union activity.[312] In others, such as sexual discrimination, the aim is more than to punish a vicious intention: the deeper aim is to change social habits and obtain true equality. No matter what the case, it is almost always difficult to prove discrimination.

416. Domestic laws and regulations contain various measures aimed at preventing acts or situations of this kind, or at making it easier for the victim to furnish proof. Thus, the law or the courts can ensure that the worker does not need to reveal facts or opinions (political, religious, etc.) that could give rise to discrimination. Belgian legislation, for example, prohibits a reference to age in employment offers. More generally, the judge must be able to examine any tests, inquiries or questionnaires that are part of the recruitment process and make sure, if they are used, that they contain no element liable to result in discrimination.

417. Much obviously depends on the system of proof adopted (accusatorial or inquisitorial) and its flexibility. This being said, it usually suffices to prove discrimination; it is not necessary to prove further the existence of a prejudice. European Union Directives 2000/43, 2000/78, and 2006/54 provide that the burden of proof shall be shared between the worker/plaintiff and the employer/respondent if the

---

311. ILC (101st Session, 2012), *Giving Globalization a Human Face, op. cit.,* paras 849 and 881.
312. *See* paras 289–293 *above.*

former establishes facts from which it may be presumed that there has been direct or indirect discrimination based on causes they mention. It is then up to the respondent to justify an act or situation, more specifically to prove that there has been no breach of the principle of equal treatment. They also protect the worker who has filed an appeal from reprisals. Sometime the legislation goes even further and lists the acts or kinds of behaviour deemed to be discriminatory, which is tantamount to having the employer prove they are legitimate. As we shall see further on, Convention No. 158 of 1982 on termination of employment also provides that the burden of proving that the dismissal was justified be either reversed or shared.[313]

II. Equality between Men and Women

418. Since its inception, ILO has had two objectives when it comes to women workers, and both are set out in its Constitution. On the one hand, the protection of women is listed as one of the improvements in working conditions that is urgently required. On the other, the Constitution also affirms the principle of equal pay for equal work.[314] This dual approach – special protection for women workers, granting them the same rights as men workers – has guided ILO's activities in this respect, even though one (special protection at the outset, equal rights today) can, at a given point in time, appear to take precedence over the other.

419. The first group of standards concerns additional guarantees granted to all women workers; it deals with the prohibition of or limits to the employment of women for certain tasks and working hours and the facilities women are granted (seats, rest rooms). It also covers the guarantees granted to women workers as mothers or future mothers (protection of maternity; special working conditions for pregnant or nursing workers; prohibition or restrictions for certain tasks).

420. These standards gave rise to lengthy debate on whether to give preference to protection or to equality of treatment with men.[315] The discussion is a longstanding one; it dates back to the early 20th century in Australia and even earlier in northern Europe. It relates to what has been and often still is considered to be one of the pillars of social protection at work; in Western Europe, for example, the first workers' laws regulated the work of women. The controversy was undoubtedly also fuelled by another bone of contention, the degree of flexibility for labour standards; the jury is still out on the effects of labour regulations on the labour market, profits and the overall performance of national economies.

421. The special protection granted women at work is also the subject of intense, even fundamental reflexion for all those concerned with labour and the conditions

313. *See* Article 9 and para. 49. *See also* the Workers' Representatives Recommendation, 1971 No. 143, para. 6(2)(e).
314. *See* the Preamble and Article 427 on General Principles of the original ILO Constitution. The two concerns are still included in the present Preamble of the ILO Constitution.
315. J.-M. Servais, *Droit en synergie sur le travail*, Brussels, Bruylant, 1997, p. 124 *et seq.*

in which people work. The question is the usefulness of and limits to the right to be different in a world of labour that is not asexual.

422. The major international institutions have broached the matter pragmatically. The 1979 United Nations Convention on the Elimination of All Forms of Discrimination against Women requires[316] that the legislation protecting women, in particular as concerns health and security (including protection of the reproductive function) be reviewed periodically in the light of scientific and technological knowledge and be 'revised, repealed or extended as necessary'. The same approach has prevailed at ILO. The CEACR considers that protective measures applicable to women's employment, based on stereotypes regarding women's professional abilities and role in society, violate the principle of equality. Safety at work provisions should aimed at protecting the health and safety of both men and women at work, while taking account of gender differences with regard to specific risks to their health. With a view to repealing discriminatory protective measures, it may be necessary to examine what other measures, such as improved health protection of both men and women, adequate transportation and security, as well as social services, are necessary to ensure that women can access these types of employment on an equal footing with men.[317]

423. The second group of instruments concerning women workers aims to afford women true equality of opportunity and treatment with their male colleagues. These standards are supplementary to the general standards set forth in Convention and Recommendation No. 111. Convention No. 100 and Recommendation No. 90 of 1951 on equal remuneration, and Convention No. 156 and Recommendation No. 165 of 1981 on workers with family responsibilities all merit special attention.[318]

424. Convention No. 100 is considered by the 1998 Declaration on Fundamental Principles and Rights at Work to be one of ILO's fundamental instruments. Article 2 provides that the States must, 'by means appropriate to the methods in operation for determining rates of remuneration, promote and, in so far as is consistent with such methods, ensure the application to all workers of the principle of equal remuneration for men and women workers for work of equal value'. It lists the means of applying that principle: legislation, legally established or recognized machinery for wage determination, collective agreements between employers and workers or a combination thereof.

425. The concept of work of equal value is broader than that of equal work. It covers in particular occupations that in practice are the preserve of women, and which are more difficult to compare with men's work. The Convention therefore

316. Article 11(3).
317. ILC (101st session, 2012), *op. cit.*, para. 840.
318. Specific standards aim at promoting women work such as the Promotion of Cooperatives Recommendation, 2002 (No. 193), para. 7. Others try to know better the situation in this regard: the Home Work Recommendation, 1996 (No. 184), para. 4, asks for detailed information, including data classified according to sex, on the extent and characteristics of home work; this information should be published and made publicly available.

encourages countries to promote objective appraisal of jobs on the basis of the work to be performed. The principle established in the Convention was reiterated in the International Covenant on Economic, Social and Cultural Rights[319] and in various regional instruments, including the Treaty on the functioning of the European Union.[320]

426. The Convention does not oblige the States to ensure that the principle is applied to all workers when doing so is not consistent with the methods in operation for determining rates of remuneration; it simply asks them in that case to encourage application. The difficulty mentioned most often by some governments is indeed that they have no direct influence on the determination of salaries in the private sector. This is why Recommendation No. 90 focuses on sectors in which the State plays a dominant role in this respect and can answer for the principle's implementation: central public administration and occupations in which the rates of remuneration are subject to regulations or public control. This is the case, the Recommendation says, for:

(a) the establishment of minimum or other wage rates in industries and services where such rates are determined under public authority;
(b) industries and undertakings operated under public ownership or control; and
(c) where appropriate, work executed under the terms of public contracts.

The means of giving effect to Convention No. 100 must correspond, need we say, to the national mechanisms for determining wages. Employers' and workers' organizations must be fully associated in the process. Recommendation No. 30 on minimum wages stipulates that women should be included in the wage-setting machinery as workers' representatives and independent persons whenever an industry (or part of an industry) employs a large number of women.

427. The gender pay gap has declined in the crisis years in most countries. However, a narrowing does not necessarily imply that the situation of women has improved. A recent ILO report refers to the case of Estonia and shows how a decline in the gender pay gap can be achieved not through improvements in the situation of women but through a deterioration of the labour market circumstances of men relative to women. If wages of part-time workers are included in the calculation, the gap can increase to much higher levels. In brief, the gender pay gap remains one of the most obvious examples of structural gender discrimination.[321]

428. Significant progress has been made in Europe and in the Americas during the last fifty years towards more equality between men and women in their working

319. Article 7 applies more broadly than to discrimination between women and men only.
320. Article 157.
321. ILO, *Global Wage Report 2012/13.Wages and Equitable Growth*, Geneva, 2013, pp. 4–7; ILC (101st session, 2012), *op. cit.*, para. 668. The gender pay gap stays at 16 per cent in the EU: *see Tackling the Gender Pay Gap in the European Union*, Luxembourg Publication Office of the European Union, 2013.

life; those developments, however, have been uneven and depend on the country concerned. Nevertheless, the traditional means of action against gender discrimination have, in many cases, reached a limit in their efficiency: women workers have certainly obtained a certain degree of equality of opportunities and treatment with their male colleagues, but it appears extremely difficult to go beyond a given border line. The question has therefore been legitimately raised whether other policies should not complement the existing ones with a view to overcoming the present blockage. Let us underline that the new measures should come in addition to – and not instead of – the still indispensable measures used until now. As strong as the commitment of the spouses (or partners) may be towards a true equality, a time occurs when they face objective differences in their personal interests when they try to accommodate professional obligations and family life. It always happens once in a while that one member of the couple has to choose between a professional opportunity, and the need to offer the same chance to the other. Those are uneasy decisions that may lead to acute conflicts. Ways and means to settle them peacefully must certainly contribute to the promotion of a real equality.

429. A number of modern domestic laws endeavour to introduce effective equality of opportunity and treatment for workers of both sexes who have children, or who are responsible for other members of their immediate family, where that responsibility restricts their possibilities of preparing for, entering, participating in or advancing in economic activity. Trade union circles in particular have pointed out that the equal rights granted in theory to men and women who work do not always have the same effect when the situation of the stakeholders is different. Indeed, who would deny that women usually still have principal responsibility for the household and raising the children? This additional task weighs on a woman's professional life and in many cases works in her 568disfavour. Those who make this point obviously do not all consider, far from it, that family responsibilities lie naturally with the women. But they observe that in the current state of many societies, those tasks fall de facto and for the most part to the woman and that special guarantees are called for as long as that is indeed the situation: in this area in any case, customs must change before the law can. What is more, the adoption of the measures provided for in these rules, such as parental leave, could hasten such a development. The question has been treated at both European and international level.

430. States ratifying the ILO Convention No. 156 must aim (and take measures to that end) to eliminate discrimination based on these constraints and, to the extent possible, conflict between employment and family responsibilities. The Convention lists areas in which measures should be taken. The States have acted mainly on support services and day care for dependants (very young children and also very old people) and working hour arrangements. Many undertakings are now realizing, that it is in their interests to support such policies in order to retain the services of the most qualified personnel – for the time being mainly women. The ILO Recommendation No. 165 adds details and makes suggestions about information and education, employment and training, employment conditions, child-care and family services and facilities, social security, and help in the exercise of family responsibilities.

431. The most innovative experiences for drawing a better balance between family and working life can been found in the field of working time. The Maternity Protection Recommendation, 2000 (No. 191) provides for parental or, as the case may be, paternity leave. Part-time work has also been promoted with – partially – the same concern in mind. It is the subject of ILO Convention No. 175 and Recommendation No. 182 of 1994. Still with a view to reconciling professional constraints and private life, some researchers have proposed considering working time in a broader perspective, namely in its relationship to 'leisure' and social times of the entire working population. They assume that a better balance between work and family responsibilities could be found by integrating new elements towards a solution. Employers and wage earners are also consumers, users, customers, parents; they want to procure the products and services (which are also public) they need when they are not at work. They have families, they want to spend their free time looking after their children or their elderly parents, and to do so with their spouse or (at least in some cases) at different times. Occupational working time arrangements are indeed a vehicle for equalizing opportunities and treatment for men and women. Governments are concerned to connect working time to employment, not only supposedly to avoid dismissals by reducing working periods, but also to encourage hiring whenever possible. It has been asked whether lengthening opening hours for shops and some offices by rotating personnel would not have a positive impact. Consideration has been given to staggering vacation time or daily schedules in order to solve traffic problems and ease the overload on public transportation. Those policies have a clear impact on the balance between family and work. In Italy, the idea emerged of trying to poll people on whether their aspirations could not be more easily met at the regional, town or neighbourhood level than by adopting a general approach to problems of work, leisure time and employment.[322] By the same token, the successful experience (based in particular on the promotion of part-time work) of a small country like the Netherlands can be explained by the perception its leaders had of the true needs of different sectors of the population.[323] France has also given thought to the future of work in all its dimensions.[324] The debate continues across Europe.[325]

322. S. Bonfiglioli and M. Mareggi (eds.), 'Il tempo e la città fra natura e storia. Atlante di progetti sui tempi della città', *Urbanistica Quaderni*, May 1997, No. 12; A. Catasta and E. Donatti, 'Conciliare cura e lavoro' in S. Bonfigliolo and M. Mareggi (eds.), 'Il tempo e la città fra natura e storia. Atlante di progetti sui tempi dellocittà', *Urbanistica Quaderni*, No. 12, May 1997, pp. 252–256.

323. In Belgium as well, there has been quite substantial legislative activities on working time. They have led, more generally, to significant changes in the vision of labour and industrial relations legislation: *see* M. Jamoulle, E. Geerkens, G. Foxhal and S. Bredael, *Le temps de travail. Transformations du droit du travail et des relations collectives du travail*, Brussels, CRISP, 1997.

324. A. Supiot (ed.), *Le travail en perspective*, Paris, LGDJ, 1998; Rapport de la Commission (Commissariat général au plan) présidée par Jean Boissonnat, 'Le travail dans vingt ans', Paris, O. Jacob, La Documentation française, 1995; D. Méda, *Le temps des femmes. Pour un nouveau partage des rôles*. Paris, Flammarion, 2001; *see also* A. Valli (ed.), *Tempo di lavoro e occupazione. Il caso italiano*, Rome, La Nuova Italia Scientifica, 1988, pp. 13–38 and 177–197.

325. A. Supiot (ed.), *Au-delà de l'emploi*, Paris, Flammarion, 1999.

§3. Employment Policy and Promotion

432. The prevention of unemployment is mentioned in Part XIII of the Treaty of Versailles, which saw the establishment of ILO. More elaborate wording is used in the Philadelphia Declaration, which was voted at the end of World War Two and appended to the ILO Constitution.[326]

433. The promotion of employment lies at the heart of ILO programmes and of the social policies adopted by its members, whether they are developing or industrialized countries. For ILO programmes, poverty cannot be eliminated 'unless the economy generates opportunities for investment, entrepreneurship, job creation and sustainable livelihoods. The principal route out of poverty is work.'[327] The strategy to eliminate poverty proposed by the ILO Director General has a number of components, all related in one way or another to both employment and international labour standards: developing skills for sustainable livelihoods; investing in jobs and the community (through labour-intensive programmes); promoting entrepreneurship; making money work (using microfinance); building local development through cooperatives; overcoming discrimination and working to end child labour; ensuring incomes and basic social security; working safely (by taking adequate steps to prevent occupational accidents and illnesses).

434. Forced inactivity also has a devastating impact in industrialized countries, both on the unemployed and on the undertakings forced to layoff workers. Forced departures leave deep scars on the undertaking's internal mechanisms and in the souls of its workers. Indeed, a company cannot divest itself of part of its staff without losing their experience and know-how. These capacities are not easily rebuilt, especially since, by definition, the time is not ripe for spending on training for those who remain employed. And yet, this is when the employer should react, adapt and innovate.

435. The scars are also psychological. In Western Europe and Japan, employment relationships were usually entered into for an unlimited time, i.e. for a very long spell if not, as in Japan above all, for the wage earner's entire working life. A moral bond of loyalty was forged between the employer and the wage earner. Dismissals sever that bond, destabilizing those who remain. Workers who were dismissed for economic reasons are sometimes given priority in re-hiring, but this makes little difference. Although those who remain may try to work better so as to protect themselves from dismissal, their perception of work changes: they disengage, or switch their priorities to activities outside work (or take a second job). Are we to believe this will not affect the bottom line?

436. The repercussions of unemployment go much further than simple cases of staff reduction. The phenomenon is a serious one. It has reached disturbing rates in

326. *See* para. 22 *et seq. above*.

327. ILC, *Working out of Poverty*, Report of the Director-General to the 91st session of the ILC (2003) (Geneva), ILO, 2003, p. 7 *et seq.*

numerous countries, including in the South of Europe. It pushes people, especially young job-seekers, to consume drugs and alcohol, and can have psychosomatic effects. If the unemployment rate grows, the social fabric holding the country together may wear thin and tear. The ILO has call for most urgent action in favour of people aged 15 to 24.[328]

437. The Philadelphia Declaration recognizes that ILO has an obligation to further among the world's nations the implementation of programmes whose aims it lists in detail. They include:

- full employment and the raising of standards of living;
- the employment of workers in the occupations in which they can have the satisfaction of giving the fullest measure of their skills;
- the provision of facilities for training and the transfer of labour, including migration.

438. How do the international labour standards promote fulfilment of these objectives? The answer is a complex one because it lies in the grey area between the law and economics. All the more reason to be specific and to render unto each discipline its due. The answer also calls for an adequate balance in policies between job creation and the protection of work; we will examine, at the end of this monograph, the solutions proposed by the ILO in its 'decent work agenda'.

439. The promotion of full, productive and freely chosen employment should be regarded, as provided in an ILO recommendation,[329] as the means of giving practical effect to the right to work. This right is programmed rather than immediately achievable, at least in countries with market economies. It is also mentioned in the United Nations International Covenant on Economic, Social and Cultural Rights,[330] in the European Social Charter[331] and in several national constitutions; it is political, 'promotional', rather than directly enforceable. The worker, it should be added, has a right, not a duty, to work.

440. The right to work is also usually construed as not imposing on the State the obligation to provide a job to anyone who wants to work. The State has a duty to act, not to succeed. It undertakes to devise and adopt an employment policy – and views differ on the value of such policies – that it will apply using economic and social measures. In terms of economic measures, at any rate, undertakings are under no special obligation. However, a genuine subjective right to obtain and retain a job corresponding to one's skills sometimes exists for targeted groups of workers (the handicapped, veterans, pregnant women, etc.).

328. European Industrial Relations Observatory, *Helping Young Workers During the crisis: Contributions by Social Partners and public Authorities. Comparative Study*, Eironline, May 2012; ILC (101st Session, 2012), *The Youth Employment Crisis: Time for Action*, Report V, Geneva, ILO, 2012.
329. The Employment Policy (Supplementary Provisions) Recommendation, 1984 (No. 169), para. 1.
330. Article 6.
331. Article 1.

441. Furthermore, legal doctrine tends to consider today that in case of doubt, the judge should choose the solution that is most likely to further attainment of the right. Anglo-Saxon scholars in particular include the right to work in the category of reflexive rights.

442. No matter what the case, in market economies provisions relating to the right to work tend to be programmatic in nature. They establish obligations of means, not of outcome. The pertinent international standards oblige the ratifying States to justify their policy in this respect. ILO Convention No. 122 on employment policy, 1964, contains such an obligation, although it does not expressly mention 'the right to work'. Recommendation No. 169 does, however, as we have said, mention that right, with the same content.

443. It goes without saying that no legal text will ever completely do away with unemployment: only an economic policy can do this. Such a policy will aim, for example, to restructure undertakings and the national (regional) production machinery as needed. But legal standards can help find a solution if, on the one hand, they set goals to be attained, recommend specific policies and programmes, create appropriate channels for those policies and programmes and, on the other, they provide for very tangible labour market measures and the means of evaluating the effectiveness thereof.

444. There are two kinds of measures: the main ones aim to lay the groundwork for an active employment policy in the longer term., others tries at short-term to alleviate the situation. They include the organization of efficient employment services, employability-enhancing measures and other labour market interventions, assistance in searching for new employment, counselling, training or re-training whenever necessary, or temporary wage subsidies.[332] Measures such as public works or other forms of employment guarantees provide certain forms of paid employment to beneficiaries. Active policies in this field are more developed in some countries, like the Nordic European Nations, than in others. Most seek nevertheless to strike what is deemed to be a satisfactory balance between the diverging interests of enterprises and job seekers.

445. In these pages we shall look at the instruments adopted for that purpose, except those on employment services, which raise other questions and are examined in the next paragraph. The following pages consider the ILO standards on social policies and job stimulation (1), termination of employment (2), vocational training and occupational retraining (3), and the role of social security in an employment policy (4). We shall see that social security benefits (sometimes conceived as compensation if the right to work cannot be achieved 'in kind') may be tied to an obligation to accept any suitable employment.

332. *See* J. Hajdú, *Social Protection of the Unemployed*, 10th European Congress of Labour Law and Social Security, General report, Seville, 21–23 September 2011, 135 *et seq.*

I. Job Stimulation and Social Policies

446. Convention No. 122 of 1964 is the principal ILO reference instrument on employment policy. It is supplemented by two recommendations: Recommendation No. 122 adopted the same year, and Recommendation No. 169 adopted in 1984. In addition, several other instruments relate in one way or another to the formulation and implementation of employment policy: Convention No. 142 and Recommendation No. 150 (1975) on human resources development; Convention No. 88 and Recommendation No. 83 (1948) on employment service; and Convention No. 168 and Recommendation No. 176 (1988) on employment promotion and protection against unemployment.

447. These instruments are very broad in scope and concern 'all who are available for and seeking work', to quote Convention No. 122.[333] The main goal it establishes for the ratifying States is an active policy designed to promote full, productive and freely chosen employment. It asks them to take the necessary measures – including consultation with interested circles – to give effect to that policy.

448. The two successive recommendations specify the general objectives of an employment policy. The first – No. 122 – lists the general and selective measures it proposes and outlines the policies to be adopted (investment and income; promotion of industrial and rural employment; population growth; action by employers and workers and their organizations; international action). It contains an annex with suggestions for methods of application. Recommendation No. 169 completes the picture with provisions on the employment of young persons and underprivileged people or groups of people, on technology and regional development policies, on the informal sector and small businesses, on investment and public works programmes. It also contains paragraphs on population policy, international economic cooperation and migration.

449. More recently, in 1998, ILO adopted Recommendation No. 189 on job creation in small and medium-sized enterprises. The Recommendation deals successively with the policy and legal framework, the development of an enterprise culture and of an effective service infrastructure and – two topics dear to ILO – the roles of employers' and workers' organizations and international cooperation.

450. Mention should finally be made of the 'Global Jobs Pact' that the ILC adopted in 2009. This soft law document has been elaborated by representatives of governments, business and labour. It proposes a set of policies and measures that countries, with the collaboration of regional and multilateral institutions, can adopt to strengthen their on-going efforts to address unemployment.

451. As we can see, most of the standards proposed are macro-economic. Hence the difficulty that has been noted for a long time by ILO[334] in overseeing their

333. Article 1, para. 2.
334. Governing Body Document GB.258/2/2, November 1993, para. 194.

application. The form for preparing the periodic reports on the application of Convention No. 122 comprises questions on the relations between employment policy objectives and other economic and social goals. It refers expressly to general and sector development policies and to the measures adopted, for example, in terms of investment, fiscal and monetary policy, trade, prices, income, wages and regional development. It also addresses the issues of educational and training policies and of labour market policies. This confirms that many aspects of employment policy are beyond the immediate purview of labour administrations and that it is wise to involve other government administrations and institutions (economic planning, finance, statistics, etc.) in the application of a convention.

452. Current economic difficulties, the latest technological developments, the growing interdependence of national economies, all make it harder to fulfil the objectives of Convention No. 122. In many cases, the internationalization of economic structures limits the governments' room for manoeuvre. But it does not paralyse them and they can always take initiatives to improve qualifications and adapt to new technologies. This being said, an employment policy is more than just legal words. Indicators, clearly economic criteria of progress are needed to analyse programmes of the same kind.

453. Other conventions deal more broadly with social policy and encourage the States to take systematic action and launch properly coordinated employment programmes. They do this either for a particular sector, such as plantations, tenants and sharecroppers, which are discussed below,[335] and cooperatives, or generally.

454. Convention No. 117 of 1962 was adopted when decolonialization brought independence to many countries. It deals with basic objectives and standards. It sets out the general principle that any policy should be directed to the people's well-being and development and to the promotion of the desire on their part for social progress. It regards the improvement of standards of living as the principal objective in the planning of economic development, and lists a series of practical measures to that end. It contains provisions on the fixing of minimum wages and the protection of those wages, on non-discrimination, and on education and vocational training; there are also several articles on migrant workers.

455. Recommendation No. 193 of 2002 considers that a balanced society requires the existence of strong public and private sectors, a strong cooperative, mutual sector and a social and non-governmental sector. It sets objectives; cooperatives should serve in particular to:[336]

(a) create and develop income-generating activities and sustainable decent employment;
(b) develop human resource capacities and knowledge of the values, advantages and benefits of the cooperative movement through education and training;

335. *See* paras 724 and 839 *et seq. below*.
336. Para. 4.

(c) develop their business potential, including entrepreneurial and managerial capacities;
(d) strengthen their competitiveness as well as gain access to markets and to institutional finance;
(e) increase savings and investment;
(f) improve social and economic well-being, taking into account the need to eliminate all forms of discrimination;
(g) contribute to sustainable human development; and
(h) establish and expand a viable and dynamic distinctive sector of the economy, which includes cooperatives, that responds to the social and economic needs of the community.

The Recommendation proposes a legal framework and outlines the role of governments and of occupational organizations and cooperatives. It suggests methods of implementing policies to promote such institutions and encourages international cooperation.

456. Two ILO instruments deal with social services for workers and housing. Recommendation No. 102 of 1956 discusses the facilities to be granted to wage earners of public and private undertakings[337] in terms of meals, rest (seats and rest rooms), recreation and transportation. Recommendation No. 115 of 1961 applies to the housing of 'manual and non-manual workers, including those who are self-employed and aged, retired or physically handicapped persons'. It defines the objectives of a national housing policy and the responsibility of the public authorities in that regard. It deals successively with the questions of housing provided by employers, the financing of housing programmes, housing standards, and measures to promote efficiency in the building industry, the link between house building and employment stabilization, and town, country and regional planning. It contains suggestions on the methods of applying the principles it establishes.

II. Enhancing Occupational Skills

457. No society can do without working to enhance knowledge and skills, to foster reflection, initiative and creativity. All studies confirm in particular that training is the best guarantee against unemployment. It has been observed that youth is divided by diploma. Of course, training is no guarantee of a job. Employment depends on very many factors. Technical qualifications are certainly important, but other factors, some of them economic, also play a role. We should not underestimate such elements as the skill to integrate the enterprise community as well as the ability to change post of work, place of work or even firm within a group. A distinction has to be made between the industrialized countries and Third World States. They cannot have the same policy: in industrialized countries, where manpower tends to be highly skilled, employment problems arise essentially in terms of adaptation and conversion in the face of changes in the production system; in the

337. Excluding workers in agriculture and sea transport.

developing countries, where manpower tends to be poorly skilled, training has to aim at creating skilled workers. It must also take account of the informal sector.

458. But who could deny the usefulness of coupling training with employment? Witness the host of approaches devised by governments in recent years, encouraging employers to hire or take on apprentices and trainees, in particular by providing financial aid. The decision by several countries to prolong compulsory education also makes the point. The employment crisis has prompted many governments to question the quality and effectiveness of their educational systems and to introduce what are sometimes thoroughgoing measures of reform affecting the reconversion of adults and ongoing training as well as the education of young people.

459. Any human resources development policy that is intended to have tangible results presupposes the implementation of an integrated training and vocational orientation scheme that reflects the choices made in terms of objectives, structures, conditions and sources of financing. Key to the success of such a policy, need we say, is the definition of specific and concrete objectives for the short and medium term. In some countries, ILO contributes to the implementation of the relevant programmes within the framework of technical cooperation projects. The concern is less to train people for a specific occupation than it is to teach the workers how to adapt to unexpected work situations, tasks and jobs, how to deal, in particular in industrialized countries, with the consequences of technological change and the adjustments and restructuring aimed at enhancing the economy. Occupational training should make wage earners more versatile and enable them to change occupation, even within the company, in the course of their working lives. It is also a means of introducing a degree of long-term flexibility into industry, commerce and offices.

460. How can international standards contribute to that process and have a positive impact on national polices (B)? Before answering that question, we shall look at the content of the pertinent standards (A).

A. *International Law on Vocational Training and Orientation*

461. The International Covenant on Economic, Social and Cultural Rights looks at vocational training from two angles: in terms of every person's right to education (established in Article 13) and of the measures that every State must take (under Article 6) to ensure full enjoyment of the right to work.

462. ILO and UNESCO took those provisions and expanded on them in more detailed international instruments. In 1974 UNESCO adopted the Revised Recommendation concerning Technical and Vocational Education; on 10 November 1989 it adopted an international convention on the same topic.. Both institutions also worked together on a 1997 recommendation on the status of higher-education teaching personnel, which contains several paragraphs on preparation for the profession and on further training. As a rule, UNESCO deals mainly with issues of education and organization, while ILO is more keenly interested in the relationship between training on the one hand and employment and work on the other.

463. The organization of vocational and technical teaching was one of the measures listed in 1919 in the Preamble to the ILO Constitution. The Philadelphia Declaration also refers to training possibilities.[338] By the 1970s ILO had adopted a series of recommendations that reflected the concerns of the time; only one, Recommendation No. 99 of 1955 on the vocational rehabilitation of the disabled, is considered relevant today.[339]

464. When the employment crisis struck most countries, ILO reconsidered all the problems relating to the development of human resources and as a result adopted new instruments including, this time, conventions. The basic texts in this area are Convention No. 142 of 1995 and Recommendation No. 195 of 2004, on human resources development; the convention placed vocational training and orientation in a global perspective, as factors of economic and social development; the recommendation underlines the need for lifelong learning. Convention No. 140 on paid educational leave established in 1974 the need for adult education. The ILO has still adopted, in 1983, Convention No. 159 and Recommendation No. 168 on the vocational rehabilitation and employment of handicapped persons, and the UN, in 2006, a general convention on the rights of persons with disabilities; that includes articles on habilitation and rehabilitation, work and employment, adequate standard of living and social protection.

465. Convention No. 142 and Recommendation No. 195 propose a true social policy for human resources development.[340] The Convention asks the States to adopt and develop comprehensive and coordinated policies and programmes of vocational guidance and training, and to establish a close link with employment policy. These concerns have already been noted. While the objectives are ambitious – the policies and programmes are to be 'comprehensive and coordinated' – Article 1 adds that the latter are to take due account of the level of economic, social and cultural development and the relationship with 'other economic, social and cultural objectives', and are to be pursued by methods that are appropriate to national conditions. The final paragraph states that these policies and programmes should both help everyone develop and use their capabilities for work and take account of the needs of society.

466. Article 2 requires the States, in order to meet those objectives, to establish and develop 'open, flexible and complementary systems' of general, technical and vocational education, educational and vocational guidance and vocational training. The States also undertake gradually to extend their systems of vocational guidance and employment information, 'with a view to ensuring that comprehensive

338. Para. III(c).
339. *See* the ILO website under 'labour standards'.
340. *See* H.H. Barbagelata (ed.), *El derecho a la formación professional y las normas internacionales*, Montevideo, CINTERFOR, 2000.

information and the broadest possible guidance' are available to all young persons and adults, 'including appropriate programmes for all handicapped and disabled persons'.

467. The States further undertake to 'extend, adapt and harmonize' their vocational training systems to meet the needs 'throughout life of both young persons and adults in all sectors of the economy and branches of economic activity and at all levels of skill and responsibility'.

468. Every State that ratifies Convention No. 140 must formulate and apply a policy designed to promote the granting of paid educational leave for the purpose of: (a) training at all levels; (b) general, social and civic education; (c) trade union education. Article 1 specifies that the term 'paid educational leave' means leave granted to a worker for educational purposes for a specified period during working hours, with adequate financial entitlement.[341] Under the Convention's preambular clauses, the leave must be conceived in terms of a policy of continuing education and training to be implemented progressively and in an effective manner. During the 1991 Conference, the employers' group stressed the high level of the Convention's requirements, which in their view reflected 'the great optimism prevailing at the time of its adoption'.[342] The convention remains, however, in the up to date instruments list.

469. Conventions Nos. 142 and 140 both insist that employers' and workers' organizations, and other interested agencies, must cooperate in the preparation and application of these policies and programmes.

470. Workers' organizations have been interested in educational issues since they first came into being. They started by demanding free and compulsory schooling for all; at the same time, they fought to prohibit child labour. More recently they have demanded training for adults. They have often themselves founded institutions for that purpose – such as the workers' universities – or sought to arrange schooling in the light of job constraints, promoting evening classes.

471. Employers usually want to work with skilled workers. In many cases they have set up, alone or in groups, their own vocational training structures. The public authorities, for their part, have every interest in associating business and its research facilities in the current forms of vocational training.

472. Employers and trade unions are both stakeholders in vocational training and retraining, which they increasingly view as essential items for collective bargaining. Some labour codes impose an obligation to negotiate the matter and list the

341. According to Article 11, a period of paid educational leave shall be assimilated to a period of effective service for the purpose of establishing claims to social benefits and other rights deriving from the employment relation.
342. Wisskirchen and Hess, *op. cit.*, p. 9.

points to be discussed. The topic gives rise to little conflict. It is one of those identified for the European social dialogue.[343]

473. Within the company or undertaking, the workers' staff committees or representatives can usually broach the matter with management. The employer is often bound by the law or the collective agreement to provide them with information or to consult them. Less often, the committees or representatives can negotiate the matter or even obtain genuine power to co-manage. On the other hand, informal or institutionalized bodies of permanent dialogue on these matters between the public authorities and occupational organizations frequently exist nationally, regionally or for branches of activity; they discuss organization, programmes, financing, draft laws and regulations.

474. It goes without saying that active cooperation between employers' associations and trade unions serves to make the system more flexible and to adapt the training more closely to the users' needs.

475. Numerous other ILO instruments contain provisions on vocational training, be it in respect of employment[344] overall, for specific sectors such as plantations[345] or for groups such as young people.[346] And generally speaking, international labour conventions and recommendations apply to apprentices in that they concern all persons employed or occupied, as the case may be, within an undertaking or at a certain task.

476. Under the terms of Convention No. 159 and Recommendation No. 168 supplementing it, the purpose of vocational rehabilitation is to enable disabled persons to secure, retain and advance in suitable employment and thereby to further their integration or reintegration into society.[347] The States must formulate, implement and periodically review a national policy to that end. In accordance with Article 3 of the Convention, employment opportunities for disabled persons should be promoted in the open labour market. Article 4 contains a second component, equality of opportunity with other workers. It adds that special positive measures aimed at effective equality of opportunity and treatment are not to be regarded as

343. The European Social Partners have signed in 2002 a framework of action for the lifelong development of competencies and qualifications. *See also*: European Centre for the Development of Vocational Training, *Social dialogue and lifelong learning: supporting industrial changes*. Results from a peer learning activity, Working paper No 2, Thessaloniki, Cedefop, December 2008; J. Winterton, 'Building Social Dialogue over Training and Learning: European and National Developments', *European Journal of Industrial Relations*, Vol. 13(3), 2007, pp. 281–300.

344. *See* for example the Discrimination (Employment and Occupation) Recommendation, 1958 (No. 111); the Employment Policy Convention (No. 122) and Recommendation (No. 122), 1964, and the Employment Promotion and Protection against Unemployment Convention (No. 168) and Recommendation (No. 169), 1988.

345. *See* the Plantations Recommendation, 1958 (No. 110), paras 5 to 8.

346. The Minimum Age Convention, 1973 (No. 138) does not apply to work done in schools or in training institutions and to trainees under certain conditions (Article 6).

347. *See also* the ILO code of practice on managing disability in the workplace, Geneva, 2002.

discriminating against other workers; we examined the issue of positive discrimination earlier.[348]

B. The Bearing of the Standards

477. Improving vocational skills is not a matter for the law: the problems encountered are above all economic and financial, they have to do with the educational system and organization. Nevertheless – and this is the second point – legal measures are required to implement the relevant policy. It is through legal texts that the principles underpinning the system are established, choices made or comprises reached between sometimes conflicting objectives. It is through them that concepts are translated into action, i.e. into training programmes and conditions for the granting of benefits, into means of stimulating workers to retrain, into administrative and financial structures, into consultations with employers' and workers' organizations. It is through legal texts that apprentices and trainees are granted certain rights and guarantees.

478. These texts tend to be legislative or regulatory, but it is worth considering the usefulness of allowing employers and trade unions, even where such is not the tradition, to conclude independent collective agreements to that effect. Doing so would make the provisions more flexible, adapt them more closely to the needs of those concerned, at any rate ensure they were more readily accepted.

479. But – and this is the third point to ponder – what is the role in this field of international legal instruments, in particular ILO standards? The texts adopted, by the mere fact of their existence, sometimes start the ball rolling, lead opinion to swing in favour of a policy to develop human resources, especially since ILO does a great deal to promote the application of its standards. Obviously, however, they do much more. Convention No. 142 and the other recent instruments on the topic propose 'models' for the harmonious development of vocational capacity. These programmatic provisions do not have the same scope as those on labour conditions or social security: they encourage a certain social policy, set goals to be reached, rather than impose immediate obligations of outcome on the States. In the same spirit, the global jobs pact of 2009[349] aims at equipping the workforce with the skills needed for today and tomorrow.

480. These standards are closely related to the economy. Their application thus depends as much if not more on practical programmes than on legal methods. Hence the importance in this field, more than in others, of ILO technical cooperation for the implementation of the international standards. ILO's International Training Centre in Turin and regional advisers provide headquarters' services with backing to that end. Practical action can also take the form of publications, meetings, seminars and internships, and of modern systems of collecting, coordinating and spreading

348. *See* paras 381 and 408 *above*.
349. *See above* para. 450.

information on vocational guidance and training. These methods help make the enhancement of vocational skills an everyday reality. The ripple effect of each of these measures taken separately or together is not to be underestimated.

481. Specific legal problems can nevertheless arise. One is the clause by which a worker agrees to stay for a certain time in the service of the employer that trained him (or to pay a penalty if he breaks the contract). In the case of abuse, the question of the compatibility of this clause with international labour standards is posed *inter alia* in 1930 Convention No. 29 on forced labour.[350]

482. Conventions Nos. 142, 140 and 159 have a universal mission and the model they propose must therefore correspond to the needs of as many countries as possible. The approach chosen, the fact that these instruments recommend certain social policies, has inevitable prompted questions on the relevance of those policies: are they suitable – even though the texts are written in general and flexible terms – for developing countries, especially their informal sector? More to the point, industrializing countries find it difficult to reconcile objectives of equity and effectiveness: they have to choose their priorities and the ensuing investments. The person most in need of training may not be the person whose training will be of greatest benefit to the community: is it not more profitable to allow a skilled worker to enhance his skills? And – again – what about the vocational education of all the workers – often the majority – in the unorganized sector?[351]

483. These questions show that appropriate economic or practical means are the only ones that will serve to assess the effective application of these instruments. Such means could figure in the report forms. Codes of practice also might supplement the international standards on vocational training by collecting and compiling in one unit the knowledge and experience of potential conflicts, real problems and compromises needed for the choices to be made, as has done, in 2001, the one on managing disability in the workplace.[352]

III. Dismissal

484. Dismissal is not the only means of breaking off the employment relationship, but it is the most frequently used. The parties also may agree on the terms of the termination of their relations, usually in return for some financial compensation, sometimes promoted by the legislation.

---

350. *See* ILC (65th session, 1979), *Abolition of Forced Labour*, Report III (Part 4B) (Geneva), ILO, 1979, paras 55–62 and 67–73.
351. *See* for example T. Alfthan, D. Bas, A. Cabral de Andrade and Cl. de Moura Castro, *The Human Resources Development Convention: Is it Applicable in Poor Countries?,* Training Policies Programme, Discussion Paper No. 28, Geneva, ILO, 1988.
352. ILO, *Code of Practice on Managing Disability in the Workplace*, Tripartite Meeting of Experts on the Management of Disability at the Workplace, Geneva, October 2001; Alfthan, Bas, de Andrade and de Moura Castro, *The Human Resources*, *op. cit.*

485. The employment relationship may also be broken off because it was for a set term fixed in advance. It has always been considered that giving the worker a term of employment allows him to plan for the future, but there is a clear risk of abuse: the period of notice can be very short, and the use of successive fixed-term contracts can be a means of avoiding the protection relating to dismissal. Convention No. 158 of 1982 requires adequate guarantees against such procedures. Recommendation No. 166, which supplements it, lists the measures to that end: limiting recourse to contracts for a specified period of time to cases in which the employment relationship cannot be of indeterminate duration (owing either to the nature of the work to be effected or to the circumstances under which it is to be effected or to the interests of the worker), or deeming contracts for a specified period of time, when renewed on one or more occasions, to be contracts of employment of indeterminate duration. Many countries have laws and regulations with provisions of this kind; the rule has in some cases also been established by case-law. However, concern to encourage this kind of employment in order to fight unemployment has led a number of legislators to liberalize recourse to fixed-term contracts.

486. It must also be remembered that the wage earner, too, can unilaterally end the employment contract. Otherwise, there would still exist forms of forced labour such as the servitude targeted by the already mentioned Code of Napoleon, Article 1780 of which provides that one's services can be hired only for a time or for a specific undertaking. In principle, the procedures are the same, no matter which party takes the initiative to break off the relationship; workers usually have to give shorter notice.

487. Convention No. 158 and Recommendation No. 166 deal with termination of employment, its justification and the procedures to follow. They apply in principle to all wage earners, except those we have mentioned above: workers engaged under a contract of employment for a specified period of time or a specified task, workers serving a period of probation and those engaged on a casual basis for a short period.

488. The Convention distinguishes between dismissals connected with the capacity or conduct of the worker and those based on the operational requirements of the undertaking or service. Of course, what needs to be considered are not the stated reasons but the real motives for the dismissal; it is up to the judge, when the case is brought before him, to discern where the truth lies.

489. That comment applies in particular to the reasons that cannot be invoked to justify a dismissal. There are basically two kinds of such reasons: the first involve discrimination of some kind, the others are based on the worker exercising a right.[353] Convention No. 158 and Recommendation No. 166 define the first category as follows:

353. *See* the very complete ILO data base on employment protection legislation, EPLex (www.ilo.org/dyn/eplex).

(a) union membership or participation in union activities 'outside working hours or, with the consent of the employer, within working hours';
(b) seeking office as or acting in the capacity of a workers' representative;
(c) the filing of a complaint or the participation in proceedings against an employer involving alleged violation of laws or regulations;
(d) race, colour, sex, marital status, family responsibilities, pregnancy, religion, political opinion, national extraction or social origin;
(e) age, 'subject to national law and practice regarding retirement'.

The second category comprises:

(a) maternity leave;
(b) absence from work because of illness or injury (the Convention specifies that the definition of what constitutes temporary absence from work, the extent to which medical certification should be required and possible limitations are to be determined at the national level);
(c) military service or other civic obligations.

490. The laws and regulations of many countries prohibit dismissals on these grounds.

491. Personal reasons for dismissal lead the employer to consider that it is impossible to continue the employment relationship. Economic motives have to do with the undertaking's profits; they affect workers individually and as a group; in the latter case, the decision takes on a special dimension.

492. Different steps can be taken to prevent collective dismissals or limit their effects. In France and Germany (where works committees play a decisive role), the law provides for the establishment of genuine planned redundancy schemes. Insertion enterprises have been set up in both countries. ILO Recommendation No. 166 of 1982 on termination of employment expressly suggests a series of steps to take. The most common include a hiring freeze, non-renewal of temporary contracts, transfers, placement in alternative employment (with retraining and/or mobility assistance as required), temporary lay-offs, part-time work, early or gradual retirement, voluntary departure (with or without a bonus), reduced overtime, etc. In Japan, the courts make sure the employer has used these procedures to retain staff before considering that economic dismissals are valid.[354]

493. As Recommendation No. 166 suggests, national laws usually establish in advance the criteria on which the workers affected are selected, their order of

354. *See* K. Sugeno: *Japanese Employment and Labor Law*, Durham, Carolina Academic Press, 2002, p. 479 *et seq.*; H. Nakakuto, 'The 2003 Revision of the Labor Standards Law: Fixed-Term Contracts, Dismissal and Discretionary-work schemes', *Japan Labor Review*, Vol. 1(2), Spring 2004, pp. 4–25. The employer may even receive, within certain limits, an allowance with a view to further training the workers concerned and to maintaining them in the enterprise: *see* T. Araki, *Labor and Employment Law in Japan*, Tokyo, The Japan Institute of Labor, 2002, p. 25 *et seq.*

priority and their relative number, giving due weight to the interests of the undertaking or service and to the interests of the workers. The criteria most frequently cited are seniority, vocational skills, personal capacity and family situation. Others include nationality, age or belonging to a protected category (workers' representatives, the disabled, veterans).[355]

494. If the employer reduces the size of the workforce, many laws and collective agreements impose, in keeping with the Recommendation, priority in rehiring on certain conditions. In addition, Recommendation No. 166 mentions two kinds of measures that are in common use today to attenuate the effects of such dismissals: compensation, which we will look at later, and assistance in finding other suitable employment.

495. The procedures to be followed are, generally speaking, an important aspect of the protection afforded dismissed workers. According to Article 11 of Convention No. 158, such workers are entitled to a 'reasonable period of notice' or compensation in lieu thereof, unless they are guilty of serious misconduct; this refers to misconduct of such a nature that it would be unreasonable to require the employer to continue the employment during the notice period. The period of notice is intended to allow the workers to start looking for another job. Many laws provide facilities to that end, in particular, as Recommendation No. 166 suggests, free time without loss of pay taken at times that are convenient to both parties.

496. Both instruments spell out the measures to be taken prior to or during termination of employment. The employer shall not terminate the relationship unless there is a valid reason to do so. If the dismissal has to do with the wage earner's person, the employer should give him a prior warning. The wage earner has the right to defend himself. Whether immediately or after a period of notice, a non-voluntary departure requires a notification indicating the employer's decision to end the contract; many countries require that this unilateral notice be given in writing, often with the mention of the date of termination, the reasons therefore, and the legal provisions on the subject (including the possibility of appeal); the periods of notice are sometimes the subject of detailed rules.[356] Lastly, the dismissed wage earner can usually ask the employer to give him a certificate of employment indicating only, as stipulated in Recommendation No. 166, 'the dates of his engagement and termination of his employment and the type or types of work on which he was employed'; nevertheless, 'and at the request of the worker, an evaluation of his conduct and performance may be given in this certificate or in a separate certificate'.

497. The Convention and the Recommendation indicate procedures to follow before or against the dismissal: internal appeals that can involve workers' representatives are supplemented with complaints to bodies that are external to the

355. *See* ILC (67th session, 1981), *Termination of Employment at the initiative of the Employer*, report VIII(i), Geneva, ILO, 1981, pp. 83–85.

356. For further details, *see* the ILO data base on employment protection legislation, EPLex (www.ilo.org/dyn/eplex).

undertaking or public service and are usually a court or board of arbitration. If the worker loses his job for economic reasons, many laws and collective agreements, and European law, require prior consultation with the workers' representatives and notification of the public authorities, in keeping with Articles 13 and 14 of the Convention.

498. The wage earner may find it difficult to prove that the dismissal is unlawful. The laws of some countries therefore shift the burden of proof; others require the judges or boards of arbitration to base their findings relating to the reasons for the dismissal on the elements provided by both parties, as we have seen in case of discrimination. Both procedures are in conformity with Article 9 of the Convention.

499. When a court or board of arbitration deems the dismissal to be unjustified, it can annul it and/or order that the worker be reinstated. That decision, which usually includes the payment of any earnings lost, is obviously difficult to execute in practice. Many countries therefore merely oblige the employer to pay compensation. Both formulas meet the terms of Article 10 of the Convention. The solution adopted varies from country to country and case to case; the compensation may be a lump sum (calculated on the basis of the previous salary and seniority), constitute complete reparation for the damages suffered (in some cases only if the law has been broken) or left to the discretion of the judge.

500. In keeping with Article 12 of the Convention, custom, collective agreements and individual contracts have gradually introduced the concept of severance pay. This kind of compensation is now part of the laws and regulations of a number of countries, subject to the principle that there has been no serious misconduct on the part of the wage earner and sometimes only if there is a reduction in the number of staff.[357]

501. Facing employment crises, national law and legislation have insisted on the worker's financial security rather than on the restrictions to dismissal, in particular the control of the cause of termination of the relationship. These developments are not in line with the convention. The ILO employers group had already pointed out for a long time that the conditions imposed by the instrument were difficult and restrictive. They have been especially critical of Articles 9 (burden of proof) and 12 (severance allowance).[358] As a consequence, the convention and the recommendation No. 166 are no more included in the list of instruments considered as up to date. There is no common point of view between employers, workers and government by now to revise them.

502. What happens if the employer goes bankrupt? In 1992 ILO set out two means of protecting the workers' claims: by means of a privilege, and by means of a guarantee institution.

---

357. For further details, *see* ILO, www.ilo.org/dyn/eplex.
358. Wisskirchen and Hess, *op. cit.*, p. 11.

503. It is a longstanding legal practice to grant preference to certain creditors, who are paid out of the insolvent debtor's assets before other, non-privileged creditors can be paid their share. This is by far the most common method of protecting workers' claims.[359] The Convention No. 173 and the Recommendation No. 180 mention the main debts to be privileged: wages and other amounts due (paid holidays, paid absences, severance pay, indemnities, social security and occupational insurance premiums, etc.). They state that the protection by privilege of workers' claims may be limited to a prescribed amount, but the Convention requires that workers' claims be given a high rank. Privilege for the payment of wages is no modern invention. In continental Europe, for example, it was introduced by the a*ncien régime*. The Code of Napoleon established privilege for the wages of domestic servants and bankruptcy law extended it to manual workers and clerks. Labour law often consolidated and further extended this kind of protection. Countries with a common-law system reacted more slowly and less comprehensively, however, and the law in those countries was initially not as developed on this point.[360]

504. The second means consists in having a third-party institution guarantee payment of the workers' claims in cases where the insolvent employer cannot settle them. Funds were created for that purpose, essentially in Western Europe,[361] and Belgium played a pioneering role in the 1960s. The above-mentioned ILO Convention set a limit to the claims thus protected (essentially the same as for privilege). The Recommendation establishes the working principles of such funds, which, it has been said,[362] are similar to those of social security schemes: they are mandatory, work on the basis of solidarity, are financed (except in some cases) by payments calculated on the basis of salary, and are managed by institutions that are administratively, financial and legally independent. In Israel and in Switzerland, the guarantee fund is an integral part of the social insurance system.

505. The privileged protection accorded to workers' wage claims in the case of the bankruptcy of the employer appears to be, on the whole, a standard feature of the general labour legislation of nearly all countries. Numerous States have even conferred preferential treatment to employment-related claims other than wages, and granted to wage claims absolute priority over all other privileged debts, including those of the State and the social security system, and, in some cases, guarantee the settlement of workers' wage claims through a wage guarantee scheme. Designed

---

359. See ILC (78th session, 1991), *Protection of Workers' Claims in the Event of Insolvency of Their Employer*, Report V(i), (Geneva), ILO, 1990; E. Yemin and A. Bronstein (eds.), *The Protection of Workers' Claims in the Event of the Employers' Insolvency*, Geneva, ILO, 1991; Paul M. Secunda, 'An Analysis of the Treatment of Employee Pension and Wage Claims in Insolvency and Under Guarantee Schemes in OECD Countries: Comparative Law Lessons for Detroit and the United States', *Fordham Urban Law Journal*, Vol. 41, 2014 (forthcoming).

360. *See* ILC, *op. cit.*, p. 20.

361. The European Directive No. 2008/94 of 22 October 2008 also deals with the matter.

362. *See* A. Bronstein, 'The protection of workers' claim in the event of the insolvency of their employer. From civil law to social security', *ILR*, Vol. 126(6), Nov.–Dec. 1987, pp. 715–731; *see also* J.V. Gruat, *Les problèmes des régimes de protection des salariés en cas de faillite de l'entreprise (étude comparative); protection contre le chômage et politique de l'emploi*, Documentation de sécurité sociale, Série européenne, No. 5 (Geneva), ISSA, 1981, pp. 171–196.

as a dual thrust instrument, Convention No. 173 strengthens the privilege system while exploring new means of protection in the form of wage guarantee institutions. The CEACR has recalled, however, that, whether there may be considerable advantages in setting up wage guarantee institutions, these are no panacea to the problems of corporate insolvency. They offer an assurance of payment which is absent under the privilege system, but they are subject to limitations, in terms of maximum length of service and the maximum amount protected; they do not totally replace the traditional bankruptcy procedures of liquidating assets and settling priority debts according to the established order of distribution; and they presuppose healthy labour institutions and sound management, and as such may not be readily applicable in many contexts.[363]

506. In addition, dismissed workers may receive an income from unemployment insurance benefits and aid to the unemployed. Some countries oblige the employer to notify dismissals to the social security funds.

IV. Unemployment Benefits and Employment

507. Employment programmes must, to be effective, fully integrate the social security system in force, first and foremost any unemployment benefits that exist. Convention No. 168 of 1988 on employment promotion and protection against unemployment insists that these policies must be properly coordinated.[364] Article 14 sets down the principle: in cases of full unemployment, benefits are be provided in the form of periodical payments calculated in such a way as to provide the beneficiary with partial and transitional wage replacement and, at the same time, to avoid creating disincentives either to work or to employment creation. Social security is discussed in another section of this monograph; at this point we shall discuss only the points relating specifically to employment.

508. Economists consider that the amount of the unemployment benefits paid in some countries was a disincentive to find work. That affirmation, no matter how relevant, is of less practical value when jobs are scarce and job-seekers many. In any case, the existing theoretical and empirical literature suggests that the strictness of eligibility criteria for unemployment benefits, which require recipients to actively look for work, take up suitable job offers or take part in active labour market programmes could play an important role in influencing unemployment outcomes, and even offset the impact of benefit generosity in increasing unemployment duration.[365]

363. ILC (91st Session, 2003), Report III (Part 1B) *General Survey of the reports concerning the Protection of Wages Convention (No. 95) and the Protection of Wages Recommendation (No. 85)*, 1949, Geneva, ILO, 2003, paras 351–353.

364. *See* also the Social Protection Floors Recommendation, 2013 No. 202, para. 10.

365. D. Venn, *Eligibility Criteria for Unemployment Benefits: Quantitative Indicators for OECD and EU Countries*, OECD social, employment and migration working papers, No. 131, DELSA/ELSA/WD/SEM(2012)1 (Org. Econ. Cooperation Dev. 2011).

509. The methods of providing unemployment benefit, the Convention No. 168 says, must contribute to the promotion of 'full, productive and freely chosen' employment, and not discourage employers from offering and workers from seeking productive employment. One significant example is Japan, where employers in difficulty can receive different kinds of subsidies in order to avoid having to dismiss workers; the funds used for that purpose come solely from the employers' contributions to the unemployment insurance scheme.[366] Article 21 allows the benefit to be refused when the person concerned refuses to accept suitable employment; this condition is usually also found in national law.

510. Recommendation No. 176 of 1988, for its part, suggests measures to be taken in response to the same concern, such as assistance for occupational mobility, easy access to temporary jobs, encouraging the unemployed to set up their own businesses or get involved in another economic activity, assistance for return undertaken of the worker's own volition, the progressive introduction of community services, including health-care services 'financed by social security contributions or by other sources'. A number of States have adopted such measures today. In some, unemployed workers who receive benefits may be obliged to take a course of vocational training.

511. The first ILO convention on unemployment – Convention No. 2 of 1919, the year the Organization was founded – asked the States to provide information, statistical or otherwise, and to open free employment agencies. It contains an additional obligation that promotes the international mobility of workers: the States that have established systems of insurance against unemployment must, upon terms being agreed between the Members concerned, make arrangements whereby workers belonging to one Member and working in the territory of another are admitted to the same rates of benefit of such insurance as those which obtain for the workers belonging to the latter. Migrant workers are covered elsewhere in this monograph.

512. In the laws and regulations of many countries, and in the above-mentioned Convention, special attention is paid to the placement of workers suffering hardship. Among these, invalids, the disabled occupy a special place. Often the legislation deals with the plight of young unemployed people, whose unemployment tends to give rise to real social problems. Convention No. 168 also refers to women, the elderly, the long-term unemployed, regular emigrants and workers affected by structural changes. The inhabitants of depressed regions sometimes benefit from specific employment programmes, including from the European Union.

513. The means of giving effect to these policies vary: some are legislative, others consensual, others a combination of the two. Article 3 of Convention No. 168 states that its provisions are to be implemented in consultation and cooperation with employers' and workers' organizations. The employers, the workers and their

366. T. Araki, 'Promotion and regulation of job creation opportunities', national report submitted to the XIV Congress of Labour Law and Social Security (Seoul, 27–30 September 1994), *Reports and Proceedings*, Vol. I, Seoul, Korean Academy of Industrial Relations, 1996, pp. 414–415.

associations sometimes but not always play a decisive role in the application of programmes. Sometimes, as in Europe, the negotiations are tripartite and the States conclude genuine social pacts with the vocational organizations; the value of such pacts is more politically than legally binding, unless they are repeated in other kinds of instruments.

514. Collective bargaining, whether bilateral or tripartite, is a very suitable means of broaching controversial issues such as the effects of working hour arrangements on employment. The parties to the talks can all find some advantage in such arrangements: for the workers, more leisure time and thus more opportunities to do other things (cultural, social, etc.) and working hours that are better suited to family life (including part-time work) or early retirement if they want, etc.; for the employer, the possibility to avoid dismissals but also an opportunity to modify the production calendar and to obtain, in some cases, the support for its policy that is the best guarantee that that policy will succeed. The parties can take the risk of broaching subjects on which they are divided: recourse to overtime (a way for the employer to avoid hiring), total or partial early or flexible retirement, timesharing.

515. Beyond this, the real issue is flexibility, the requisite flexibility and the indispensable protective nature of labour standards. The problem is acute when it comes to precarious forms of employment.[367] Everyone agrees that it is better dealt with through dialogue than through confrontation, but there are sometimes few (good) intentions to materialize the standards.

516. The worker's departure can also trigger the right to other benefits, to an old-age pension (which can be early) in particular.

517. These ILO conventions on social security supplement the programmatic instruments promoting employment. The legislation of a number of countries provides in addition for a guaranteed minimum income for the poorest. This is also the objective of the Social Protection Floors Recommendation, 2012 (No. 202); the instrument that we will examine in the chapter dealing with social security, include concrete proposals in this regard. Some authors dare to imagine that more could be done and propose the preparation of a true charter of State duties towards their citizens in terms of guaranteeing a minimum income. The protagonists behind this idea see it as a fresh way of averting the excesses of an overly mechanical, dehumanized functioning of the production machinery, of making sure that machinery does not crush the poorest, of promoting a form of development that truly associates economic progress and social justice. Of course, adequate forms of financing remain to be found.

§4. Labour Administrations

518. It does not suffice to proclaim policies or adopt rules, they have to be implemented as well. This is a matter of credibility, of confidence in the State and its

367. *See* para. 176 *et seq. above*.

agencies, of respect for the legal system (for the "rule of law") and the judicial bodies in place. In this respect, the vigour with which the fight against fraud and corruption is waged and the accessibility of the judicial system are highly revelatory indicators.

519. In order to conduct its programmes and monitor respect for its standards, the State needs top-notch institutions.[368] Any public service, however, implies users seeking quality services at the best price and taxpayers concerned about the financial burden those services create. Whether or not such institutions are public or private is in many respects predicated on the tension between these two aspects of every citizen's relationship with the State.[369]

520. The sections below look successively at the traditional spheres of action of a public labour administration as defined in ILO instruments, in particular 1978 Recommendation No. 158. They start with employment, move on to monitoring of labour conditions, industrial disputes and international labour relations, and conclude with a number of more general comments.

I. Employment Services

521. At the outset, public employment services dealt essentially with vocational guidance and the unemployed. As they grew, their activities became more systematic: they categorized occupations, analysed positions, looked for and distributed recruitment information. As the State stepped up its role in many countries in the economic and social fields, it adopted new means of action. After the Second World War in particular, the target of many governments was full employment and this prompted them to act – or try to act – as employment market regulators; in fact, the results fluctuated with each country's economic health. In the 1960s, the States further expanded their field of action and integrated these activities into their overall policies and programmes.[370]

522. The labour standards drawn up by ILO on this subject reflect those developments. In 1948, the International Labour Conference adopted Convention No. 88 on employment service and supplementary Recommendation No. 83, both of which consider full employment to be the natural outcome of a rationally organized employment market. In 1964, Convention No. 122 and Recommendation No. 122 on employment policy called on the States to undertake far-reaching programmes of action. The trend continued, the accent increasingly being placed on an active and

368. ILC, *Working out of Poverty*, *op. cit.*, pp. 80–81.
369. J.-M. Servais, 'Labour and employment agencies: Pubic or private management?', in J.R. Bellace and M.G. Rood (eds.), *Labour Law at the Crossroad: Changing Employment Relationships, Studies in Honour of Benjamin Aaron*, The Hague, Kluwer, 1997, pp. 167–181.
370. *See* S. Ricca, Introduction to public employment services (Geneva), ILO, 1994, p. 5 *et seq.*; ILO, *Strategies developed by the Public Employment Service in response to structural changes in the labour market*, Acts of the Interregional Technical Meeting, WAPES/ILO, 23–24 January 1997, ILO, Geneva, 1997.

global policy. Recommendation No. 158 of 1978 on labour administration underscored the need for coordination between employment services, programmes to create and promote jobs, occupational guidance and vocational training, and unemployment benefit schemes. Although to a certain extent it repeated the terms of the 1948 instruments, the Recommendation emphasized that the services, systems and programmes had to be implemented by means of an overall policy. Recommendation No. 169 of 1984 completed the arsenal of measures put forward by ILO.

523. Since the last decade of the 20th century, however, the tendency has been for the State to pull back. This has rekindled discussion of whether placement agencies should be privately or publicly managed. The point has never really been decided, although those who favour prohibiting private offices as a matter of principle appeared to hold sway at one time and the situation has been reversed today. Witness the fact that in 1933 – i.e. during the great economic crisis – ILO adopted a convention (No. 34) on fee-charging employment agencies stipulating that such agencies were to be abolished within three years from the coming into force of the Convention for the Member concerned. The Convention was considered to be too rigid, however, and was revised in 1949 by a new convention (No. 96) that left the ratifying countries the choice either of prohibiting the existence of such agencies (Part II) or of regulating their activities (Part III). For the better part of a century, therefore, the public authorities played an active part in the placement of workers in order to put a stop, initially, to well-known abuses. Many countries prohibited private employment agencies, granting the State a monopoly.[371]

524. The debate continued. The doubts expressed about the effectiveness of certain public employment agencies were obviously one aspect, the practices of certain private agencies another. In 1997, the International Labour Conference finally adopted a new convention (No. 181) and a supplementary recommendation (No. 188) on private employment agencies allowing the latter to operate while protecting the workers concerned from possible forms of abuse.

525. The new instruments define the term 'private employment agency' as 'any natural or legal person, independent of the public authorities, which provides one or more of the following labour market services:

(a) services for matching offers of and applications for employment, without the private employment agency becoming a party to the employment relationships which may arise there from;
(b) services consisting of employing workers with a view to making them available to a third party, who may be a natural or legal person (referred to below as a 'user enterprise') which assigns their tasks and supervises the execution of these tasks;

371. Governing Body Document GB.25/2/1, November 1992, para. 88 *et seq.*; ILC (81st session, 1994), *The Role of Private Employment Agencies on the Functioning of Labour markets*, Report VI (Geneva), ILO, 1994.

(c) other services relating to job seeking, determined by the competent authority after consulting the most representative employers' and workers' organizations, such as the provision of information, that do not set out to match specific offers of and applications for employment'.

526. Convention No. 181 considers cases in which the parties to the labour relationship are either the private agency itself or the user enterprise. National legislation and practice must specify the respective responsibilities of the agency and the enterprise. Indeed, Article 12 stipulates this in respect of a wide range of subjects: collective bargaining; minimum wages; hours of work, working time and other working conditions; statutory social security benefits; access to training; occupational safety and health; compensation in case of occupational accidents or diseases; compensation in case of insolvency and protection of workers' claims; maternity and parental protection and benefits. National law provides for shared responsibility in some cases.

527. The Convention authorizes States to prohibit recourse to private agencies for certain categories of workers and certain branches of activity; it also authorizes the exclusion of certain workers from the scope of the Convention provided that 'adequate protection is otherwise assured for the workers concerned'. Recommendation No. 188 adds that private agencies are not to make available to enterprises workers to replace workers who are on strike.

528. The Recommendation calls on the States to combat unfair advertising practices and misleading advertisements, including advertisements for non-existent jobs, and requires the agencies not knowingly to recruit workers for jobs involving unacceptable hazards or risks. It recommends that the contract be written. The Convention, for its part, requires that the agencies not charge directly or indirectly, in whole or in part, any fees or costs to workers.

529. Several of the Convention's articles deal with the protection of the workers recruited by the agency. These guarantees concern fundamental labour rights (freedom of association and right to collective bargaining, equality of opportunity and treatment, no child labour) and the processing of personal data (which should be limited to matters related to the qualifications and professional experience of the workers concerned and any other directly relevant information). The Recommendation specifies that the agencies should store such data only for so long as justified and that the workers should be able to obtain and examine a copy of the data and to correct any errors. Unless directly relevant to the requirements of a particular occupation and with the express permission of the worker concerned, the agencies should not require, maintain or use information on the medical status of a worker.

530. The Convention requires adequate protection for workers employed by the agencies in all the major areas of labour law and social security already mentioned in respect of the responsibilities those agencies share with the user enterprises. Migrant workers must also be given sufficient safeguards. National legislation must ensure that adequate machinery and procedures, involving as appropriate the most representative employers' and workers' organizations, exist for the investigation of complaints, alleged abuses and fraudulent practices concerning the activities of private employment agencies.

531. National legislation seeks to prevent unscrupulous agencies from having recourse to reprehensible practises and stipulates, for example, the conditions for delivering and withdrawing operating licences and the possibility for legally recognized agencies to form an association or federation. Article 3 of the Convention states that the legal status of private employment agencies is to be determined in accordance with national law and practice, and after consulting the most representative organizations of employers and workers; the conditions governing the operation of private employment agencies are in principle determined in accordance with a system of licensing or certification.

532. The only thing left to determine is the nature of the relationship between such agencies, any regulatory authority and public employment services (or any other public employment market regulator). This is the subject of Article 13 of the Convention. Private employment agencies must provide the public authorities with the information they require, with due regard to the confidential nature of such information, to be aware of the structure and activities of such agencies and for statistical purposes. The competent authorities compile that information and, at regular intervals, make it publicly available. According to the Recommendation, co-operation between public employment services and private agencies can include:

(a) pooling of information and use of common terminology so as to improve transparency of labour market functioning;
(b) exchanging vacancy notices;
(c) launching of joint projects, for example in training;
(d) concluding agreements between the public employment service and private employment agencies regarding the execution of certain activities, such as projects for the integration of the long-term unemployed;
(e) training of staff;
(f) consulting regularly with a view to improving professional practices.

The Convention stipulates that more generally cooperation is based on the principle that the public authorities retain final authority for formulating labour market policy and for utilizing or controlling the use of public funds earmarked for the implementation of that policy. It would indeed be hard to imagine the complete privatization of employment services, in particular those participating in the government's strategies to fight unemployment.[372]

533. The States also have the obligation, if they have ratified ILO Convention No. 88, to maintain and ensure the maintenance of a free public service for this

372. *See* for example S. van Eck, 'Revisiting Agency Work in Namibia and South Africa: Any lessons from the Decent Work Agenda and the Flexicurity Approach?' *IJCLLIR*, Vol. 30(1), March 2014, pp. 49–66.

purpose. That provision was already contained in Convention No. 2 on unemployment, adopted in 1919. Convention No. 88 in particular aims to strengthen and heighten the effectiveness of national public employment services. With Recommendation No. 83, it calls for improved information on the labour market and occupational guidance; it encourages activities promoting geographical and occupational mobility. Workers' and employers' representatives must be associated in the functioning of such services and in policy implementation.

534. Labour administrations carry out active labour market policies.[373] They do this in different ways: by granting transportation allowances and bonuses for mobility, by subsidizing the costs of finding a new job, and by providing special subsidies for workers said to be a priority, occupational internships, advice for enterprises, priorities with a view to placement, etc. Several of these tasks are part of the basic mission of the modern State. In some countries, the employment services advise and coach the job seeker.

535. Labour administrations, or more specialized units, are in charge of the vocational rehabilitation and promoting the recruitment of disabled persons, as stated in other ILO conventions and one recommendation.[374] The recommendation stresses the link between the training, rehabilitation and placement of these disadvantaged workers and the social security system.

536. In terms of placement in general, the legislation of many countries requires jobseekers to meet certain conditions, such as accepting a job with a minimum number of working hours per week, for them to be able to register with public offices.

II. Monitoring Employment Conditions

537. Ever since 1919, how to monitor the application of labour standards has been at the heart of ILO's concerns: the last article of Part XIII of the Treaty of Versailles includes, among the methods and principles for regulating labour conditions intended to guide the policy of the future International Labour Organization, a provision according to which 'each State should make provision for a system of inspection in which women should take part, in order to ensure the enforcement of the laws and regulations for the protection of the employed'.

538. For labour standards to be effective they must be monitored and, in a more modern vision of labour inspection, information on their content must be made widely available. This is the object of Convention No. 81 of 1947, which is supplemented by the 1995 Protocol and Recommendation No. 81, also of 1947. The two 1947 instruments concern industry and commerce; the Protocol expands the scope

373. OECD, 'Activating the Unemployed What countries do?', Chapter 5, *Employment Outlook 2007*, Paris, 2007, pp. 207–241.

374. *See in particular* the Vocational Rehabilitation and Employment (Disabled Persons) Convention (No. 159) and Recommendation (No. 168), 1983 and para. 476 *above*.

of application to 'activities in the non-commercial services sector'. Convention No. 129 and Recommendation No. 133 concern labour inspection in agriculture.

539. Convention No. 81 defines the functions of inspectors:

- to secure the enforcement of the legal provisions relating to conditions of work and the protection of workers while engaged in their work; this is the most traditional task;
- to bring defects or abuses to the notice of the competent authority; this is its natural corollary;
- to supply technical information and advice to employers and workers concerning the most effective means of complying with the legal provisions; this corresponds, as we have seen, to a more recent development in labour law: employers and wage earners, especially in small businesses, are often ignorant of the complexities of the rules; in some cases they are reluctant to comply because of the cost or for other reasons; the role of the inspector is to explain the law and its underlying principles.

540. It is no easy task to perform all these functions satisfactorily.[375] The inherent weaknesses of labour inspectorates are well known: scant resources, understaffing (and what personnel there is may be asked to do other jobs as well), poor training, lack of transportation for reaching far-flung workplaces. Articles 10 and 11 of Convention No. 81 require that this situation be remedied; this is a daunting undertaking, especially for a developing country. And yet, the credibility of labour law hangs in the balance.

541. Article 6 provides that the inspection staff is to be composed of public officials whose status and conditions of service are such that they are assured of stability of employment and are independent of 'changes of government and of improper external influences'. The effectiveness of their work depends on this. Article 15 stipulates that labour inspectors must have no interests in the enterprises they inspect and have a duty of discretion (concerning the source of any complaint). Article 7 and the articles that follow deal with the recruitment conditions ('with sole regard to their qualifications for the performance of their duties') and make-up of the corps of inspectors ('both men and women shall be eligible for appointment'; 'ensure that duly qualified technical experts and specialists … are associated in the work of inspection').

542. As representatives of the public authorities, the inspectors have substantial powers of supervision and injunction. The Convention[376] empowers them freely to

375. ILC (100th session, 2011), *Labour Administration and Labour Inspection*, Report V, Geneva, ILO, 2011.

376. Articles 12 *et seq.* Convention No. 129 contains similar provisions for agriculture. The 1995 Protocol provides for special arrangements in the case of essential government administration and public security services.

enter establishments liable to inspection and to carry out checks by means of interrogations or by controlling documents, postings and the materials and substances used. These powers are to be found in the legislation of most countries. The controls can lead to prosecution, in some countries on the direct initiative of the inspector, in others after the competent body has been asked to set legal proceedings in motion.

543. The inspectors also have powers of injunction. Convention No. 81 and subsequently the legislation of many countries open two avenues for action: either the employers are given a deadline to take steps with a view to remedying the shortcomings observed, or they are asked to take immediate steps if there is an imminent danger to the health or safety of the workers. However, national legislation and practice does not always give such sweeping functions to the inspectors, even though Article 13 states that inspectors have the right to apply to the competent authority for the issue of orders or for the initiation of measures with immediate executory force. In any event, the inspector's decisions can usually be appealed to the courts.[377]

544. The labour inspectorate is to be notified of industrial accidents and cases of occupational disease (Article 14). Its members are required to submit periodical reports on the results of their inspection activities, and the central inspection authority to publish an annual general report (Articles 19 to 21). If they are well written, these reports are an invaluable source of information on the implementation of social policies.

545. The difficulties encountered by inspectors in the performance of their tasks have led to greater emphasis being placed on their preventive mission[378]. Recommendation No. 81 contains several paragraphs on this topic; they concern in particular the opening of industrial or commercial undertakings and major changes in their activities, of which the labour inspectorate must be informed. By the same token, plans for new plants or new procedures must be submitted to the labour inspectorate for its opinion.

546. Other paragraphs cover cooperation on occupational health and safety of the employers and the workers, as they are directly concerned. The Recommendation encourages the conclusion of arrangements for that purpose, for example the health and safety committees that exist in many countries, in particular in Europe[379]. The members of such committees must be able to work directly with the labour inspectorate.

---

377. *See* ILC (95th Session, 2006), *Labour Inspection,* Report III (Part 1B), Geneva, ILO, 2006, paras 108 and 114.
378. On the role of labour inspection in developing countries, *see* S. Lee and D. McCann, (eds.), *Regulating for Decent Work. New Directions in Labour Market Regulation*, Geneva, ILO, 2011, p. 23 and the chapter by R. Rocha and C. Pires, pp. 313–338.
379. *See* §7 on health and safety at work.

547. The Recommendation proposes that employers and workers be given advice and instruction in labour legislation and questions of industrial hygiene and safety.

III. The Settlement of Labour Disputes

548. International labour law is understandably somewhat discreet on this point. Strikes are a core issue in industrial disputes. In the absence of a consensus on how best to regulate strikes, ILO delegates have always been reluctant to take any standard-setting action. They have preferred to leave it to the parties concerned to establish means of settling disputes.

549. Strikes and the procedures for settling disputes were discussed earlier in respect of the standards on freedom of association. Here we shall take a closer look at the role of labour administrations in settling disputes.

550. Recommendation No. 158 of 1978 on labour administration recalls the importance of the administration's functions. It must foster a good climate for industrial relations, which implies that it must help ensure that the parties are free to exercise their right of association and promote voluntary bargaining procedures between them. It should also provide conciliation and mediation facilities in case of collective disputes.[380] It provides in particular, to the extent that it is authorized to do so, the information the workers and the employers need. It frequently plays a relatively discreet role in collective discussions when the parties find it difficult to reach an agreement. Its mission ranges from that of mere technical adviser to that of conciliator and mediator, in some cases of arbiter if the parties agree to submit a matter to it. If the problems to be solved have grave economic implications, other ministries (finance, planning, economy) may also step in.

551. In several countries (Germany, Japan and Switzerland, for example), the law considers the jobs of inspector and conciliator to be incompatible; the same person cannot hold both positions. Elsewhere, as in France, the opposite position has prevailed on the basis of positive past experience. Conventions Nos. 81 and 129 are silent on this point. Ratifying them therefore does not imply a strict international obligation in this regard. However, their supplementary recommendations, No. 81 more firmly than No. 133 on agriculture, suggest that the functions be separate. Countries such as Belgium, the United States and Sweden have separate conciliation services.

552. As we have seen,[381] Recommendation No. 92 on voluntary conciliation and arbitration, 1951 and Recommendation No. 130 on the examination of grievances, 1967, also deal with the settlement of disputes.

---

380. Paras 7 to 10 of the Recommendation.
381. *See* Part II, Chapter 1 *above*.

IV. International Labour Relations

553. Financial and commercial exchanges are rapidly becoming more and more globalized, as is the market economy and hence also labour issues. In many cases, labour problems slip out of the grasp of national structures and any real control by the authorities of the country concerned. Hence the heightened importance of international reflection and the joint preparation by the States of programmes, rules, an international social framework for the economic apparatus.

554. Neighbouring countries quite naturally forge relationships. In this respect, the European Union has played a pioneering role, and the Council of Europe has taken significant action. Other groups of nations have shown great creative drive: the association of Canada, the United States and Mexico that emerged from the NAFTA treaty and MERCOSUR in Latin America's southern cone are prime examples. In all these cases, economic considerations are inseparable from social concerns.

555. The institutions do not leave much room for non-governmental organizations, including workers' and employers' organizations. It is an original trait of ILO – a global structure created much earlier, in 1919 – that it has welcomed employers and trade unions into its managing bodies and activities since its inception. This characteristic has clearly been richly rewarding.

556. Article 8 of Convention No. 150 of 1978 on labour administration exhorts national labour administrations to help frame the national policy on international relations, to help represent the State and to help prepare the measures to be taken in this connection. National employers' and workers' confederations in fact have similar responsibilities, relating chiefly to their participation in the International Labour Conference and, for some of them, in ILO's Governing Body.

557. Convention No. 144 on tripartite consultation to promote the implementation of international labour standards, and supplementary Recommendation No. 152, both adopted in 1976, seek to stimulate cooperation between the three major social players to that end. Convention No. 144 obliges the States, on ratification, to operate procedures which ensure effective consultations between representatives of the government (which provides administrative support), of employers and of workers (the latter on an equal footing); the discussions must centre on ILO standard-setting work. Recommendation No. 152 extends the scope of the consultations to legislative and other measures intended to give effect to international labour standards, and to the resolutions and conclusions of the Organization's bodies, its technical cooperation programmes, and the dissemination of information on its activities in general.

V. An Efficient Labour Administration

558. Convention No. 150 and Recommendation No. 158 provide for a structure, general guidelines and an institutional framework enabling the labour administration to perform its tasks efficiently.

559. The Convention underscores that it is in the interests of the administration's work to associate its users, namely the employers and the workers grouped in their respective organizations. It even leaves the States free to delegate or entrust some of their activities to non-governmental organizations such as employers' or workers' associations (or employers' or workers' representatives). By the same token, some aspects of national labour policy may be decided by direct negotiation between the parties.[382]

560. Major efforts have been made to improve the aptitude of national administrations to perform their mission. Those efforts aim to enhance the quality of the services provided and of relations with the 'customers'. They concern rearrangement of administrative structures in order to ensure both real control by the central authorities and enhanced cooperation between units of the labour ministry or with departments whose mission is economic. This coordination reflects the principles expressed in the above instruments.[383]

561. The goal is to put together a competent and sophisticated social welfare administration as the best means of preparing, coordinating and executing an overall social policy, an administration that is able to give instructions to the operational units and to ensure they are applied. As Article 10 of the Convention states, this requires qualified staff that are decently treated. The administration must also have the information it needs to build its action on technically sound grounds and to stimulate creativity. This presupposes serious research into labour and employment (paragraph 18 of Recommendation No. 158 suggests that a genuine policy be adopted on this point) and reliable statistics.

562. Convention No. 160 and Recommendation No. 170, adopted in 1985, deal with labour statistics. The Convention obliges the States regularly to collect, compile and publish basic labour statistics, which must progressively be extended to cover the main labour-related data: working population, employment, unemployment and (if possible) visible under-employment; earnings and hours of work; wages; labour costs; consumer price indices; household expenditure and income; occupational injuries and diseases; industrial disputes. The Recommendation adds statistics on productivity; it emphasizes the importance of classifying the data according to sex, age group, occupational group or level of qualifications, branch of economic activity, geographical area and status in employment (such as employer, own-account worker, employee, unpaid family worker, member of producers' cooperative).

382. Articles 2, 3 and 5 of the Convention.
383. Article 9 of Convention No. 150 and paras 19 *et seq.* of the Recommendation No. 158.

§5. WORKING TIME

I. General Overview

563. This topic has been with us for decades and is a wellspring of contradictions, one of the reasons it is highly controversial. It is the point at which many social policy issues converge.

564. When countries first drew up national legislation on working time,[384] political and trade union pressure was exerted to limit the hours put in by workers, including children, out of concern to protect their physical health. This was also the spirit of the relevant provisions of Part XIII of the Treaty of Versailles, the ILO's future constitution: the Preamble spoke of the urgent need to regulate the hours of work and to establish a maximum working day and week; the general principles stated in Article 427 include 'the adoption of an eight hours day or a forty-eight hours week as the standard to be aimed at where it has not already been attained' and 'the adoption of a weekly rest of at least twenty-four hours, which should include Sunday wherever practicable'.

565. The first convention adopted by the newly established ILO did indeed set the standard of 8 hours per day and 48 hours per week in industry, and spelled out the limits of the authorized exceptions and the system of overtime. Convention No. 30 did the same but in somewhat greater detail for commerce and offices in 1930. One of the merits of those conventions, which have had a lasting influence on labour codes or their equivalent and on many collective agreements, is to have rationalized the issue and shown to what extent it all boils down in the end to a matter of proper organization in the workplace.

566. More recently, the International Covenant on Economic, Social and Cultural Rights required the States to recognize the right of everyone to the enjoyment of just and favourable conditions of work which ensure, in particular (Article 7d), 'rest, leisure and reasonable limitation of working hours and periodic holidays with pay, as well as remuneration for public holidays'.

567. ILO Convention No. 47, adopted in 1935, i.e. towards the end of the long depression that ravaged the industrialized countries between the 20th century's two world wars, had another aim: to combat unemployment by reducing working time. It was followed[385] by several sector instruments and Recommendation No. 116 of 1962, which is discussed in §5.II.

384. For more details, *see* ILC (93rd Session, 2005), *Hours of Work: From Fixed to Flexible?* Report III (Part 1B), Geneva, ILO, 2005, para. 3 *et seq*.

385. In 1934 already, Convention No. 43 provided that the hours of work will not exceed an average of 42 hours per week in Automatic Sheet-Glass Works. Convention No. 46, 1935, was more concerned with the manner to calculate the hours of work *in* an *underground* coal mine (7 hours 45 minutes a day), in view of the time required for the descent and the ascent.

568. Working time, whether to reduce it, daily, weekly, monthly, yearly arrangements of working time, part-time work and chosen time, early or late retirement, are all discussed in many forums and publications today. In many instances the matter is broached from the point of view of the workers and the protection they need (via legal standards such as those of ILO) or from the employer's perspective (underscoring the flexibility that is crucial for the employer to improve the production process).

569. These are definitely fundamental concerns. Bridging the gap between them, reconciling positions is no easy task. Evidence for this is to be found in the aborted attempts to review the ILO instruments on working time. We repeat, the task is no easy one, yet people often dream of working less – and of spending more time with their families, on their leisure activities, even just doing nothing – but grow anxious if work is in short supply. They have to guarantee an income for themselves and their families and crave recognition of their social status.

570. In order to reconcile these conflicting points of view (illustrated in France by the disputes over the 35-hour work week), some people would like to consider the subject from a broader perspective, namely the relationship of working time and leisure time for the entire working population. By integrating other factors, they believe, a solution could be found. Employers and wage earners are also consumers, users, customers; they want to procure the products and services (which are also public) they need when they are not at work. They have families, want to spend their free time looking after their children or their elderly parents, and to do so with their spouse or (at least in some cases) at different times. Occupational working time arrangements are also more generally a vehicle for equalizing opportunities and treatment for men and women. Some people, for reasons that include health, education and retraining, hope to reduce their working time.

571. Governments are concerned to connect working time to employment, not only to avoid dismissals by reducing working periods, but also to encourage hiring whenever possible. All too rarely has it been asked whether lengthening opening hours for shops and some offices by rotating personnel would have a positive impact. All too rarely has consideration been given to staggering vacation time or daily schedules in order to solve traffic problems and ease the overload on public transportation. In Italy the idea emerged of trying to poll people on whether their aspirations could not be more easily met at the regional, town or neighbourhood level than by adopting a general approach to problems of work, leisure time and employment.[386] By the same token, the successful experience (based in particular on the promotion of part-time work) of a small country like the Netherlands can be explained by the perception its leaders had of the true needs of different sectors of the population.

---

386. S. Bonfiglioli and M. Mareggi (eds.), 'Il tempo e la città fra natura e storia. Atlante di progetti sui tempi della città', *Urbanistica Quaderni*, No. 12, May 1997.

572. France has also given thought to the future of work; this has been expressed in particular in the writings of Alain Supiot, Dominique Méda and the team set up in connection with the Boissonnat report.[387] The debate has continued across Europe and at international level.[388]

573. ILO law has noted these changes and tried to integrate them where a consensus is discernible among its managing bodies. This was the case in 1974 in connection with paid educational leave (Convention No. 140 and Recommendation No. 148), followed in 1981 by Convention No. 156 and Recommendation No. 165 on workers with family responsibilities, in 1994 by Convention No. 175 and Recommendation No. 182 on part-time work and in 1996 by Convention No. 177 and Recommendation No. 184 on home work. These instruments are examined elsewhere in this monograph.[389]

574. These pages will focus on three main themes: hours of work, their reduction and arrangement (II), night work and the priority given, in respect of women, to equality in protection (III) and paid leave (IV).

II. Hours of Work

575. Recommendation No. 116[390] requires each Member to formulate and pursue a national policy designed progressively to reduce hours of work to 40 hours per week, without loss of pay; where the duration of the normal working week exceeds 48 hours, immediate steps should be taken to bring it down to this level.

576. The measures adopted should take account of:

(a) the level of economic development attained and the extent to which the country is in a position to bring about a reduction in hours of work without reducing total production or productivity, endangering its economic growth, the development of new industries or its competitive position in international trade, and without creating inflationary pressures which would ultimately reduce the real income of the workers;

387. A. Supiot (ed.), *Le travail en perspective*, Paris, LGDJ, 1998; *Rapport de la Commission* (Commissariat général au plan) *présidée par Jean Boissonnat*, 'Le travail dans vingt ans', Paris, O. Jacob, La Documentation française, 1995; *see also* A. Valli (ed.), *Tempo di lavoro e occupazione. Il caso italiano*, Rome, La Nuova Italia Scientifica, 1988, pp. 13–38 and 177–197.

388. A. Supiot (ed.), *Au-delà de l'emploi*, Paris, Flammarion, 1999; Sangheon Lee, Deirdre McCann and J. C. Messenger, *Working Time Around the World*, London/New York, Routledge, 2007; J. C. Messenger and N. Ghosheh, *Work Sharing during the Great Recession New Developments and Beyond*, Geneva, ILO, 2013.

389. *See* paras 428–429 and 461 *above* and paras 740–751 *below*.

390. This Recommendation does not apply to agriculture, to maritime transport and to maritime fishing. Para. 23 adds that special provisions should be formulated for these branches of economic activity.

(b) the progress achieved and which it is possible to achieve in raising productivity by the application of modern technology, automation and management techniques;
(c) the need in the case of countries still in the process of development for improving the standards of living of their peoples; and
(d) the preferences of employers' and workers' organizations in the different branches of activity concerned as to the manner in which the reduction in working hours might be brought about.

The principle of the progressive reduction of hours of work can be applied by stages or by gradually encompassing other branches of activity; heavy or dangerous industries and occupations should be given priority.

577. The Recommendation defines the normal hours of work in terms of national legislation and, by default, as 'the number of hours in excess of which any time worked is remunerated at overtime rates or forms an exception to the recognized rules or custom of the establishment or of the process concerned'. The hours are in principle calculated per week, except when special conditions in certain branches of activity or technical needs justify an exception; in such cases, the maximum length of the period of calculation should be determined. The authorities can draw up special measures with regard to processes which, by reason of their nature, have to be carried on continuously by a succession of shifts; in that case, the normal hours of work as an average should not exceed in any case the normal hours of work fixed for the economic activity concerned.

578. National institutions are to determine the circumstances and limits in which exceptions to the normal hours of work are permitted:

(a) permanently –
  (i) in work which is essentially intermittent;
  (ii) in certain exceptional cases required in the public interest;
  (iii) in operations which for technical reasons must necessarily be carried on outside the limits laid down for the general working of the undertaking, part of the undertaking, or shift;
(b) temporarily –
  (i) in case of accident, actual or threatened;
  (ii) in case of urgent work to be done to machinery or plant;
  (iii) in case of *force majeure*;
  (iv) in case of abnormal pressure of work;
  (v) to make up time lost through collective stoppages of work due to accidents to materials, interruptions to the power supply, inclement weather, shortages of materials or transport facilities, and calamities;
  (vi) in case of national emergency;
(c) periodically –
  (i) for annual stocktaking and the preparation of annual balance sheets;
  (ii) for specified seasonal activities.

579. All hours worked in excess of the normal hours are deemed to be overtime, 'unless they are taken into account in fixing remuneration in accordance with custom'. Except for cases of *force majeure*, limits to the total number of hours of overtime which can be worked during a specified period are to be determined by the national authorities; due consideration must be given to the special circumstances of young persons under 18 years of age, of pregnant women and nursing mothers and of handicapped persons. Overtime should be remunerated at a rate that is at least 25 per cent higher than the salary.

580. The Recommendation states that the authorities must make a practice of consulting the most representative employers' and workers' organizations and underscores the importance of supervision. Supervision comprises adequate inspection and a system of penalties, but the employers have a further dual obligation: to notify the workers concerned, by the posting of notices or by other methods, of the times at which work begins and ends; to keep a record of the hours of work, wages and overtime for each worker.

III. Night Work

581. The history of the rules governing night work[391] is a compelling example of the problems posed by the issue of equality between men and women,[392] namely whether it is the women workers' protection or equality of treatment that should take precedence.

582. The prohibition of night work for women in industry was the subject of one of the first two international labour conventions adopted in Berne in 1906. The International Labour Conference returned to the matter in 1919 and regulated it in greater detail by adopting Convention No. 4, which defined night as a 'period of at least eleven consecutive hours, including the interval between ten o'clock in the evening and five o'clock in the morning'. The Convention was successively revised in 1934 (Convention No. 41) and 1949 (Convention No. 89), in order to allow greater flexibility in the calculation of the night period and to authorize exceptions for certain categories of women workers.[393]

583. Since the late 1980ies, the International Labour Office reflects, in general terms, on the best possible balance to strike between protection and equality in legislation on the work of women. The experts have recommended that the standards be reviewed in the light of the most recent scientific knowledge and technical developments. The review is to take account of the biological condition of women and

391. The focus is here on night work of adults. The prohibition of night work of young persons is examined together with the other measures required for the protection of these workers: *see* para. 370 *above*.
392. *See* para. 418 *above*.
393. For further details, *see* Valticos, *op. cit.*, paras 31–32 and 586 *et seq.*

men, of concerns to provide equal but appropriate protection, and of the factors inherent in each country (level of guarantees, cultural and religious factors, etc.).[394] It has led to the adoption in 1990 by the International Labour Conference of more modern instruments on night work: a protocol that eased the prohibition and Convention No. 171 and Recommendation No. 178 containing standards to improve the conditions of night work for both men and women.

584. In the meantime, another question has appeared within the problematic of night work. The modern organization of goods and services production, the use of new technologies and the progressive disappearance of the economic borders have a significant impact on the professional work schedule. More than others, the persons acting within networks have to adapt their rhythm of life to the globalization of the markets, to the need to keep in touch with counterparts located in countries with different hours.

A. Convention No. 89 (Revised), on Night Work (Women), 1948

585. The Convention prohibits[395] the employment of women, without distinction of age, during the night in any public or private industrial undertaking, or in any branch thereof, other than an undertaking in which only members of the same family are employed. Article 2 defines[396] 'night' as a period of at least eleven consecutive hours, including, except in certain cases, an interval of at least seven consecutive hours falling between ten o'clock in the evening and seven o'clock in the morning.[397]

586. The prohibition does not apply in cases of force majeure or to work that has to do with materials subject to rapid deterioration (where night work is necessary to preserve the said materials from certain loss). The prohibition can be suspended by the government, after consultation with the employers' and workers' organizations concerned, when in a serious emergency the national interest so requires.

587. The night period may be reduced:

- to ten hours on sixty days of the year in industrial undertakings influenced by the seasons and in all cases where exceptional circumstances demand it;
- in countries where the climate renders work by day particularly trying if compensatory rest is accorded during the day.

394. ILO, *Special Protective Measures for Women and Equality of Opportunity and Treatment*. Meeting of Experts (10–17 October 1989) (Geneva), 1989, para. 93.
395. Article 3.
396. A definition of the term 'industrial undertaking' can be found in Article 1.
397. *See* however Article 9.

588. The Convention does not apply to women holding responsible positions of a managerial or technical character and to women employed in health and welfare services who are not ordinarily engaged in manual work.[398]

B. The 1990 Protocol to Convention No. 89

589. The Protocol relaxes the prohibition of night work for women on condition, in principle, that the relevant employers' and workers' organizations concur. It reflects a trend in national legislation to authorize exceptions even to imperative rules, in particular in terms of arrangements for hours of work, by agreement between the social partners.

590. The Protocol authorizes variations in the duration of the night period (Article 2 of the Convention) and exemptions from the prohibition of night work (Article 3 of the Convention) by means of an agreement concluded either for the branch of activity or occupation, or for one or several enterprises; in the latter case, a simple procedure of consultation is acceptable in some cases.

591. Special rules, including a prohibition of dismissal, apply to pregnant workers or those who have just given birth.

C. Convention No. 171 and Recommendation No. 178

592. The new Convention breaks with the previous rules on several fronts: it applies to all wage earners, men as well as women; it does not prohibit night work, but rather tries to improve the conditions in which night work is performed; it covers not only industry but most branches of activity, the only[399] exceptions being agriculture, animal husbandry, fishing, maritime transport and inland navigation.

593. Convention No. 171 defines 'night' more loosely than Convention No. 89 as a period of not less than seven consecutive hours, including the interval from midnight to 5 a.m. It defines 'night worker' as an employed person whose work requires performance of a substantial number of hours of night work which exceeds a specified limit. On the other hand, the authorities can determine the meaning of the term 'night' and any limit to night hours only after consulting the most representative organizations of employers and workers or by collective agreements.

594. Articles 4 to 10 of the Convention list the specific measures required by the nature of night work in order to protect workers' health (including in the event of maternity), ensure their safety, assist them to meet their family and social

---

398. The Permanent Court of International Justice considered that the Night Work (Women) Convention, 1919 (No. 4) applied to women who hold positions of supervision or management and are not ordinarily engaged in manual work: *see* para. 144 *above*.
399. A flexibility clause authorizes the exclusion of limited categories of workers: *see* Article 2, para. 2.

responsibilities, provide opportunities for occupational advancement, and compensate them appropriately in terms of hours of work, salary and other similar benefits. It requires the establishment of social services.

595. Before introducing work schedules requiring the services of night workers, the employer must consult the workers' representatives concerned on the details of the schedules, on the forms of organization that are best adapted to the establishment and its personnel and on the occupational health measures and social services required; this consultation must take place regularly.

596. Recommendation No. 178 contains additional proposals on hours of work and rest periods, financial compensation, health and safety and social services; special measures are required in some cases, such as that of a wage earner who has been engaged for many years in night work.

IV. Leave Periods

597. Leaves comes in many varied forms, some of which have been or will be discussed elsewhere in this monograph: when they are linked for example with an educational programme or relates to the protection of pregnant women, young mothers and their babies. ILO has adopted no standards that deal directly with public holidays,[400] whereas Article 7 of the International Covenant on Economic, Social and Cultural Rights requires that such holidays be paid. It has, however, adopted standards on weekly rest (A) and on paid leave (B).

A. Weekly Rest

598. The main standards are laid down in Convention No. 14 (1921) for industry, and in Convention No. 106 (1957) and supplementary Recommendation No. 103 for commerce and offices.

599. According to these instruments, the personnel of all establishments concerned[401] is in principle entitled to an uninterrupted weekly rest period of not less than 24 hours in the course of each period of seven days. The weekly rest period should, wherever possible, be the same for everyone and coincide with the day of rest established by tradition or local customs.[402] Both Conventions, the more recent

400. *See* however the provisions contained in Convention No. 132 and in Recommendation No. 98 on holidays with pay, Recommendation No. 184 on home work, Convention No. 172 on working conditions in hotels, restaurants and similar establishments, and Convention No. 175 on part-time work. They are examined together with the other rules concerning those questions.
401. *See* Article 1 of Convention No. 14 and Articles 2 to 5 of Convention No. 106.
402. Article 6 of Convention No. 106 states that the traditions and customs of religious minorities shall, as far as possible, be respected.

in greater detail, allow partial or total exceptions for economic or humanitarian reasons, after consultation with the employers' and workers' organizations concerned. In particular, Convention No. 106 allows temporary exemptions:

(a) in case of accident, actual or threatened, force majeure or urgent work to premises and equipment, but only so far as may be necessary to avoid serious interference with the ordinary working of the establishment;
(b) in the event of abnormal pressure of work due to special circumstances, in so far as the employer cannot ordinarily be expected to resort to other measures;
(c) in order to prevent the loss of perishable goods.[403]

National law must provide for special rest schemes or compensatory rest. Convention No. 106 adds that application of the standards should result in no reduction of income 'in so far as wages are regulated by laws and regulations or subject to the control of administrative authorities'.[404]

600. Recommendation No. 103 is more detailed on the calculation of weekly rest and suggests that it should comprise at least thirty-six hours and be, whenever practicable, uninterrupted. The weekly rest should be calculated so as to include the period from midnight to midnight and should not include other rest periods immediately preceding or following the period from midnight to midnight. Paragraph 3 provides special guarantees if special rest schemes are applied, and paragraph 4 states that young persons under 18 years of age should be granted an uninterrupted weekly rest of two days, with no exceptions, even temporary.

601. Both Convention No. 14 for industry and Recommendation No. 103 for commerce and offices oblige the employer to provide certain information on the system of rest[405] by means of notices and on exceptions by a roster established for that purpose. This is also intended to facilitate the work of labour inspectors and the application, if required, of the appropriate penalties under Article 10 of Convention No. 106.

B. Paid Leave

602. ILO standards concern two very different kinds of paid leave: that granted for educational purposes (Convention No. 140 and Recommendation No. 148, which were discussed earlier),[406] and that corresponding to holidays (chiefly Recommendation No. 98 of 1954 and Convention No. 132 of 1970).

403. Article 8, para. 1.
404. Article 9; *see also* para. 7 of Recommendation No. 103.
405. In any establishment in which the weekly rest period for any of the persons employed is other than the period established by national practice, as far as the recommendation is concerned: *see* para. 5.
406. *See* para. 468 *above*.

603. Both of the latter two instruments are broadly applicable, but not to seafarers or, in the case of the Recommendation, to agricultural workers or family undertakings; a flexibility clause in the Convention serves to exclude limited categories of wage earners.

604. All the workers covered are entitled to annual paid leave; the length of that leave[407] should be at least three weeks for one year of service and should be reduced proportionately for a shorter period of work. A minimum period of service may be required for entitlement to any annual holiday with pay. If the employment relationship is terminated, the worker is entitled to a holiday with pay proportionate to the period of service performed during which he had no leave or to compensation in lieu thereof or to the equivalent holiday credit.[408]

605. Absences for reasons over which the worker has no control, such as illness, accident or maternity, are counted in the period of service. Statutory holidays ('public or customary') and periods of incapacity for work resulting from sickness or injury are not to be counted as part of the minimum annual holiday with pay.[409] The Recommendation adds[410] that annual paid leave can increase with seniority.

606. Article 8 of the Convention authorizes the division of the annual holiday with pay into parts; one of the parts must nevertheless consist of at least two uninterrupted working weeks. That part must be granted and taken no later than one year, and the remainder of the annual holiday with pay no later than eighteen months, from the end of the year in respect of which the holiday entitlement has arisen. The exact period is in principle to be determined by the employer after consultation with the worker or his representatives.[411]

607. When he takes his holiday, the wage earner must receive – in advance, unless an agreement has been reached otherwise – at least his normal or average remuneration (including the cash equivalent of any part of that remuneration which is paid in kind).[412]

608. Agreements to relinquish the right to the minimum annual holiday with pay prescribed in the Convention or to forgo such a holiday, for compensation or otherwise, should be null and void or prohibited. Special rules may be laid down in respect of cases in which the employed person engages, during the holiday, in a gainful activity conflicting with the purpose of the holiday.[413]

---

407. Articles 3 to 5 of the Convention; *see also* paras 4 and 10 of the Recommendation.
408. Article 11 of the Convention.
409. Articles 5 and 6 of the Convention and paras 5, 7 and 8 of the Recommendation.
410. Paragraph 6.
411. Articles 9 and 10 of the Convention; *see also* para. 9 of the Recommendation.
412. Unless if it is not a permanent benefit continuing whether or not the person concerned is on holiday: Article 7 of the Convention; *see also* para. 11 of the Recommendation.
413. Articles 12 and 13 of the Convention.

609. Both instruments provide for consultation with employers' and workers' organizations, in particular prior to the framing of the applicable laws and in the operation of any bodies established.[414]

610. The Recommendation requires that workers be notified of the date at which their annual holiday with pay is to begin sufficiently in advance so that they can make use of their holidays in an appropriate manner. The employer should keep a record for that purpose,[415] also, again, in order to facilitate the work of the inspector.[416]

§6. WAGES

611. Freedom of contract is the legal reason the parties to the labour relationship are empowered themselves to decide on the remuneration for the service provided. They do this in their individual relationship or, more commonly, in collective bargaining with trade unions. Concerns to avoid competition between countries and between enterprises based on starvation wages explains however the efforts made to harmonize rules on salary protection that contribute to antipoverty policies.

612. The State authorities are not indifferent to how wages are determined. Too much is at stake: concern to keep control of changes in prices and incomes; the will to bring about equal pay for equal work; concern to step in for an insolvent employer who leaves the worker without a job but also without an income for the work already done. A number of aspects of the pay issue – in respect of the limits of collective bargaining, the fight against discrimination and job security – were considered earlier.[417] The following pages look at another aspect: the safeguards preventing the employer from taking advantage of the wage earner's often weak position. Some safeguards concern wage protection (II), others the establishment of a minimum wage (III). We shall start, however, by taking a quick look at the international legislation on the subject.

I. Overview of International Legislation

613. Article 7 of the International Covenant on Economic, Social and Cultural Rights requires the States parties to recognize:

> the right of everyone to the enjoyment of just and favourable conditions of work which ensure, in particular: (a) Remuneration which provides all workers, as a minimum, with: (i) Fair wages and equal remuneration for work of

414. Paras 13 and 14 of the Recommendation, Articles 2 para. 2 and 9 para. 3 of the Convention.
415. Paras 9, subparas 2, and 12 of the Recommendation.
416. On the inspection, *see* Article 14 of the Convention.
417. *See* paras 272 and 275, 397, 424–427 and 499 *above*.

equal value without distinction of any kind, in particular women being guaranteed conditions of work not inferior to those enjoyed by men, with equal pay for equal work; (ii) A decent living for themselves and their families in accordance with the provisions of the present Covenant.

614. Note the concept of a 'decent' living, which corresponds to ILO's view that the point is to create not just jobs but jobs that are of acceptable quality: there is no separating the level of employment and its quality.[418] The same notion also appeared in 1919 in ILO's Constitution, the Preamble to which speaks of the provision of an adequate living wage. Earlier, Article 427 of the Treaty of Versailles, which contains general principles, mentioned as one of those principles the payment to the employed of a wage adequate to maintain a reasonable standard of living 'as this is understood in their time and country'. More recently, the Philadelphia Declaration included[419] ensuring 'a just share of the fruits of progress to all, and a minimum living wage to all employed and in need of such protection' in the programmes to be carried out with ILO support. In ILO's view, adequate wages are therefore a basic requirement. Of course, those wages then need to be actually paid. Hence the adoption of standards on both the minimum level of pay and the protection of wages.

615. The following pages focus on general standards. Specific provisions exist for certain branches of activity such as plantations[420] or domestic work.[421]

II. Wage Protection

616. Wages are the main counterpart for the service provided within the framework of a labour relationship, to the point that the employee is called the 'wage earner'. This remuneration, which is often the worker's only source of income, has been protected since the inception of labour law. As early as the 19th century European States enacted legislation governing the payment of wages in kind and company stores.[422] The literature and history recount singularly unpleasant instances of abuse in this regard.

617. The International Labour Conference, contrary to the legislation of many countries, first focused on the level of pay – introducing, as we shall see, mechanisms to establish minimum wages – before adopting standard-setting instruments

418. ILC, Report of the Director General, *Decent Work*, 87th Session, ILO, Geneva, 1999, pp. 3–4.
419. Para. IIId.
420. The Plantations Convention, 1958 (No. 110), and the 1982 Protocol, Articles 24 to 35; the Plantations Recommendation, 1958 (No. 110), paras 9–26.
421. The Domestic Workers Convention, 2011, Aricles 11 and 12; the Domestic Workers Recommendation, 2011, paras 6, 14 and 15.
422. And even before: it seems that the oldest legislation prohibiting the truck system in England is dated 1464: *see* ILC (91st session, 2003), *General Survey of the reports concerning the Protection of Wages Convention (No. 95) and the Protection of Wages Recommendation (No. 85), 1949*, Geneva, ILO, 2003, para. 96.

on the protection of wages. The main text in this respect is Convention No. 95, adopted in 1949 and supplemented by Recommendation No. 85. The same year, the Conference adopted Convention No. 94 and Recommendation No. 84 on labour clauses in public contracts, which contain important provisions on pay.

618. Convention No. 95 deals with remuneration or earnings capable of being expressed in terms of money and fixed by mutual agreement or by law, which are payable in virtue of a contract of employment[423] by an employer for services rendered or to be rendered.

619. The Convention applies to all persons to whom wages are 'paid or payable'. The competent authorities of the State ratifying the Convention may, after consultation with the organizations of employers and employed persons, exclude from the application of all or any of the provisions of the Convention categories of workers who are not employed in manual labour or are employed in domestic service or work similar thereto.

620. The Convention considers five main means of paying wages: in cash, by bank cheque, by postal cheque or money order, and in kind. Other forms of payment, such as bank and postal transfers, which are common practice today, are not expressly mentioned. The Convention requires payment in cash to be in legal tender, but prohibits promissory notes, vouchers or coupons. Payment in kind is accepted in limited conditions; the payment may cover only part of the wages, and only in branches of activities where this form of payment 'is customary or desirable because of the nature of the industry or occupation concerned'. In cases in which payment in kind is authorized, appropriate measures must be taken to ensure that it is appropriate for the personal use of the worker and his family and in his interests (liquor and noxious drugs are prohibited). The value attributed to such allowances must be fair and reasonable.[424]

621. The history of labour relations connects, as we have said, the appearance of company stores with remuneration in kind. Such stores were subsequently prohibited by law in Western Europe and the United States. In spite of this, the matter prompted lively debate at the Conference when the draft instruments were being discussed.[425] Article 7 of the convention ultimately adopted stipulates that workers are to be free from any coercion to make use of works stores or services. It also stipulates that where access to other stores or services is not possible, measures must be taken to ensure that goods are sold and services provided at fair and reasonable prices, and that the stores established and services operated are not operated for the purpose of securing a profit but for the benefit of the workers concerned. Recommendation No. 85 suggests that representatives of the workers concerned, and more particularly members of works welfare committees or similar bodies, participate in the general administration of works stores or services.

423. Article 2 of Convention No. 95.
424. For further details, *see* ILC, *op. cit.*, para. 65 *et seq.*
425. ILC, *op. cit.*, para. 94 *et seq.* and 192 *et seq.*

622. Generally speaking, the wages are in principle paid directly to the worker concerned. The employer can in no way restrict the worker's freedom to use his wages as he pleases. Thus, the obligation to buy and wear a uniform should not put too much strain on the worker.[426]

623. The amount the worker brings home is usually smaller than the gross pay to which he is theoretically entitled: deductions are made for contributions to social security schemes and for other purposes. According to Article 8 of the Convention, such deductions are permitted only under conditions and to the extent prescribed by national laws or fixed by collective agreement or arbitration award; the workers must be duly informed. Paragraphs 1 to 3 of the Recommendation require limits to the deductions permitted. The first limit should go without saying: not to exceed 'the extent deemed to be necessary to safeguard the maintenance of the worker and his family'. The other limits concern the conditions applicable to the deductions made for the reimbursement of loss of or damage to the goods or installations of the employer and to the furnishings and equipment made available to the workers. Article 9 of the Convention prohibits deductions made with a view to ensuring a payment to an employer or an intermediary for the purpose of obtaining or retaining employment.

624. The Convention further stipulates that wages may be attached or assigned, if the worker is in debt, only in a manner and within limits prescribed by national laws; again, the wages must be protected to the extent deemed necessary for the maintenance of the worker and his family.[427]

625. The wage earner must be paid at regular intervals,[428] not less often than twice a month in the case of workers whose wages are calculated by the hour, day or week, and not less often than once a month in the case of employed persons whose remuneration is fixed on a monthly or annual basis.[429] National law, the collective agreement or an arbitration award usually determines the intervals at which wages are paid and the terms of final settlements when the contract expires. In the latter case, a final settlement of all wages is to be made within a reasonable period of time 'having regard to the terms of the contract'.[430]

626. In the event of the bankruptcy or judicial liquidation of an undertaking, the workers must, according to Article 11, be treated as privileged creditors. We know that in 1992 Convention No. 173 and Recommendation No. 180 strengthened the protection of the workers' claims if the employer was insolvent.[431]

426. See U. Coiquaud, 'Le droit du travail: générateur de pauvreté? Le cas du Canada', in P. Auvergnon (ed.), *Droit social et travailleurs pauvres*, Brussels, Bruylant, 2013.
427. Article 10 of the Convention.
428. Article 12, para. 1 of the Convention.
429. Para. 4 of the Recommendation. Paragraph 5 suggests that the maximum intervals for the payment of wages should be 16 days in the case of workers whose wages are calculated on a piece-work or output basis and of workers employed to perform a task.
430. Article 12, para. 2 of the Convention.
431. *See* para. 502 *et seq. above*.

627. The payment of wages in cash must take place on working days only and at or near the workplace; it is prohibited in taverns or other similar establishments and, where necessary to prevent abuse, in shops or stores for the retail sale of merchandise and in places of amusement.[432]

628. The Convention and the Recommendation contain several provisions to the effect that the workers must be fully informed, before and during their employment, of the conditions in respect of their wages and of the particulars of those wages. They must know about the applicable legislation and records of pay must be maintained in all appropriate cases.[433] The Recommendation specifies the information to be provided, *inter alia* the rates of wages payable, the method of calculation, the periodicity and the place of payment, and the conditions under which deductions may be made.[434]

629. Most observations issued by the CEACR have to do with problems of back wages and the failure of certain governments to meet their obligation to guarantee that wages are regularly paid. Other ILO supervisory bodies have had to comment on the same points, notably the Conference Committee on the Application of Standards and, in response to grievances filed under Article 24 of the Constitution, the Governing Body. The phenomenon affects many countries in Central and Eastern Europe, Africa and Latin America.[435]

630. The Committee of Experts has also commented[436] on the concept of wages to be protected: although the wage component of the amounts paid to workers can vary under national laws, the Committee considers that all earnings, no matter what they are called or how they are dealt with when calculating basic pay, including benefits and allowances, are entitled to protection. The Committee has also underscored that the obligation to reach a rapid final settlement at the end of the employment relationship applies to all wage earners, no matter what the nature of their contract, the reasons it was terminated or their nationality.

III. Labour Clauses in Public Contracts

631. In 1949 the International Labour Conference also adopted Convention No. 94 and Recommendation No. 84 on labour clauses in the contracts concluded by the public authorities. Those instruments echo the steps taken in more than one industrialized country. The basic idea is as follows: in a free-market State, the public authorities can only intervene in a limited manner – essentially in time of crisis or to prevent abuse – when it comes to determining the conditions of employment. However, when they forge commercial ties with private undertakings, they have the

432. Article 13 of Convention No. 95.
433. Articles 14 and 15 of the Convention.
434. Paras 6 and 7 of the Recommendation No. 85.
435. ILC, *op. cit.*, para. 356 *et seq.*
436. *See* G.P. Politakis, 'The ILO and the protection of wages', *Labour Education* (ILO), No. 128, 2002/3, pp. 5–7.

option of inserting into the contract a clause obliging the undertaking to afford its personnel decent pay and conditions of work.

632. The Convention applies to contracts in which one of the parties is a public authority and which involve the expenditure of public funds and employment of workers by the other party to the contract. The contract may concern public works, the manufacture, assembly, handling or shipment of materials, supplies or equipment, or the performance or supply of services. The Convention also applies to subcontractors. Exemptions are allowed for contracts involving the expenditure of limited public funds, after consultation with the organizations of employers and workers concerned. Recommendation No. 84 suggests that similar provisions should apply in cases where private employers are granted subsidies or are licensed to operate a public utility.

633. Public contracts must include clauses ensuring to the workers concerned wages (including allowances), hours of work and other conditions of labour which are not less favourable than those established for work of the same character, in the branch of activity in the district where the work is carried out, by collective agreement, arbitration award or law (Article 2). The Recommendation adds that labour clauses should prescribe the normal and overtime rates of wages, the manner in which hours of work are to be regulated and holiday and sick leave provisions. The Convention further provides that the workers concerned must benefit from fair and reasonable conditions of health, safety and welfare (Article 3).

634. The CEACR has pointed out that the European Directive No. 96/71 of 16 December 1996, especially as interpreted by the Court of Justice of the EU in the Rüffert case,[437] limits the application of domestic law in the case of foreign posted workers. The Commission has recalled European countries like the Netherlands bound by both instruments that the Convention requires the inclusion of labour clauses of the type provided for in Article 2 in all circumstances.[438] On the contrary, it has considered that the then in force European Directives No 2004/17 and No 2004/18 opening public contracts to European competition do not contain provisions violating the Convention.[439]

635. Article 4 contains provisions on the information to be provided to the workers and on the maintenance of records indicating the hours worked and the wages paid; those records should facilitate the task of inspection. Article 5 requires, in the

437. *Rüffert, Dirk,* 3 April 2008, case C-346/06, http://eur-lex.europa.eu (case-law, 2008).

438. ILC (102nd session, 2013), *Report of the Committee of Experts for the Application of Conventions and Recommendations*, Report III (part A), Geneva, ILO, 2013, pp. 689–690; *see also* pp. 690–691 (Norway).

439. ILC (97th session, 2008), *Report of the Committee of Experts for the application of Conventions and Recommendations*, Report III (part 1B), para. 248. *See* K. Ahlberg and N. Bruun, 'Public Procurement and Labour Rights: Governance by Scaremongering?' in S. Evju (ed.), *Regulating Transnational Labour in Europe: The Quandaries of Multilevel Governance,* Department of Private Law, University of Oslo. Publications Series No. 196, 2014, pp. 239–261.

event of an infringement, the application of adequate sanctions 'by the withholding of contracts or otherwise'; it adds that appropriate measures must be taken, 'by the withholding of payments under the contract or otherwise', to enable the workers concerned to be paid the wages to which they are entitled.

IV. Fixing the Minimum Wage

636. On the minimum wage, economists remain divided between the relatively traditional camps of *laissez-faire* practitioners and interventionists. The proponents of *laissez-faire* policy praise the virtues of the market; the interventionists underscore its imperfections and the need to correct them for the benefit of the weakest. Their arguments in favour of setting a minimum wage centre on protecting the purchasing power of wage earners, a policy aimed at eliminating exploitation and reducing poverty, at avoiding downward competition between job seekers, at ensuring greater equality of pay and at preventing social unrest.[440] The other camp highlights the risk of inflation and greater unemployment.

637. There are few decision-makers, especially in developing countries, who question the principle of setting a minimum wage. They nevertheless consider that the level of that wage must be reasonable and any increases modest. They tend to criticize the mechanism used rather than the principle itself.[441] Hence the relevance of ILO's standards on the subject. There are many such standards, the first dating back to 1928. We shall nevertheless focus on those ILO considers to be most current, 1970 Convention No. 131 and Recommendation No. 135 on minimum wage fixing.

638. In both developed and developing countries minimum wages have been recently reactivated to reduce the social tensions resulting from the growing inequalities in the poorer half of the labour market. Perhaps most symbolic of the revival of the institution in industrialized States is the case of the United Kingdom which, after dismantling its system of industry-level minimum wages in the 1980s, adopted a new minimum salary with national coverage in 1999. The following year, Ireland introduced a similar system, for the first time in its history,[442] as Germany did more recently.

440. OECD, *Growing Unequal? Income Distribution and Poverty in OECD Countries*, Paris, OECD, 2008; ARPLA, *Minimum Wage Laws and Administration: the Widening Gap*, Bangkok, ILO, 1990, p. 12; see C. Saget, 'Fixing minimum wage levels in developing countries: Common failures and remedies', *International Labour Review*, 2008/1.

441. *See* D. Card and A.B. Krueger, *Myth and Measurement: The Economics of the Minimum Wage*, Princeton University Press, 1995, especially pp. 240–275; *see also* H. Suzuki, 'Background paper on minimum wage fixation and enforcement: the Asian experience', in ARPLA, *op. cit.*, p. 21 *et seq.*

442. ILO, *Global Wage Report: Minimum Wages and Collective Bargaining. Towards policy coherence*, Geneva, 2008, pp. 34–36; ILO, documents GB.303/ESP/1, Geneva, November 2008, §13–14 and GB.304/ESP/3, Geneva, March 2009.

639. Each State which ratifies the Convention undertakes to establish and maintain a system for fixing and adjusting the minimum wages of groups of protected workers. According to the Recommendation, the wage fixing machinery may take the form of a statute, decisions of the competent authority, decisions of wages boards or councils, court rulings or acts giving force of law to provisions of collective agreements. The Convention stipulates that minimum wages must have force of law, with 'penal or other sanctions' be applied in case of violations.

640. Representatives of employers and workers are to be fully consulted in connection with the establishment, operation and modification of minimum wage machinery and, the Recommendation adds, in connection with the selection and application of the criteria for determining the level of minimum wages, the rate or rates of minimum wages to be fixed, their adjustment, the problems encountered and the collection of useful data and information. Wherever appropriate, the same representatives should also help give effect to the machinery, as should persons having recognized competence for representing the general interests of the country. The Recommendation asks the States, to the extent possible, to devote sufficient resources to the collection of statistics and other data needed for the relevant analytical studies.

641. Fixing minimum wages must be an essential component of any policy aimed at reducing poverty and meeting the needs of workers and their families.[443] There are many different ways of setting the minimum wage, with a distinction between those that apply to all workers and those that centre on a branch of activity, a region or an occupational category.[444] The general trend, including in the instruments discussed here, is to fix a general minimum wage.[445]

642. The Convention and the Recommendation list the criteria to take into account in setting the level of minimum wages: the needs of workers and their families, the general level of wages in the country, the cost of living and fluctuations in it, social security benefits, and the relative living standards of other social groups. There are also economic factors, including the requirements of economic development, productivity and the desirability of maintaining a high level of employment.[446] It is no easy matter to come up with the best possible combination of these diverse elements, especially since the right to collective bargaining must also be respected.[447] ILO experts suggest avoiding too complex minimum wage-fixing machinery because it could disturb the collective bargaining process, the minimum wages complementing by the establishment of a threshold, rather than substituting collective agreements. Minimum wage rates need to be adjusted from time to time to take account of changes in the cost of living and general economic conditions;

443. Recommendation No. 135, para. 1.
444. ILC (79th session, 1992), *Minimum Wages. Wage-fixing Machinery, Application and Supervision* (Geneva), ILO, 1992, para. 152 *et seq.*
445. I LC (103rd session, 2014), *Minimum Wage Systems*, report III (Part 1B), Geneva, ILO, 2014, para. 198; ILO, *Global Wage Report, op. cit.*, pp. 50–55. *See* however para. 5 of the Recommendation.
446. Article 3 of the Convention and para. 3 of the Recommendation.
447. Article 2 para. 2 of the Convention; *see also* para. 275 *above*.

the Recommendation suggests that periodical surveys be carried out to that end. The levels of minimum salaries and of social security benefits should however be disconnected with a view to dispelling the fear to create or increase the deficit of the social protection regime.[448]

643. In brief, the international labour standards ask the ratifying States to create a mechanism for fixing and adjusting basic wages; they do not indicate any minimum amount. The only exception relates to the able seamen for whom precise minimum pay is provided in Guideline B2.2.4 of the Maritime Labour Convention, 2006.[449]

644. The many difficulties encountered undoubtedly stem from the effective application of the machinery set up. For it to function smoothly, not only do all the elements just mentioned genuinely have to be taken into account (including the problems specific to SMEs and the agricultural sector), an adequate system of inspection must exist and specific measures such as those suggested by the Recommendation have to be adopted: widely available information on minimum wage rates, simple and non-bureaucratic procedures, easy access of the workers concerned to appeal procedures and protection against any reprisals, an administration of adequately trained and well organized staff, and the association of employers' and workers' organizations in efforts made to obtain effective application of the relevant legislation.

§7. Health and Security at Work

645. The employment contract is peculiar in that it is the wage earner himself who physically executes it. Intolerable situations arose in the 19th century, at the beginning of the industrial era, because people lost sight of this fact. Hence the adoption of standards to protect life and limb at work. Hence also a need emerged more recently to guarantee its privacy.

646. National lawmakers were the first to react. International instruments followed in the 20th century. One of the first international labour conventions, adopted in Bern in 1906, prohibited work with white phosphorous, a highly toxic product used in the manufacture of matches. The Preamble to the Constitution of ILO, which was established in 1919, refers to 'the protection of the worker against sickness, disease and injury arising out of his employment'. Since its inception, the Organization has drawn up conventions and recommendations to that end.

647. Occupational health and safety remains a matter of acute concern. There are no global standardized systems for collecting accurate and comprehensive data. Very little information is available on developing countries, and the estimates and projections based on the information collected in the industrialized countries and a

448. ILO, *op. cit.*, pp. 51–52.
449. *See* para 867 *below*.

few others are not reliable enough to constitute a universal statistical base. It is nevertheless estimated that every day some 6,300 people die as a result of work-related injuries or diseases – more than 2.3 million deaths per year. Each of the 337 million workplace accidents that occur each year commonly results in extended absences from work. New occupational safety and health risks have appeared in a world of work undergoing rapid transformation. Many occupational hazards remain hidden and ignored, particularly in the informal economy.[450]

648. The enactment of protective legislation has always been one of the chief means of fighting this endemic scourge. These pages contain a brief overview of the relevant international rules on safety at work (I), then centre on changes in ILO standards on occupational health and safety (II) and on the problems of national implementation (III). They end with some developments on the protection of privacy (IV).

I. The International Dimension of Regulations on Occupational Health

649. The adoption, in December 1966, of the International Covenant on Economic, Social and Cultural Rights recalled, in legal terms, the fundamental point that, above and beyond satisfying certain albeit respectable claims, above and beyond even protecting workers from certain forms of abuse, what counts is human dignity. Work is made to serve man, and not the other way round. Every worker has the right to be treated as a human being, and the State the corresponding duty.

650. More specifically, the Covenant requires the States to recognize 'the right of everyone to the enjoyment of just and favourable conditions of work which ensure, in particular: … Safe and healthy working conditions'.[451] It also refers to the right of everyone to enjoy the highest attainable standard of physical and mental health.

651. The States parties agreed that the international measures aimed at achieving the rights recognized in the Covenant included *inter alia* – and this is key to understanding the relationship between United Nations and ILO activities in this field – the conclusion of conventions, the adoption of recommendations, the furnishing of technical assistance and the holding of regional and technical meetings, organized in conjunction with the governments concerned, for the purpose of consultation and study.[452] ILO's role quite naturally proceeds from this: to implement, at universal level, the rights thus granted to workers.[453]

---

450. ILO, *Emerging Risks and New Patterns of Prevention in a Changing World of Work*, Geneva, 2010, pp. 1 and 10.
451. Article 7.
452. Article 23.
453. *See* for example J.M. Thouvenin and A. Trebilcock (ed.), *Droit international social*, vol. II, Brussels, Bruylant, 2013, pp. 1002 *et seq.* R. Nunin, 'Ambiente e lavoro', in L. Mazzetti (ed.), *Manuale di diritto ambientale*, Milan, CEDAM, 2001, p. 1179 *et seq.*

652. The ILO has done this in particular by adopting, pursuant to expert reports, a series of conventions and recommendations dealing with health as it relates to work. The instruments dealing directly with the issue comprise some that are general in scope and some that consider specific factors. The first group includes:

- Convention No. 155 and Recommendation No. 164, 1981, on occupational safety and health; the Protocol to Convention No. 155, 2002;
- Convention No. 161 and Recommendation No. 171, 1985, on occupational health services;
- Convention No. 174 and Recommendation No. 181, 1993, on the prevention of major industrial accidents;
- Recommendation No. 97, 1953, on the protection of workers' health.
- Convention No. 187 and Recommendation No. 197, 2006, concerning the promotional framework for occupational safety and health.

The risk factors are toxic substances and agents,[454] machines,[455] loads,[456] air pollution, noise and vibrations,[457] HIV and AIDS.[458]

653. Several conventions and recommendations deal with a specific branch of activity;[459] others concern a category of workers it was felt should benefit from additional guarantees: children and young people, elderly workers, migrants, women.

654. In fields as technical as these, data collection and analysis, research and exchanges between experts are all vital steps in the preparation of new international labour standards. Although the examination of national laws and their effectiveness is, here again, a crucial part of the process of formulating instruments, those instruments are less a synthesis of the most recent legislation than in other areas.

---

454. The Annex to Recommendation No. 197 considers relevant for the promotional framework it establishes the following instruments of this group: the Radiation Protection Convention (No. 115) and Recommendation (No. 114), 1960; the Occupational Cancer Convention (No. 139) and Recommendation (No. 147), 1974; the Asbestos Convention (No. 162) and Recommendation (No. 172), 1986; the Chemicals Convention (No. 170) and Recommendation (No. 177), 1990.
455. The Guarding of Machinery Convention (No. 119) and Recommendation (No. 118), 1963 however are not mentioned in the annex to Recommendation No. 197.
456. The Maximum Weight Convention (No. 127) and Recommendation (No. 128), 1967 are not mentioned neither in the annex to Recommendation No. 197.
457. The Working Environment (Air Pollution, Noise and Vibration) Convention (No. 148) and Recommendation (No. 156), 1977 are included in the list of the above-mentioned annex.
458. The HIV and AIDS Recommendation, 2010 (No. 200).
459. The following instruments included in the annex to Recommendation No. 197: the Hygiene (Commerce and Offices) Convention (No. 120) and Recommendation (No. 120), 1964; the Safety and Health in Construction Convention (No. 167) and Recommendation (No. 175), 1988; the Safety and Health in Mines Convention (No. 176) and Recommendation (No. 183), 1995; the Safety and Health in Agriculture Convention (No. 184) and Recommendation (No. 192), 2001; the Occupational Safety and Health (Dock Work) Convention (No. 152) and Recommendation (No. 160), 1979.

655. The above provisions are supplemented with less binding measures: resolutions adopted by the International Labour Conference, what were once model codes and are now codes of practice.[460] There are guides and handbooks to help the people in charge of giving effect to the measures called for. The Organization's occupational health and safety programmes include much more than standard-setting activities: they also encompass research, data collection and dissemination, technical advice and assistance for the Organization's constituents and technical cooperation programmes. The standards adopted are also the fruit of these deliberations and reflections.[461]

656. It must not be forgotten that what has been accomplished at the universal level is supplemented by regional, in particular European, standards.

II. Changes in ILO Standards on Occupational Health

657. The approach to the legal protection of occupational health has not always been the same. This is reflected in the broadened scope of application of ILO conventions and recommendations (A). More importantly, it is apparent from the very concept of the protection (B). It is manifested, lastly and at a later stage, in the globalization of preventive methods (C).

A. The Changing Field of Application

658. The first instruments adopted by the International Labour Conference on occupational health and safety aimed to shield the workers concerned from daunting illnesses (carbon and lead poisoning) and from the risks inherent in especially harmful products (white lead, white phosphorus). How many people know, for example, that phossy jaw, which is caused by the use of white phosphorus in the manufacture of matches, was the first occupational disease done away with thanks to international action, following the implementation of the above-mentioned Bern Convention?[462] In some cases, certain tasks were prohibited for workers deemed to be more vulnerable because of their age (young people under the age of 18) or their sex;[463] one of the 1919 conventions gave women the right – in some respects the obligation – to leave work for a determined period before and after giving birth.[464]

659. The International Labour Conference subsequently voted instruments on compensation for occupational accidents and diseases; this had an obvious

460. *See* paras 213–214 *above* and the ILO website http://www.ilo.org/safework/info/standards-and-instruments/codes/lang–en/index.htm.

461. *See* the ILO website on safety and health at work as well as the online edition of the *Encyclopaedia of Occupational Health and Safety.*

462. *See* Servais, *Droits en synergie sur le travail, op. cit.*, p. 82.

463. *See* the Lead Poisoning (Women and Children) Recommendation, 1919 (No. 4), paras 1 and 2; the White Lead (Painting) Convention, 1921 (No. 13), Article 3 and the Underground Work (Women) Convention, 1935 (No. 45).

464. The Maternity Protection Convention, 1919 (No. 3), Article 3.

preventive effect (management having wanted to shrug off its obligation to compensate workers). In the late 1920s, it drew up safety rules for highly exposed economic sectors: industry in general, with Recommendation No. 31 on the prevention of industrial accidents, 1929; work in ports, with the three conventions and three recommendations dating from 1929 to 1932. Several years later, in 1937, it voted instruments on building.

660. Other instruments were adopted after the Second World War. New standards provided enhanced protection against specific risks (radiation, benzene, carcinogenic substances and agents, asbestos, chemical products, etc.). Several instruments stipulated that young people under 18 or 21 years of age, as the case may be,[465] had to undergo a medical examination, and Recommendation No. 125 of 1965 regulated the conditions of employment of young persons working underground in mines. Other sector standards on hygiene and safety were adopted, in particular for commerce and offices, for seafarers and farm workers, for work in ports, in construction and in mines. All these rules are to be found in the national laws of many countries.

661. At the same time, however, the Conference was breaking new ground, adopting, after 1946, general standards from the point of view of both the workers covered and the risks dealt with. Examples are Recommendation No. 97 on the protection of workers' health, 1953, and Convention No. 174 and Recommendation No. 181 on the prevention of major industrial accidents, 1993. Convention No. 155 and Recommendation No. 164 of 1981 deal with occupational safety and health and the working environment; they cover all branches of activity and all workers in those branches, although the States ratifying the Convention may invoke what are known as flexibility clauses and allow certain exceptions. Similarly, under the terms of Convention No. 161 and Recommendation No. 171 on occupational health services, the States undertake progressively to develop occupational health services for all workers in all branches of economic activity and all undertakings.

B. Changes in the Methods of Protecting Health

662. The first instruments adopted by ILO contained essentially provisions that prohibited the use of certain products, severely regulating their utilization and issuing instructions on the precautions to take. Very soon, however, under the influence of doctrines which, as in the United States, emphasized voluntary effort and individual responsibility, a broader concept prevailed. As early as 1929, Recommendation No. 31 listed, for industrial undertakings, most of the modern principles of occupational accident prevention. Those principles can be summed up as follows: the importance of determining causes and circumstances, the role of physical,

465. The Medical Examination of Young Persons (Industry) Convention, 1946 (No. 77); the Medical Examination of Young Persons (Non-Industrial Occupations) Convention, 1946 (No. 78), the Medical Examination of Young Persons Recommendation, 1946 (No. 79), the Medical Examination of Young Persons (Underground Work) Convention, 1965 (No. 124).

physiological and psychological factors, advance examination by the authorities of plans to build or transform establishments, consultation with workers' organizations on the drafting of safety rules, cooperation between all the parties concerned, notably employers and workers, the responsibility of employers, workers and their organizations, the formation of the right attitude towards safety, etc.[466]

663. It was not until much later, however, in 1953, that the first standards were adopted that dealt with all the problems of preventing health risks in the workplace. Those standards are contained in Recommendation No. 97, which does not stop at listing protective measures: it seeks more thoroughly to improve occupational hygiene as well, and it establishes the basic rules for safeguarding people's health at work. It requires both that technical protective measures be taken (including measures such as regular analysis of the atmospheric conditions on the premises and the use of individual protective equipment) and that medical examinations and first aid be provided. These provisions imply recourse to specialists, engineers, doctors and hygienists in particular. The Recommendation was quite naturally supplemented shortly after by another one, on occupational health services.[467] The instruments adopted since – such as Convention No. 176 and Recommendation No. 183 on health and safety in mines, 1995 – accentuated the trend.

664. Efforts to improve occupational health and safety did not stop there. Ergonomics has served to give effect to the principles brought out earlier and systematically to analyse all reactions, in short, man's behaviour in the working environment, his mental faculties and physical capabilities, his possibilities to adapt, to form relationships, his emotions. It considers the working environment and the tools, materials and methods used, as well as how the work is organized, drawing on physiology and labour psychology, psycho-sociology and even business economics. It has shown that preventing occupational accidents and diseases is more than just identifying the immediate causes and that the many circumstances surrounding work had to be considered as a whole, with one acting on the other.

665. Poor working conditions, such as too many or badly organized hours, an excessive pace of work or stress, can, just as easily as unsafe installations, cause accidents and ill health. The connections with the general protection of the environment, of the population as a whole, are strikingly clear when disaster strikes. The distance between home and work, traditions, social structures, individual health and malnutrition are other factors to be taken into account.[468]

---

466. *See* M. Robert and L. Parmeggiani, 'Fifty years of international collaboration in occupational safety and health', *ILR*, Vol. 99, No. 1, January 1969, p. 93; *see also* L. Bougnol: 'L'action de l'OIT en matière d'hygiène et de sécurité du travail', *Revue française des affaires sociales*, April–June 1969, p. 144 *et seq.*; ILC, *op. cit.*, para. 46 *et seq.*

467. The Occupational Health Services Recommendation, 1959 (No. 112). In 1985, the ILO Conference adopted the Occupational Health Services Convention (No. 161) and Recommendation (No. 171); the latter supersedes Recommendation No. 112: *see* para. 48.

468. *See* J.M. Clerc (ed.), *Introduction to Working Conditions and Environment* (Geneva), ILO, 1985, p. 7 *et seq.* and 20 *et seq.*

666. All of the above are reasons for having a global approach to problems of occupational health and safety and for establishing a coherent system of protection in order to remedy them. This is the concept that gradually emerged and inspired all international standard-setting activity.

667. Take Convention No. 155 and Recommendation No. 164, on occupational health and safety and the working environment, which were adopted in 1981. The Convention lays the foundations of national policy in this respect. It lists the main spheres of action: the material elements of work, relationships between those elements and the persons who carry out or supervise the work, the training, qualifications and motivations of those in charge of safety and health, communication and cooperation, the protection of workers and their representatives from disciplinary measures as a result of actions properly taken by them in conformity with the policy. It determines the responsibilities of the authorities (prohibition, administrative supervision and authorizations, procedures for declaring illnesses and accidents, inquiries, statistical analyses, systems of investigation and inspection, coordinating of services) and of the manufacturers and sellers of materials and products. It establishes the responsibilities of the employer (the terms of the obligation to ensure safety) and of the worker and his representatives (the obligations to cooperate, to receive the necessary information and training, to point out any dangerous situations). It refers to the worker's right not to return to work after having signalled that it presents 'an imminent and serious danger to his life or health' (and to be protected from reprisals in that case).

668. Under what has become a classic procedure, Recommendation No. 164 supplements the Convention, for example by spelling out the technical measures to be taken and by suggesting the appointment of workers' safety delegates or safety and health committees.

669. This global approach is to be found in other ILO instruments. Convention No. 148 and Recommendation No. 156 of 1977, in particular, deal with the protection of workers from the occupational risks of air pollution, noise and vibrations at the workplace. Both instruments deal less with structural and institutional matters and more with the types of measures to be taken against these risks: technical and administrative measures, organization of work, medical surveillance and individual protective equipment, training, information, research.

C. A Modern Vision of Occupational Health Standards

670. The translation into legal terms of this modern concept of occupational health required, obviously, different formulations, more flexible wording of the standards in this field: the new texts focus on the results to be obtained and are less explicit on the means of doing so. Flexibility was also needed to make sure the standards could keep up with increasingly rapid technological change and the sometimes dizzying prospects they presented for the future. In addition, the pace of change made it more and more difficult to regulate each case, to provide satisfactory responses for all situations.

671. This is why modern ILO standards require that national policies and measures be periodically reviewed in the light of scientific and technical progress. Convention No. 187 of 2006 for instance, provides[469] that 'each Member shall formulate, implement, monitor, evaluate and periodically review a national programme of safety and health in consultation with the most representative organizations of employers and workers'. This approach had already been adopted in Convention No. 115 of 1960 on protection from radiation. It is to be found in numerous more recent instruments. In those cases, the convention or the supplementary recommendation refers to the elements that will help update the measures adopted to give effect to the convention. Recommendation No. 194 on the list of occupational diseases, 2002, even contains an annex listing the occupational diseases to be regularly reviewed and updated through tripartite meetings of experts.[470] Recommendation No. 197 adds[471] that the national programme should be based on principles of assessment and management of hazards and risks. Many experts consider today that this approach is part of good enterprise governance.

672. There was another reason, at the international level, for introducing greater flexibility into the wording of labour standards. The developing States insisted that the International Labour Conference should draw up provisions that were applicable everywhere, even in places where the degree of economic development made implementation an especially nettlesome problem. Different means[472] were used to do this depending on the objective: exempting branches of activity or kinds of undertakings from the instrument's field of application, making exceptions for certain categories of workers, allowing States to ratify only some parts of the instruments, using expressions such as 'as needed', 'in the light of national conditions and practice', 'wherever circumstances so require', which left the authorities in charge of implementing the convention a wide margin for interpretation. Greater flexibility was also introduced into the methods of applying an instrument; Convention No. 161, for example, provides that occupational health services may be established by law, by collective agreement or in any other manner approved by the authorities after consultation with the representative organizations of employers and workers concerned. In addition, the Conference has often limited the rules a convention contains to the essential principles and relegated more specific and detailed standards to a supplementary recommendation, whose provisions are not binding. In fact, some articles in recent conventions in this field are programmatic in nature in that they invite the States to adopt policies and draw up programmes, but do not impose specific, immediately applicable legal obligations on the States concerned.

469. Article 5.
470. *See* Part II, chapter 3, §2, I *below*.
471. Para. 7.
472. *See* paras 1112–1113 *below*.

673. There are limits, obviously, to how flexibly ILO conventions can be drafted if they are to be sufficiently binding to prompt the governments to act. The problem of strict versus flexible standards appears in very many fields of international (and national) labour law. In this case, however, it is a key factor in the development of the rules.

III. National Implementation of the Standards

A. *The Obstacles Overcome and Lasting Difficulties*

674. Remarkable progress has been made in some case, far less in others: the implementation of ILO standards on occupational health has met with varied results. Some substantial improvements have been made, and the CEACR has on several occasions noted a positive change.[473] In spite of the slow but steady progress made in many countries, occupational accidents and diseases and major industrial accidents remain frequent, and they take a heavy human and economic toll.

675. Much therefore remains to be done. The number of ratifications of the principal conventions in this field is, on average, fairly low. True, the impact of those conventions, is greater than the number of ratifications would lead one to believe. That impact could be greater, however.

676. Amongst the criteria used by the CEACR to ask for more frequent reports on the application of a given convention, are included workers' health and safety problems and their seriousness.[474] Some of the obstacles have to do with discrepancies between the law and the ILO standard, others with State practice.

677. The discrepancies can be major. For example, limits to the scope of application of the laws – labour codes or specific statutes – protecting the workers' physical integrity can affect branches of activity, categories of undertakings or groups of workers. They are not necessarily all incompatible with a given convention, which itself may contain flexibility clauses allowing limits, through a declaration, to the instrument's field of application in certain conditions. No matter what the case, exceptions deprive many workers of any protection. Those most frequently excluded (and not only in developing countries) include small enterprises or family businesses, home workers or the self-employed, and all those doing 'odd jobs' in the unstructured sector in towns and in the countryside.

678. The law may not apply to the entire national territory, or not respect the requirements – of age in particular – set by the international standard, or not afford the beneficiaries an appropriate level of protection. The CEACR has noted, for

473. *See in particular* K.-M. Felderhoff, I. Kröner-Moosmann and T. Samuel, 'Occupational Safety and Health' in ILO, *International Labour Standards: A Global Approach* Geneva, 2001, p. 430 *et seq.*
474. ILC (102nd session 2013), *Report of the Committee of Experts for the application of Conventions and Recommendations*, General report, Geneva, ILO, 2013, paras 68–69.

example, that while most countries prohibit the use of machines that do not have adequate protective guards, extending that prohibition to the sale, hire, transfer or exhibition of such machines has been an impediment to the implementation of Convention No. 119 on guarding of machinery, of 1963. It has also observed in respect of Convention No. 148 on the working environment (air pollution, noise and vibrations), 1977, that several countries had not established criteria and limits for exposure to air pollution, what undermines the effectiveness of any other protective measures that might be taken[475].

679. Secondly, laws are worthless if they are not applied. The implementation of a legal text usually implies checks by a labour inspectorate and therefore a properly trained corps of sufficient public servants. This is often far from being the case. Practical difficulties can arise from the cost of safety measures for companies, especially those of modest size, or lack of technical knowledge. In some cases the problem is the attitude of certain workers, who are disinclined to be bothered at work by sophisticated equipment, or, more generally speaking, the weight of habit or superstitions that are always difficult to overturn. Hence the usefulness of making everyone aware of the risks inherent in work and of determining responsibilities, because the objective or social causes must not cover up mistakes made through carelessness, lack of proper precautions or negligence. Hence also the importance of informing the workers and their representatives, of consultations, and even of true cooperation between employers and workers. The national laws of several European countries call for the appointment, for that purpose, either of workers' safety delegates or of (workers' or joint) health and safety committees.[476]

680. The International Labour Conference discussed the future of ILO's standard-setting activities in the field of occupational health and safety, in what they termed an integrated approach.[477] The delegates confirmed[478] the need for a systematic occupational health and safety management strategy. The Organization's programme of action should remain based on technical assistance and cooperation, on the promotion of a culture of prevention, advocacy and mobilization of energy and on standard-setting instruments.

681. The Convention No. 187 focus on promoting occupational health and safety: the matter is to be a national priority and the object of a political commitment to conceive and give effect to strategies associating employers' and workers'

475. *See* ILC (102nd session 2013), *Report of the Committee of Experts for the Application of Conventions and Recommendations*, General report, Geneva, ILO, 2013, pp. 733 (Guinea) and 742 (Sierra Leone); ILC (101st session, 2012), *Report of the Committee of Experts on the Application of Conventions and Recommendations*, Report III (Part 4B), Geneva, ILO, 2012, pp. 826 and 828 (Ecuador) and 837 (Hungary).

476. *See also* the Occupational Safety and Health Recommendation (No. 164), adopted by the ILO in 1981, para. 12.

477. *See* para. 78 *above*.

478. *See* the conclusions of the discussions regarding standards-related activities in ILC (91st session, 2003), *Provisional Record*, No. 22 (Geneva), ILO, 2003.

organizations in the development of a 'culture' of prevention and of modern management systems in this area. A framework rather than a technical document, the instrument promotes the influence of existing conventions and recommendations and the continued improvement of national schemes.

682. The delegates also identified the standards worth revising. Above all, they called for new instruments on ergonomics and biological risks. They suggested that new practical guidelines be prepared.

B. The Cost of Occupational Health Standards

683. One objection has nevertheless been voiced, and it is a serious one because it casts doubt on the progress made and the goals set: are these standards, or some of them, not too expensive in the face of stepped-up competition in a globalized economy.

684. Some people are shocked at this argument: we are talking about human beings, their lives, their health, the happiness of their loved ones. It is nevertheless to the point. We shall consider the general problem of the cost of international labour standards at the end of this monograph,[479] but we can already make a few remarks here relating more directly to occupational health and safety.

685. The first is that the cost of the standards protecting the physical integrity of workers is in many cases a mere fraction of the total amount invested in machines and equipment; rationalization can in some cases reduce it even further. It is nevertheless true that these costs can be deemed high in countries just starting on the path of economic development.

686. Secondly, the medium term must not be sacrificed for the short term, or even the very short term; indeed, these standards are ultimately often, contrary to what many people think, a source of benefit for the State concerned. The precautions taken against work-related illnesses and accidents can save what may be substantially higher costs further down the line, because in the long run those illnesses and accidents are expensive for the employer and the nation.[480] Besides financial compensation for the injury suffered (in the form of social security or other benefits) and the provision of benefits in kind (medical care, medicines, etc.), other, admittedly indirect but very real costs have to be taken into account:[481] possible

---

479. *See* paras 1104–1107 and 1153–1154 *below*.

480. *See* Clerc, *Introduction to Working Conditions, op. cit.*, p. 17 *et seq.*; *see also* A. Gladstone, *The Manager's Guide to International Labour Standards* (Geneva), ILO, 1986, pp. 53–54; Mary A. Jansen, 'Emotional disorders and the labour force. Prevalance, costs, prevention and rehabilitation', *ILR*, Vol. 125(5), September–October 1986, pp. 606–607; K.S. Kilimnik (ed.), *Health and Safety Regulations*, Vol. I (Deventer), Kluwer, 1994, p. 11 *et seq.*

481. *See* already D. Andreoni, *The Cost of Occupational Accidents and Diseases*, Geneva, ILO, 1986.

repairs to the material and equipment, the immobilization of machines, the disruption to the production programme caused by the worker's absence. More seriously, such illnesses and accidents can, if they occur frequently, affect the country's productive potential and ultimately its economic development. Enhanced prevention is a sign of good management for the company and, for the country, a criterion for a successful economic and social policy. The employer cannot easily and immediately replace an injured or sick worker who has the training and experience needed for the job. What is more, a safe working environment is obviously a major factor of worker satisfaction and therefore leads to increased productivity, not to mention the tension and social conflicts that would inevitably erupt in the presence of serious industrial risks.

687. Even if the last element is not taken into account, it is estimated that at least 4 per cent of global gross national product is lost in compensation, unworked days, production interruptions, rehabilitation, medical expenses, etc.[482] And, in response to those who rather brutally purport that the cost of these illnesses and accidents is in the final analysis insignificant for many developing countries (because of the sheer number of unemployed and failures in the system of compensation), it has been pointedly said that such absences are even more damaging to the economies of such countries, where skilled labour, like material resources, is in short supply: it usually takes longer to replace the worker than in industrialized countries. In addition, the community to which the injured or sick worker belongs will in any case have to bear the consequences, even if social security is poor and the 'cost' must be borne by the victim himself or his family.

§8. Protection of Workers' Privacy

688. Both the International Covenant on Civil and Political Rights and the European Convention on Human Rights provide that everyone has the right to respect for his privacy. The question concerns *inter alia* the collect by the firm of information about its employees.[483] The European Union Charter of fundamental rights, adopted on 7 December 2000, refers more specifically, in chapter 2, to the protection of personal data; the reform agreed upon in October 2007 has given to this instrument the same value as a treaty, for all Member States except for Poland and the United Kingdom. Work on computers raises, however, specific problems. Which

---

482. ILC (91st session, 2003), *ILO Standards-related Activities in the Area of Occupational Safety and Health, op. cit.*, para. 24.

483. Convention No. 181 on private employment agencies (*see* para. 529 above) and Convention No. 186 on maritime labour provide guarantees concerning the processing of personal data. *See* also the Council of Europe Recommendation No. R (89) 2 on the protection of personal data for employment purposes. More general International or European instruments also apply to employers and workers, such as the OECD Guidelines governing the Protection of Privacy and Transborder Flows of Personal Data, the Council of Europe Convention for the protection of individuals with regard to automatic processing of personal data or the European Directives 95/46 on the protection of individuals with regard to the processing of personal data and on the free movement of such data and 2002/58 on privacy and electronic communications.

limits if any, for instance, to impose to the use of the equipment for private purposes within the enterprise, or even during the working hours? More and more company work rules deal with the question; their answers vary greatly. Regulation in this regard exists mainly at the national level.[484] The European Social partners have discussed another topic, i.e. telework. A framework agreement has been signed on 16 July 2002.[485] It also includes the protection of personal data.

689. ILO Convention No. 181 and Recommendation No. 188 on private employment agencies, 1997 as well as ILO Convention No. 186 on maritime labour, from 2006, cover the protection of workers' personal data. The ILO Recommendation No. 171 on occupational health services includes several paragraphs dealing specifically with the confidentiality of employees' medical records. The Recommendation on Decent Work for Domestic Workers also includes provisions on the protection of personal data used for employment purposes[486]. More generally, in 1996, the Organization prepared a set of practical guidelines on protecting workers' personal data. They cover the ways the information is collected and stored, as well as the security, use, and communication of the data. Workers should be regularly informed about the existence and processing of data concerning them, able to consult the information free of charge and correct it, if necessary, as well obtain assistance in these operations.

§9. Non-standard Forms of Work

690. For many years contracts without limits of time were the most usual form of employment relationship. New methods of organizing work, often born of the desire to give undertakings more flexible structures, fostered later variations in the forms of employment. The phenomenon grew under the pressure of competition, linked to the internationalization of the market economy, and scientific and technical progress. The employers' determination to make their companies more profitable, to lower their costs, pushed them to explore and use all possible combinations. At the same time, the public authorities often encouraged varieties of employment in order to absorb an employment crisis they could not solve by other means.

---

484. R. Blanpain and M. Van Gestel, *Use and Monitoring of E-mails, Intranet and Indirect Facilities at Work Law and Practice*, The Hague, Kluwer, 2004; 'Information technology and workers' privacy', *Comparative Labor Law & Policy Journal*, special issue, Vol. 23, No. 2, winter 2002; J.F. Siqueira Neto, 'Derecho del trabajo y derechos humanos fundamentales', *Libro de informes generales*, XVII Congreso mundial de derecho del trabajo y de la seguridad social (Montevideo, 2–5 September 2005), Montevideo, Asociación Uruguaya de derecho del trabajo y de la seguridad social, 2003, p. 179 *et seq*. J. Craig, *Privacy and Employment Law*, Oxford, Hart Publishing, 1999.
485. *See also* R. Blanpain (ed.), *European Framework Agreemenst and Telework: Law and Practice. A European and Comparative Study*, The Hague, Kluwer, 2007; T.P. Larsen and S.K. Andersen, 'A new mode of European regulation? The implementation of the Autonomous Framework Agreement on Telework in five countries', *European Journal of Industrial Relations*, Vol. 13, No. 2, 2007, pp. 181–198.
486. See para. 3(a).

691. The circumstances explain, therefore, why many people associate other forms of employment with precarious work, even if that assimilation is not always accurate: a mother can ask to work half-time and maintain her open-ended contract. Nevertheless, the workers concerned are usually more vulnerable because their job is not secure, their social protection is weak and they find it difficult to organize in trade unions. More specifically, they are often paid less, benefit from hardly any additional social benefits and have only limited access to common social security schemes (pension, unemployment, family allowance, etc.). They tend not to be included in collective bargaining processes and therefore do not enjoy the guarantees that supplement the individual contract. Another aspect is the absence of career prospects and occupational investment. Many women hold jobs of this kind, as do, although apparently to a lesser extent, young and elderly workers, immigrants and all those looking for a second or third job when they find that the first does not pay enough.

692. The terms and conditions of segmented employment – the search for greater flexibility; the often precarious situation of the workers concerned – explain the difficulties, at national and international level, of finding adequate legal provisions for regulation.

693. In terms of the law, the fact that there is a variety of forms of employment stems chiefly from contractual autonomy, i.e. the freedom everyone has to undertake to perform a task for another person and the faculty each of the parties has to give the ensuing relationship the shape they wish, subject to the limits of the law. There are many possible combinations. The main variables concern whether the relationship is a subordinate one or not, where the work is done (the case of homework, including telework), the time factor (temporary work, part-time work, fixed-term work) and the method of remuneration (in kind, at least partially, for apprentices and for au pair workers).

694. Do international labour standards apply to all these forms of employment? The answer is neither yes or no, but lies somewhere in between. The method we have chosen is to review, subject by subject, the main fields of international labour and social security law and ask whether the relevant standards apply to certain forms of employment (1).

695. One remark, however: the founders of the Organization stated that the International Labour Conference had a duty to introduce flexibility into the legal texts it adopted:

> In framing any Convention or Recommendation of general application the Conference shall have due regard to those countries in which climatic conditions, the imperfect development of industrial organization, or other special circumstances make the industrial conditions substantially different and shall

suggest the modifications, if any, which it considers may be required to meet the case of such countries.[487]

Their successors therefore introduced into the instruments they adopted what are known as flexibility clauses that made it possible *inter alia* to exclude certain branches of activity or given categories of workers from the protection thus granted. Those exceptions frequently affect the people considered here: the self-employed, apprentices, home-workers, those working in the informal economy, and so on. Care must therefore be taken not to go too far and thereby deprive the workers concerned of all forms of guarantee. Hence the need to adopt specific standards (2).

I. The Applicability of International Labour Standards to the Various Forms of Work

A. *Freedom of Association*

696. Conventions Nos. 87 and 98 and the other instruments adopted by ILO in connection with freedom of association apply in principle to all workers, no matter what the form of employment. They cover, for example, home workers, temporary workers and even the self-employed. In practice, however, it is a well-known fact that many of these workers find it difficult to join an association because they are dispersed, because their work is unstable and because of all the circumstances that render their work precarious. Sometimes, in fact, the conditions established by national law for the creation of a workers' organization – for example a minimum number of workers at the workplace or a certain number of years of experience in the occupation or company – prevent some groups from forming a union, even if that was not the original intention.

697. The same observations can be made for the provisions on collective bargaining and industrial relations, whether in the company, in the branch of activity, or nationwide. Convention No. 135 and Recommendation No. 143 on workers' representatives in the undertaking and the facilities they are to be granted encounter clear practical problems of implementation when it comes to specific forms of employment. Nor is it any easier to apply the principles of the right to collective bargaining, even if there is nothing to prevent discussions of and agreements on non-traditional categories of workers. Examples exist, but they are few and far between.

698. In fact, organized labour tends to be absent from these forms of work. No country has to date really found the means of incorporating underprivileged categories of people into a renewed social dialogue at national level.

487. Article 19, para. 3 of the Constitution and paras 1112–1113 *below*.

B. Labour and Employment

1. Forced Labour and Child Labour

699. The term 'forced or compulsory labour' is broadly defined in Conventions Nos. 29 and 105: work or service which is exacted from any person under the menace of any penalty and for which the said person has not offered himself voluntarily. There is no distinction made, as can be seen, for whether the worker is a wage earner or not, whether he works part-time, for a limited time or on an open-ended basis, etc.

700. Most of the instruments on young workers (minimum age, prohibition of night work, medical examination, etc.) expressly cover wage earners and the self-employed. In Convention No. 182 on the prohibition and immediate action for the elimination of the worst forms of child labour, 'the term *child* shall apply to all persons under the age of 18'.

2. Equality of Opportunity and Treatment

701. Conventions Nos. 100, on equal remuneration, 1951, and 111, concerning discrimination (employment and occupation), 1958, and the corresponding recommendations define the principle of equality in general terms: there are no provisions limiting their scope in terms of either people or occupations. The same holds true for Convention No. 156 and Recommendation No. 165 of 1981 on equality of opportunity and treatment for workers of either sex with family responsibilities.

702. Recommendation No. 165 is particularly solicitous with regard to the categories of employment looked at here. It states[488] that in order to protect part-time workers, temporary workers and homeworkers, many of whom, it adds, have family responsibilities, the conditions on which these types of employment are performed should be adequately regulated and supervised. The terms and conditions of employment, including social security coverage, of part-time workers and temporary workers should be, to the extent possible, equivalent to those of full-time and permanent workers respectively; in appropriate cases, their entitlement may be calculated on a pro rata basis.

3. Employment Policy and Promotion

703. Convention No. 122 and the other instruments on employment policy are very broad in scope: they concern 'all who are available for and seeking work'[489]

488. Para. 21.
489. Article 1, para. 2 of Convention No. 122.

and contain several provisions relating more specifically to the types of employment of concern here: seasonal work,[490] and family or independent work.[491] Recommendation No. 169 recognizes the importance, as a provider of jobs, of the informal sector, 'that is economic activities which are carried on outside the institutionalized economic structures'.[492]

704. Every employment policy must comprise occupational guidance and training. That is the object, as we have seen, of Convention No. 142 and Recommendation No. 150, which deal with both salaried employment and independent work. It is also covered by the labour standards on the vocational rehabilitation and employment of the disabled. Convention No. 159 covers 'an individual' – a generic term if ever there was one – 'whose prospects of securing, retaining and advancing in suitable employment are substantially reduced as a result of a duly recognized physical or mental impairment'; Article 1 adds, as though it were necessary, that the Convention applies 'to all categories of disabled persons'. The measures spelled out in supplementary Recommendation No. 168 include provision of part-time employment and other job arrangements adapted to the capabilities of people for whom full-time employment is not immediately, and may not ever be, practicable.[493]

705. Convention No. 158 on termination of employment applies in principle to all wage earners, but allows exceptions some of which relate more specifically to our subject: workers engaged for a specified period of time or a specified task, workers serving a period of probation and workers engaged on a casual basis for a short period.[494]

706. It has traditionally been considered that fixing a term to the contract enables the worker, as we have said, to make plans for the future. However, the period of notice may be short and the employer may try to get around the protection provided in contracts without limit of time in matters such as notice and just cause by having repeated recourse to fixed-term contracts. Convention No. 158 requires adequate safeguards against this, and its supplementary recommendation[495] lists measures to that effect: limiting recourse to fixed-term contracts to cases in which the employment relationship cannot be of indeterminate duration (owing either to the nature of the work to be effected or to the circumstances under which it is to be effected or to the interests of the worker); or deeming such contracts to be contracts of employment of indeterminate duration, *inter alia* when renewed on one or more occasions.

707. Convention No. 181 on private employment agencies applies to all categories of workers and all branches of economic activity, except seafarers.[496] As we

490. The Employment Policy Recommendation, 1964 (No. 122), para. 12.
491. The Employment Policy (Supplementary Provisions) Recommendation, 1984 (No. 169), para. 27(2).
492. *Ibid.*, para. 27(1).
493. Para. 11(b).
494. Article 2.
495. Recommendation No. 166, para. 3(2).
496. Article 2.

have said, the standards it contains protect the workers concerned from abuse but do not, contrary to earlier instruments, prohibit the existence in principle of profit placement offices.

4. Labour Administration

708. Convention No. 150 on labour administration, although it concerns essentially wage earners, also covers, when national conditions so require, self-employed workers, members of cooperatives and worker-managed undertakings, etc.[497] Convention No. 160 on labour statistics and its supplementary recommendation (No. 170) also cover the entire working population.[498]

709. The standards on labour inspection deal first with the situation of wage-earning workers employed in industrial and commercial undertakings, in non-commercial services and in agriculture.[499] However, Convention No. 129 on labour inspection in agriculture provides for the extension of the inspection system to tenants, sharecroppers, cooperators and other persons working in the undertaking, such as members of the operator's family.[500]

5. Conditions of Work

710. The standards on labour conditions were also drafted essentially to cover the situation of persons employed in industrial, commercial or agricultural undertakings. However, a legal analysis of these instruments can lead to the conclusion that they apply to all workers, even those who are self-employed. This is particularly true for occupational safety and health, where the extension is easiest to operate; certain ILO recommendations say this expressly.[501]

711. The standards on the protection of women workers (the prohibition for women to do certain jobs; maternity guarantees) are essentially conceived for situations where the women are subordinates. Nevertheless Convention No. 183 of 2000 on maternity protection expressly covers women employed 'in atypical forms of dependent work'.[502]

---

497. Article 7; *see also* Article 6(2)(b).
498. *See in particular* Article 1 of the Convention and para. 1 of the Recommendation.
499. The Labour Inspection Convention, 1947 (No. 81) and its Protocol of 1995; the Labour Inspection (Agriculture) Convention, 1969 (No. 129).
500. Article 5.
501. *See* the following Recommendations: the Working Environment (Air Pollution, Noise and Vibration) Recommendation, 1977 (No. 156), para. 1(1); the Occupational Safety and Health Recommendation, 1981 (No. 164), para. 1(1); the Occupational Health Services Recommendation, 1985 (No. 171), para. 2(2); the Asbestos Recommendation, 1986 (No. 172), para. 1(2); the Safety and Health in Construction Recommendation, 1988 (No. 175), para. 2(2)(d); the Chemicals Recommendation, 1990 (No. 177), para. 4.
502. Article 2(1).

712. Conventions Nos. 97 and 143 define migrant workers, in terms of the protection they grant, as people who migrate from one country to another with a view to being employed otherwise than on their own account.

713. Recommendation No. 162 on older workers, of 1980, applies to wage earners and independent workers.

C. *Social Security*

714. The conventions on social security adopted since the end of the Second World War deal, using various formulas, with categories either of wage earners or more broadly the working or resident population; some stipulate that they apply to apprentices.[503] It is nevertheless true that workers in unstable situations find it very difficult to join social security schemes.

715. Such workers are sometimes among those the instruments make exceptions for; such is the case of casual workers but also, in respect of occupational accidents and diseases, of homeworkers.[504] The supplementary recommendations frequently ask that these restrictions be waived, gradually if needed.

716. What is more, these workers find it difficult to meet the conditions to receive benefits, in particular the obligation to have worked or contributed for a minimum period (or worked for a minimum number of hours or paid a minimum amount of contributions). Convention No. 102 on social security (minimum standards), 1952, and more recent conventions, like national rules, authorize qualifying periods, although the supplementary recommendations usually ask that those qualifying periods be waived.

717. Another difficulty is that in national social security schemes the amount of the benefits usually depends on the earned salary and among 'atypical' workers that amount is often modest. This is not the only method of calculation, however. Convention No. 102 and the subsequent instruments authorize – and themselves use for their 'average' standards for determining the minimum amount – techniques that are not directly related to the wage received.

718. The rules sometimes contain special adjustments for the specific employment conditions of certain groups of workers. Convention No. 102, for example, has a special provision on unemployment benefits for seasonal workers.[505] Generally speaking, States should revise their pensions and social insurance systems so that they are no longer tied to continuous employment. In the USA the system must be delinked from any particular employer and permit the beneficiary to keep the acquiring rights when he/she has no job or to transfer them to the new employer.

503. *See* Conventions No. 121 (Article 4), No. 128 (Articles 9 and 22) and No. 130 (Article 10).
504. *See* Convention No. 121, Article 4(2)(b).
505. Article 24, para. 4.

719. The fundamental problem is to adapt social security – which is a guarantee of income – to new categories of workers (at least in terms of their numbers) who have few resources and for whom social welfare schemes cannot, for one reason or another, make suitable provision. Sometimes, in order to promote hiring, the State acts as a substitute, at least in part, for the parties concerned when it comes to financing social benefits for these workers; EU countries should keep an eye in this case on the case-law of the CJEU regarding the free competition. The Income Security Recommendation, 1944 (No. 67) and the Medical Care Recommendation, 1944 (No. 69) had already established the principle of a comprehensive coverage of the whole population by a social protection scheme associating measures of social insurance, social assistance and public services.The Social Protection Floors Recommendation, 2012 (No. 202) promotes a guaranteed minimum income for the poorest. Those instruments will be examined in the chapter dealing with social security.

II. The Specific Standards

720. We shall first consider independent work, family work and apprenticeship, for which no specific instruments have been adopted but which are the subject of standards including or excluding them from more general legal texts. We shall then turn to homework, part-time work and domestic workers on which conventions and recommendations have been adopted. Temporary work is analysed in the study on private employment agencies, and the reader will be referred to the appropriate sections.[506]

A. Independent Work

721. Work that is legally independent occupies a separate place in the pantheon of employment situations. We know that labour law was developed to afford protection for wage earners; it did not apply to workers who were subordinate to no one. However, it gradually became clear that there was a need to extend at least some of the guarantees to the self-employed,[507] since the demarcation line between wage-earners and independent workers is not always easy to determine, as in the so-called gig economy or crowd work. In some cases, the legal status of independence could even camouflage genuine economic dependence.

722. Whether or not an international labour standard applies to independent workers depends on how the relevant text is worded and, of course, on its object; it is hard to imagine how some standards could apply to such work. What is more, a

506. *See* para. 524 *et seq. above*.
507. *See* already G. Lyon-Caen: *Le droit du travail non salarié* (Paris), Sirey, 1990 and also for example A. Supiot, 'L'avenir d'un vieux couple: travail et sécurité sociale', *Droit social*, Nos. 9–10, Sept.–Oct. 1995, pp. 823–831; B. Langille and G. Davidoff (eds.), *Boundaries and Frontiers of Labour Law*, Oxford, Hart Publishing, 2006.

situation that is to all appearances one of independent work can dissimulate salaried employment. Attempts have been made in various bodies of national law, with varying degrees of success, to shed light on the true nature of these relations. In such cases, as in others where there is no fraud, certain laws provide that there shall be a presumption of salaried work; the contrary presumption also exists, as in the French Labour Code.

723. Many ILO instruments, as we have already pointed out, use the word 'worker' without qualifiers, i.e. without limiting the meaning, directly or indirectly, to wage earners.[508] Some, such as Convention No. 141 on rural workers' organizations, refer explicitly to people working on their own account. Convention No. 111, too, on discrimination (employment and occupation) targets, as its title indicates, both the occupation and the job and therefore applies to self-employed workers.

724. Recommendation No. 192 of 2001 requires that Convention No. 184 on health and safety in agriculture, also adopted in 2001, be extended progressively to self-employed farmers. Recommendation No. 132 of 1968 concerns the improvement of conditions of life and work of tenants, sharecroppers and similar categories of agricultural workers.[509]

725. Recommendation No. 132 states that it should be an objective of social and economic policy to promote a progressive and continuing increase in the people covered and to assure them the greatest possible degree of stability and security of work and livelihood. The measures to take should focus on good farming techniques, access to land, the establishment and development, on a voluntary basis, of organizations representing their interests, the formation of cooperatives, credit facilities, general and vocational education, the development of rural employment and health, social, cultural and recreational services. The Recommendation specifically requests that rent be kept to a decent level, recommends protection from the imposition to perform personal services, the enforcement of protective legal rules (to 'encourage the spirit of initiative' and promote well-being and the rapid settlement of disputes) and the application, if possible, of adequate social security schemes; the parties concerned should be protected, as far as possible and practicable, against risks of loss in income resulting from natural calamities. The contracts between the workers and the landowners should be in writing, respect certain forms and contain specific indications; the workers' rights should be duly recorded. The Recommendation also contains provisions on the housing the landowners are encouraged to provide, on the use of some land for the workers to grow food for themselves and their families, on the terms on which the employment may be terminated, including compensation for damages suffered, and on the right to make improvements to the holding, with compensation for the value of such improvements on giving up the holding.

---

508. ILC (77th session, 1990), *The Promotion of Self-employment*, report VII (Geneva), ILO, 1990: *see* Chapter IV relating to international labour standards.
509. The scope of the Recommendation is indicated in paras 1 to 3.

726. It is best not to generalize, however: this is an exceptional set of rules. Many of the social security conventions adopted since the end of the Second World War do, it is true, offer the States that ratify them the possibility of protecting specific categories of residents or of the working population (including, therefore, independent workers); the States also have the choice, however, of covering only wage earners. Other conventions, such as Convention No. 71 on seafarers' pensions, 1946, expressly authorize the exclusion of people working exclusively on their own account[510] or limit their scope to those bound by a subordinate working relationship (for example, Convention No. 175 and Recommendation No. 182 on part-time work, 1994). There are many examples of provisions that implicitly exclude the self-employed because the situation they cover does not concern them. This is the case, obviously, of Convention No. 95 on protection of wages, 1949, and Convention No. 158 on termination of employment, 1982. It is also the case of standards on industrial relations, such as Recommendation No. 94 on cooperation at the level of the undertaking, 1952, and Recommendation No. 130 on the examination of grievances, 1967. Many texts, although they do not formally exclude independent workers and are not totally inapplicable to them, are clearly not conceived for that kind of employment. They can nevertheless call for the extension, progressively if need be, and with the necessary adaptations, of their scope to such workers. Such is the case, for example, of Convention No. 150 on labour administration, 1978 – which incidentally refers expressly to self-employed workers 'occupied in the informal sector'[511] – and Convention No. 119 on the guarding of machinery, 1963.[512]

727. The ILO Recommendation No. 198 on Employment Relationship Recommendation was adopted in 2006, after a long-lasting and difficult debate. While the standards are finally contained in a not binding recommendation, employers' circles have expressed reservations about its content. The document focuses on the demarcation line between the contract of services and the contract for services. It does not deal with the grey area in-between, i.e. the relationships called *parasubordinazione* by the Italians, where the dependence is more economic than legal. Germany, Spain, and some other countries know this intermediate category of workers; the persons concerned received some protection in line with the waged employees, with regard to their employment conditions and social security.

728. According to the Recommendation, the determination of the existence of an employment relationship should be guided primarily by the facts relating to the performance of work and the remuneration of the worker, notwithstanding how the relationship is characterized in any contrary arrangement, contractual or otherwise, that may have been agreed between the parties. For facilitating the determination, Members should allow a broad range of means for determining the existence of an employment relationship and of providing for a legal presumption or assimilation, like in France and in other countries with regard to home-based work, that an employment relationship exists where one or more relevant indicators is present.

510. Article 2(2)h.
511. Article 7.
512. Article 13.

729. Members should clearly precise the conditions applied for determining the existence of an employment relationship, basically subordination or dependence. They should also remove incentives to disguise an employment relationship and define specific indicators of the existence of an employment relationship. Those indicators, as can be seen in numerous case-laws, might include:

(i) the fact that the work is carried out according to the instructions and under the control of another party, involves the integration of the worker in the organization of the enterprise, is performed mainly for the benefit of another person, must be carried out personally by the worker, is carried out within specific working hours or at a workplace specified or agreed by the party requesting the work, is of a particular duration and has a certain continuity, requires the worker's availability, or involves the provision of tools, materials and machinery by the party requesting the work;
(ii) periodic payment of remuneration to the worker; the fact that such remuneration constitutes the worker's sole or principal source of income; provision of payment in kind, such as food, lodging or transport; recognition of entitlements such as weekly rest and annual holidays; payment by the party requesting the work for travel undertaken by the worker in order to carry out the work; or absence of financial risk for the worker.

730. The Recommendation calls on Members to review at appropriate intervals and, if necessary, clarify and adapt the scope of relevant laws and regulations, in order to guarantee effective protection for persons who have an employment relationship, in particular the ones especially affected by the uncertainty as to its existence, as women workers, young and older workers, workers in the informal economy, migrant workers and workers with disabilities. National policy should at least include measures to:

(i) provide guidance for the parties concerned, in particular employers and workers, on effectively establishing the existence of an employment relationship and on the distinction between employed and self-employed workers;
(ii) combat disguised employment relationships in the context of, for example, other relationships that may include the use of other forms of contractual arrangements that hide the true legal status, noting that a disguised employment relationship occurs when the employer treats an individual as other than an employee in a manner that hides his or her true legal status as an employee, and that situations can arise where contractual arrangements have the effect of depriving workers of the protection they are due;
(iii) ensure standards applicable to all forms of contractual arrangements, including those involving multiple parties, so that employed workers have the protection they are due;
(iv) ensure that standards applicable to all forms of contractual arrangements establish who is responsible for the protection contained therein;
(v) provide effective access of those concerned, in particular employers and workers, to appropriate, speedy, inexpensive, fair and efficient procedures and

mechanisms for settling disputes regarding the existence and terms of an employment relationship;

(vi) ensure compliance with, and effective application of, laws and regulations concerning the employment relationship; and

(vii) provide for appropriate and adequate training in relevant international labour standards, comparative and case law for the judiciary, arbitrators, mediators, labour inspectors, and other persons responsible for dealing with the resolution of disputes and enforcement of national employment laws and standards.

Such a policy should not interfere with true civil and commercial relationships.

731. In the context of the transnational movement of workers, where workers are recruited in one country for work in another, the Members concerned may consider concluding bilateral agreements to prevent abuses and fraudulent practices which have as their purpose the evasion of the existing arrangements for the protection of workers in the context of an employment relationship. Members should establish specific national mechanisms in order to ensure that employment relationships can be effectively identified within the framework of the transnational provision of services. Consideration should be given to developing systematic contact and exchange of information on the subject with other States.

B. *Family Work*

732. This expression basically covers two hypotheses: work in family undertakings, i.e. usually in establishments where the only employees are members of the same family, and the work of a special category of workers, the members of the employer's family, no matter what the undertaking.

733. Many of ILO's earlier instruments on labour conditions (hours of work, weekly rest, paid leave, work of women, of young people) do not apply to family undertakings[513] or, more flexibly, authorize the exclusion of such undertakings.[514] Such exceptions are usually not to be found in the conventions on occupational safety and health.

513. *See for example*: the Hours of Work (Industry) Convention, 1919 (No. 1), Article 2; the Holidays with Pay Recommendation, 1954 (No. 98), para. 3; the Maternity Protection Convention, 1919 (No. 3), Article 3; the Night Work of Young Persons (Industry) Convention, 1919 (No. 6), Article 2; the Medical Examination of Young Persons (Sea) Convention, 1921 (No. 16), Article 2; the Minimum Age (Sea) Convention (Revised), 1936 (No. 58), Article 2.

514. *See in particular*: the Hours of Work (Commerce and Offices) Convention, 1930 (No. 30), Article 1(3); the Weekly Rest (Industry) Convention, 1921 (No. 14), Article 3; the Night Work of Young Persons (Non-Industrial Occupations) Convention, 1946 (No. 79), Article 1(4): 'in family undertakings in which only parents and their children or words are employed'; the Night Work of Young Persons (Industry) Convention (Revised), 1948 (No. 90), Article 1(3): *idem*; the Medical Examination of Young Persons (Non-Industrial Occupations) Convention, 1946 (No. 78), Article 1(4): *idem* at certain conditions; the Weekly Rest (Commerce and Offices) Convention, 1957 (No. 106), Article 5: 'who are not or cannot be considered to be wage earners'.

734. Provisions exist allowing derogations for small undertakings or, in the maritime and fishing sectors, for small boats. These undertakings (and boats) are usually family undertakings (or vessels) which are thereby excluded from the benefits of the instruments or subject to special provisions.[515]

735. The social security exemptions allowed are aimed more often than not at members of the employer's family,[516] usually on condition that they live under the same roof as he does and work for him.[517] Similar possibilities for exemptions exist in other fields.[518] In some cases, however, the ILO recommendation drafted to supplement a convention on a given subject expressly suggests that the same protection be granted to this specific category of worker. Examples are Recommendation No. 79 on medical examinations of young people and children, 1946,[519] and, in the field of social security, Recommendations Nos. 131 and 134.[520] Convention No. 129 on labour inspection (agriculture), 1969, also expressly provides for this possible extension.[521]

736. Several instruments explicitly stipulate that they apply, on terms and conditions that vary, to family work: for example, Convention No. 153 on hours of work and rest periods (road transport), 1979 (unless the Convention states otherwise);[522] Recommendation No. 132 on tenants and sharecroppers, 1968;[523] and Recommendation No. 170 on labour statistics, 1985.[524]

C. Apprenticeship

737. Few instruments exclude from their scope apprentices or other people undergoing practical training. Convention No. 114 on fishermen's articles of agreement, 1959, excludes from its definition of the term 'fisherman' cadets and 'duly

515. *See* for example: the Paid Educational Leave Convention, 1974 (No. 140), Article 9; the Plantations Convention, 1958 (No. 110) and its Protocol of 1982, Article 1 (which refers to both family and small-scale enterprises) and a number of maritime conventions (in particular Conventions Nos. 53, 71, 73, 91, 92, 133, 147, 165) and Recommendation No. 140. With regard to fishing, *see in particular* the Conventions Nos. 113, 125, 126.
516. With regard to seamen, *see* the Shipowners' liability (Sick and Injured Seamen) Convention, 1936 (No. 55).
517. *See* the Employment Injury Benefits Convention, 1964 (No. 121), Article 4; the Invalidity, Old-Age and Survivors' Benefits Convention, 1967 (No. 128), Article 37; the Medical Care and Sickness Benefits Convention, 1969 (No. 130), Article 5.
518. *See* the Minimum Wage Fixing Machinery (Agriculture) Convention, 1951 (No. 99), Article 1, para. 3.
519. Paragraph 1(2).
520. The Invalidity, Old-Age and Survivors' Benefits Recommendation, 1967 (No. 131), paras 2 and 3; the Medical Care and Sickness Benefits Recommendation, 1969 (No. 134), paras 2 and 11.
521. Article 5.
522. Article 1, para. 2.
523. Para. 1.
524. Para. 2.

indentured' apprentices.[525] The same holds true for Convention No. 22 on seamen's articles of agreement, 1926.[526]

738. The provisions on minimum age usually allow exceptions to the prohibition to work before having attained a given age for tasks performed in the framework of vocational training,[527] for obvious reasons.

739. Elsewhere, international labour standards apply to apprentices in that they concern all persons employed or occupied, as the case may be, in an undertaking or at a specific task. Some conventions and recommendations stipulate this expressly, such as Convention No. 106 on weekly rest in commerce and offices, 1957,[528] and several social security conventions.[529]

D. Homework

740. Some ILO instruments explicitly cover homeworkers: for example, Convention No. 26 on minimum wage-fixing machinery, 1928. Several early social security conventions contained both provisions that mentioned homeworkers (who were therefore in principle included in the scope of the Convention) and others that excluded them. This is still the case for Convention No. 121 of 1964 on employment injury benefits, which authorizes exceptions to the general scheme in respect of homeworkers.[530] More generally speaking, most international labour conventions and recommendations are written in terms that are sufficiently all-encompassing to comprise this kind of employment. There are exceptions, which are also broadly formulated, that make it possible to exclude them.

741. On the other hand, many standards do not apply to homework, because of the way in which they are worded or even by their very nature. One example is Convention No. 13 on the use of white lead in painting, of 1921, which prohibits the use of white lead and sulphate of lead in the internal painting of buildings. Other standards do not formally exclude homeworkers but were clearly not conceived for such workers and do not take account of their specific needs. Hence ILO's decision to draft specific rules; these took the form in 1996 of Convention No. 177 and Recommendation No. 184.[531]

525. Article 2.
526. Article 2.
527. *See* the Minimum Age Convention, 1973 (No. 138), Article 6.
528. Article 2.
529. *See* the Employment Injury Benefits Convention, 1964 (No. 121), Article 4; the Invalidity, Old-Age and Survivors' Benefits Convention, 1967 (No. 128), Article 9; the Medical Care and Sickness Benefits Convention, 1969 (No. 130), Article 10.
530. Article 4(2)(b).
531. An overview of the national legislations in force at that time can be found in ILC (82nd session, 1995), *Home work*, Report V (Part 1) (Geneva), ILO, 1994; *see* Chapter III.

742. Convention No. 177 does not apply to independent workers working at home, i.e. to persons who have 'the degree of autonomy and of economic independence necessary' to be considered independent workers under national laws or court decisions.[532] The situation of independent workers in general was discussed earlier.[533]

743. States ratifying the Convention undertake to adopt, implement and periodically review a national policy aimed at improving the situation of homeworkers. They must promote equality of treatment between homeworkers and other wage earners, 'taking into account the special characteristics of homework' and conditions applicable to similar work carried out in an enterprise. Equality of treatment is to be promoted in particular in respect of:

(a) the homeworkers' right to establish or join organizations of their own choosing and to participate in the activities of such organizations;
(b) protection against discrimination in employment and occupation;
(c) protection in the field of occupational safety and health;
(d) remuneration;
(e) statutory social security protection;
(f) access to training;
(g) minimum age for admission to employment or work; and
(h) maternity protection.[534]

744. A number of difficulties quickly become apparent, and they are interrelated. The first has to do with the applicability of general legislation. Implementing rules on hours of work is no easy task. One may be tempted to apply the same reasoning to occupational health and safety, but other considerations intervene, namely the incidence of certain practices on the life and health of the worker, his spouse and his family. Specific action therefore seems to be required; indeed, the obligation of safety incumbent on the employer of a homeworker does not appear to be the same as that of the head of a small or large undertaking in respect of those working in his premises. Article 7 of the Convention provides that 'national laws and regulations on safety and health at work shall apply to homework, taking account of its special characteristics, and shall establish conditions under which certain types of work and the use of certain substances may be prohibited in homework for reasons of safety and health'. As concerns hours of work, Recommendation No. 184 simply requests that the deadline to complete a work assignment not deprive a homeworker of the possibility to have daily and weekly rest comparable to that enjoyed by other workers; national laws and regulations should establish the conditions under which homeworkers are entitled to benefit, as other workers, from paid public holidays, annual holidays with pay and paid sick leave.[535]

---

532. Article 1(a).
533. *See* paras 721–730 *above*.
534. Article 4.
535. Paras 23 and 24.

745. The second difficulty consists in the fact that the applicable rules cannot be supervised in the same way. Generally speaking, admission to inhabited premises is subject to the authorization of the person occupying those premises; that person can refuse entry, perhaps simply because of an ill-defined fear of supervision. This is why the Recommendation insists[536] that labour inspectors be allowed to enter 'the parts of the home or other private premises in which the work is carried out'.

746. It is not enough to know the rules: information on or awareness of the risks to health and the usefulness of protective rules are of signal importance here. Several countries have set up bodies of inspectors specially trained for this kind of employment, such as the *Entgeltprüfer* for homework in Germany. Recommendation No. 184 suggests a number of means of reinforcing the effectiveness of inspection. The home worker should be kept informed of the specific conditions of employment in writing or by other means;[537] employers, or the intermediaries used by them, should be registered (and provide the information requested); they should be required to notify the competent authority when they give out homework for the first time and should keep a register of all home workers, classified according to sex, to whom they give work; they should also keep a record of the time allocated for a given task and of the rate of remuneration.[538] The inspector then has to supervise, not only compliance with the applicable rules but also, in a way, the validity of the contract and respect for its content. The implementation of the Recommendation's provisions can lead to a return to a certain degree of formalism in the framing of the contract for homework: the obligation to set the conditions of employment down in writing is a recognized guarantee for the worker; registration, an invaluable aid for the labour inspector.

747. When the use of intermediaries is permitted, the respective responsibilities of employers and intermediaries must be determined; where such an intermediary is used, the latter and the employer should be made jointly and severally liable for payment of the remuneration due to home workers.[539] The Recommendation deals with other matters, as well: the right to organize and to collective bargaining and the settlement of disputes; remuneration, minimum age, occupational health and safety, protection in the event of dismissal, protection of maternity and social security. The laws of some countries have original mechanisms, such as ad hoc committees, to make up for the inevitable defects in this sector of collective bargaining of employment conditions, in particular wages. The Recommendation further encourages information and training programmes and access to the necessary facilities. The Convention requires that labour statistics cover this kind of employment.[540]

---

536. Para. 8 in addition to Article 9 of the Convention whose wording is not very specific.
537. Para. 5.
538. Paras 6 and 7.
539. Article 8 of the Convention and paragraph 18 of the Recommendation respectively.
540. Article 6.

E. Part-Time Work

748. Part-time work is another form of employment subject to specific rules, at national, European and international level. It is the subject of Convention No. 175 and Recommendation No. 182 of 1994.

749. The Convention seeks to provide the persons concerned with the same protection as that granted to full-time workers in terms of freedom of association, equality of opportunity and treatment, occupational health and safety and equivalent conditions of maternity protection, annual holidays with pay and paid public holidays, sick leave and the termination of employment. It requires that part-time workers not receive a basic wage – the Recommendation adds compensatory allowances – which, calculated proportionately on an hourly, performance-related, or piece-rate basis, is lower than the basic wage of comparable full-time workers. The Recommendation suggests that part-time workers benefit on 'an equitable basis' from the facilities and services intended for their welfare.

750. This type of employment requires adjustments to working hours and paid leave and in terms of training, careers and vocational mobility. Part-time workers can find themselves excluded from the social security schemes promoted by Convention No. 102 and later ILO instruments. They may not fit the definition of people covered or meet the conditions to qualify for benefits (minimum period of work or earnings).[541] Both these instruments and those on part-time work nevertheless propose that, if the country's financial resources permit, certain requirements be waived, thresholds lowered, minimum allowances established and other means adopted to circumvent such limits.

751. The Recommendation provides part-time workers with a guarantee granted to home workers, namely to be informed of their specific conditions of employment in writing (or by another means). It also discusses how to count part-time workers in the total number of company wage earners (for the purposes of certain social laws). Several provisions in the Convention and the Recommendation deal with facilities of access to this kind of employment (with, if needed, reconsideration of the legislative provisions preventing such access) and with the transfer from full-time to part-time work and vice versa.[542]

F. Domestic Workers

752. The ILO has adopted in June 2011 a Convention (No 189) and a Recommendation (N0 201) on domestic work, i.e. work performed in or for a household

541. *See* para. 714 *et seq. above*.
542. *See also* J. Murray, *Transnational Labour Regulation: The ILO and EC Compared*, The Hague, Kluwer, 2002, p. 156 *et seq.*

or households.[543] In accordance with the Convention, the domestic workers should be informed of their terms and conditions of employment, in an appropriate, verifiable and easily comprehensible manner, preferably through written contracts. They should enjoy, like workers generally, fair terms of employment and decent working conditions including, if they reside in the household, decent living conditions that respect their privacy. They should receive effective protection against all forms of abuse, harassment and violence. In particular, national and migrant domestic workers recruited or placed by an employment agency need to be effectively protected against abusive practices, including by establishing the respective legal liability of the household and the agency. Each Member should ensure that domestic workers, either by themselves or through a representative, they have effective access to courts, tribunals or other dispute resolution procedures.

753. Among the domestic workers, the foreigners are often the victims of more abuses. The Convention states that national laws and regulations should require that migrant domestic workers receive a written job offer or a contract of employment containing minimum terms and conditions of employment agreed upon prior to crossing national borders. The Recommendation adds that each Member should consider specifying the conditions under which migrant domestic workers are entitled to repatriation, at no cost to the worker, upon the expiry or termination of the employment contract. Let us examine now more generally the standards on migrant workers.

§10. Foreign Workers

754. UN global migration statistics indicate that 232 million international migrants are living abroad worldwide[544]. Real figures may even be more as taking into account clandestine manpower keeps problematical. The population mobility has grown considerably for political, humanitarian, family or other reasons, but the first cause keeps the search of a bread-job. The focus in the following pages will be on migrant workers together with some other categories of foreign workers such as frontier, seasonal and posted workers.

755. The country of origin may impede, restrict or control the departure of their nationals. Nevertheless emigration is a substantial source of income for poor States whose citizens abroad earn money they would be unable to get otherwise and send home some of their earnings; the authorities of the countries concerned therefore do not oppose normally the departure of their citizens. At the very most, they will try to ensure they have decent living and working conditions. When the move however

543. See D. Dutoit (ed.), *Exploited, Undervalued and Essential: Domestic Workers and the Realization of their Rights*, Pretoria University Press, 2013; M. Oeltz, 'The ILO's Domestic Workers Convention and Recommendations: A Window of Opportunity for Social Justice', *ILR*, Vol. 143 (1), 2014, pp. 143 *et seq*.

544. UN, *International Migration 2013*, New York/Geneva, 2013; ILC (103rd Session, 2014), *Fair migration: Setting an ILO agenda*, Geneva, ILO, 2014, para. 50.

concerns the most qualified graduates, it may affect the economic capacity of the State. The brain drain today does not regard only developing countries.

756. The free movement of labour is not a right, even if some international meetings have claimed it is. Receiving countries regulate immigration out of natural concern to protect their employment markets; they oblige foreigners to obtain both an authorization of residence and a work permit and do their best, insofar as possible, to prevent foreigners from working clandestinely. Their concern is shared by national workers, especially when unemployment is high. The legalization of the illegal workers permits on the contrary to collect taxes and social insurances contributions, and, more generally, to compensate for the reduction in the births and the ageing of the population.

757. Another issue is the emigrants' integration in the host country. In some cases, the host country authorities are against integration because it runs counter to their religion or the vision they have of their country. This is the case of Israel and many Arab countries. Sometimes the workers concerned hope one day to go home, once their material situation has stabilized; all they ask is to live without being harassed or discriminated against. A majority nevertheless end up melting into the societies that have taken them in. Whatever the case, the new arrivals often come to work in branches of activity – agriculture, construction, hotels and restaurants, domestic work – scorned by national workers because the jobs are precarious, difficult and poorly paid. They are therefore vulnerable workers at a time when they are already susceptible to problems because of their situation as emigrants, cut off from their families.

758. The migratory policy proposed by an international institution must strike a balance between these different, and rather contradictory, concerns. It is therefore hardly surprising that the national legislation in this field is often reworked and that international standards are the object of more or less strenuous opposition. The most recent ILO convention on the subject, Convention No. 143 of 1975, had (as at 12 June 2014) been ratified by only 23 countries, few of them (Italy, Norway, Sweden) economic heavyweights. And the United Nations Convention on the Protection of the Rights of All Migrant Workers and Members of Their Families, adopted in 1990, has only obtained on 1 July 2003 the twentieth ratification required for its entry into force.[545]

759. The first bilateral labour agreements, such as that signed by France and Italy in 1904,[546] were concluded to provide protection to foreign workers. In 1919, the Preamble to the ILO Constitution listed as one of the issues to be dealt with by the Organization, 'protection of the interests of workers when employed in countries other than their own', and one of the general principles listed in Article 427 of

545. As at 28 November 2016, it has been ratified by 49 countries.

546. S.G. Nagel and Ch. Thalamy, *Le droit international de la sécurité sociale,* Paris, PUF (Que sais-je?), 1993, pp. 8 and ff.; Valticos, *op. cit.*, paras 153 and 219.

the Treaty of Versailles[547] was that 'the standard set by law in each country with respect to the conditions of labour should have due regard to the equitable economic treatment of all workers lawfully resident therein'. Protection and the struggle against clandestine immigration were also among the core concerns of ILO's founding fathers; they are obviously interrelated.

760. The International Labour Conference subsequently adopted a series of instruments dealing specifically with foreign workers (2) or containing specific provisions on them (3). The ones on social security will not be dealt with here but in the next chapter. The ILO has also adopted, in 2006, a Multilateral Framework on Labour Migration: non-binding principles and guidelines for completing its labour standards on the matter. In 1990, the United Nations General Assembly, for its part, adopted an international convention protecting the rights of all migrant workers and the members of their families (1). Most ILO general instruments do not specifically mention foreigners; the general terms in which they are formulated mean that they can usually be construed to apply fully to such workers.

I. The International Convention on the Protection of the Rights of All Migrant Workers and Members of Their Families

761. Part I of the Convention defines its field of application: all migrant workers and members of their families without distinction of any kind and the entire migration process, comprising preparation for migration, departure and return. It defines the term 'migrant worker' ('a person who is to be engaged, is engaged or has been engaged in a remunerated activity in a State of which he or she is not a national') and mentions eight particular categories: frontier workers, seasonal workers, seafarers, workers on offshore installations, itinerant workers, self-employed workers, project-tied and specified-employment workers.

762. Article 7, the only article in Part II, contains a clause of non-discrimination in respect of the rights recognized in the Convention.

763. Part III lists the rights and freedoms to which migrant workers and their families are entitled, whether or not their situation is regular and no matter which category they belong to. Those rights and freedoms include the fundamental human rights, such as the right to adhere to a trade union and to participate in its activities (Article 26) and the right to enjoy treatment not less favourable than that which applies to nationals of the State of employment in respect of remuneration and other conditions of employment, including social security (Articles 25 and 27). Other matters discussed in Part III are, for example, the right of access of the children of migrant workers to public pre-school educational institutions or schools (Article 30, this right applies no matter what the situation of the parent, the child or both), respect for the cultural identity of migrants (Article 31) and the right to transfer back

547. *See* para. 13 *above*.

their incomes and savings to their home country when they leave the receiving country (Article 32).

764. Part IV lists the rights of migrant workers in a regular situation. They have the right to form an association or a trade union (Article 40), to enjoy equality of opportunity and treatment in respect of a good number of social and economic services (Articles 43, 45 and 48), of the protection against the dismissal and of the unemployment benefits (Article 54), and, subject to certain restrictions and conditions, freely to choose their remunerated activity (Article 52). The authors of the Convention felt that these rights could only be granted to migrants who were lawfully in the country of employment. The crucial distinction between the rights to which all migrants should be entitled (Part III) and the rights applicable only to migrants in a regular situation (Part IV) is clear when certain rights are juxtaposed. Thus, all migrants in a legal situation, and they alone, are also entitled, to transfer regularly their incomes and savings to their country of origin (Article 47) All migrants benefit from a number of rights in terms of the expulsion procedure (Part III, Article 22); migrants in a regular situation also enjoy broader security, in that they cannot usually be expelled (Part IV, Article 56). The latter provision is one of the more innovative aspects of the Convention. Previously, there were really no limits to the power of the States to expel foreigners if they respected guarantees of procedure, were equitable, compassionate, etc. Henceforth, Article 56 stipulates that a State 'may not' expel a migrant worker in a regular situation or a member of his family except for 'reasons defined in the national legislation of that State' and never 'for the purpose of depriving a migrant worker or a member of his or her family of the rights arising out of the authorization of residence and the work permit'.

765. Part V specifies which provisions of Part IV are applicable as such or in modified form to six of the eight categories of workers defined in Article 2 of the Convention. Frontier, seasonal and itinerant workers are granted rights 'by reason of their presence and work in the territory of the State of employment'. Thus, because frontier workers usually live in another State, they cannot claim equality of opportunity and treatment in terms of 'access to housing' under Article 43(d), but they can form a trade union in their country of employment (Article 40). Another generic formula applying to self-employed migrant workers specifies which rights under Part IV are applicable to them (*see* Article 63). The Convention contains an exhaustive list of the articles applicable in whole or in part to project-tied and specified-employment workers (posted workers). Two of the categories of workers the Convention is intended to protect, namely foreign seafarers and workers on offshore installations, are not among those whose rights are specified in Part V. In view of the objections raised by several countries employing seafarers, it was decided: (a) that the Convention would not apply to foreign non-resident seafarers and workers on offshore installations (*see* Article 3(f)), and (b) that Part V should contain no articles on foreign seafarers and workers on offshore installations admitted to take up residence in the State in which the vessel was registered or under whose jurisdiction the installation was run.

766. Part VI focuses on the measures the States parties must take to promote sound, equitable, humane and lawful conditions of international migration. The main idea underpinning this part of the Convention is not to promote migration but rather to fight illegal movements and illegal employment of foreigners, to make sure than any migration is lawful under the terms of the Convention. The Preamble already refers to the matter (paragraphs 13, 14 and 15); the clause of non-discrimination also applies to migrants in an irregular situation (Article 7); the rights to liberty and security of person, to equality with nationals of the State concerned before the courts and tribunals, to protection from unauthorized confiscation of documents, to equality of treatment in working and other employment conditions, and in respect of social security (Articles 16, 18, 21, 25 and 27) were worded in such a way as to render the presence and work of those in an irregular situation unattractive from the economic and administrative points of view, as opposed to workers in a regular situation (see also Article 70). According to Article 25(2), it is not 'lawful to derogate in private contracts of employment from the principle of equality of treatment'. In Part VI, three provisions are aimed at strengthening the fight against illegal migration and employment (*see* Articles 67(1), 68 and 69).

767. Since this is a United Nations treaty, the ILO's supervisory procedures do not apply. Part VII therefore indicates the steps to be taken to supervise application and the procedure to follow in the event of grievances, which are basically the purview of a special committee established by virtue of Article 72.

768. Part VIII contains general provisions on rules more favourable to the migrants, the prohibition on renouncing rights, the possibility to exercise an effective remedy and the follow-up measures to be taken. It also contains a compatibility clause covering ILO.

II. ILO Instruments on Migrant Workers

769. It is within this general framework that ILO standards on migrant workers must be considered. The reference instruments are Convention No. 97 and Recommendation No. 86, adopted in 1949 and supplemented by Convention No. 143 and Recommendation No. 151 in 1975, and Recommendation No. 100, 1955, for developing countries. Three other instruments will be examined in the chapter on social security: Convention No. 118 of 1962 on equality of treatment of nationals and non-nationals in social security, and Convention No. 157 and Recommendation No. 167 of 1982 concerning the establishment of an international system for the maintenance of rights in social security.

770. The provisions analysed here deal with the conditions of access to foreign employment markets, the protection of the migrant workers who have entered and are lawfully employed in the host countries (equality (a) of opportunity and treatment; (b) of working conditions) and their integration into the society of the country to which they emigrated. We shall start by looking at the field of application of the relevant instruments.

A. Field of Application

771. All these instruments apply to migration for the purposes of employment, a term which, in its present-day acceptation, does not cover self-employed workers who are thereby excluded.[548] Convention No. 97 and Recommendation No. 86 state this expressly; they also exclude frontier workers, seafarers and short-term entry of 'members of the liberal professions and artistes'. Part II of Convention No. 143, on equality of opportunity and treatment,[549] contains an identical provision; it also excludes all persons coming specifically for purposes of training or education and those who have been admitted temporarily to the country at the request of their employer to undertake specific duties or assignments.

B. Conditions of Access to Foreign Employment Markets

772. The States ratifying Convention No. 143 undertake to suppress clandestine migration and illegal employment of migrants. To that end, they must cooperate with other Member States and take the necessary measures for that purpose. Article 8 adds, however, that migrant workers residing legally in a country cannot be regarded as being in an irregular situation by the mere fact of the loss of their employment.[550] On the contrary, they must enjoy equality of treatment with nationals in respect of guarantees of security of employment and of alternative employment, relief work and retraining. A wage earner who is subject to an expulsion order must have a right of appeal during which the order is suspended (subject to duly justified reasons of public order or national security). He should enjoy, whether his stay has been regular or not, rights arising out of past employment as regards remuneration, social security and other benefits.[551]

773. Convention No. 97, for its part, calls for the Member States to exchange information with each other and with ILO and for cooperation between employment services. The States should have a free service to assist migrant workers, in particular to provide them with accurate information (Article 3 requires them to combat misleading propaganda). The Convention further suggests that measures be taken as appropriate to facilitate the departure, journey and reception of migrants for employment and to offer them appropriate medical assistance. Two of the annexes to the Convention deal with the recruitment of migrant workers under government-sponsored arrangements for group transfers or otherwise. The third annex deals with the importation of migrants' personal effects, tools and equipment.

---

548. ILC (87th session, 1999), *Migrant Workers*, Report III (Part 1B), Geneva, 1999, para. 110.
549. The first part of the Convention deals with migrations in abusive conditions; it applies to all migrant workers illegally 'employed' within the country.
550. *See also* Article 8 of Convention No. 97 (illness contracted or injury sustained subsequent to entry), para. 18 of Recommendation No. 86 and para. 30 *et seq.* of Recommendation No. 151.
551. *See* Article 9 of Convention No. 143 and paras 8 and 34 of Recommendation No. 151.

774. Recommendation No. 86 contains other suggestions in this respect for the stated purpose of facilitating 'the international distribution of manpower and in particular the movement of manpower from countries which have a surplus of manpower to those countries that have a deficiency'.[552] The measures proposed include advice for migrants in a language they understand, facilities in completing administrative formalities, preparatory courses, help with housing, access to schools and vocational training, facilities for transferring funds, medical assistance, etc.[553]

775. The Recommendation goes on to say that any intermediary who recruits migrant workers must obtain a written warrant from the employer. In addition, if the migrant workers or the members of their families return to their country of origin, that country should admit them to the benefit of the assistance measures for nationals and the unemployed without a waiting period.

776. More generally, the Recommendation suggests that bilateral agreements be concluded on the temporary and permanent migration of workers, including refugees and displaced persons, and proposes a model agreement in an annex.[554]

777. Recommendation No. 100 contains further suggestions for the protection of migrant workers from developing countries and the members of their families during their journeys out and in and prior to the period of employment (means of transportation, rest camps, cost of the trip, medical follow-up, etc.). It suggests means of discouraging migratory flows that are undesirable; measures to be taken already include economic development and vocational training programmes.[555]

C. Equality of Protection

778. The Recommendation also contains detailed standards on guarantees during the employment period, in particular the determination of wages, access to skilled jobs, occupational health and safety, social security and trade union activities.

779. Convention No. 97 establishes that lawful immigrants must receive, without discrimination in respect of nationality, race, religion or sex, treatment no less favourable than that applied to nationals in respect of the following matters:

(a) in so far as such matters are regulated by law or regulations, or are subject to the control of administrative authorities –
   (i) remuneration, including family allowances where these form part of remuneration, hours of work, overtime arrangements, holidays with pay, restrictions on home work, minimum age for employment, apprenticeship and training, women's work and the work of young persons;

552. Para. 4; *see also* para. 14.
553. *See also* para. 54 of Recommendation No. 100.
554. *See also* Article 10 of the Convention.
555. Paras 16–19.

(ii) membership of trade unions and enjoyment of the benefits of collective bargaining;
(iii) accommodation;

(b) social security (that is to say, legal provision in respect of employment injury, maternity, sickness, invalidity, old age, death, unemployment and family responsibilities, and any other contingency which, according to national laws or regulations, is covered by a social security scheme), subject to the following limitations:
(i) there may be appropriate arrangements for the maintenance of acquired rights and rights in course of acquisition;
(ii) national laws or regulations of immigration countries may prescribe special arrangements concerning benefits or portions of benefits which are payable wholly out of public funds, and concerning allowances paid to persons who do not fulfil the contribution conditions prescribed for the award of a normal pension;

(c) employment taxes, dues or contributions payable in respect of the person employed; and

(d) legal proceedings relating to the matters referred to in this Convention.[556]

Many migrants face multiple discrimination, as nationality often intersects with other grounds and it may be difficult to determine whether discriminatory treatment faced by migrant workers is exclusively based on their nationality, or on racial, ethnic, religious or other grounds.[557]

780. Recommendation No. 86 stipulates that migrants and the members of their families authorized to accompany them should be admitted to employment in the same conditions as nationals; their conditions of employment should be specially supervised. Convention No. 143 goes further; it obliges the States to declare and pursue a national policy of equality of opportunity and treatment for migrants and their families who are lawfully within their territory in respect of employment,[558] social security, trade union and cultural rights and individual and collective freedoms. Article 12 lists various means of ensuring application of this principle, in particular the need to associate employers' and workers' organizations in those efforts.

781. Recommendation No. 151 is more specific about the areas in which there must be effective equality:[559]

> (a) access to vocational guidance and placement services; (b) access to vocational training and employment of their own choice on the basis of individual suitability for such training or employment, account being taken of

---

556. Article 6.
557. See International Labour Conference (101st Session, 2012), *Giving Globalization a Human Face*, *op. cit.*, §821.
558. Under the conditions of Article 14.
559. Para. 2; *see also* para. 20 of Recommendation No. 100.

qualifications acquired outside the territory of and in the country of employment; (c) advancement in accordance with their individual character, experience, ability and diligence; (d) security of employment, the provision of alternative employment, relief work and retraining; (e) remuneration for work of equal value; (f) conditions of work, including hours of work, rest periods, annual holidays with pay, occupational safety and occupational health measures, as well as social security measures and welfare facilities and benefits provided in connection with employment; (g) membership of trade unions, exercise of trade union rights and eligibility for office in trade unions and in labour-management relations bodies, including bodies representing workers in undertakings; (h) rights of full membership in any form of cooperative; (i) conditions of life, including housing and the benefits of social services and educational and health facilities.

Paragraph 3 *et seq.* list the measures to be taken to give effect to this provision. They include providing information on rights (if possible in a language the migrants understand) and the possibility to learn the host country's language.

782. It remains that migrant workers are often engaged in the most precarious forms of work and in hazardous jobs. The danger of abuses are therefore more present, as illustrated in Günter Wallraff's famous book *Lowest of the Low*.[560] The risks of work accidents and professional diseases are generally higher, while the wages stay at the minimum.

D. Policy of Integration and Respect for Identity

783. Here more than anywhere else, it is both important and difficult to strike a balance between the elimination of various kinds of discrimination and respect for the right to be different. Let the reader judge for himself.

784. Article 12(f) of Convention No. 143 asks the States to take all steps to encourage the efforts of migrant workers and their families to preserve their national and ethnic identity and their ties with their country of origin; it specifically mentions the possibility for children to receive instruction in their mother tongue. Recommendation No. 100 mentions facilities for the remittance of funds, the exchange of correspondence and the performance of customary obligations the migrant worker wishes to observe.[561]

785. By the same token, the States ratifying Convention No. 97[562] undertake to permit the transfer of all or part of the earnings and savings of the migrants for employment to their country of origin. Where a migrant worker who has been employed for at least one year in a country of employment cannot be joined by his

560. Methuen, London, 1988.
561. Para. 48.
562. Article 9.

family in that country, he should be entitled to visit the country of residence of his family without losing any rights or to be visited by his family for a period corresponding at least to the annual holiday with pay to which he is entitled.[563]

786. Several provisions of Recommendation No. 100 deal with the right of migrant workers, and where applicable of the members of their families, to return home at the recruiter's or employer's expense in the event of a death, if they become incapacitated for work or if their work contract expires.[564]

787. The Recommendation nevertheless immediately[565] goes on to say that migrant workers should be free to waive the right to repatriation or to postpone it for a determined period. As we know,[566] ILO standards also provide migrant workers with protection against automatic expulsion if they lose their job. Recommendation No. 151 provides that a migrant who has lost his job should be allowed sufficient time to find alternative employment, at least for a period corresponding to that during which he may be entitled to unemployment benefit; if he has lodged an appeal against the termination of his employment, he should be allowed sufficient time to obtain a final decision and, if he wins his case, he should benefit, on the same terms as national workers, to reinstatement, compensation and access to a new job.[567]

788. There are many other rules aimed at facilitating the integration of foreigners who have worked lawfully in the host country.

789. The first concern family reunification. Convention No. 143 and Recommendation No. 86 require the States to allow the spouse and dependent children and parents to come and live with the migrant workers.[568] Measures must be taken to enable the worker to obtain adequate housing.[569]

790. More generally, Recommendation No. 100 advises the States in principle to seek the stabilization of the workers and their families in or near the employment centres. Where such action is not contrary to their policy, they should afford migrant workers who have been resident for a period of not less than five years all opportunities of acquiring citizenship of the country of immigration.[570]

791. From another point of view, Recommendation No. 151 asks that account be taken of the special needs of migrant workers until they are adapted to the society of the country of employment. The policy to that end should be based, in particular, on an examination not only of conditions in the host country but also of those in the

563. Recommendation No. 151, para. 17.
564. Paras 10 to 12.
565. Para. 13.
566. *See* para. 772 *above*.
567. Para. 31 and 32.
568. Article 13 of Convention No. 143 and para. 15 of Recommendation No. 86.
569. Paras 13 and 16 of Recommendation No. 151; 21 and 22 of Recommendation No. 100.
570. Paras 50 to 52.

countries of origin.[571] The measures cited include the protection of health (with special understandable instructions and training for that purpose) and the assistance of social services.

792. Recommendation No. 86[572] adds that it is advisable to provide migrants and the members of their families with assistance in obtaining access to recreation and welfare facilities, including through special facilities made available during the initial period of settlement. Recommendation No. 100 also considers the material, intellectual and moral welfare of migrants;[573] it contains provisions on thrift and protection from usury.

III. The Provisions on Migrant Workers in ILO General Instruments

793. A number of these instruments deal with social security, an area in which it is vital but complex to integrate foreigners.[574] Others regard health and security at work: Recommendation No. 197 asks States to provide appropriate measures for the protection of all workers, but in particular, the ones vulnerable or in high-risk sectors, such as migrants.[575] HIV and AIDS Recommendation No. 200 mentions specifically migrant workers when it states that testing programmes must respect international guidelines on confidentiality, counselling and consent; the results should not endanger access to jobs, tenure, job security or opportunities for advancement. Training, safety instructions and any necessary guidance in the workplace should be provided in a clear and accessible form. Countries of origin, of transit and of destination should ensure access to HIV prevention, treatment, care and support services; the countries concerned should conclude agreements, whenever appropriate.[576]

794. As already mentioned,[577] Employment Relationship Recommendation No. 198 asks States to ensure effective protection to workers especially affected by the uncertainty as to the existence of an employment relationship, including migrant workers, and to prevent abuses.[578]

795. The Human Resources Development Recommendation No. 195 insists on the special needs of workers such as migrants; provisions should ensure recognition and certification of their skills and qualifications. [579]

796. We have also mentioned, in the previous paragraph, the provisions of Convention No.189 and Recommendation No. 201 that refer to domestic migrant

571. Paras 9 and 10; *see also* the two following paragraphs.
572. Para. 11.
573. Para. 49; *see also* para. 12.
574. *See* the next chapter.
575. Para. 3.
576. Paras 24–28, 40 and 47.
577. *See* paras 727–731 *above*.
578. Paras 5 and 7.
579. Paras 5 and 12.

workers that, more than others, may be abused.[580] In another field, Convention No. 110 on plantations (1958) states that it applies to all workers without distinction of nationality;[581] that specification may be legally superfluous, but not from the social policy point of view when one considers the problems encountered by migrants in that sector.

§11. Special Categories of Workers

797. Our examination of the different fields of international labour law reveals that some instruments deal specifically with groups of workers such as rural workers, miners or public servants. We shall not return to them. However, we shall consider the standards adopted in respect of special categories because of their personal condition[582] (women, elderly workers), or the specific nature of their profession (seafarers, dockworkers and fishermen, plantation workers, nursing staff, hotel and restaurant workers). ILO has also drawn up instruments for the protection of aboriginal and tribal people; those instruments are considered in Section III.

I. Specific Standards Owing to Personal Conditions

A. *Women Workers*

798. Most ILO conventions and recommendations apply to women and men without distinction. Women and men workers are also covered, in principle, by the standards adopted on general employment conditions (wages, working hours, safety and health), social security, employment, industrial relations and fundamental human rights. Besides these generally applicable rules, the Organization has also adopted others that deal specifically with the work of women.

799. We have mentioned[583] the two concerns that the founders of ILO included in the Preamble to the Constitution: special protection in certain cases and the guarantee of true equality. This dual concern is also to be found in the International Covenant on Economic, Social and Cultural Rights: Article 7 requires that women be guaranteed conditions of work not inferior to those enjoyed by men, and Article 10 calls for special protection for mothers 'during a reasonable period before and after childbirth'; during that time, working mothers should be accorded 'paid leave or leave with adequate social security benefits'.

800. The standards promoting equality of opportunity and treatment have already been dealt with.[584] They concern chiefly equal pay for work of equal value

580. Articles 8 and 15 of the Convention; paragraphs 20–23 and 26 of the Recommendation.
581. Article 2.
582. On youth employment: *see* §§347 *et seq.*
583. *See* para. 418 *above*.
584. *Ibid.*

and the reconciliation of work-related and family responsibilities. We have also seen[585] that the new standards on night work apply equally to workers of both sexes. In this section we shall examine specific rules of protection for women.

801. A first group of rules accords guarantees to pregnant workers and new mothers. A second concerns women workers in general.

802. Convention No. 183 and Recommendation No. 191, adopted in 2000, are the main instruments in the first group, although they are supplemented by others on certain points. Convention No. 183 applies to all employed women, including those 'in atypical forms of dependent work'.[586]

803. The Convention provides that pregnant and breastfeeding women may not be obliged to perform work which is dangerous or prejudicial to the health of the mother or the child. The Recommendation cites in particular:

(a) arduous work involving the manual lifting, carrying, pushing or pulling of loads;
(b) work involving exposure to biological, chemical or physical agents which represent a reproductive health hazard;
(c) work requiring special equilibrium;
(d) work involving physical strain due to prolonged periods of sitting or standing, to extreme temperatures, or to vibration.[587]

It further states that pregnant or nursing women should not be obliged to do night work if a medical certificate declares such work to be incompatible with pregnancy or nursing.[588]

804. Some ILO standards prohibit pregnant women and new mothers from doing certain jobs and limit the exercise thereof. This is the case for plantations,[589] benzene,[590] chemical products[591] and the nursing profession.[592]

---

585. *See* para. 584 *above*.
586. *See also* the Part-Time Work Convention, 1994 (No. 175), Article 7; the Home Work Convention, 1996 (No. 177), Article 4, para. 2 and the complementary Recommendation (No. 184), para. 26; the Private Employment Agencies Convention, 1997 (No. 181), Article 11 (which also deals with parental protection and benefits).
587. Para. 6(3).
588. Para. 6(4). A similar provision can be found in the Protocol of 1990 to the Night Work (Women) Convention (Revised), 1948 (No. 89). The Protocol lifts all the normally authorized variations and exemptions during a period before and after childbirth of at least 16 weeks. *See also* the Night Work Convention, 1990 (No. 171), Article 7.
589. Article 47, para. 8 of the Plantations Convention, 1958 (No. 110).
590. Article 11 of the Benzene Convention, 1971 (No. 136) and para. 19 of the complementary Recommendation (No. 144).
591. Para. 25(4) of the Chemicals Recommendation, 1990 (No. 177).
592. *See* the Nursing Personnel Recommendation, 1977 (No. 157), para. 50 (the provision refers to pregnant women and *parents* of young children, broadening so the scope of protection) and Annex, para. 26.

805. Women should retain the right to return to their jobs (or equivalent jobs) as soon as it is safe for them to do so; they should be allowed to leave the workplace, after notifying the employer, for the purpose of undergoing medical examinations relating to the pregnancy.[593]

806. Recommendation No. 116 of 1962 on the reduction of hours of work provides that in arranging overtime, due consideration should be given to the special circumstances of pregnant women and nursing mothers. More specifically, Convention No. 183 provides women workers with the right to one or more daily breaks or a daily reduction of hours of work to breastfeed their children; the breaks or the reduction must be counted as working time and remunerated accordingly.[594] Recommendation No. 191[595] suggests that provision should be made for the establishment of facilities for nursing under adequate hygienic conditions at or near the workplace.

807. On production of a medical certificate or other appropriate certification, a woman worker is entitled to a period of maternity leave of not less than 14 weeks; that period must include a period of six weeks' compulsory leave after childbirth; the prenatal portion of maternity leave is extended, if necessary, until the actual date of childbirth, without reduction in any compulsory portion of postnatal leave. Recommendation No. 191 extends the maternity leave granted under Convention No. 183 to a minimum of 18 weeks, extends the maternity leave in the event of multiple births, and allows the woman to choose the time at which any non-compulsory portion of maternity leave is taken.[596] Additional leave must be granted in the case of illness, complications or risk of complications.[597] The Recommendation also provides for paternity or parental leave in the following instances:

(a) in the case of the death of the mother before the expiry of postnatal leave, the employed father should be entitled to take leave of a duration equal to the remaining period;
(b) in the case of sickness or hospitalization of the mother after childbirth and before the expiry of postnatal leave, and where the mother cannot look after the child, the employed father should be entitled to leave of an equal duration;
(c) the employed mother or the employed father should be entitled to parental leave following the expiry of maternity leave.

808. Women on maternity or sickness leave are entitled to receive cash benefits at a level ensuring that they can maintain themselves and their children 'in proper conditions of health and with a suitable standard of living'.[598] Where the cash benefits are based on previous earnings, they must not be less than two-thirds of the

593. Recommendation No. 191, para. 6(5 and 6).
594. *See also* Recommendation No. 191, paras 7 and 8.
595. *See also* the Safety and Health in Agriculture Recommendation, 2001 (No. 192), para. 10(c).
596. *See also* the Article 11 of the Convention.
597. Article 5 of the Convention.
598. Article 6 of Convention No. 183; *see also* Article 11.

previous earnings; where other methods are used to determine the cash benefits, their amount must be comparable.[599] The States must ensure that the conditions to qualify for cash benefits can be satisfied by a large majority of women workers; women who do not meet those conditions must be entitled to benefits out of social assistance funds, subject to the means test required for such assistance. A State whose economy and social security system are insufficiently developed can provide cash benefits at a rate no lower than a rate payable for sickness or temporary disability in accordance with national laws and regulations.

809. The woman and her child must receive medical benefits that include prenatal, childbirth and postnatal care, as well as hospitalization care when necessary.[600]

810. The cash benefits must in principle be provided through compulsory social insurance or public funds; the employer must not be individually liable for the direct cost of any such benefits, except in certain cases.[601] Any contribution and tax raised for the purpose of providing such benefits, whether paid by both the employer and the employees or by the employer, should be paid in respect of the total number of men and women employed.[602]

811. Women are guaranteed the right to return to the same position or an equivalent position paid at the same rate at the end of maternity leave.[603] The Convention stipulates that it is unlawful to terminate the employment of a woman during her pregnancy or absence or during a period following her return to work to be prescribed by national laws or regulations, except on grounds unrelated to the pregnancy or birth of the child and its consequences or nursing; the burden of proof consequently rests on the employer.

812. The Member States must adopt appropriate measures to ensure that maternity does not constitute a source of discrimination. The Convention lists measures the States can take to that effect, including the prohibition to require a test for pregnancy or a certificate of such a test, except in respect of work that is prohibited or restricted for pregnant or nursing women or where there is a 'recognized or significant' risk to the health of the woman and child.[604] The Recommendation further requires that the period of leave be considered as a period of service for the determination of rights.

599. The Recommendation raises the cash benefits to the full amount of the women's previous earnings.
600. According to para. 3 of Recommendation No. 191, the medical benefits should include: 'a) care given in a doctor's office, at home or in a hospital or other medical establishment by a general practitioner or a specialist; b) maternity care given by a qualified midwife or by another maternity service at home or in a hospital or other medical establishment; c) maintenance in a hospital or other medical establishment; d) any necessary pharmaceutical and medical supplies, examinations and tests prescribed by a medical practitioner or other qualified person; and e) dental and surgical care.'
601. Article 6 of Convention No. 183.
602. Para. 4 of Recommendation No. 191.
603. Article 5 of Convention No. 183.
604. Article 9.

813. Where national law and practice provide for adoption, adoptive parents should have access to the same protection, especially regarding leave, benefits and employment protection.[605]

814. The second group of standards provides additional guarantees to women workers no matter what their status. These provisions are regarded with greater reluctance in many countries and in their case-law because they are not physiological in origin.

815. ILO has not deemed it necessary to adopt a convention or a recommendation on sexual harassment. Only the Indigenous and Tribal People Convention (No. 169) [606] provides that workers belonging to these peoples should enjoy equal opportunities and equal treatment in employment for men and women, and protection from sexual harassment. The CEACR has addressed sexual harassment as a prohibited form of sex discrimination under the Discrimination (Employment and Occupation) Convention (No. C111).[607] Harassment may be indeed, like the refusal to recruit or to promote, a discriminatory conduct if it based on a gender reason. It should be clear however that it is an unacceptable attitude in all cases whatever the reason is and it may affect the mental or the physical health of the victim in the meaning of Occupational Safety and Health Convention No 155.

816. This second group includes standards that restrict the exercise of certain activities or prohibit them outright. Again, this is the case of night work in industry, as stipulated in Convention No. 89 of 1948 and the 1990 Protocol modifying it; the matter has already been examined.[608] It is also the case for the prohibition or restriction of certain tasks, in some cases to protect the reproductive function of women: jobs that can result in lead poisoning,[609] the use of white lead in industrial painting,[610] underground work in mines,[611] manual transport of loads,[612] agricultural work,[613] or work with radiation.[614]

817. Recommendation No. 116 of 1962 states that in carrying out measures for progressively reducing hours of work, priority should be given to industries and occupations which involve a particularly heavy physical or mental strain or health risks for the workers concerned, particularly where these consist mainly of women (and young persons).

605. Para. 10, subpara. 5 of Recommendation No. 191.
606. Article 20, 3(d).
607. ILC (101st Session, 2012), *Giving Globalization a Human Face*, Report III (Part 1B), Geneva, ILO, 2012, paras. 789–794.
608. *See* para. 581 *et seq. above.*
609. The Lead Poisoning (Women and Children) Recommendation, 1919 (No. 4).
610. The White Lead (Painting) Convention, 1921 (No. 13).
611. The Underground Work (Women) Convention, 1935 (No. 45).
612. Th Maximum Weight Convention (No. 127) and Recommendation (No. 128), 1967.
613. The Safety and Health in Agriculture Convention (No. 184) and Recommendation (No. 192), 2001.
614. The Radiation Protection Recommendation, 1960 (No. 114), para. 16; *see also* the ILO Code of practice, adopted in 1987, para. 23(13).

818. Recommendation No. 102 of 1956 on welfare facilities requires that seats and rest rooms be made available in particular to women workers in undertakings. Recommendations Nos. 183 on mines and 192 on agriculture stipulate that the employers must maintain in good condition sanitary and changing facilities which are gender-specific. Convention No. 81, of 1947, states that inspection staff must include both men and women, as special duties may be assigned to men and women inspectors where necessary.

B. Older Workers

819. The problem of protection versus equality is relevant to older workers, as it is every time a given group receives extra guarantees. The context varies, however. In this case, the issue is the time and above all the terms of the transition from a working life to retirement. This is the subject of Recommendation No. 162 of 1980 on older workers, which is analysed below. ILO instruments on old-age pensions are examined in the following chapter, on social security.

820. Should there be a mandatory retirement age? As life expectations are longer today, the experts consider[615] that social expenditure could be sharply cut by prolonging the wage earner's working life and that the working capacity of many older people is largely sufficient and gives the undertaking employing them an advantage. Indeed, Recommendation No. 162 states that, wherever possible, retirement should be voluntary and take place in a framework allowing for a gradual transition from working life to freedom of activity; the qualifying age for an old-age pension should therefore be flexible and the legislative and other provisions making the termination of employment at a specified age mandatory should be reviewed. The argument of equality of opportunity and treatment is also invoked here.

821. Older workers who are fit for work should be able to defer their claim to an old-age benefit beyond the normal age, for example for the purpose of satisfying the qualifying conditions for benefit or with a view to receiving a higher benefit. Alternatively, older workers who have been unemployed for a long time, are recognized as being unfit for work or have been engaged in occupations that are deemed arduous or unhealthy should have the possibility of early retirement.[616] The Recommendation also suggests that retirement preparation programmes be implemented that provide the people concerned with information on benefits for the elderly, the opportunities for continuing an occupational activity, measures to attenuate the ageing process, how to use leisure time and adult education facilities.[617]

---

615. OECD, *Ageing and Employment Policies/Vieillissement et politiques de l'emploi. Live Longer, Work Longer*, Paris, 2006. See also F. Hendricks (ed.), *Active Ageing and Labour Law. Contributions in Honour of Roger Blanpain,* Cambridge, Intersentia, 2012.

616. Recommendation No. 162, para.. 25.

617. Para. 30.

822. The Recommendation, which applies both to occupations and to employment, and therefore also to self-employed workers,[618] considers that the problems it addresses should be dealt with in the context of an overall and well-balanced strategy for full employment, due attention being given to all population groups.[619]

823. It is therefore within the framework of its general policy to promote equality of opportunity and treatment that a Member State must take measures to prevent any discrimination in employment and occupation in respect of older persons. It should associate employers' and workers' organizations in the preparation, promotion and application of such programmes. The areas targeted by the Recommendation include access to employment, vocational training and guidance, placement services, fair distribution of tasks and promotions, job security, remuneration for work of equal value, working conditions, social security, and access to social services, housing and health institutions.[620] The workers concerned and their organizations, as well as the employers and their associations, should have access to the bodies in charge of considering grievances in this respect.

824. Do older workers cost the undertaking more? Do they produce less or less well? Do they really create an opening for young people if they leave their jobs? Recent studies show that nothing could be less sure, that the heterogeneity of the group means that there is no single answer to these overly simplistic questions, that many older workers have invaluable experience and know-how.[621] Of course, if a flexible policy is adopted on retirement age, the risks to health of the job and the employment conditions that accelerate the aging process need to be identified and eliminated.

825. The Recommendation therefore suggests that studies be undertaken to identify the types of activity likely to hasten the ageing process or in which older workers encounter difficulties in adapting to the demands of their work, to determine the reasons, and to devise appropriate solutions. It proposes measures to remedy those conditions of work that are likely to hasten the ageing process:[622]

- modify the forms of work organization and working time which lead to stress or to an excessive pace of work, in particular by limiting overtime;
- adapt the job to the worker by recourse to all available technical means and, in particular, to ergonomic principles;
- provide for more systematic supervision of the workers' state of health;
- provide for on-site supervision appropriate for preserving the workers' safety and health.

618. Para. 1.
619. Para. 2.
620. For further details, *see* para. 5.
621. OECD, *op. cit.*
622. Paras 13 and 14.

826. Measures can be taken to apply to older workers systems of remuneration adapted to their needs and to make available other employment opportunities in their own or in another occupation in which they can make use of their talents and experience.[623]

827. The Recommendation ends by emphasizing the importance of proper information for older workers, those in charge of employment and vocational training and the public in general.[624]

II. Specific Occupation-related Standards

A. Hotel and Restaurant Workers

828. The goal of Convention No. 172 of 1991 is to improve working conditions in a notoriously painful sector in order to bring hotels, restaurants and similar establishments in line, as supplementary Recommendation No. 179 specifies, with those in other fields of activity. In particular, workers in this rapidly growing branch must not be excluded from any of the minimum rules adopted by the States in favour of workers in general, including those relating to social security.

829. The Convention focuses on three issues: hours of work, remuneration and access to employment; the Recommendation also considers training. The Convention stipulates that the normal hours of work – i.e. in principle the periods during which the workers are at the disposal of the employer – and the overtime provisions be 'reasonable'; the same applies to daily and weekly rest periods. The Recommendation is more explicit: working hours and overtime work must be properly calculated and recorded (and each worker have access to his or her record); overtime work should be compensated by time off with pay or by a higher rate of remuneration; split shifts should be progressively eliminated; the number and length of meal breaks should be determined in the light of the customs and traditions of each country or area and according to whether the meal is taken in the establishment itself or elsewhere; the average daily rest period should be 10 consecutive hours and the weekly rest not less than 36 uninterrupted hours. According to the Convention, the workers should, whenever possible, have sufficient advance notice of working schedules to enable them to organize their personal and family life accordingly.

830. The work is also humanized in terms of public holidays and annual holidays with pay: the former must be compensated in time or remuneration, the latter are to be determined by collective bargaining or in accordance with national law or practice. If the period of service is not sufficient to qualify them for full annual leave, the workers concerned are entitled to paid leave proportionate to the length of service or payment of wages in lieu. The Recommendation states that annual paid leave is to be brought progressively to a level of four weeks.

623. Paras 16, 17 and 18.
624. Paras 32 and 33.

831. Regardless of tips, the workers concerned must receive a basic remuneration that is paid at regular intervals. This provision runs counter to the well-known practice whereby the workers' sole wages are whatever sums they are given voluntarily by a customer, in addition to the amount paid for the services received. Sometimes, the worker has to pay to obtain the job; this is another practice prohibited by the Convention.[625]

832. The Recommendation ends by suggesting the establishment, in consultation with the employers' and workers' organizations concerned, of policies and programmes of vocational education and training and of management development. The objectives should be to improve skills and the quality of job performance and to enhance the career prospects of the participants.

B. Nursing Personnel

833. The same concerns about hours of work, remuneration, access to employment and training are reflected in Convention No. 149 and Recommendation No. 157 of 1977 on nursing personnel. The Recommendation, however, contains more detailed provisions on participation, health protection and social security. Here, too, at a more basic level, the dual concern is to promote quality of care and services ('for attaining the highest possible level of health for the population') and the career prospects of nurses by guaranteeing conditions of employment 'likely to attract persons to the profession and retain them in it'.[626]

834. Nursing personnel must enjoy conditions at least equivalent to those of other workers in the country concerned in terms of: (a) hours of work (including regulation and compensation of overtime, 'inconvenient hours' and shift work); (b) weekly rest; (c) paid annual holidays; (d) educational leave; (e) maternity leave; (f) sick leave; (g) social security.[627] The Recommendation contains detailed provisions on hours of work, rest periods and social security. In addition, each State must, if necessary, endeavour to improve existing laws and regulations on occupational health and safety by adapting them to the special nature of nursing work.[628]

835. More generally speaking, the conditions of employment and work are to be determined preferably by negotiation between employers' and workers' organizations, and in the event of a dispute through independent and impartial machinery such as mediation, conciliation and voluntary arbitration. In addition, the participation of nursing personnel in the planning of nursing services and consultation with them on decisions concerning them is strongly encouraged.[629]

---

625. *See* Articles 6 and 7.
626. Article 2 of the Convention; *see also* para. 4 of the Recommendation.
627. Article 6.
628. Article 7 of the Convention; paras 44 *et seq.* of the Recommendation.
629. Article 5 of the Convention; paras 19 and 20 of the Recommendation.

836. The Recommendation deals in depth with career development and remuneration; it considers the possibility of temporary and part-time employment.[630]

837. Both the Convention and the Recommendation discuss the basic requirements of education and training and their supervision. The Convention stipulates that education and training are to be coordinated with the education and training of other workers in the field of health. It states that national laws or regulations must specify the requirements for the practice of nursing.[631] The Recommendation contains a number of supplementary standards on education and training, on students learning the profession, on the practice of the profession and on the classification of personnel (professional nurses, auxiliary nurses and nursing aids) and on international coordination in this respect.

838. The Recommendation comprises an annex with suggestions for practical application.

C. Plantation Workers

839. Certain manual tasks have drawn ILO's attention because of their arduous nature. Such is the case of work on plantations.

840. Several ILO instruments that deal more generally with agricultural workers were examined in the sections on freedom of association,[632] labour inspection,[633] occupational health and safety[634] and independent work;[635] their aim was either to extend the protection granted in industry to that particular sector or to arrange general standards or deal with the problems specific to such workers.

841. The standards adopted with regard to plantations – Convention No. 110 and Recommendation No. 110 of 1958, and a protocol to the Convention in 1982 – are different in that they cover a vast array of aspects of labour and social security law. The Convention is divided into the following parts:

- the engagement and recruitment of migrant workers;
- contracts of employment and the abolition of penal sanctions;
- wages;
- annual holidays with pay;
- weekly rest;
- maternity protection;
- workmen's compensation;

630. On the nursing personnel who gives services on a voluntary basis, *see* para. 3 of the Recommendation.
631. Articles 3 and 4.
632. The Rural Workers' Organizations Convention (No. 141) and Recommendation (No. 149), 1975.
633. The Labour Inspection (Agriculture) Convention (No. 129) and Recommendation (No. 133), 1969.
634. The Safety and Health in Agriculture Convention (No. 184) and Recommendation (No. 192), 2001.
635. The Tenants and Share-croppers Recommendation, 1968 (No. 132).

- the right to organize and collective bargaining;
- freedom of association;
- labour inspection;
- housing;
- medical care.

The ratifying State can opt to be bound by only five of the twelve parts, three of which are specified (those relating to wages, the right to organize and collective bargaining and labour inspection). The Protocol allows for the exclusion of undertakings the area of which covers not more than 5 hectares and which employ not more than ten workers.

842. The Recommendation considers questions of wages, workmen's compensation and labour inspection in greater detail. It contains several paragraphs on equal pay, accident prevention, social security and compensation for occupational diseases. It also considers hours of work and overtime, social services and vocational training.

D. Dockworkers

843. Handling cargo in docks presents obvious risks that are considered in Convention No. 152 and Recommendation No. 160 of 1979, which were discussed in the section on occupational health and safety. An earlier convention, No. 27 of 1929, requires that the weight be indicated on large parcels transported by ship.

844. More generally speaking, Convention No. 137 and Recommendation No. 145 of 1973 deal with the social repercussions of new methods of cargo handling in docks. The Convention applies to persons who are regularly available for work as dockworkers and who depend on their work as such for their main annual income. It outlines a policy for the sector. The Recommendation considers the subjects dealt with in greater depth and adds others.[636]

845. The policy has two main aspects.[637] First, national policy should be to encourage all concerned to provide permanent or regular employment for dockworkers; in any case, dockworkers are to be assured minimum periods of employment or a minimum income. Registers are to be established and maintained; registered dockworkers are to be available for work and are to have priority of engagement. The strength of the registers is to be periodically reviewed, so as to achieve levels adapted to the needs of the port; any necessary reduction in the strength of a register must be accompanied by measures designed to prevent or minimize detrimental effects on dockworkers.

---

636. On both instruments, *see* ILC (90th session, 2002), *Dock Work*, Report III (Part 1B) (Geneva), ILO, 2002.
637. Articles 2 to 5 of the Convention.

846. In order to secure the greatest social benefit from new methods of cargo handling, national policy must, secondly, encourage employers or their organizations and workers' organizations to improve the efficiency of work in ports, with the participation, as appropriate, of the competent authorities.

847. The Convention concludes by requiring the States to ensure that appropriate safety, health, welfare and vocational training provisions apply to dockworkers.

848. Recommendation No. 145 calls for regular and systematic assessments in each country and, as appropriate, each port, of the probable impact of changes in cargo-handling methods, including the impact on the occupational structure in ports, the employment opportunities for, and the conditions of employment of, dockworkers. It then considers, in greater detail than the Convention, the means of regularizing employment and income (possibilities for permanent or regular employment; other employment or income guarantees; registration; adjustments to the strength of registers; allocation; temporary and seasonal dockworkers),[638] the organization of work in ports and the conditions of work and life.[639] It also covers issues of labour-management relations,[640] referring to Conventions Nos. 87 of 1948 and No. 98 of 1949 on the right to organize and collective bargaining, and to Recommendation No. 130 of 1967 on the examination of grievances.

E. Fishermen

849. ILO general standards apply to fishermen except where the text provides otherwise. The maritime conventions usually specify that they do not cover this category of seafarer. On the other hand, the International Labour Conference has drafted the Work in Fishing Convention (No. 188) and Recommendation (No. 199), 2007, to deal with their specific problems.[641] The Convention gives a broad definition of the fisher: 'every person employed or engaged in any capacity or carrying out an occupation on board any fishing vessel, including persons working on board who are paid on the basis of a share of the catch'; it excludes *inter alia* pilots, other persons in the permanent service of a government, shore-based persons carrying out work aboard and fisheries observers. The Convention revises previous instruments.

850. Fishing is a hazardous occupation. The Convention contains provisions on minimum requirements for work on board fishing vessels (minimum age, and medical examination); on conditions of service (manning and hours of rest, crew list, fisher's agreement, repatriation, recruitment and placement, payment of fishers, accomodation and food); and on medical care, health protection and social security

638. Paras 7 to 22 and 36.
639. Paras 28 to 30 and 31 to 35.
640. Paras 23 to 27.
641. For more details about the preparatory work, *see* ILC, *Conditions of Work in the Fishing Sector: A Comprehensive Standard (a Convention supplemented by a Recommendation) on Work in the Fishing Sector*, 92nd Session, Report V(1), ILO, Geneva, 2003.

(including occupational accident prevention and protection in the case of work-related sickness, injury or death). Recommendation No. 199 complements the Convention on those issues.

851. The vessel owner has the overall responsibility to ensure that the skipper is provided with the necessary resources and facilities to comply with the obligations of the Convention. The latter has the responsibility for the safety of the fishers on board and the safe operation of the vessel. He will not be constrained by the owner from taking any decision in this respect which, in his professional judgement, is necessary. Fishers shall comply with the lawful orders of the skipper and applicable safety and health measures.[642] A State which has ratified the Private Employment Agencies Convention, 1997 (No. 181)[643] may allocate to them certain responsibilities. The vessel shipping owner, however, shall be liable in the event that such an agency defaults on its obligations to a fisher for whom he is the user enterprise.[644]

852. Convention No. 188 contains standards on the fishers' work agreement. The States must adopt laws, regulations or other measures requiring that fishers working on vessels flying their flag have the protection of an agreement that is comprehensible to them and is consistent with the provisions of the Convention. They should also specify the minimum particulars to be included in the agreements, in accordance with the provisions contained in an annex to the Convention. Procedures should exist for ensuring that a fisher has an opportunity to review and seek advice on the terms of the agreement before it is concluded.[645]

853. Every fishing vessel must carry a crew list, a copy of which shall be provided to authorized persons ashore prior to departure, or communicated ashore immediately after departure. The States must adopt laws, regulations or other measures requiring that owners of fishing vessels flying their flag ensure that their vessels are sufficiently and safely manned for the safe navigation and operation of the vessel and under the control of a competent skipper. Fishers shall be given regular periods of rest of sufficient lengh to ensure safety and health[646].

854. States must ensure that fishers on a fishing vessel that flies their flag and that enters a foreign port are entitled to repatriation in the event that their work agreement has expired or has been terminated for justified reasons by fishers or by the owner, or that fishers is no longer able to carry out his duties. The cost of repatriation must be borne by the owner, except where the fisher has been found to be in serious default of his/her work agreement obligations. If an owner fails to provide for the repatriation, the State whose flag the vessel flies shall arrange for it and shall be entitled to recover the cost from him.[647]

642. Article 8.
643. *See* paras 524–532 above.
644. Article 22, para. 5.
645. Articles 16 and 17.
646. Articles 15 and 13.
647. Article 21.

855. Fishers who are paid a wage shall be ensured a monthly or other regular payment. They shall be given a means to transmit all or part of it, including advances, to their families at no cost.[648]

856. The State must adopt laws, regulations or other measures for fishing vessels that fly its flag with respect to accommodation, food and potable water on board. Accommodation shall be of sufficient size and quality and appropriately equipped for the service of the vessel and the length of time fishers live on board. The food, of a sufficient nutritional value, quality and quantity, and potable water of sufficient quality and quantity, shall be provided by the owner at no cost to the fisher, except if the collective agreement governing a share system or the fisher's work agreement so provides.[649] Annex III contains very detailed rules in this regard, including planning, control, design and construction.

F. Seafarers [650]

857. ILO standards on seafarers have a truly original drafting process (they are the subject of special sessions of the Conference)[651] and content. We have already, for example, discussed the special conditions for the entry into force of instruments in this field.[652]

858. The ILO has adopted in 2006 a new instrument to regroup most previous maritime instruments. The consolidated convention, 'MLC' No. 186, is original from several points of view.[653] From the point of view of structure, it distinguishes four levels. The first is presented in the same form as classic international labour conventions, with articles concerning basic rights and the provisions on the instrument as a whole (such as its entry into force and the revision procedure). The next consists of 'regulations' listing the rights and obligations of the persons concerned and the obligations of the ratifying States. The third and fourth levels (called together the 'code') contain the details for the implementation of the regulations; it comprises mandatory standards (part A) and non-mandatory guidelines (part B) on how to give effect to the requirements of the convention. The ratifying State undertakes to respect the rights and obligations set out in the regulations and to apply them in the manner set out in the corresponding provisions of Part A of the code; in addition it must give due consideration to implementing its responsibilities as provided for in Part B (Article VI of the Convention).

---

648. Articles 23 and 24.
649. Articles 25–27.
650. The Hours of Work (Inland Navigation) Recommendation, 1920 (No. 8) is the only instrument dealing with inland navigation.
651. On the grounds for a difference, *see* Valticos, *op. cit.*, para. 77 and footnote 99, and para. 634.
652. *See* paras 108 and 110 *above*.
653. *See* Documents GB.286/ LILS/8 and GB.286/3/2 of the ILO Governing Body (Geneva), March 2003. See also: 'Revue de droit comparé du travail et de la sécurité sociale', *La mise en œuvre de la Convention du travail maritime de l'OIT: Espoirs et défis*, special issue, No. 2013/2.

859. In another innovation, the procedure for amending the consolidated convention has been simplified.[654] Changes may be introduced in the convention itself and in the regulations by amendments rather than by the adoption of a revised convention or a protocol. Modifications to the code, as in 2016, can be tacitly agreed by the States that have ratified the Convention, a procedure based on that established for the instruments of other international organizations, in particular the International Maritime Organization (IMO).

860. The working of the Convention is kept under continuous review by a tripartite committee, established by the ILO Governing Body, with special competence in the area of maritime labour standards (Article XIII). This committee recommended in 2014 the ILC to adopt amendments in order to better address the problems faced by abandoned seafarers and their families and to elaborate on the requirement in the instrument, for ship-owners to provide financial security to assure compensation in the event of death or long-term disability of a seafarer due to occupational injury, illness or hazard.[655]

861. Title V of the regulations part of the consolidated convention regroups (on the basis of Article V of the first part) the different aspects of compliance and enforcement at the national level. The roles of the parties concerned – the flag State (which plays a paramount role), the port State and the labour-supplying State – are defined in this respect. Each State has effective jurisdiction and control over vessels flying its flag. It ensures that such vessels carry a certificate and a compliance document duly issued by the competent authority. It should clearly establish the objectives and standards governing the operation of inspection and certification systems and adequate general procedures to evaluate the degree of compliance with those objectives and standards. A vessel to which the Convention applies can be inspected by the authorities of a State other than the flag State, when the vessel weighs anchor in its port. The State must ensure that seafarers on ships calling at a port in its territory, who allege a breach of their rights or of other requirements of the Convention, are entitled to report such a complaint in order to facilitate a prompt and practical means of redress (Regulation 5.2.2). Each State shall exercise effective jurisdiction and control over the engagement of seamen and over placement services on its territory. By thus increasing the number of parties tasked with ensuring effective implementation, the consolidated convention aims at universal application, even if certain recalcitrant States fail to ratify it.

862. The Convention has three objectives: to lay down, in its Articles and Regulations, a firm set of rights and obligations; to allow, through the Code, flexibility in the way States implement them; to ensure that those rights and obligations are properly complied with and enforced. There are two main areas for flexibility in application. One is the possibility to give effect to the detailed requirements of Part A of the Code through substantial equivalence (Article VI, paras 3 and 4). The second is provided by formulating the mandatory requirements of many provisions in Part A

---

654. *See* Articles XIV and XV, and para. 105 *above*.
655. ILC, *Provisional Record*, No. 2A, 103rd Session, Geneva, 2014.

in a general way, thus leaving a wider scope for discretion as to the precise action to be taken at the national level. In such cases, guidance on implementation is given in the non-mandatory Part B of the Code.[656]

863. National law and regulations must respect the rights mentioned in the ILO Declaration on Fundamental Principles and Rights at Work[657] i.e. freedom of association and the right to collective bargaining, the abolition of forced and child labour and the elimination of discrimination in respect of employment and occupation (Article III). Equality between men and women in employment is still a problem in a number of countries as they have maintained the prohibition of females to work on board ship.

864. Article IV provides that the seafarers have the right to a safe and secure workplace, to fair terms of employment, to decent working and living conditions on board ship, and to health protection, medical care, welfare measures and other forms of social protection. The Regulations and the Code contain detailed rules on such rights and obligations under five titles: minimum requirements for seafarers to work on a ship; conditions of employment (including hours of work and of rest, entitlement to leave, career and skill development and opportunities); accommodation and recreational activities (design and construction, ventilation, heating, lighting, sleeping rooms, mess rooms, sanitary and hospital accommodation, prevention of noise and vibration, mail, ship visit arrangements, etc.), food and catering (to ensure access to good quality food and drinking water provided under regulated hygienic conditions); health protection, medical care, welfare and social security protection;[658] compliance and enforcement.

865. Seafarers must not work on a ship unless they are certified to be medically fit (Regulation 1.2), trained or certified as competent or otherwise qualified, and have successfully completed training for personal safety on board ship (Regulation 1.3). They must have access to an efficient, adequate and accountable system for finding employment without charge to them (Regulation 1.4). The terms and conditions for employment must be referred to in a clear written legally enforceable agreement and agreed to by the seafarer under conditions which ensure that he has an opportunity to review and seek advice, and freely accepts them before signing. To the extent compatible with national law and practice, the agreements are understood to incorporate any applicable collective bargaining agreements (Regulation 2.1). Each State must require that all ships that fly its flag have a sufficient number of seafarers employed on board to ensure that ships are operated safely, efficiently and with due regard to security under all conditions, taking into account concerns about crew fatigue and the particular nature and conditions of the voyage (Regulation 2.7).

656. Explanatory note to the Regulations and Code of the Convention, attached to the text, paras 8 and 9.
657. Article III. *See* paras 203–210 *above*.
658. O. Fotinopoulou Bazurko, 'La indemnización por daños y el accidente de trabajo marítimo', *Revista General de Derecho del Trabajo y Seguridad Social*, No. 31, July 2012.

866. Regulation 4.2 establishes a ship-owners' liability: the States must ensure that measures, in accordance with the Code, are in place on ships that fly their flags to provide seafarers with a right to material assistance and support from the ship-owner with respect to the financial consequences of sickness, injury or death occurring while they are serving or arising from their employment. Seafarers have a right to be repatriated at no cost to themselves in the circumstances and under the conditions specified in the Code. States must prohibit ship-owners from requiring that they make an advance payment towards the cost of repatriation at the beginning of their employment, and also from recovering the cost from the wages or other entitlements, except where the seafarer has been found to be in serious default of his obligations. They must require ships that fly their flags to provide financial security to ensure due repatriation (Regulation 2.5 and Standard A2.5). Seafarers are also entitled to adequate compensation in the case of injury, loss or unemployment arising from the ship's loss or foundering; in such circumstances, the ship-owner must pay an indemnity against the resulting unemployment (Regulation 2.6 and Standard A2.6).

867. All seafarers should be paid regularly and in full accordance with their employment agreements (Regulation 2.2). The ship-owners shall take measures to provide seafarers with a means to transmit all or part of their earnings to their families or dependants or legal beneficiaries (Standard A2.2, para. 3). Guideline B2.2.4 deals with the minimum monthly wages. Contrary to the ILO general standards on the matter, it provides for the amount of basic pay. More precisely, it stipulates that the minimum wages for a calendar month of service for an able seafarer should be no less than the amount periodically set by the Joint Maritime Commission or another organ authorized by the ILO Governing Body.[659]

868. The upsurge in terrorist activity in the early years of this century have heightened concern to deliver reliable identity documents to seamen. Convention No. 185 thus revised an earlier convention in 2003. Article 2 requires each State to issue to each of its nationals who is a seafarer and makes an application to that effect a seafarer's identity document conforming to the provisions of the Convention; a record of each seafarer's identity document issued, suspended or withdrawn by it must be stored in an electronic database. The documents are intended to allow the bearers to obtain permission to leave ship more easily during a stopover or for transit to transfer purposes.

III. Indigenous and Tribal Peoples

869. As indicated in the name itself of this category, the standards on indigenous and tribal peoples go beyond the framework of labour to deal with the general problem of development. Hence the especially close cooperation with the United Nations and specialized agencies.

---

659. *See* para. 643 *above*.

870. Convention No. 169 of 1989 defines the populations to which it applies as follows (Article 1):

(a) tribal peoples in independent countries whose social, cultural and economic conditions distinguish them from other sections of the national community, and whose status is regulated wholly or partially by their own customs or traditions or by special laws or regulations;
(b) peoples in independent countries who are regarded as indigenous on account of their descent from the populations which inhabited the country, or a geographical region to which the country belongs, at the time of conquest or colonization or the establishment of present state boundaries and who, irrespective of their legal status, retain some or all of their own social, economic, cultural and political institutions.

2. Self-identification as indigenous or tribal shall be regarded as a fundamental criterion for determining the groups to which the provisions of this Convention apply.
3. The use of the term *peoples* in this Convention shall not be construed as having any implications as regards the rights which may attach to the term under international law.

871. These peoples raise an issue already seen with migrant workers. They live in a society within which they are a minority; they must therefore try to integrate. But at the same time, many of them want to keep their values, which are part of their history and their identity. The first convention adopted by ILO in this field, Convention No. 107 of 1957, emphasized policies of assimilation. Convention No. 169, which revised it, takes greater account of the peoples' aspirations to attain control of their institutions, their lifestyle and their own economic development, and to maintain their identity, language and religion within the context of the States in which they live.[660] Recommendation No. 104, which was also adopted in 1957, nevertheless continues to be considered to have priority, although it again stresses the promotion of factors of integration, even in its title. Once again, a balance is sought between these antinomical views.

872. Convention No. 169 invites the governments to protect the rights of such peoples and to respect their integrity. Article 2, paragraph 2 stipulates that the systematic action to be taken must include:

(a) ensuring that members of these peoples benefit on an equal footing from the rights and opportunities which national laws and regulations grant to other members of the population;
(b) promoting the full realization of the social, economic and cultural rights of these peoples with respect for their social and cultural identity, their customs and traditions and their institutions;

---

660. *See* the Preamble of Convention No. 169. *Comp.* P.G. McHugh, *Aboriginal Title: The Modern Jurisprudence of Tribal Land Rights,* Oxford University Press, 2011, p. 227 *et seq.*

(c) assisting the members of the peoples concerned to eliminate socioeconomic gaps that may exist between indigenous and other members of the national community, in a manner compatible with their aspirations and ways of life.

873. The Convention addresses peoples as communities, as beneficiaries, rather than as individual persons. This underscores the programmatic nature of these standards. Thus, it is the indigenous and tribal people that must enjoy the full measure of human rights and fundamental freedoms 'without hindrance or discrimination' (Article 3). In applying the provisions of the Convention (Article 5):

(a) the social, cultural, religious and spiritual values and practices of these peoples shall be recognized and protected, and due account shall be taken of the nature of the problems which face them both as groups and as individuals;
(b) the integrity of the values, practices and institutions of these peoples shall be respected;
(c) policies aimed at mitigating the difficulties experienced by these peoples in facing new conditions of life and work shall be adopted, with the participation and cooperation of the peoples affected.

The governments must also recognize the rights of ownership and possession of the peoples concerned over the lands which they traditionally occupy (Articles 13 to 19).

874. The Convention requires that the peoples concerned participate in the policies and programmes of interest to them and be entitled to decide on their own development priorities. The coordination of this specific effort with the fundamental ILO option of associating employers' and workers' organizations in all its activities has not always been problem-free. These problems can obviously only be solved – and indeed have been – to the satisfaction of the Organization's constituents.

875. Other articles of the Convention concern the members of these peoples. They prohibit the exaction of compulsory personal services, whether paid or unpaid (Article 11) and provide for the possibility of legal proceedings for the effective protection of rights; such proceedings may be instituted either individually or through representative bodies (Article 12). The same holds true for the provisions (Articles 20 *et seq.*) on labour issues: recruitment and conditions of employment; vocational training; handicrafts and rural industries; social security and health.

876. Recommendation No. 104 deals with the same topics in greater detail. Both the Convention and the Recommendation also contain provisions on education, means of communication and cross-border cooperation.

Chapter 3. Social Security

877. Not only did the social question and its answer in legislation give birth to labour law in respect of both individuals and groups, they also resulted in wage earners being provided with a guaranteed source of income to cope with the variables of working life (loss of employment, illness, accident, retirement, etc.). Labour law and social security law are therefore closely connected, despite the obvious differences in legal techniques; in fact, they are growing steadily closer, as we saw in our examination of the employment policies.[661] What is more, wage-earning and the guarantees it affords are not to be sneezed at in this day and age; indeed, the self-employed workers who once tended to feel socially superior now seek to benefit from an equivalent system or to be integrated into it,[662] a trend in which social security has no doubt played no small part.

878. The trend concerns national legislation as much as it does the ILO law discussed here. This chapter considers first the general principles of social security (§1) before moving on to the guarantees afforded by its different branches (§2); the last paragraph (§3) discusses social security for foreign workers.

§1. General Principles

I. Historical Markers

879. Right from the outset, the ILO's Constitution underscored the need to fight unemployment, to protect workers from general and occupational diseases and accidents in the workplace, to establish pension and disability benefits.[663] In 1944, the Philadelphia Declaration expressly mentioned the war against want and required that social security measures be extended 'to provide a basic income to all in need of such protection and comprehensive medical care'.[664] Echoing the point, the International Covenant on Economic, Social and Cultural Rights calls on the States to recognize 'the right of everyone to social security, including social insurance'.[665] It adds that working mothers should be accorded, during a reasonable period before and after childbirth, paid leave or leave with adequate social security benefits.[666]

880. The first ILO conventions and recommendations on the subject – and, subsequently, national legislation in general[667] – established what were known as 'social' insurance schemes, i.e. they provided obligatory coverage for work-related risks. In some cases (in connection with employment injury), they simply stipulated

661. *See* para. 507 *et seq. above.*
662. *See* R. Castel, *Les métamorphoses de la question sociale. Une chronique du salarial*, Paris, Fayard, 1995.
663. *See* the Preamble.
664. Paras I(d) and III(f). *See* para. 21 *et seq. above.*
665. Article 9.
666. Article 10, para. 2. *See* paras 808–810 *above.*
667. Valticos, *op. cit.*, para. 517.

the employer's responsibility, leaving it up to him to choose the means of fulfilling his obligation.

881. The Great Depression of 1929–1933, the 1939–1945 war and the concomitant ruinous periods of inflation cast a different light on social security. The first signs of change were a 1935 American statute and legislation adopted in 1938 by New Zealand. Lord Beveridge's landmark 1942 report, prepared at the behest of the British Government, marked a turning point. ILO had assisted both the Americans and the British.[668] On the European Continent, a number of countries had nationalized the private social insurances that were unable to face their financial commitments. Those developments culminated in the social security system promoted by ILO and since adopted by many countries, with the State itself assuming responsibility, at least as a substitute for the employer, the scope of benefits being broadened and the different branches of social security being incorporated into one unified and coordinated system.

882. The first ILO instruments to reflect this shift were two recommendations adopted in 1944. Recommendation No. 67 calls for income security schemes that relieve want and prevent destitution by restoring, up to a reasonable level, income which is lost by reason of inability to work ('including old age') or to obtain remunerative work or by reason of the death of a breadwinner. It considers that income security should be organized as far as possible on the basis of compulsory social insurance, whereby insured persons fulfilling prescribed qualifying conditions are entitled to benefits in consideration of the contributions they have paid to an insurance institution. Provision for needs not covered by compulsory social insurance should be made by social assistance; certain categories of persons (such as dependent children and needy invalids, aged persons and widows) should be entitled to reasonable allowances; social assistance appropriate to the needs of the case should be provided for other persons in want.[669] The Recommendation lists the various contingencies that should be covered by compulsory social insurance. Social insurance should afford protection to employed and self-employed persons, together with their dependants; its administration should be unified or coordinated within a general system of social security services; contributors should, through their organizations, be represented on the bodies 'which determine or advise upon administrative policy and propose legislation or frame work regulations'.[670] An annex contains suggestions for the application of these guiding principles.

883. The second recommendation, No. 69, concerns medical care, which it suggests should fully cover all members of the community. It should be provided either

668. B. Kahil-Wolff and P. Y. Greber, *Sécurité sociale. Aspects de droit national, international et européen*, Bâle, Helbing and Lichtenhahn, 2006, paras 291–300 and 305; Valticos, *op. cit.*, para. 518 and footnote; G. López Morales, R. Silva and A. Egorov, 'Social security' in ILO, *International Labour Standards: A Global Approach* (Geneva), ILO, 20, 2001, p. 452; M. Humblet and R. Silva, *Standards for the XXIst Century: Social Security*, Geneva, ILO, 2002, pp. 1–2.
669. Paras 1 to 4.
670. Paras 5 to 27.

through a social insurance medical care service with supplementary provision by way of social assistance, or through a public medical care service.[671]

884. Both instruments served as a basis for the standard-setting work carried out thereafter until the adoption, in 1952, of Convention No. 102 establishing minimum standards for social security. Their provisions are still very similar to the anti-poverty policies adopted by countries like Brazil or India. Thus the Indian Parliament has adopted the National Rural Employment Guarantee Act, No. 42 of 2005.[672] It aims at paying 100 employment days per year to any adult rural household whose member(s) would accept to do some manual unskilled work and applies already in 200 districts from all States of the country. In India also, the Self-Employed Women Association (SEWA) has established a pension fund supplied by fees paid by its members who are women rural informal workers; other successful experiences exist in Brazil,[673] India again, Iran and Tanzania.[674] The Brazilian government has launched in 2003 a new programme called Bolsa Familia. It gives financial support to poor families who observe some development requirements, including in terms of schooling, vaccination, food control and ante- and postnatal tests. The initiative covers millions of families. It could be improved because too many beneficiaries still are not really poor. It has nevertheless permitted a significant reduction in the number of citizens living below the poverty line.[675]

885. Microfinance is another means to help the wretched. It does so while trying to maintain the profitability of the system. The ILO and other international institutions have underlined the potentialities of the mechanism[676] and pointed out particular successes like the one of the Grameen Bank in Bangladesh.[677] The successful experiences provide for a dual system. They include guarantees in case of specific contingencies, such as sickness, accident, old age and death. They also contain anti-poverty measures such as free or subsidized food supply and accommodation, medical assistance, prevention campaign and public employment programmes.

886. Convention No. 102 establishes, as its title suggests, a general system whose scope is (gradually) extended to all sectors of activity and to the entire

671. Paras 8, 19 and 5.
672. *The Gazette of India*, No. 48, 7 September 2005.
673. S. Rocha, *Pobreza no Brasil. A final, de que se trata?*, Rio de Janeiro, Editora FGV, 2003.
674. ISSA, *Coping with the Crisis: Managing Social Security in Uncertain Times*, 2012; T. Akson, 'Extension de la couverture du système de sécurité sociale en Tanzanie. Les leçons de l'Inde et de l'Iran', *Bull. droit comparé travail sécurité sociale*, 2008, pp. 65–81.
675. ILO, *Bolsa Família in Brazil: Context, Concept and Impacts*, Social Security Department, Geneva, March 2009.
676. B. Balkenhol (ed.), *Microfinance and Public Policy: Outreach, Performance and Efficiency*, Geneva, ILO, 2007; ILO, *Microfinance for Employment Creation and Enterprise Development*, Geneva, 2002; ILO, *Micro-finance in Industrialized Countries. Helping the Unemployed to Start a Business*, Genève, 2002; A. Noya et E. Clarence (ed.), *Social Economy: Building Inclusive Economies*, Paris, OECD, 2007; C. Churchill (ed.) *Protecting the Poor: A Micro insurance Compendium*, Geneva, ILO and Munich Re Foundation, 2006; L. Mayoux, *Microfinance and the Empowerment of Women. A Review of the Key Issues*, Geneva, ILO, 2000.
677. *See* www.grameen-info.org/.

population. It comprises the nine main kinds of benefits that become due at the appearance of specific contingencies: medical care, and sickness, unemployment, old-age, employment injury, family, maternity, invalidity and survivors' benefits. On 1 February 2014, Convention No. 102 had been ratified by 50 countries, including a number of developing countries.

887. The instruments drawn up since are based on Convention No. 102, but provide broader protection in terms of the persons covered and the amount of the benefits. They cover specific areas of social security or problems inherent in international transfers of labour. Besides a number of countries have completed the social protection benefits by a guaranteed minimum income, often coupled with measures for the reintegration into the labour market and calculated in such a way as to provide the beneficiary with partial and transitional wage replacement and, at the same time, to avoid creating disincentives either to work or to employment creation.[678] This system is a part of social security[679] and should be distinguished from the social assistance in that it grants legal entitlements to beneficiaries which are considered as a given category of persons. On the contrary, the need for social aid is assessed on a case by case basis for each individual.[680]

II. Extending to the Poorest

888. Recent research has emphasized the pivotal role of social security in achieving a fair globalization, facilitating economic development and structural change, and managing crises.[681] In the early 2000, the ILO has renewed its commitment to the extension of social security coverage and to the improvement of the governance, financing and administration of the schemes. The Organization had reaffirmed the importance of Recommendations No. 67 and No. 69 for the development of a modern system of social security; they establish the principle of a

678. P. Horusitzky, K. Julienne, M. Lelièvre, 'Un panorama des minima sociaux en Europe', *Problèmes économiques*, 24 December 2008, pp. 21–27; La documentation française, Du RMI au RSA: une refonte des politiques d'insertion et d'aide sociale, http://www.ladocumentationfrancaise.fr/dossiers/rmi-rsa-insertion-aide-sociale/index.shtml?xtor=EPR-528=.
679. See the judgment of the European Court of Justice in the case *Vera Hoecks*, No. 249/83, 27 March 1985, Rec. p. 973.
680. See the judgment of the European Court of Justice in the Case *Frilli*, No. 1/72, 22 June 1972, Rec. p. 457; *see also* Case *Notebaum*, No. 101/04, 20 January 2005, Rec.I, p. 771.
681. ILO, *World Social Protection Report 2014/15: Building economic recovery, inclusive development and social justice*, Geneva, 2014; E. Kalula and E. Levy, 'Accès aux soins de santé et aux systèmes de santé en Afrique du Sud', *Bull. droit comparé travail sécurité sociale*, 2008, pp. 161–185; E. Fourie, 'The Informal Economy, Social Security and Legislative Attempts to Extend Social Security Protection', in R. Blanpain, W. Bromwich, O. Rymkevich, S. Spattini (eds.), *The Modernization of Labour Law and Industrial Relations in a Comparative Perspective* (Bulletin of Comparative Labour Relations, No. 70), Alphen aan den Rijn, Kluwer, 2009, pp. 271–293; M. Olivier, 'Extension of Labour Law and Social Security Protection to the Informal Sector: Developing Countries Perspectives with Specific Reference to Southern Africa', *ibid.*, pp. 241–293; ISSA, *Dynamic Social Security for Africa*: An Agenda for *Development*, Geneva, 2008; *ibid.*; *Coping with the Crisis: Managing Social Security in Uncertain Times*, 2012.

comprehensive coverage of the whole population by a scheme associating measures of social insurance, social assistance and public services. They offers a broader legal and institutional framework than the one proposed by Convention No. 102.[682]

889. Difficulties should not be underestimated. The problems of the social security systems in developing countries are well-known. They relate to the size of the informal economy, to the limited income of the State and maybe still more to the weakness of the management provoked by numerous factors. Some are connected with the confusion between the State and the social security budgets, with corruption and more often than not with the bureaucracy and wasting. Some regards the incapacity of the State to collect all dues and to invest them in a safe and profitable way. Some other are linked to the incapacity to adjust the benefits to the inflation rate, to obtain the same economies of scale than industrialized countries and to use a performing data processing system. Reference is also made to clientelism and to the absence of a 'work culture', as a consequence of a bad application of social policies. In summary, a sustainable system of social protection requires some basic conditions: a sound economic (financial) basis, an efficient state structure and a strong sense of solidarity among the people concerned.

890. The Organization has launched a 'Global Campaign on Social Security and Coverage for All' and developed a two-dimensional strategy. The 'horizontal' dimension comprises the extension of income security and access to health care, starting at a modest level, to the whole population. It echoes the idea of the transfer component of the Social Protection Floor (SPF), developed by the United Nations Chief Executives Board for Coordination, which promotes a set of basic transfers or entitlements enabling persons to access essential goods and services; the SPF extends the initiative to such other essential services as drinkable water, adequate food, sanitation, health, education and lodging. The second, 'vertical', dimension has sought to provide higher levels of income security and health protection in line with economic and social development, when people were faced with fundamental life contingencies such as unemployment, ill health, disability, maternity, loss of breadwinner and old age.

891. The ILO, together with the World Health Organization (WHO), has been given a leading role in the SPF. The collaboration with other agencies aims at building a coalition of international agencies and donors supporting countries to plan and implement sustainable social protection schemes. The SPF approach was incorporated into the Global Jobs Pact, adopted by the International Labour Conference in 2009. It was endorsed by the 2010 United Nations Summit on the Millennium Development Goals which stressed that 'social protection systems addressing and reducing inequality and social exclusion are essential for protecting the gains

682. *See* ILC, *Social Security for Social Justice and a Fair Globalization* (Report VI), Geneva: 100th Session, ILO, 2011; ILC, *Social Security and the Rule of Law*. Report of the Committee of Experts on the Application of Conventions and Recommendations, Report III (Part 1B) 100th Session, 2011, ILO, Geneva, 2011.

towards the achievement of the Millennium Development Goals'.[683] Since then the World Bank Group and the ILO have joined forces: a new Global Partnership for Universal Social Protection was announced during the 2016 UN General Assembly; it aims to help countries reach all poor and vulnerable groups with a variety of measures to ensure that nobody lacks access to key forms of support when needed.[684]

892. The International Labour Conference has voted in June 2012 a new Recommendation on social protection floors that synthesizes the renewed approach. The text is of programmatic character, stimulating Member States to adopt a certain policy and to take the necessary measures of implementation. It provides guidelines to develop a social security strategy compatible with, and supportive of, wider national economic and social policy strategies and seeks in particular to contribute poverty reduction and the formalization of informal employment[685]. States should put in place and complete as rapidly as possible, and maintain, their social protection floors that comprise basic social security guarantees ensuring at a minimum that, over the life cycle, all in need have access to essential health care and to basic income security. The social protection floors goes beyond the traditional social security schemes; it should include access to goods and services, defined as necessary at the national level, which constitute essential health care, including in the case of maternity, and access for children to nutrition, education, care and any other necessary goods and services.

893. The new instrument focuses on the extension of coverage to wider groups of the population (horizontal extension of coverage). With respect to progressively ensuring higher levels of protection (vertical extension of coverage), the Recommendation encourage States to ratify and to ensure the effective implementation of the Social Security (Minimum Standards) Convention, 1952 (No. 102) and other up-to-date ILO social security instruments. The text specifies a number of guidelines for the design and implementation of national social security strategies. To give the necessary flexibility in the choice of the methods and policies for achieving the intended social protection outcomes, schemes providing such benefits may include universal benefit schemes, social insurance schemes, social assistance schemes, negative income tax schemes, public employment schemes and employment support schemes. The instrument encourages Members to close coverage gaps of populations with contributory capacity through contributory schemes.

894. Interestingly, the Recommendation has established a system of monitoring the progress made by the States in implementing social protection floors and achieving extension strategies of national social security systems. It suggests the setting up of nationally defined mechanisms involving representative organizations of

683. United Nations: *Keeping the promise: United to achieve the Millennium Development Goals*, General Assembly Resolution A/65/L.1, adopted on 22 September 2010 (New York, 2010), para. 51.
684. http://www.social-protection.org/gimi/gess/NewYork.action (21 September 2016).
685. *See also* ILC, *Transitioning from the informal to the formal economy*, Report V (1), Geneva, ILO, 2014, paras. 72 and 157.

employers and workers and, as appropriate, representatives of other organizations and persons concerned. Special attention has to be given to the concepts, definitions and methodology used in the production of social security data, statistics and indicators as well as to their collection, compilation and publication, with due regard to privacy. Information, experiences and expertise on social security strategies, policies and practices should be exchanged among Members and with the ILO.

III. Common Principles

895. All recent ILO instruments on social security share the same vision and have therefore in common a number of principles.[686] They implement the human right to social security contained in the various UN treaties. They are based on solidarity and compulsory affiliation; their coverage is universal and their provision sufficiently flexible to apply to a large variety of countries; they are financed by payments calculated on the basis of salary or by taxes and are managed by institutions that are administratively, financial and legally autonomous. The Beneficiaries' Right follows the same pattern.

A. Social Security as a Human Right

896. It has often been underlined that social security pertains to that minimum protective threshold below which human beings could not live and work with dignity.[687] The International Covenant on Economic, Social and Cultural Rights not only formally recognize the right to social security as a human right in the International Covenant on Economic, Social and Cultural Rights, but also refer to the protection and assistance to the family and to the right of everyone to an adequate standard of living, including adequate food, clothing and housing, and to the continuous improvement of living conditions.[688] The right is enshrined as such in other international[689] and regional legal instruments.[690] Each State Party undertakes to

686. J.M. Servais, *International Social Security Law* in W. van Eeckhoutte (ed.), International Encyclopaedia for Social Security Law, The Hague, Kluwer, 2013. Some of the so-called principles mentioned in para. 3 of Recommendation No. 202 are rather sound and prudential guidelines of management.

687. J. van Langendonck 'The Right to Social Security and Allied Rights' in F. Ruland, B.von Maydell, (eds.), *Verfassung, Theorie und Praxis des Sozialstaats Festschrift für Hans F. Zacher zum 70 Geburtstag*, Karlsruhe, C.F. Müller Juristischer Verlag, 1998, pp. 477–488; J.M. Thouvenin and A. Trebilcock (eds.), *Droit international social*, vol. 2, Brussels, Bruylant, 2013, pp. 1664-1680.

688. Articles 9–11 of the Covenant.

689. In particular, in several United Nations instruments: the Convention on the Elimination of All Forms of Discrimination against Women, 1979, Articles 11(1)(e), 11(2)(b) and 14(2)); the Convention on the Rights of the Child, 1989, Articles 26, 27(1), 27(2) and 27(4); the International Convention on the Elimination of All Forms of Racial Discrimination, 1965, Article 5(e)(iv); the International Convention on the Protection of the Rights of All Migrant Workers and Their Families, 1990, Articles 27 and 54; the Convention on the Rights of Persons with Disabilities, 2006, Articles 25 and 28 in particular.

690. Such as the European Social Charter, adopted by the Council of Europe in 1961 and its Revised version of 1996.

implement these rights progressively, upon ratification, i.e. to take steps towards the full realization of the relevant rights 'to the maximum of its available resources', while ensuring immediate protection against discrimination.[691] The ILO Recommendation No. 202 concerning national floors of social protection, 2012, also reaffirms that the right to social security is a human right and an economic and social necessity for development and progress.

897. The impact of the ILO conventions and that of Convention No. 102 in particular, should therefore not only be measured in terms of the number of ratifications: over the years, Convention No. 102 has had, and continues to have, substantial influence on the development of social security in the various regions of the world. The ILO technical cooperation activities in the field of social security are based on its principles. Many States, like China, Latvia or Lebanon, take its provisions into account when drafting their own legislation, even if they have not yet ratified. The social security systems of nearly all European countries and many Latin American and Caribbean countries follow the pattern set out in Convention No. 102 and in the higher social security standards. The influence of these standards has also been felt in Japan and in the Republic of Korea as well as in Tunisia and Morocco. Furthermore, the Convention has influenced the development of formal social security systems in low-income countries: more than thirty African countries have set up pensions schemes modelled on it. Although these countries' formal social security systems cover only a small portion of the population, Convention No. 102 constitutes a development goal and is a reference used in documents setting long-term objectives with regard to the levels of protection and social security needed to be attained.[692]

898. Article 67 of Convention No. 102 states that the benefits should 'be sufficient to maintain the family of the beneficiary in health and decency'. Articles 65(10) and 66(8) adds that the rates of current periodical payments in respect of old-age, employment injury (except in case of incapacity for work), invalidity and death of breadwinner, shall be reviewed following substantial changes in the general level of earnings where these result from substantial changes in the cost of living.

899. According to paragraph 8 of Recommendation No. 202, basic income security should allow life in dignity. Nationally defined minimum levels of income may correspond to the monetary value of a set of necessary goods and services, national poverty lines, income thresholds for social assistance or other comparable thresholds established by national law or practice, and may take into account regional differences. The levels of basic social security guarantees should be regularly reviewed through a transparent procedure that is established by national laws and regulations.

691. Article 2 of the Covenant.

692. Such as the Southern African Development Community (SADC) Code of Social Security, or a number of national social security policy documents, for example in the United Republic of Tanzania and Zambia. See Intl. Lab. Conf., *Social Security for social Justice and a Fair Globalization, above.* at paras. 40–41.

Representative organizations of employers and workers and, as appropriate, representatives of other organizations and persons concerned should be involved in the establishment and review of the levels of these guarantees.

B. Obligation of Solidarity

900. Social security systems are one of the most powerful institutional expressions of social solidarity. Friendly societies were formed at the rise of the industrial revolution where the employees helped each other by putting voluntarily contributions in common. Some categories of solidarity still exist in other parts of the world. Spontaneous community forms of mutual aid are usually based, in Africa for example, on family ties, religious or ethnic adherence, or ancestral activities, such as managing common land, shared work or crisis resolution. More structured solidarities can be observed in the different regions. They have a personal or territorial basis, like tontines, or an occupational one, like cooperatives or mutual benefit associations. They cover field from health care to the micro-insurance.[693] They might be further studied as alternative means of insuring social protection when more sophisticated social security cannot be reached in near future.

901. International labour standards in this field aim to strengthen social cohesion by promoting this solidarity between active and non-active members of society, between rich and poor and between present and future generations. The old-age pension constitutes an excellent example. Formal social security pensions are deeply rooted in long-standing values of inter-generational solidarity; they rapidly became an important part of inter-generational arrangements and were considered a necessary supplement to informal arrangements.[694] The ILO conventions and recommendations base social security systems on such organizational principles as risk pooling and collective financing by the members of the community through contributions or taxes, and guaranteeing a minimum level of protection sufficient to maintain the family of the beneficiary in health and decency. They also reduce the risk of social and political upheavals and allow a more stable development of democratic institutions and the rule of law.[695]

902. The solidarity principle can difficultly be realized within a large community if affiliation is not obligatory. At the system level, the political commitment of high coverage, adequate benefits and sustainable financing can only be reached through dialogue and consensus. How to reach such a balance is a major component in the debates on the reforms needed to adjust social security systems to demographic changes. At each individual level however, the challenges remain, and there

693. ILO, *Standards-related Activities and Decent Work: Prospects in the Field of Social Security* 5 (ILO, Mar. 2005). Proposals made by the independent experts, social security policy and development branch.
694. Intl. Lab. Conf., Social *Security for Social Justice and a Fair Globalization, op. cit.* para. 231.
695. *Ibid.*, paras. 34, 109, 162, 164 and 443.

is an ongoing need to enforce in the daily practice the compulsory nature of the contributions. As has been said, fraud corrupts solidarity.

C. Flexibility towards Universality

903. Recommendation No. 202 underlines[696] the principle of universality of protection, based on social solidarity. The progressive incorporation of different categories into the social security schemes, even in countries where they evolve towards universal coverage, is not an easy task. That is why Convention No. 102 puts forward targets to meet rather than describing the applicable techniques. It is worded flexibly enough to be adapted to the different systems used by the Member States and to the development process. In addition, the minimum rate of benefit is based on the level of wages in the country concerned. The ILO conventions provide a range of ratification options for countries whose economic development does not allow for full implementation of the instruments considered; such countries do not need to wait until general coverage has been extended to all branches of activity and all categories of persons, and can offer limited levels of benefits. The conventions on social security contain several flexibility clauses.[697]

904. Several conventions have distinct parts, only some of which must be accepted on ratification. As we have just said, such is the case of Convention No. 102: the ratifying State must accept at least three of its nine parts (corresponding to the nine branches of social security), including at least one of the following five: unemployment, old age, employment injury, invalidity, survivors. It can subsequently notify ILO that it has accepted one or several other parts. Likewise, Convention No. 118, 1962, on equality of treatment (social security) allows Members to accept the obligations it sets forth in respect of only one of the nine branches of social security. Convention No. 128, 1967, on invalidity, old-age and survivors' benefits, allows the States to apply only one of those three branches; Convention No. 168, 1988, on employment promotion and protection against unemployment, allows them to exclude the provisions on new applicants for employment from the obligations accepted on ratification.

905. Convention No. 102 and the conventions adopted later allow other exceptions in terms of beneficiaries:

(a) Convention No. 102 does not apply to seamen or sea fishermen,[698] and the State does not itself have to exclude them. Convention No. 128, which we have already mentioned, and Conventions Nos. 121, 1964, on employment injury benefits, and No. 130, 1969, on medical care and sickness benefits, permit the

696. Para. 3.

697. *See also* M. Humblet and R. Silva, *Standards for the XXIst Century: Social Security*, Geneva, ILO, 2002, pp. 7–15.

698. With regard to seafarers, *see* the Seafarers' Pension Convention, 1946 (No. 71) and the Social Security (Seafarers) Convention (Revised), 1987 (No. 165).

exclusion of seafarers, including sea fishermen, if those categories are protected by special schemes which provide benefits that are at least equivalent;

(b) all three conventions, Nos. 128, 121 and 130, authorize the exclusion of public servants under the same conditions. Convention No. 168 states that public employees whose employment up to normal retiring age is guaranteed by national laws or regulations may be excluded from protection;

(c) Conventions Nos. 121, 128 and 130 also authorize the exclusion of members of the employer's family living under the same roof, if they work for him, and of casual workers.[699] Convention No. 121 also provides an exemption for home-workers, and Conventions Nos. 128 and 130 for wage earners in the agricultural sector;

(d) all three conventions authorize the exclusion of other categories of workers whose number should not exceed 10 per cent of all wage earners, and Convention No. 183 of 2000 on maternity protection of 'limited categories of workers' when its application to them 'would raise special problems of a substantial nature'.[700]

906. More generally, countries whose economy and medical facilities are insufficiently developed can cover a more limited number of protected persons if they make a declaration to that effect on ratification. In such cases, Convention No. 102 allows the States to determine the number of protected persons with sole reference to the workers employed in industrial undertakings of a certain size; it also authorizes the Member State to afford benefits that are not as great or for a limited time. These are temporary derogations and the country that avails itself of them must regularly indicate whether the reasons for doing so remain valid or whether it ceases to avail itself of them. Other, similar temporary derogations are to be found in Conventions Nos. 121, 128, 130 and 168.

D. *Financing: Contributory and Non-contributory Systems*

907. Social security systems should be financed in such a manner as to ensure their long-term financial sustainability. No comprehensive scheme can be maintained without a stable revenue basis. Expenditure on health and pension predominates everywhere. According to Recommendation No. 202, national SPFs should be financed, in principle, by national resources; however, members whose economic and fiscal capacities are insufficient to implement the entire set of guarantees may seek international assistance that complement their own efforts. States should consider using different methods to mobilize the necessary resources to ensure

699. The formula used by Article 4 of Convention No. 121 ('persons whose employment is of a casual nature and who are employed otherwise than for the purpose of the employers' trade or business') differs from the one of Conventions No. 128 (Article 37) and No. 130 (Article 5): 'persons whose employment is of a casual nature'.

700. Article 2, para. 2.

financial, fiscal and economic sustainability of national SPFs, taking into account the contributory capacities of different population groups. Such methods may include, individually or in combination, effective enforcement of tax and contribution obligations, reprioritizing expenditure, or a broader and sufficiently progressive revenue base.[701]

908. The main choice for the financing of public programmes remains how far they should be organized as contributory social insurance and how far as non-contributory institutions accessible to all residents or all residents in a specified category (such as to be active). The success of the various approaches largely depends on labour market structure, the proportion of formal wage and salary employment in total employment, and the extent of the informal economy. However, the size of social security investment depends also on the prevailing political and social will. In many cases, this is the result of different, often historically influenced societal preferences.[702]

909. Convention No. 102, in the same way as the later instruments, accepts varying methods for the provision of protection through the mechanisms of social insurance, social assistance or universal public service, so as to leave more options to Member States. Each country may apply the Convention through a combination of contributory and non-contributory benefits, general and occupational schemes, compulsory and voluntary insurance, through different methods for the administration of benefits, and public and private participation. The Convention only sets out a series of objectives based on commonly accepted principles establishing a minimum social threshold for all Member States.[703]

910. Convention No. 102[704] establishes a general framework for the financing of benefits: the cost of the benefits and of their administration is to be borne collectively by way of insurance contributions or taxation. It also specifies how the burden is to be shared: in a manner which avoids hardship to persons of small means; in contributory schemes, the total of the insurance contributions borne by the employees protected must not exceed 50% of the total of the financial resources allocated to the protection. In all other respects, the Member States are free to adopt the system they want. The Convention merely requires that they take account of the economic situation of the country and of the beneficiaries. Conventions Nos. 121, 128 and 130 contain no further indications. Convention No. 168 specifies[705] that the system chosen may be contributory or non-contributory or a combination of the two.

701. Paras 11 and 12.
702. ILC, *Social Security for Social Justice and a Fair Globalization*, *op. cit.*, paras. 102, 107, 110–111 and 375; Ch. Hiessl, 'Employer-Centred Benefits and Atypical Workforce', *IJCLLIR*, Vol. 30 (1), March 2014, pp. 67–85.
703. ILC, *Social Security and the Rule of Law*, *op. cit.*, paras 58 and 67.
704. Article 71.
705. Article 12.

E. Organization and Administration: Public or Private Management?

911. ILO drafted Convention No. 102 and most of the subsequent conventions in such a way as to allow the States great leeway in organizing the systems by which benefits are provided. Article 72 of Convention No. 102, for example, provides that the system may be regulated by the public authorities, by a government department or by any other body, under prescribed conditions. Those instruments nevertheless set forth basic rules that must be respected no matter what system is used.[706] The CEACR recalled this in its consideration of the compatibility of a private pension scheme with Convention No. 102. It considered that the co-existence in a social security system of both a private and a public scheme was not incompatible with the Convention, which 'allows the minimum level of social security to be attained through various means'.[707] That flexibility must nevertheless be accompanied by the adoption of clear rules on organization and administration. The principles of good management concern in particular the State's ultimate responsibility, the participation of the insured and the financing of benefits.[708]

912. Both Convention No. 102 and the subsequent instruments state that the State bears general responsibility for the proper administration of social security systems.[709] That responsibility extends to the benefits service. Convention No. 102 adds that the State must ensure, where appropriate, that the necessary actuarial studies and calculations concerning financial equilibrium are made periodically and, in any event, prior to any change in benefits, the rate of insurance contributions, or the taxes allocated to covering the contingencies in question.[710] The CEACR has stated, in respect of old-age benefits, that the State's recognized power of oversight or control should not lead it to draw in any way on the funds constituted for purpose of paying such benefits[711] with a view to making up a budget deficit. Likewise, Convention No. 168 stipulates that in cases where subsidies are granted by the State or the social security system in order to safeguard employment, steps must be taken to ensure that the subsidies are expended only for the intended purpose and to prevent fraud or abuse by the beneficiaries.[712]

913. If there is one area in which public institutions[713] and private bodies have long collaborated, it is in the area of social security. The distribution of functions between State and employer, workers, their respective organizations, as well as

706. López Morales, Silva and Egorov, *op. cit.*, pp. 472–473.
707. ILC (86th session, 1998): *Report of the Committee of Experts for the Application of Conventions and Recommendations*, Report III (Part 1A) (Geneva), ILO, 1998, pp. 279–283.
708. Humblet and Silva, *op. cit.*, pp. 11–14.
709. Articles 72 of Convention No. 102, 24–25 of Convention No. 121, 35 of Convention No. 128, 30 of Convention No. 130 and 28 of Convention No. 168. It is not the case of the Maternity Protection Convention, 2000 (No. 183).
710. Article 72.
711. ILC (76th session, 1989), *Social Security Protection in Old Age*, Report III (Part 4B) (Geneva), ILO, 1989, para. 210.
712. Article 30.
713. They include in Germany social insurances managed jointly by trade unions and employers associations.

other interested groups, is a traditional issue, as is the role of the private sector with profit-making objectives (as for example for complementary pensions) and the professions.[714] Where administration is not entrusted to an institution regulated by the public authorities or to a government department responsible to a legislature, representatives of the beneficiaries must participate in the management, or be associated therewith in a consultative capacity; national laws or regulations may likewise decide as to the participation of representatives of employers and of the public authorities.[715]

914. We have already mentioned[716] the specific case of Convention No. 183 on maternity protection. Like the earlier standards, Article 6 states that the benefits due in respect of maternity or sick leave are to be provided through compulsory social insurance or public funds, or in a manner determined by national law and practice; however, the employer is not individually liable for the direct cost of such benefits to a woman employed by him or her. The aim is to protect the situation of women workers in the labour market, to ensure, in respect of a long-standing concern, that maternity protection does not add to the employer's burden or make him prefer to hire men workers. There are three exceptions: if the employer expressly agrees to bear those costs; if the national law or practice of a Member State provided thus prior to the date of adoption of the Convention; if the government and the representative organizations of employers and workers subsequently so agree.

F. Entitlements

1. Method for Calculating Cash Benefits

915. The conventions make allowances for differences in economic development by defining the minimum level of benefits in terms of the wages in the country. They provide three formulas for evaluating the extent to which the benefits granted under national laws and regulations attain the rates required.[717] The formulas, from which the States can choose, are based on the methods of calculation most often used in practice:

- Under the first, the minimum amount of the benefits must correspond, for a standard beneficiary, at a given percentage of the previous earnings of the beneficiary

---

714. See ILC (76th Session 1989), *General Survey of the Reports Relating to the Social Security (Minimum Standards) Convention (no. 102) 1952* Report III (Part 4 B), Geneva, ILO, 1989, paras 47–49. *See also* A. Nußberger, *Sozialstandards im Völkerrecht*, Duncker u. Humblot, Berlin, 2005, p. 331 (Case of Chile) and p. 333 (Case of Peru); M. Voirin, *L'organisation administrative de la sécurité sociale. Un enjeu social et politique*, Geneva, ILO, 1991.

715. Articles 72 of Convention No. 102, 24 of Convention No. 121, 36 of Convention No. 128, 29 of Convention No. 168. Article 31 of Convention No. 130 requires the participation of employers 'where appropriate'.

716. *See* para. 810 *above*.

717. Convention No. 102 uses these formulas for all social security branches with the exception of family benefits. Conventions Nos. 168 and 183 provide for other rules.

or breadwinner. The percentage must be attained if the previous earnings of the beneficiary or breadwinner are equal to or lower than the wage of a skilled manual male employee; a maximum limit may be prescribed for the rate of benefit or for the earnings taken into account.[718]

- Under the second, the rate of benefits, for a standard beneficiary, must attain a specified minimum amount in relation to the wage of the ordinary adult male labourer.[719]
- The third formula consists in setting the rate of benefit using a prescribed scale that may depend on the other resources of the beneficiary's family. In this case, the rate must not be less than that calculated using the previous formula. This method can only be used for systems covering all residents.

No matter what the formula chosen, the rate of benefit must therefore attain, for a 'standard beneficiary', a certain percentage of the reference wage or earnings. The standard beneficiary is defined differently for each contingency and serves only as a reference for comparing the rate of benefit provided in national laws and regulations and the provisions of the conventions. The States remain free to adopt their own rules for calculating the rate of benefit, subject to the sole condition that it be at least equal to the rate established by the instruments.

916. A number of legislation, like in Germany, deal with the share of the old-age, invalidity and survivors' benefits in case of divorce. Others consider however that those women today are fully integrated to the labour market and have a direct entitlement to a pension, and not a right dependent on a breadwinner husband.

2. Suspension, Refusal, Withdrawal of Benefits

917. Convention No. 102 and the subsequent conventions[720] recognize three instances in which benefits may be suspended: (a) if the beneficiary is absent from the country in which the rights were acquired; (b) if he is maintained at public expense, or at the expense of a social security institution or service, or if he receives another social security cash benefit; (c) if the beneficiary's personal conduct is open to doubt: for example, if he makes a fraudulent claim, if the contingency arose from a crime, offence or wilful misconduct, if he neglected to call on the appropriate services (medical care, placement, guidance and training services).

918. Conventions Nos. 102, 121 and 128 further provide for the suspension of survivors' benefits as long as the surviving spouse is living with another person as spouse. Conventions Nos. 121, 128 and 130, however, stipulate that part of the cash benefit otherwise due is to be paid to the dependants of the person concerned.

---

718. On the concept, *see* Article 65 of Convention No. 102.
719. On the concept, see Article 66 of Convention No. 102.
720. Articles 69 of Convention No. 102, 22 of Convention No. 121 and 32 of Convention No. 128; Articles 28 of Convention No. 130 and 20 of Convention No. 168.

919. Under the terms of Convention No. 168 on employment promotion and protection against unemployment, benefits may be refused, withdrawn or suspended not only in the above three cases (for example, if the person concerned deliberately contributed to his or her own dismissal or left employment voluntarily without just cause), but also 'during the period of a labour dispute, when the person concerned has stopped work to take part in a labour dispute or when he or she is prevented from working as a direct result of a stoppage of work due to this labour dispute'.[721]

3. The Beneficiaries' Right of Appeal

920. The principle of the right of appeal is set down in Convention No. 102 and in the subsequent conventions.[722] Conventions Nos. 102, 121 and 130 restrict the right of appeal when it comes to medical care if the administration of medical care is entrusted to a government department responsible to a legislature; in that case, the right of appeal may be replaced by a right to have a complaint concerning the refusal of medical care or the quality of the care received investigated by the appropriate authority. The preparatory work for Conventions Nos. 121 and 128 contain additional indications on the nature of the appeal: it does not suffice to allow the person concerned to ask the administrative authority that took the decision to reconsider the matter; an independent authority must render a decision.[723] According to Convention No. 168, the claimants must be informed in writing of the procedures available, which must be simple and rapid. Both Conventions No. 168 and 128 stipulate that the claimant must be able to be represented or assisted by a qualified person of his choice or by a delegate of a representative workers' organization.

§2. The Branches of Social Security

921. The following pages look in succession at the nine branches of social security listed in Convention No. 102 and the other instruments ILO considers to have priority. The minimum income security will be added. For each branch, we shall define the contingency, i.e. the risk to which the protected person is exposed, the personal field of application, i.e. the beneficiaries, the scope of the benefits and the conditions of their allocation. The reference texts will be mentioned in each case at the beginning.[724]

---

721. Article 20(d).
722. Articles 70 of Convention No. 102, 23 of Convention No. 121, 34 of Convention No. 128, 29 of Convention No. 130 and 27 of Convention No. 168.
723. ILC (48th session, 1964), *Report V(2)* (Geneva), ILO, 1964, p. 60; *ibid.*, (50th session, 1966), *Report V(I)* (Geneva), ILO, 1966, p. 68. Compare with Article 70(3) of Convention No. 102 and Article 23(3) of Convention No. 121.
724. *See* also López Morales, Silva and Egorov, *op. cit.*, p. 453 *et seq.* and on Humblet and Silva, *op. cit.*, p. 17 *et seq.*

I. Employment Injury

922. In addition to Convention No. 102 (Part VI), the reference texts are Convention No. 121 and Recommendation No. 121, 1964, on employment injury benefits, and Recommendation No. 194, 2002, on the list of occupational diseases. Mention should also be made of Recommendation No. 67.

A. Definition of the Contingency

923. The contingency comprises morbid condition, incapacity for work, invalidity and loss of faculty resulting from an employment injury. It also covers loss of support as a result of the death of the family breadwinner for the same reasons; in that case, the beneficiaries are the widow and children for Convention No. 102; for Convention No. 121, the beneficiaries are, under the terms of national laws and regulations, the widow, the disabled dependent widower, the deceased's dependent children and any other person designated by national law (parents, grandparents, etc.).

924. Convention No. 121 requires the States to define the term 'industrial accident', including the conditions under which a commuting accident is considered to be an industrial accident. It suggests three means by which the States can determine what are occupational diseases: (a) by prescribing a legal list of recognized occupational diseases, comprising at least the diseases enumerated in Schedule I to the Convention; (b) by including in their legislation a general definition of occupational diseases broad enough to cover the diseases enumerated in Schedule I; (c) by prescribing a list of diseases supplemented by a general definition. The left-hand column of Schedule I lists 29 categories of occupational diseases (the list was updated in 1980) and the right-hand column the types of work involving an exposure to risk. If a protected person contracts one of the diseases listed and is employed in a job involving exposure to the corresponding risk, the disease is presumed to be occupational in origin. Recommendation No. 121 specifies in which cases accidents are always to be considered 'industrial' and the conditions under which a disease is presumed to be occupational in origin. Recommendation No. 194 invites States to draw up a list of occupational diseases for the purposes of prevention, registration, declaration and reparation;[725] the list should contain at least those diseases listed in Schedule I to Convention No. 121; it can also cover the diseases listed in an annex to the Recommendation, which calls for the lists to be periodically updated.[726]

B. Beneficiaries

925. Convention No. 102 applies to wage earners; protection must comprise prescribed classes of employees, constituting not less than 50 per cent of all

725. *See* the 1996 Code of practice on the recording and notification of occupational accidents and diseases.
726. This was most recently done in 2010.

employees.[727] Convention No. 121 has a broader field of application: all wage earners; it specifies that the term covers employees from both the private and the public sectors, from cooperatives and apprentices.[728] As we learned from the principles common to all social security standards, the conventions authorize derogations. Recommendation No. 121 provides for the gradual extension of the benefits provided to any categories that were excluded. It also suggests that the States secure the provision of employment injury or analogous benefits, if necessary through voluntary insurance, to categories of workers who are not wage earners, including self-employed workers.[729]

926. If the family breadwinner dies as a result of the employment injury, the beneficiaries are the widow (the right to benefit may be made conditional on her being presumed to be incapable of self-support) and children for Convention No. 102; for Convention No. 121, the beneficiaries are, under the terms of national laws and regulations, the widow, the disabled dependent widower, the deceased's dependent children and any other person designated by national law (parents, grandparents, etc.).

C. Benefits

927. Conventions Nos. 102 and 121 grant cash medical and other benefits both to the victims and to their dependents in the case of death.

928. Medical care is provided with a view to maintaining, restoring or improving the health of the victim and his ability to work and attend to his personal needs. It must comprise:[730]

(a) general practitioner and specialist in-patient care and out-patient care, including domiciliary visiting;
(b) dental care;
(c) nursing care at home or in hospital or other medical institutions;
(d) maintenance in hospitals, convalescent homes, sanatoria or other medical institutions;
(e) dental, pharmaceutical and other medical or surgical supplies, including prosthetic appliances, kept in repair, and eyeglasses; and
(f) the care furnished by members of such other professions as may at any time be legally recognized as allied to the medical profession, under the supervision of a medical or dental practitioner.

Convention No. 121 adds on-the-spot emergency treatment of persons sustaining a serious accident and follow-up treatment of those whose injury is slight (and does

727. Article 33.
728. Article 4.
729. Para. 3.
730. Articles 34 of Convention No. 102 and 10 of Convention No. 121.

not entail discontinuance of work). The States authorized to make temporary derogations from this list provide more limited treatment.[731]

929. The cash benefits to be paid in the event of incapacity for work, loss of earning capacity (or corresponding loss of faculty), or death of the family breadwinner must take the form of periodic payments.[732] In the case of temporary incapacity for work and of total loss of earning capacity likely to be permanent (or in the case of corresponding loss of faculty), the amounts of the payments for a standard beneficiary (i.e. a man with a wife and two children) must be 50 per cent of the reference wage under Convention No. 102 and 60 per cent under Convention No. 121; Recommendation No. 121 suggests that the amount of the benefits not be less than two-thirds of the victim's previous earnings. In the case of a partial loss of earning capacity,[733] likely to be permanent, the amount of the benefit should correspond to a fair proportion of that which is due in the case of total loss.

930. These instruments allow the benefits due for permanent incapacity to be converted into a lump-sum payment[734] when the incapacity is slight or there is a guarantee that the sum paid will be wisely used. Convention No. 121 underscores the exceptional nature of this possibility and makes it subject to the victim's agreement. It does, however, allow States to make such payments if they do not have the administrative resources required to make regular periodic payments.

931. The survivors' benefits for a widow with two children must amount to at least 40 per cent of the reference wage under Convention No. 102 and 50 per cent under Convention No. 121.

932. In addition, Convention No. 121 stipulates that periodic payments may not be lower than a minimum prescribed amount. Both conventions provide that the benefits are to be reviewed following substantial changes in the general level of earnings or in the cost of living.

933. Convention No. 121 underscores preventive measures and calls for additional protection as follows:

(a) victims whose condition requires the constant assistance of a third party must receive extra benefits;
(b) national laws and regulations must provide for a funeral benefit that is not less than the normal cost of a funeral;
(c) the States must organize rehabilitation services and facilitate the placement of the disabled in suitable employment.

731. *See* Articles 34 of Convention No. 102 and 12 of Convention No. 121.
732. On the manner to calculate the periodical payment, *see* Articles 36, 65 and 66 of Convention No. 102 and Articles 13, 14, 19 and 20 of Convention No. 121.
733. Convention No. 121 refers to *substantial* partial loss of earning capacity, in excess of a prescribed degree: Article 14(3).
734. It corresponds to the actuarial equivalent of the periodical payment.

D. *Conditions of Allocation*

934. There is no waiting period for any of the benefits discussed here. Entitlement exists as of the occurrence of the contingency. Convention No. 102 nevertheless accepts that the benefit need not be paid for the first three days of incapacity for work (resulting from an employment injury, accident or occupational disease) in each case of suspension of earnings.[735] Convention No. 121 is more restrictive and allows for a delay[736] in two cases only: if the State benefits from temporary derogations, or where its legislation provided for a waiting period at the date on which the Convention came into force. Recommendation No. 121 suggests that all waiting periods be eliminated.

934bis. Convention No. 121 authorizes the suspension of the benefits as long as a surviving spouse is living with another person as spouse.

II. Medical Care

935. The reference texts here are Part II of Convention No. 102, and Convention No. 130 and Recommendation No. 134, 1969, on medical care and sickness benefits. Recommendation No. 69 also deals with medical care.

A. *Definition of the Contingency*

936. Here as in the previous contingency, medical care is afforded with a view to maintaining, restoring or improving the health of the person protected and his ability to work and attend to his personal needs.[737] The State must also guarantee medical care of a preventive or curative nature and the needs associated with pregnancy, confinement and their consequences.[738]

B. *Beneficiaries*

937. The State has the option of protecting a certain percentage of wage earners, of the economically active population or of residents,[739] as follows:

(a) 'wage earners' option: 50 per cent at least of all wage earners, plus their spouses and children, under Convention No. 102, and all wage earners (their spouses and children), including apprentices, under Convention No. 130;

---

735. Article 38.
736. Article 9.
737. Article 10, para. 3 of Convention No. 102; Article 9 of Convention No. 130.
738. Articles 7 of Convention No. 102 and 8 of Convention No. 130.
739. Article 9 of Convention No. 102 and Article 10 of Convention No. 130.

(b) 'working population' option: prescribed classes of the working population, constituting not less than 20 per cent of all residents (and their wives and children) under Convention No. 102, and prescribed classes of the working population, constituting not less than 75 per cent of the entire working population (and their wives and children) under Convention No. 130;
(c) 'residents' option: not less than 50 per cent of all residents under Convention No. 102, not less than 75 per cent under Convention No. 130.

Recommendation No. 134 suggests that medical care be extended by stages to the entire working population and to all residents.

C. Benefits

938. Convention No. 102 requires that the benefit include at least, in the case of sickness, general practitioner care (including domiciliary visiting), specialist care, essential prescribed pharmaceutical supplies and hospitalization where necessary.[740] Convention No. 130 adds[741] dental care and medical rehabilitation, including the supply, maintenance and renewal of prosthetic and orthopaedic appliances, and Recommendation No. 134, the supply of medical aids, such as eyeglasses, and services for convalescents.

939. Both Conventions No. 102 and No. 130 allow that the beneficiaries may be required to share in the cost of the medical care. Cost-sharing should not, however, result in hardship or, according to Convention No. 130 only, 'prejudice the effectiveness of medical and social protection'.

D. Conditions of Allocation

940. In order to prevent abuse, the States may make entitlement to benefits subject to a qualifying period,[742] i.e. a period of contribution, a period of employment, a period of residence, or a combination thereof. Recommendation No. 134 calls for the elimination of qualifying periods.

941. Once the entitlement to benefits has been recognized, the beneficiary must receive the medical care throughout the contingency. In particular, the benefit cannot be suspended while a sickness benefit continues to be paid or for as long as the case must be extended for diseases recognized as entailing prolonged care. On these conditions, Convention No. 102 nevertheless authorizes the States to limit the duration of the benefit to 26 weeks in each case, or to 13 weeks in countries whose economy and medical facilities are insufficiently developed. Convention No. 130

740. *See* Article 10 which also refers to medical care in case of pregnancy and confinement and their consequences.
741. *See* Article 13 which refers to the 'necessary' rather than 'essential' pharmaceutical supplies.
742. Articles 11 of Convention No. 102 and 15 of Convention No. 130.

allows the benefit to be limited to 26 weeks only where the beneficiary ceases to belong to the categories of persons protected, but the sickness started while he belonged to the said categories.[743]

III. Sickness Benefits

942. This branch and the previous one are obviously interrelated and are therefore dealt with in the same international instruments: Convention No. 102 (in this case Part III), Convention No. 130 and Recommendation No 134. Recommendation No. 67 should be added.

A. *Definition of the Contingency*

943. The contingency covered comprises incapacity for work resulting from a morbid condition and involving suspension of earnings.[744] Recommendation No. 134 suggests that cash benefits should also be paid in cases of absence from work for the following reasons:[745]

(a) curative or preventive medical care;
(b) isolation for the purpose of quarantine;
(c) placement under medical supervision for the purpose of rehabilitation;
(d) convalescent leave.

B. *Beneficiaries*

944. The State can chose, as for medical care, between protecting:[746]

(a) at least 50 per cent of all wage earners (Convention No. 102) or all wage earners, including apprentices (Convention No. 130);
(b) prescribed classes of the economically active population, constituting not less than 20 per cent of all residents (Convention No. 102), or 75 per cent of the whole economically active population (Convention No. 130); or
(c) all residents whose means during the contingency do not exceed prescribed limits.

Recommendation No. 134 suggests that the right to benefits should gradually be extended to casual workers, members of the employer's family living in his house,

743. Articles 12 of Convention No. 102 and 16 of Convention No. 130.
744. Article 14 of Convention No. 102 and Article 7(b) of Convention No. 130.
745. *See* para. 8 of Recommendation No. 134.
746. Article 15 of Convention No. 102 and Article 19 of Convention No. 130.

in respect of their work for him, and more broadly all economically active persons.[747]

C. *Benefits*

945. The method for calculating periodic payments was explained in §1 above, on general principles. The amount of sickness benefits must correspond, for a standard beneficiary (a man with a wife and two children) to a percentage of the reference wage fixed at, at least, 45 per cent in Convention No. 102 and 60 per cent in Convention No. 130.[748] The latter stipulates that in the event of the beneficiary's death, the survivors (or the persons who bore the expense of the funeral) must receive a funeral benefit.

D. *Conditions of Allocation*

946. The State can, as in the case of the previous branch, make entitlement to benefits subject to a qualifying period.[749] Once that condition has been met, the beneficiaries must receive the benefit throughout the contingency. All three reference instruments nevertheless allow that it may not be granted for the first three days of suspension of earnings (waiting period) and that it may be limited in the event of sickness either to 26 weeks (Convention No. 102) or to 52 weeks (Convention No. 130). States whose economy and medical facilities are insufficiently developed can reduce the minimum duration of benefits in each case of incapacity to 13 weeks (Convention No. 102) or 26 weeks (Convention No. 130).

IV. Invalidity Benefits

947. The relevant instruments for this branch of social security are Convention No. 102 (Part IX), Convention No. 128 and Recommendation No. 131.

A. *Definition of the Contingency*

948. The risk covered is the inability to engage in any gainful activity, when said inability is likely to be permanent or persists after the exhaustion of sickness benefit.[750] Recommendation No. 131 requires that account be taken of the incapacity to engage in an activity involving substantial gain.[751]

747. Para. 11.
748. Articles 65 to 67 of Convention No. 102 and 22 to 24 of Convention No. 130.
749. Articles 17–18 of Convention No. 102 and 25–26 of Convention No. 130.
750. Article 54 of Convention No. 102 and Article 8 of Convention No. 128.
751. Para. 4.

B. Beneficiaries

949. The formula is unchanged. The State must protect either:[752]

(a) 50 per cent of employees (Convention No. 102) or all employees, including apprentices (Convention No. 128);
(b) prescribed classes of the economically active population, constituting not less than 20 per cent of all residents (Convention No. 102) or not less than 75 per cent of the whole economically active population (Convention No. 128); or
(c) all residents (Convention No. 128), or residents whose means during the contingency do not exceed prescribed limits (Conventions Nos. 102 and 128).

Recommendation No. 131 encourages the States to extend benefits to casual workers and more broadly to all economically active persons.[753]

C. Benefits

950. The benefits take the form of periodic payments the amount of which must correspond, for a standard beneficiary (a man with a wife and two children) to a given percentage of the reference wage: 40 per cent under Convention No. 102, 50 per cent under Convention No. 128 and 60 per cent under Recommendation No. 131.[754] The Recommendation adds[755] that national legislation should fix minimum amounts of benefits so as to ensure a minimum standard of living; increments in benefits should be provided for persons requiring the constant help of another person.

951. The benefits should be paid throughout the contingency or until an old-age benefit becomes payable. They should be periodically adjusted to take account of changes in the general level of earnings or the cost of living.[756]

952. Convention No. 128 further requires the State to provide rehabilitation and placement services enabling the disabled to resume their occupational activity; this obligation does not apply to countries benefiting from temporary derogations.[757]

D. Conditions of Allocation

953. Both Convention No. 102 and Convention No. 128 make entitlement to benefits contingent on a qualifying period:[758] 15 years of employment or

752. Articles 55 of Convention No. 102 and 9 of Convention No. 128.
753. Para. 2.
754. Articles 56 of Convention No. 102 and 10 of Convention No. 128; para. 22 of Recommendation No. 131.
755. Paras 23 and 25.
756. Articles 58, 65, 66 of Convention No. 102 and 12 and 29 of Convention No. 128; para. 24 of Recommendation No. 131.
757. Article 13.
758. Articles 57 of Convention No. 102 and 11 of Convention No. 128.

contribution or 10 years of residence. Where the benefit is conditional upon a minimum period of contribution, employment or – according to Convention No. 128 – residence, a reduced benefit must be secured to persons who have completed a qualifying period of five years of contribution, employment or residence. Where the national system protects all workers, more flexible rules apply for complete and reduced invalidity benefits.

V. Survivors' Benefits

954. The reference texts for this branch are Convention No. 102 (Part X), Convention No. 128 and Recommendation No. 67 and No 131.

A. Definition of the Contingency

955. The risk consists[759] in the loss of support suffered by the widow or child as the result of the death of the breadwinner. The benefits therefore cover the husband's dependent wife, and the mother or father's dependent children, if the deceased was the family breadwinner. As we may see, they have a strong gender bias.

956. Convention No. 102 subordinates the widow's entitlement to benefits to the presumption that she cannot meet her own needs. Convention No. 128 further specifies[760] that entitlement may be made conditional on the attainment of a prescribed age; that age may not, however, be higher than the age prescribed for old-age benefit. No requirement of age may be made if the widow is invalid or is caring for a dependent child of the deceased. Both Conventions also stipulate that a minimum duration of marriage may be required in certain circumstances.

957. The term 'child' refers to children under school-leaving age or under 15 years of age, whichever is higher. Convention No. 128 raises the age if the child is an apprentice or student or has a chronic illness or infirmity disabling him for any gainful activity.[761]

B. Beneficiaries

958. The persons protected must comprise either:[762]

(a) 'employees' option: the wives and children of employed breadwinners belonging to classes that constitute not less than 50 per cent of all employees

759. Article 60 of Convention No. 102 and 21 of Convention No. 128.
760. On the conditions of means: *see* Article 22(1).
761. *See* the meaning of term 'child' for the purpose of the convention.
762. Articles 61 of Convention No. 102 and 22 of Convention No. 128.

(Convention No. 102); the wives, children and, as may be prescribed, other dependants of all breadwinners who were employees or apprentices (Convention No. 128);

(b) 'economically active population' option: the wives and children of breadwinners in classes of the economically active population, which classes constitute not less than 20 per cent of all residents (Convention No. 102); the wives, children and, as may be prescribed, other dependants of breadwinners in classes of the economically active population constituting not less than 75 per cent of the whole economically active population (Convention No. 128); or

(c) 'residents' option: all resident widows and children who have lost their breadwinner and whose means do not exceed prescribed limits (Convention No. 102); all widows, children and other prescribed dependants who have lost their breadwinner, who are residents and, as appropriate, whose means during the contingency do not exceed prescribed limits (Convention No. 128).

959. In the case of a widow, Convention No. 102 authorizes the right to benefit to be made conditional on her being presumed to be incapable of self-support. Recommendation No. 131 extends entitlement to benefits to the wives, children and other dependants of casual workers and of any economically active person. It does the same for invalid and dependent widowers.[763]

C. Benefits

960. The benefits take the form of periodic payments the amount of which must correspond,[764] for the standard beneficiary (widow with two children), to a percentage of the reference wage: 40 per cent under Convention No. 102, 45 per cent under Convention No. 128 and 55 per cent under Recommendation No. 131. The latter further requires national legislation to fix minimum amounts, as in the case of invalidity benefits, so as to ensure a minimum standard of living and to increment the benefit when the beneficiary's condition requires the constant assistance of another person.

961. Entitlement to benefits is maintained throughout the contingency. They may be suspended for the widow as long as she is living with a man as his wife. As for invalidity benefits, the amount should be periodically adjusted to take account of changes in the general level of earnings or the cost of living.

D. Conditions of Allocation

962. Both conventions impose qualifying periods that the breadwinner must, as appropriate, have completed in order for the benefits to be due at the prescribed

763. Paras 2 and 12.

764. Article 62 of Convention No. 102, Article 23 of Convention No. 128 and para. 22 of Recommendation No. 131.

level.[765] The qualifying period must in principle not exceed 15 years of contribution or employment, or ten years of residence.

963. Where the granting of benefits is conditional on a qualifying period of contribution or employment, the persons protected are entitled, as in the case of invalidity, to receive reduced benefits if the breadwinner has completed five years of contribution, employment or residence. When the national system protects the women and children of all working persons, more flexible rules apply for full and reduced benefits. Convention No. 128, however, in the case of a widow, authorizes the right to a survivors' benefit to be made conditional on the attainment of a prescribed age.

VI. Old-age Benefits

964. Here again, the standards are set down in Convention No. 102 (Part V), Convention No. 128 and Recommendations No.67 and No 131.

A. *Definition of the Contingency*

965. The contingency covered is survival beyond a prescribed age, usually 65.[766] The reference conventions allow that a higher age may be set on the basis of objective criteria: working ability under Convention No. 102, demographic, economic and social criteria demonstrated statistically (life expectancy, rate of activity of elderly persons, etc.) under Convention No. 128.

966. If the age of retirement is 65 years or higher, Convention No. 128 requires that it be lowered for persons engaged in occupations that are deemed to be arduous or unhealthy. Recommendation No. 131 also calls for the pensionable age to be lowered for prescribed categories of persons on social grounds.[767]

B. *Beneficiaries*

967. The beneficiaries must comprise:[768]

(a) 'employees' option: classes of employees constituting not less than 50 per cent of all employees (Convention No. 102), or all employees, including apprentices (Convention No. 128);
(b) 'economically active population' option: classes of the economically active population constituting not less than 20 per cent of all residents (Convention

765. Articles 63 of Convention No. 102 and 24 of Convention No. 128.
766. Articles 26 of Convention No. 102 and 15 of Convention No. 128.
767. Paragraph 7.
768. Article 27 of Convention No. 102 and 16 of Convention No. 128.

No. 102), or 75 per cent of the whole economically active population (Convention No. 128);

(c) 'residents' option: all residents (Convention No. 128) or all residents whose means do not exceed prescribed limits (Conventions Nos. 102 and 128).

Recommendation No. 131 suggests for this branch as well that the right to a pension be extended by stages to casual workers and to all economically active persons.[769]

C. Benefits

968. The goal of the ILO standards is to ensure that the beneficiaries have decent means of existence for the rest of their lives. The level of the pension paid periodically must be, for a standard beneficiary (a married man), a fixed percentage of the reference wage at the end of a maximum qualifying period: 40 per cent under Convention No. 102, 45 per cent under Convention No. 128 and 55 per cent under Recommendation No. 131. As in the case of invalidity and survivors' benefits, the Recommendation invites the States to fix minimum amounts of old-age benefits so as to ensure a minimum standard of living and to increment them for beneficiaries whose condition requires the constant assistance of another person.[770]

969. An important goal is obviously to maintain the pensioners' purchasing power, as inflation can chip away at what is the main or only source of income for many pensioners. Both conventions therefore establish the principle that the amount of the benefits are to be reviewed following substantial changes in the general level of earnings or in the cost of living.[771]

D. Conditions of Allocation

970. Again, the ILO standards provide for qualifying periods to obtain a pension. In the first place, the State can require a specific qualifying period to benefit from pensions attaining the (minimum) amount prescribed in Conventions Nos. 102 and 128: in principle,[772] a maximum period of 30 years of contribution or employment or 20 years of residence. More flexible rules apply when all working persons are protected.

971. The conventions also establish (minimum) qualifying periods for entitlement to a pension. Thus, the State must secure reduced pensions for persons who

769. Para. 2.
770. Paras 23 and 25.
771. Articles 65 and 66 of Convention No. 102; Article 29 of Convention No. 128; *see also* para. 24 of Recommendation No. 131.
772. Articles 29 of Convention No. 102 and 18 of Convention No. 128.

have contributed or been employed for 15 years. Convention No. 128[773] also authorizes the payment of a pension that is 10 per cent lower than the prescribed level if the benefits are secured to any person protected after a maximum qualifying period of ten years of employment or contribution or five years of residence.

VII. Maternity Benefits

972. Convention No. 102 (Parts II and VIII), Convention No. 183 and Recommendation No. 191 are the main instruments in this field; Convention No. 183 revises in particular an older convention – No. 103 of 1952 – on the same subject. They are also dealt with in Recommendation No 67.[774] Maternity benefits must be viewed as part of the broader issue of the protection of women workers, which was discussed in the preceding chapter.[775]

A. *Definition of the Contingency*

973. The contingency is defined in Article 47 of Convention No. 102: pregnancy and confinement and their consequences, and suspension of earnings resulting therefrom.

B. *Beneficiaries*

974. Convention No. 102 provides for two options:[776]

(a) women in classes of employees constituting not less than 50 per cent of all employees and, for maternity medical benefit, also the wives of men in these classes; or
(b) women in classes of the economically active population constituting not less than 20 per cent of all residents, and, for maternity medical benefit, also the wives of men in these classes.

Convention No. 183 applies to all employed women, including those 'in atypical forms of dependent work'.[777]

C. *Benefits*

975. The benefits are medical care and cash.

773. Article 18 para. 3.
774. Annex, para. 10.
775. §10 I.A.
776. Article 48.
777. Article 2, para. 1.

976. Under Convention No. 102, medical care must comprise at least[778] hospitalization where necessary, and pre-natal, confinement and post-natal care either by medical practitioners or by qualified midwives. Recommendation No. 191 broadens the protection to:[779]

(a) care given in a doctor's office, at home or in a hospital or other medical establishment by a general practitioner or a specialist;
(b) maternity care given by a qualified midwife or by another maternity service at home or in a hospital or other medical establishment;
(c) maintenance in a hospital or other medical establishment;
(d) any necessary pharmaceutical and medical supplies, examinations and tests prescribed by a medical practitioner or other qualified person; and
(e) dental and surgical care.

977. The benefits paid in respect of suspension of earnings (resulting from maternity) must correspond, according to Convention No. 102,[780] to 45 per cent of the reference wage. Convention No. 183 requires that cash benefits enable the woman to maintain herself and her child 'in proper conditions of health and with a suitable standard of living'. Where the amount of the benefits is based on previous earnings, it must not be less than two-thirds of the woman's previous earnings; if other methods of calculation are used, the amount must be comparable. States whose economy and social security system are insufficiently developed can limit the level of benefits to that granted in the event of sickness or temporary incapacity for work. Recommendation No. 191 encourages the States to raise the cash benefits to the full amount of the woman's previous earnings.[781]

D. Conditions of Allocation

978. Convention No. 102 allows the States to make entitlement to benefits contingent on a qualifying period if they consider this necessary to preclude abuse. Once the entitlement to the benefits has been recognized, the beneficiaries must receive it throughout the contingency; the benefits may be limited to the length of the maternity leave and to a minimum of 12 weeks if the leave is not longer.[782]

979. Convention No. 183 also sets conditions for entitlement to benefits. The States must nevertheless ensure that the conditions can be satisfied by a large majority of the women to whom the Convention applies; women who do not meet those conditions are entitled to adequate benefits out of social assistance funds (subject to the means test required for such assistance).[783]

---

778. *See* Articles 10(b) and 49.
779. Para. 3; *see also* Article 4, para. 7 of Convention No. 183.
780. Article 50.
781. Articles 6 (paras 2 to 4) and 7 of Convention No. 183; para. 2 of Recommendation No. 191.
782. Articles 51 and 52 of Convention No. 102.
783. *See* Article 6, paras 5 and 6.

VIII. Family Benefits

980. The only reference standards are contained in Convention No. 102 (Part VII).

A. Definition of the Contingency

981. The contingency covered concerns the maintenance of children (i.e. children under school-leaving age or under 15 years of age).[784] The wording of Article 40 of Convention No. 102 ('The contingency covered shall be responsibility for the maintenance of children as prescribed') allows national laws and regulations to limit the number of children in respect of which benefits are payable.

B. Beneficiaries

982. Children as such are not entitled to family benefits: the beneficiaries are not the children themselves but rather the persons in whose charge they are. The beneficiaries must comprise,[785] in accordance with the now familiar formula:

(a) classes of employees constituting not less than 50 per cent of all employees;
(b) classes of the economically active population constituting not less than 20 per cent of all residents; or
(c) all residents whose means during the contingency do not exceed prescribed limits.

C. Benefits

983. The Convention provides for benefits in kind (food, clothing, housing, holidays or domestic help), cash benefits or a combination of the two. Unlike the other branches of social security, here the level of benefits is calculated overall and not in terms of a standard beneficiary. More specifically, the total value of the benefits must represent[786] either:

(a) three per cent of the wage of an ordinary adult male labourer, multiplied by the total number of children of persons protected; or
(b) 1.5 per cent of the said wage, multiplied by the total number of children of all residents.

---

784. *See* Articles 1 and 40 of the Convention.
785. Article 41.
786. Article 44.

D. *Conditions of Allocation*

984. Entitlement to benefits is contingent on a qualifying period of three months of contribution or employment, or one year of residence.[787] The benefits are granted throughout the contingency, i.e. until the child reaches the age of 15 or is no longer obliged to attend school.[788]

IX. Unemployment Benefits

985. The reference instruments in this case are Recommendation No 67, Convention No. 102 (Part IV), Convention No. 168 and Recommendation No. 176. The latter two also cover employment promotion, an area discussed earlier.[789]

A. *Definition of the Contingency*

986. The contingency is the suspension, reduction or loss of earnings due to inability to obtain suitable employment in the case of a person protected who is capable of, and available for, work;[790] in order to link the unemployment benefit to employment promotion, Convention No. 168 requires that the beneficiary actually be seeking work.

987. Convention No. 102 deals with full unemployment. Convention No. 168 also deals with partial unemployment and the suspension or reduction of earnings due to a temporary suspension of work; it requires the States to endeavour to pay benefits to part-time workers who are actually seeking full-time work.[791]

B. *Beneficiaries*

988. The persons protected must include:[792]

(a) 'employees' option: classes of employees constituting not less than 50 per cent of all employees (Convention No. 102), or classes of employees constituting not less than 85 per cent of all employees, including public employees and apprentices (Convention No. 168); or
(b) 'residents' option: all residents whose means during the contingency do not exceed prescribed limits (Conventions Nos. 102 and 168).

---

787. Article 43.
788. Article 45.
789. *See* Chapter 2, §3.IV.
790. Articles 20 of Convention No. 102 and 10 of Convention No. 168.
791. When their social security system is not sufficiently developed, Member States may defer the extension of the protection to those contingencies: *see* Article 10(4) of Convention No. 168.
792. Articles 21 of Convention No. 102, 11 and 12 of Convention No. 168.

Recommendation No. 176 invites the States gradually to extend the application of their legislation on unemployment benefits to all wage earners.[793]

C. *Benefits*

989. The benefits are periodic payments the amount of which must correspond, for a standard beneficiary (a man with a wife and two children), to a fixed percentage of the reference wage.[794] Under Convention No. 102 the figure is 45 per cent; under Convention No. 168 it is 45 per cent for countries benefiting from temporary derogations and 50 per cent for all others. The benefits are in respect of full unemployment and, as Convention No. 168 stipulates, of suspension of earnings due to a temporary suspension of work without any break in the employment relationship.[795]

990. Recommendation No. 176 contains numerous provisions on partial unemployment, workers who experience hardship during the qualifying period, persons newly seeking work and part-time workers.

D. *Conditions of Allocation*

991. The law may make entitlement to benefits contingent on the expiry of a qualifying period, which must be no longer than needed to preclude abuse.[796]

992. Convention No. 168 contains a special section on new applicants for employment. The States must take account of the following categories of persons seeking work who have never been, or have ceased to be, recognized as unemployed or have never been, or have ceased to be, covered by schemes for the protection of the unemployed:

(a) young persons who have completed their vocational training;
(b) young persons who have completed their studies;
(c) young persons who have completed their compulsory military service;
(d) persons after a period devoted to bringing up a child or caring for someone who is sick, disabled or elderly;
(e) persons whose spouse had died, when they are not entitled to a survivor's benefit;
(f) divorced or separated persons;
(g) released prisoners;
(h) adults, including disabled persons, who have completed a period of training;

793. *See* para. 16.
794. On the reference wage for the purpose of Convention No. 168: *see* Article 15; for the purpose of Convention No. 102, *see* Article 22.
795. In case of labour conflict, *see* Article 20(d) and para. 919 *above*.
796. Articles 23 of Convention No. 102 and 17 of Convention No. 168.

(i) migrant workers on return to their home country, except in so far as they have acquired rights under the legislation of the country where they last worked;
(j) previously self-employed persons.

Three at least of these ten categories must receive social benefits.[797]

993. Both Convention No. 102 and Convention No. 168 allow[798] the States to make payment of benefits contingent on a waiting period. That period is not to exceed 7 days in principle for each case of suspension of earnings, ten days for countries benefiting, under Convention No. 168, from temporary derogations. For seasonal workers, the period must be adapted to their occupational circumstances.

994. Once the entitlement has been recognized, the beneficiary must receive the benefits in principle throughout the contingency. Both conventions nevertheless authorize limits:

(a) Convention No. 102 (Article 24):
  - where classes of employees are protected, to 13 weeks within a period of 12 months; or
  - where all residents (whose means do not exceed prescribed limits) are protected, to 26 weeks within a period of 12 months;

(b) Convention No. 168 (Articles 19 and 5):
  - the initial duration of payment of the benefit may be limited to 26 weeks in each spell of unemployment, or to 39 weeks over any period of 24 months;
  - the duration of payment of benefit may be limited to 13 weeks over any periods of 12 months for States benefiting from temporary derogations;[799]
  - in the event of unemployment continuing beyond the initial period of benefit, the duration of payment of benefit, which may be calculated in the light of the resources of the beneficiary and his or her family, may be limited to a prescribed period.

995. Under Convention No. 168, when an unemployed person has received severance pay[800] from the employer or from any other source, the unemployment benefit may be suspended or the severance pay reduced by an amount corresponding to the total value of the unemployment benefit.

996. Under Convention No. 168, it is also possible to refuse (withdraw, suspend or reduce) benefits if the beneficiary refuses to accept suitable employment.[801] It lists the points to be taken into account in assessing the suitability of employment: age, length of service in the former occupation, experience, the length of the period of unemployment, the labour market situation, the impact of the employment in

797. Article 26.
798. Articles 24 of Convention No. 102 and 18 of Convention No. 168.
799. *See also* Article 19, para. 4.
800. Article 22 of Convention No. 168.
801. Article 21.

question on the person's personal and family situation and whether the employment is vacant as a direct result of a stoppage of work due to an ongoing labour dispute. Recommendation No. 176[802] considers that the concept of suitable employment should not apply to situations such as employment involving a change of occupation that does not take account of the person's abilities and qualifications, a change of residence ('to a place in which suitable accommodation is not available'), or conditions and remuneration that are appreciably less favourable than those generally granted in the occupation and district. The concept of suitable employment is also to be found in Convention No. 102 (in the definition itself of the contingency), which therefore authorizes the suspension of benefits should such employment be refused.[803] Recommendation No. 67 distinguishes between an initial period 'reasonable in the circumstances of the case' and a later period when employment involving a change of occupation or of residence, or employment under conditions less favourable, may be deemed to be suitable.[804]

X. Minimum Income Security

997. Most social insurance schemes aim at replacing a certain percentage of the beneficiary's previous income, which would allow the beneficiary to maintain a minimum acceptable standard of living in relation to previous standard of living. The primary objective therefore is not only to provide a minimum benefit level, but also to maintain a certain level of living in the event of the loss of earned income due to specific contingencies, including unemployment. Convention No. 102 and subsequent instruments on social security have then their limitations when it comes to ensuring a defined minimum benefit package; they neither define priority benefits nor require universal coverage.[805] The Income Security Recommendation, 1944 (No. 67) brought together in a single instrument all provisions for income maintenance in case of inability to work or to obtain work and recommended the extension of these provisions to all workers, whether employed, self-employed, urban or rural, as well as to their dependants. The instrument relies on social insurance as the main protection mechanism. It was however the first to define social assistance as a complement to social insurance extending protection to the vulnerable and needy population.[806] It has been completed the same year by the Medical Care Recommendation (No. 69), already mentioned. More recently, Recommendation No. 202, 2012 promote the establishment and maintenance of national floors of social protection.

802. Para. 14.
803. Article 20.
804. Annex, para. 14.
805. ILC, *Social Security for Social Justice and a Fair Globalization,* (Report VI), Geneva: 100th Session, ILO, 2011, paras. 99 and 439.
806. ILC, Social *Security and the Rule of Law*, Report of the Committee of Experts on the Application of Conventions and Recommendations, Report III (Part 1B) 100th Session, 2011, ILO, Geneva, 2011, paras. 39 and 40.

§3. Definition of the Contingency

998. Income security schemes should relieve want and prevent destitution by restoring, up to a reasonable level, income which is lost by reason of inability to work (including because of old-age) or to obtain remunerative work or by reason of the death of a breadwinner. The income security regime should be organized as far as possible on the basis of compulsory social insurance, whereby insured persons fulfilling prescribed qualifying conditions are entitled, in consideration of the contributions they have paid to an insurance institution, to benefits payable at rates, and in contingencies, defined by law.

999. Compensation should be provided in cases of incapacity for work and of death resulting from employment. In order that the benefits provided by social insurance may be closely adapted to the variety of needs, the contingencies covered should be classified as follows:

- sickness, i.e. the loss of earnings due to abstention from work necessitated on medical grounds by an acute condition, due to disease or injury, requiring medical treatment or supervision;
- maternity, i.e. the loss of earnings due to abstention from work during prescribed periods before and after childbirth;
- invalidity, i.e. the inability to engage in any substantially gainful work by reason of a chronic condition, due to disease or injury, or by reason of the loss of a member or function;
- old-age, i.e., the attainment of a prescribed age, which should be that at which persons commonly become incapable of efficient work, the incidence of sickness and invalidity becomes heavy, and unemployment, if present, is likely to be permanent;
- death of the breadwinner, i.e., the loss of support presumably suffered by the dependants as the result of the death of the head of the family;
- unemployment, i.e., the loss of earnings due to the unemployment of an insured person who is ordinarily employed, capable of regular employment in some occupation, and seeking suitable employment, or due to part-time unemployment;
- emergency expenses, i.e., extraordinary expenses, not otherwise covered, incurred in cases of sickness, maternity, invalidity and death;
- employment injury, i.e., a traumatic injury or disease resulting from employment and not brought about deliberately or by the serious and wilful misconduct of the victim, which results in temporary or permanent incapacity or death.[807]

Recommendation No. 202[808] refers to benefits for child and family and survivors in addition to benefits in case of sickness and health care, disability, maternity, old-age, unemployment and employment guarantees, and employment injury.

807. Paras 6–7, 9–16 of Recommendation No. 67.
808. Para. 9.

1000. Benefits should not be payable at the same time for more than one of the following contingencies: invalidity, old-age and unemployment.[809]

1001. Provision for needs not covered by compulsory social insurance should be made by social assistance; certain categories of persons, particularly dependent children and needy invalids, aged persons and widows should be entitled to allowances at reasonable rates according to a prescribed scale. Social assistance appropriate to the needs of the case should be provided for other persons in want.[810]

§4. Beneficiaries

1002. Social insurance should afford protection, in the contingencies to which they are exposed, to all employed and self-employed persons, together with their dependants, in respect of whom it is practicable to collect contributions without incurring disproportionate administrative expenditure and to pay benefits with the necessary cooperation of medical and employment services and with due precautions against abuse.

1003. Persons employed for remuneration should be insured against the whole range of contingencies covered by social insurance as soon as the collection of contributions in respect of them can be organized and the necessary arrangements can be made for the administration of benefit. The employer should be made responsible for collecting contributions in respect of all persons employed by him, and should be entitled to deduct the sums due by them from their remuneration at the time when it is paid.

1004. Self-employed persons should be insured against the contingencies of invalidity, old-age and death, under the same conditions as employed persons, as soon as the collection of their contributions can be organized. Consideration should be given to the possibility of insuring them also against sickness and maternity necessitating hospitalization, sickness which has lasted for several months, and extraordinary expenses incurred in cases of sickness, maternity, invalidity and death.[811]

1005. Recommendation No. 202 also provides[812] for basic income security, at least at a nationally defined minimum level, for children, for persons in active age who are unable to earn sufficient income, particularly in case of sickness, unemployment, maternity and disability, and for persons in old-age.

---

809. Para. 7 of Recommendation No. 67.
810. Paras 3–4 of Recommendation No. 67.
811. Paras 17, 18, 20, 21 of Recommendation No. 67.
812. Para. 5.

§5. Benefits

1006. The range of contingencies to be covered by compulsory social insurance should embrace all contingencies in which an insured person is prevented from earning his living, whether by inability to work or inability to obtain remunerative work, or in which he dies leaving a dependent family, and should include certain associated emergencies, generally experienced, which involved extraordinary strain on limited incomes, insofar as they are not otherwise covered.[813]

1007. Free pre-natal and post-natal medical care for the most vulnerable should be considered.[814] Supplements for each of the first two children should be added to all benefits payable for loss of earnings, provision for further children being left to be made by means of children's allowances payable out of public funds or under contributory schemes.[815]

1008. The benefits should replace lost earnings, with due regard to family responsibilities, up to as high a level as is practicable without impairing the will to resume work where resumption is a possibility, and without levying charges on the productive groups so heavy that output and employment are checked. They should be related to the previous earnings of the insured person on the basis of which he has contributed, provided that any excess of earnings over those prevalent among skilled workers may be ignored for the purpose of determining the rate of benefits, or portions thereof, financed from sources other than the contributions of the insured person. Benefits at flat rates may be appropriate for countries where adequate and economical facilities exist for the population to procure additional protection by voluntary insurance. Such benefits should be commensurate with the earnings of unskilled workers.[816]

1009. Social Assistance mechanisms should complement social insurance designed to secure the well-being of dependent children, as well as to provide special maintenance allowances at prescribed rates in favour of invalids, aged persons and widows who are not receiving social insurance benefits because they or their husbands were not compulsorily insured, and whose incomes do not exceed a prescribed level. Appropriate allowances in cash or partly in cash and partly in kind should also be provided for all persons who are in need and do not require internment for corrective care.[817]

§6. Conditions of Allocation

1010. The right to social insurance benefits other than compensation for employment injuries should be subject to contribution conditions designed to prove that the

813. Para. 5 of Recommendation No. 67.
814. Para. 8 (a) of Recommendation No. 202.
815. Para 8 of Recommendation No. 67.
816. Paras 22–24 of Recommendation No. 67.
817. Paras 28–30 of Recommendation No. 67.

normal status of the claimant is that of an employed or self-employed person and to maintain reasonable regularity in the payment of contributions, provided that a person should not be disqualified for benefits by reason of the failure of his employer duly to collect the contributions payable in respect of him. The cost of benefits, including the cost of administration, should be distributed among insured persons, employers and taxpayers in such a way as to be equitable to insured persons and to avoid hardship to insured persons of small means or any disturbance to production.[818]

§7. The Social Security of Migrant Workers

1011. The ILO standards in respect of the social security of migrant workers have two objectives: to ensure equal treatment in this fundamental area between national and foreign workers, and to ensure that a change in residence does not result in a loss of acquired rights or rights in the course of being acquired.

1012. These problems are dealt with in general instruments. Convention No. 102 on minimum standards of social security, 1952, sets forth the principle of equality of treatment for non-national residents. It nevertheless allows for two limitations:

- the first concern benefits (or portions of benefits) payable wholly or mainly out of public funds and in respect of transitional schemes: the States can adopt special rules for non-nationals (and for national born outside the territory);
- the second concern contributory social security schemes: the nationals of another State bound by the Convention (or by part of it) are entitled to the same rights (arising from the Convention or the part of it) as nationals; the application of this rule can nevertheless be made contingent on the existence of a bilateral or multilateral agreement of reciprocity. [819]

Conventions Nos. 121 on employment injury benefits, 1964, and 130 on medical care and sickness benefits, 1969, require the Member States to ensure, within their territory, that non-nationals who normally reside or work there have equality of treatment with their own nationals as regards the right to benefits.[820]

1013. The Maritime Labour Convention, 2006[821] asks States, to the extent consistent with their national law and practice, to cooperate, through bilateral or multilateral agreements or other arrangements, to ensure the maintenance of social security rights, provided through contributory or non-contributory schemes, which have been acquired, or are in the course of acquisition, by all seafarers regardless of residence. The corresponding guidelines[822] add that where seafarers are subject to

818. Paras 25–26 of Recommendation No. 67.
819. Article 68.
820. Articles 27 of Convention No. 121 and 32 of Convention No. 130.
821. Standard A4.5. 8.
822. Guideline B4.5. 5.

more than one national legislation covering social security, the countries concerned should cooperate in order to determine by mutual agreement which legislation is to apply, taking into account such factors as the type and level of protection under the respective legislations which is more favourable to the seafarer concerned as well as the seafarer's preference. Every State which has national seafarers, non-national seafarers or both serving on ships that fly its flag should provide the social security protection in the Convention as applicable, and should periodically review the branches of social security protection, with a view to identifying any additional branches appropriate for the seafarers concerned.

1014. We shall now turn to Convention No. 118, 1962, on equality of treatment of nationals and non-nationals in social security, on the one hand, and Convention No. 157, 1982, and Recommendation No. 167, 1983, on the maintenance of social security rights in that respect, on the other.[823] Both Conventions consider the nine branches of social security, but on different terms. A State can accept the obligations of Convention No. 118 for one or several branches.[824] Convention No. 157, however, requires that the Convention apply to the branches of social security for which the State has legislation in force.[825] Both conventions offer the States the possibility of derogating from their provisions by special arrangements concluded between them, on condition that the arrangements do not affect the rights and obligations of other States parties and settle the maintenance of rights on terms which, in the aggregate, are at least as favourable as those of the Convention.[826] Recommendation No. 167 encourages the States to conclude bilateral or multilateral agreements covering the nine branches of social security and to coordinate the (bilateral or multilateral) instruments by which they are respectively bound. Its annexes contain model provisions for the conclusion of such instruments and a model agreement for their coordination. The International Organization for Migration (IOM), based in Geneva, plays an important role for the development of international cooperation.

I. Equality of Treatment

1015. Pursuant in particular to Convention No. 102, Convention No. 118 establishes the principle of equality of treatment for non-nationals, as regards both coverage and the right to benefits, in respect of each of the nine branches of social security for which a State has accepted the obligations of the Convention. It makes this principle subject to a condition of reciprocity: it applies only to the nationals of a State that has also ratified Convention No. 118,[827] but it applies to refugees and stateless persons without any condition of reciprocity.[828] However, a State can

823. *See* Kahil-Wolff and Greber, *op. cit.*, paras 413–430; López Morales, Silva and Egorov, *op. cit.*, p. 476 *et seq.* and Humblet and Silva, *op. cit.*, pp. 41–45.
824. Article 2.
825. Article 2.
826. Articles 8 and 9 of Convention No. 118, 4 and 17 of Convention No. 157.
827. Article 3.
828. Article 10.

refuse equality of treatment, by way of retaliation, in respect of the benefits of a branch of social security to the nationals of another State which has legislation relating to that branch but does not grant equality of treatment in respect thereof to the nationals of the first State. Convention No. 157 also imposes implicitly a condition of reciprocity: while Article 1 considers as Member means any State member of the ILO that is bound by the Convention, Articles 6 and 9 in particular relate the obligations of each ratifying State only to the ones of other Members.

1016. Equality of treatment must in principle be assured without condition of residence. This does not mean that the benefits must be granted to non-nationals without a condition of residence, but that the requirement of residence cannot be imposed only on foreigners.[829]

II. Maintenance of Acquired Rights and Provision of Benefits Abroad

1017. Convention No. 118 stipulates a direct obligation to maintain acquired rights in respect of long-term benefits (such as invalidity, old-age, survivors' or employment injury benefits): that obligation does not depend on an agreement between the States concerned. If a State is party to Convention No. 118, it must provide the benefits abroad, for a specific branch, for both its own nationals and those of any other State that has accepted the obligations of the Convention for the same branch, no matter what the beneficiary's place of residence.[830] Convention No. 157 establishes a similar obligation, but in respect of all branches for which the States concerned have enacted legislation (since those States cannot, contrary to what is the case under Convention No. 118, exclude some of them).[831] Both instruments states expressly that this rights are granted to refugees and stateless persons without condition of reciprocity.

1018. The obligation to maintain acquired rights is mediate with regard to short-term benefits: the States must endeavour to participate in schemes for the maintenance of the acquired rights.[832] The obligation must be ensured, within the framework of Convention No. 118, within the limits of its field of application (the nationals of any other State for which the Convention is also in force, and for all branches of social security accepted by the States concerned). The same applies, and even more broadly, for Convention No. 157 (all branches of social security in respect of which the States concerned have enacted legislation). In any event, the duty is 'to endeavour', an obligation of means:[833] if the negotiations are conducted in good faith, their failure cannot be interpreted as a fault. It is binding on the 'States

829. For further details, including on possible additional conditions, *see* Article 4 of Convention No. 118.
830. *See* Article 5 and, with regard to family benefits, Article 6.
831. Article 9 which authorizes however the States concerned to guarantee the provision of such benefits through bilateral or multilateral instruments.
832. Article 7 of Convention No. 118 and Article 10 of Convention No. 157.
833. López Morales, Silva and Egorov, *op. cit.*, pp. 478–480.

concerned', i.e. on those between which there are movements of people that justify such arrangements.[834]

III. Maintenance of Rights in Course of Acquisition

1019. If a migrant worker changes country, he may lose the benefit of periods of employment, contribution or residence needed to be entitled to benefits (qualifying period) or taken into account when calculating the amount of the benefits. He may therefore be obliged to complete another qualifying period, or may receive only a reduced pension for a long working life. Conventions Nos. 118 and 157 therefore require that the States endeavour to participate in a scheme to maintain rights in course of acquisition in conditions similar to those described above for the maintenance of acquired rights.

1020. Such schemes should provide, in particular, for the totalization of periods of insurance, employment or residence and of assimilated periods for the purpose of acquiring, maintaining or recovering rights and for the calculation of benefits. They should also provide for the sharing of the cost of invalidity, old-age, survivors' and employment injury benefits.[835]

IV. Applicable Legislation

1021. ILO standards do not as a rule deal with problems of identifying the applicable law or competent court. Convention No. 157 establishes an exception for the social security of migrant workers, given the importance of preventing disputes and their undesirable consequences for the concerned parties (by either lack of protection or on the contrary a plurality of contributions and benefits). The formula it proposes consists of requiring the States concerned to conclude agreements on the legislation to apply. Article 5 establishes the basic rules:

(a) employees who are normally employed in the territory of a Member shall be subject to the legislation of that Member, even if they are resident in the territory of another Member or if the undertaking which employs them has its registered office, or their employer has his place of residence, in the territory of another Member;
(b) self-employed persons who normally engage in their occupation in the territory of a Member shall be subject to the legislation of that Member, even if they are resident in the territory of another Member;
(c) employees and self-employed persons sailing on board a ship flying the flag of a Member shall be subject to the legislation of that Member even if they are resident in the territory of another Member or if the undertaking which employs

834. Humblet and Silva, *op. cit.*, pp. 43–44.
835. Article 7 of Convention No. 118; Articles 6 to 8 of Convention No. 157.

them has its registered office, or their employer has his place of residence, in the territory of another Member;

(d) persons who are not part of the economically active population shall be subject to the legislation of the Member in whose territory they are resident, in so far as they are not protected in virtue of subparagraphs (a) to (c) of this paragraph.

Notwithstanding these provisions, as the Article states, the Members concerned may agree that certain categories of persons, in particular self-employed persons, are subject to the legislation of the Member in whose territory they are resident. The States are even authorized to establish other derogations by mutual agreement in the interests of the persons concerned.

1021bis. The guidelines corresponding to the MLC state that where seafarers are subject to more than one set of national legislation covering social security, the countries concerned should cooperate in order to determine by mutual agreement which legislation is to apply, taking into account such factors as the type and level of protection under the legislation which is more favourable to the seafarer concerned as well as the seafarer's preference.[836]

V. Mutual Administrative Assistance and Assistance to Persons

1022. Both Convention No. 118[837] and Convention No. 157[838] call on the Members to afford each other administrative assistance with a view to facilitating the application of the Convention and the execution of their respective social security legislation.

1023. Convention No. 157 also calls on the Members to promote the development of social services to assist the persons concerned in their dealings with the authorities, institutions and jurisdictions, and to facilitate the award and receipt of benefits, the exercise of their right of appeal and the improvement of their personal and family welfare.[839]

836. Guideline B4.5, 3.
837. Article 11.
838. Article 12.
839. Articles 14 and 13 (the latter provides that the claimant may present his claim validly to the institution of his place of residence, which will forward it to the institution – or institutions – referred to in the claim).

Part III. The Effectiveness of International Labour Standards

1024. The impact of ILO standards is predicated on very sophisticated supervisory machinery made up of a system of complex yet complementary elements. One procedure comprises the analysis of mandatory government reports; it covers, in theory if not in practice, all situations experienced by a country in respect of a convention it has ratified. Other procedures are set in motion by complaints and are therefore random. Examination of complaints centres on the specific points alleged; it can bring to light tangible problems, but does not entail the systematic approach of regular supervision.

1025. As we shall learn, these mechanisms involve both tripartite representative bodies (an International Labour Conference committee, the Conference itself, the Governing Body of the International Labour Office or a committee established from among its members) and bodies made up of independent experts, eminent persons chosen for their specific field of authority and impartiality. In all cases, therefore, supervision encompasses both a thorough technical examination of the situation and a discussion that is political in nature, where the willingness to talk and win over clearly takes precedence over the threat of sanctions. For cases where the usual methods of supervision have failed to solve the problems raised, special procedures of inquiry have been established.

1026. The legal methods of implementing the standards are fittingly bolstered by the means of promotion available to the Organization. In fact, legal procedures, practical activities and the spread of information should always converge. As we shall see, this is in many ways the case.

1027. Lastly, we shall take a more general look at the obvious difficulties of application encountered by States, especially developing countries, and how they are overcome. Clearly, labour regulation must keep pace with the increasingly rapid globalization of the market economy; the risk should it fail to do so is disorder of a kind that would be prejudicial to the majority. We have yet to find the right answers to these pressing issues.

Chapter 1. The Supervision and Promotion of ILO Standards

1028. The application of standards is supervised via the Member States' obligations under the Constitution (§1) and, in the case of special procedures (§2), the decisions taken by the Organization's managing bodies. The latter have also stressed that supervision should not be limited to *ex post* control and that implementation of the standards should be proactively promoted. We shall therefore reflect on the significance of supervision (§3) and of the other means of promoting ILO instruments (§4).

§1. General Supervisory Procedures

I. Regular Supervision

1029. Regular supervision consists in collecting all possible information on the manner in which a country meets its commitments. The main source of information is the reports that the States are obliged to submit to that end, copies of which they must also communicate to the representative employers' and workers' organizations so that the latter can, if they wish, add to the information provided therein.[840]

1030. The governments must provide information on four points:

- the measures taken to bring the conventions and recommendations adopted by the International Labour Conference before the competent national authorities,[841] with particulars of the authorities and of the action taken by them;
- the effect given to ratified conventions;[842] this is the principal obligation, the backbone of ILO's system of verification. Over time, a sophisticated system has been put in place for the dual purpose of obtaining as much data as possible while making sure that national administrations and the International Labour Office are not overtaxed. How often the reports must be made and the amount of detail they contain depends on whether the report is the country's first or second, or a later report, and on the priority of the instrument. Complete reports can always be required if needed, in particular in response to comments from employers' or workers' organizations. Report forms, approved by the Governing Body, help the governments provide the information required on the situation from the legal and practical points of view;
- the effect given to ratified conventions in non-metropolitan territories;[843]

840. Article 23, para. 2 of the Constitution.
841. Article 19, paras 5(c), 6(c) and 7(a), (b)(iii) of the Constitution.
842. Article 22 of the Constitution; ILO, *Handbook of Procedures Relating to International Labour Conventions and Recommendations*, Rev. 2012, Geneva, ILO, p. 20 *et seq.*
843. Article 35 of the Constitution.

– the position of national law and practice in regard to conventions that have not been ratified and to recommendations.[844] Every year the Governing Body chooses one or several conventions or recommendations and asks the member countries to report on the recommendations and on the conventions they have not ratified; the information thus provided must cover the state of the country's legislation and practice, the effect given to the instruments concerned, including any modifications in that respect, and the difficulties preventing or delaying the ratification of a convention. The aim of this procedure is to promote the ratification and application of the instruments; it serves to bring to light the fact that a given country needs assistance or that an instrument requires revision.

1031. The fact that all these documents are communicated to the representative employers' and workers' organizations affords an extra guarantee of effective supervision. In order to ensure compliance with this provision, the report forms require the governments to list the organizations that have received a copy of the reports. In addition, ILO directly informs the organizations of their government's obligation to submit a report, of the comments concerning the government made by the supervisory bodies, etc. The social partners are thus able to remind the public authorities of their obligations and to start a dialogue with them on any measures to be taken. They can communicate their views to ILO directly or through their government.[845]

1032. The reports and comments, and any other information that is available, are examined by a committee of independent experts. If the implementation of a convention gives rise to difficulties, the committee makes comments which it communicates directly to the government concerned and, in the most important cases, publishes in the report it submits every year to the International Labour Conference. At each session, the Conference sets up a committee from among its members that is specifically in charge of the application of standards and which discusses, with a representative of the government concerned, the most serious situations and the means of overcoming the shortcomings observed. It reports to the Conference plenary, where a case can be further discussed.

A. *The Committee of Experts on the Application of Conventions and Recommendations*

1033. The Committee is made up of distinguished experts – normally they number 20 – from different countries and cultures. The experts are appointed by the Governing Body on the proposal of the Director-General in the light of their professional and moral qualities: confirmed legal authority, and demonstrated impartiality and independence of mind. Their term of office is three years and is renewable; many of them have in fact remained members of the Committee for many years.

---

844. Article 19, paras 5(e), 7(a), (b)(iv), 6(d), 7(a)(b)(v) of the Constitution. *See* paras 117 and 194 *above* and 1165 *below*.

845. For further details on the role of employers' organizations in this regard, *see* Wisskirchen and Hess, *op. cit.*, pp. 28–29.

1034. It is incumbent on the Committee members to make a preliminary technical examination of the reports received from the governments and of the other information available, and thus to gauge the extent to which countries have met their obligations. Their comments take the form of requests for explanations sent directly to the governments concerned or, in the event of serious or persistent non-conformity, of observations collected in a document that is made public and communicated to the International Labour Conference. That document also contains general comments and a general survey of the laws and practices in respect of one or several specific instruments (on the basis of the information submitted under Article 19 of the Constitution and Articles 22 and 35 for the conventions and recommendations selected).

B. The International Labour Conference Committee on the Application of Conventions and Recommendations

1035. Every year the Conference appoints a tripartite committee whose role is specifically to monitor application of conventions and recommendations.[846] The Committee considers the report of the Committee of Experts, in particular the observations on individual countries. It draws up a list of cases on which it wishes to focus its deliberations; the governments concerned can submit written responses or may be invited to express themselves orally. A debate can then take place in which the employer and worker groups in particular are involved.

1036. The Committee reports to the Conference plenary. Its report contains a summary of the statements made and the deliberations. The Committee provides information on the discussions of how some States fail seriously to comply with a ratified Convention and how they observe specific obligations (sending reports and information, submitting instruments to the competent authorities, etc.). It also points out progress made.

1037. During the plenary, the Conference delegates have a further opportunity – which they use in serious cases – to draw attention to certain aspects of the Committee's deliberations. The report is published in the Conference Record; it also appears in an offprint communicated to the governments. The governments' attention is drawn to the specific questions mentioned by the Committee as requiring examination and to the discussion of individual cases, so that due account is taken of them in the preparation of subsequent reports.

II. Representations and Complaints

1038. Any workers' or employers' organization can make a 'representation' to the International Labour Office,[847] alleging that a member country is not properly

846. Article 7 of the Standing Orders of the ILC.
847. Articles 24 and 25 of the Constitution.

executing a ratified convention. In that case, the Governing Body can establish from among its members a tripartite committee that conducts an initial examination of the case and presents its conclusions. The Governing Body can invite the government in question to express its views and help examine the matter. Should it fail to receive a satisfactory response, the Governing Body can make the representation and any response public.

1039. For many years, the employers' and workers' associations hardly ever had recourse to this procedure. The situation has changed in recent years; at the initiative of the unions, numerous grievances have been examined in the recent past.

1040. Following such an examination, or otherwise, the Governing Body can launch a commission of inquiry. It can also be asked to do so, in one of two ways. Any member country can file a complaint against another State that has violated a convention both have ratified, and a delegate to the International Labour Conference can also introduce a complaint.[848] This is one of the rare instances – and the only one within the ILO context – in which a complaint can be made by an individual, although the latter is, of course, part of a government, employer or trade union delegation.

1041. As in the case of representations, the Governing Body can start by inviting the government to express its views on the complaint. If it does not consider it necessary to do this, or if it does not receive a satisfactory response, it can establish a commission of inquiry to examine and report on the case. Every Member State is then obliged, 'whether directly concerned in the complaint or not', to place at the disposal of the commission all the information in its possession which bears upon the subject-matter of the complaint.[849]

1042. The commissions of inquiry established in the past have been made up of three members, appointed on the proposal of the Director-General of the Organization. In every case, they were distinguished persons chosen in their personal capacity and known for their impartiality and independence of mind. The commission examines the complaint in depth and usually holds hearings and makes an on-site visit; it then sets down its observations in a report containing all the points of fact that serve to specify the scope of the complaint and any recommendations on the measures to be adopted and the timetable for their implementation.

1043. The Director-General communicates that report to the Governing Body and to all the governments involved in the dispute; he makes sure the report is published. Each of the governments must inform him within three months whether or

848. Articles 26 *et seq.* of the Constitution. Article 30 provides for a special procedure in case of failure to submit the newly adopted Conventions and Recommendations to the competent authorities: any other Member State is entitled to refer the matter to the ILO Governing Body; in the event of the Governing Body finding that there has been such a failure, it will report the matter to the ILC. The article lacks interest in practice since the Committee of Experts considers systematically, and reports to the ILC on, the observation of this obligation of submission by the Member States.

849. Article 27 of the Constitution.

not it accepts the recommendations and, if not, whether it intends to refer the matter to the International Court of Justice. The Court can affirm, vary or reverse any of the findings or recommendations of the commission of inquiry; its decisions are final. To date, no government has ever had recourse to the Court.

1044. If a member country fails to carry out, within the time specified, the recommendations, if any, contained in the report of the commission of inquiry, or in the decision of the International Court of Justice, the Governing Body can recommend to the Conference 'such action as it may deem wise and expedient to secure compliance therewith'.[850] This provision constitutes a last resort that has rarely been invoked. A recent case must nevertheless be mentioned. The Government of Myanmar had failed to execute the recommendations of the 1998 Commission of Inquiry, which had spoken of the 'pervasive use of forced labour imposed on the civilian population' throughout the country. It had repeatedly been asked to respond positively. Finally, at its June 2000 session the Conference adopted a resolution listing a series of measures to be taken if the government did not change course. Those measures, which were in the end adopted, aimed in particular at alerting the international community to the situation in the country, at asking it to reconsider its relations with Myanmar in view of that situation, and to keeping the matter on the agenda of various international forums. The government subsequently agreed to a programme of cooperation on the matter and to the appointment of an international liaison officer whose presence has had a deterrent effect. The situation having evolved positively, the ILC have lifted in June 2013 all remaining ILO restrictions on Myanmar, while continuing to follow up the case[851].

1045. According to Article 34 of the Constitution, the defaulting government may at any time inform the Governing Body that it has taken the steps necessary to comply with the recommendations and may request it to constitute a commission of inquiry to verify its contention. In this case, the same procedure applies. If the report of the commission (or the decision of the Court) is in favour of the defaulting government, the Governing Body must forthwith recommend the discontinuance of any action taken.

§2. Special Procedures

I. The Complaints Procedure for Violations of Freedom of Association

1046. We know[852] what importance ILO has always attached to fundamental labour rights, especially since the end of World War Two. Freedom of association for employers and workers is especially crucial for an organization made up not

850. Article 33 of the Constitution.
851. International Labour Conference (102nd Session, Geneva, June 2013), *Provisional Record*, No 17, Geneva, ILO, 2013.
852. *See* paras 26–28 *above*.

only of government but also of employer and trade union representatives. ILO therefore established, after having concluded an agreement with the United Nations in 1950, a special procedure that is complementary to – but does not replace – the general supervisory machinery. Indeed, it has all the hallmarks of the general complaints procedure.

1047. The main organism is the Committee on Freedom of Association, a tripartite body (chaired by an independent person) constituted by the Governing Body from among its members. The role of the Committee consists in promoting, with the help of all the parties concerned, effective compliance, in law and in practice, with the principles set forth in the relevant ILO instruments. It reports to the Governing Body on the very many matters submitted to it, usually pursuant to a complaint by a trade union (although the States and employers' associations can also refer matters to it). In exceptional circumstances, the Governing Body returns the file to a fact-finding and conciliation commission, another body made up of independent persons whose mission is to investigate the facts alleged and to examine, with the government concerned, the possibilities of overcoming the problems encountered before submitting a report to the Governing Body.

1048. This procedure does not – and therein lies its originality – require the ratification by the State concerned of any convention on freedom of association.[853] It does not even require the consent of the State in the case, except for the establishment of a fact-finding and conciliation commission.[854]

1049. The conditions stipulated for filing complaints against governments and for their examination by this committee reflect concern to avoid excessive formalism: allegations can be submitted as simply as by telegram or on a post card. Certain guarantees have nevertheless been provided for. The Committee cannot accept just any protest: the entire procedure would have lost credibility and the Committee's already considerable workload would have increased even further. In order to be admissible, the complaints must issue from a genuine workers' organization – and not an ephemeral group such as a strike committee – or association of employers which, if it is national, has a direct interest in the outcome; they can also come from an international workers' or employers' federation if the problem affects one of its branches, or from one of the major employers' or workers' confederations whose interests can be presumed in that they have consultative status at ILO.

1050. There are guarantees in favour of the 'accused', of the government denounced for having infringed trade union rights. The government always has the possibility of having the final word in the exchange of communications between the parties. It receives, so that it can respond, the allegations and any supplementary information provided by the complainant. Its own comments are no longer as a rule transmitted to the complainants; however, if the Committee decides to transmit them, the complainants' new observations are forwarded to the government. The

853. *See* para. 90 *above*.
854. When the conditions required for the setting up of a Commission of Inquiry are not met.

Committee is also concerned to protect the governments from unfounded accusations and it has rejected allegations that were not backed by sufficient evidence.

1051. More generally, the Committee's working methods must instil trust in the States. The States must understand that it is ultimately in their interests to respond to the accusations against them, to refute unfounded allegations and demonstrate the exaggerated character of others, to explain the obstacles encountered in implementing the principles of freedom of association. Their cooperation while the case is being considered (as, later, in following up any recommendations) guarantees that due account will be taken of the situation they face and is key to the successful conclusion of the procedure.

1052. The Committee has various means of inciting a government to agree to a dialogue: the more or less pressing appeals it makes of the government or of the head of State through its report, and hence publicly, the contacts the Committee chairman makes with the delegates of the government concerned at the International Labour Conference, and the contacts established with the help of ILO's duty stations. Should these means fail, the Committee can examine a case by default, i.e. in the absence of the expected response; it can also draw public attention to the allegations, to the recommendations made and to the government's negative attitude.

1053. If, moreover, the allegations are very serious, the Director-General can, as soon as the complaint has been received, appoint a representative whose task is to make preliminary on-site contacts, to obtain initial information and to underscore the importance of full cooperation throughout the various stages of the procedure.

1054. The Committee must rule on the basis of sufficient information. It can invite the complainants or the government to provide further information. What is more, although the procedure is in principle written and the Committee rules on the basis of the facts before it, other methods have been found of obtaining more detailed and specific information. In particular, the Committee has invited the governments concerned to receive what are known as 'direct contacts' missions, a method that is also extensively used in the periodic examination of ratified conventions. If the response is positive, an ILO representative, who may or may not be an International Labour Office staff member, travels to the spot to investigate and find a solution. These missions are in no way international inquiries; on the contrary, they enable the person chosen for his impartiality and objectivity to forge a dialogue with the parties concerned, to discuss the problems encountered less formally, to clarify the situation and to foster a climate that is favourable to finding solutions. In other, less frequent, cases the Committee has decided to hear one or both parties with a view to obtaining more complete information and, again, to examining possible remedies, to striving for conciliation on the basis of the principles of freedom of association.

1055. The Committee of Experts on the Application of Conventions and Recommendations (CEACR) and the Committee on Freedom of Association (CFA) are key components of ILO's supervisory machinery. They meet regularly, and both are the first instance of recourse in a considerable number of situations. It is therefore best to describe their respective roles accurately.

1056. The role of the CEACR is to determine whether the rules of a given convention, in particular a convention on freedom of association, are being observed, to ascertain whether or not the convention is being fully applied. Its task is fundamentally legal in nature. Although it is not called on to provide a definitive interpretation of the international labour conventions,[855] to discharge its mandate it nevertheless needs to examine the meaning of certain provisions of those conventions and to express its views on them. It must also inquire into the meaning and scope attributed, especially in practice, to certain national provisions; it examines the decisions taken in the country concerned and determines whether or not they are compatible with the requirements of the convention. [856]

1057. The CFA, for its part, has often been asked to consider matters relating to the exercise of trade union rights that are not expressly set down in the conventions on freedom of association.[857] It has been asked to formulate conclusions and propose solutions for the disputes submitted to it, on the basis of ILO standards but by drawing on principles more closely adapted to the situation at hand. It has been widely recognized that it is in the general interest to have alleged violations of trade union rights examined, impartially and dispassionately, by an international body. This can help ease both international and social tensions. The method employed allows a body made up in such a way as to ensure a reasonable balance between divergent points of view and interests to examine complaints informally; it can in no way be compared to a procedure of inquiry conducted in the context of legal proceedings against a State at which an accusing finger has been pointed.[858] Here, the functions of conciliation and mediation must have the upper hand.

1058. Both bodies coordinate their activities. The CEACR has made it a rule,[859] if another ILO body is examining a case, to wait for its conclusions before reaching its own. It nevertheless regularly refers to the conclusions and recommendations adopted, even on an interim basis, by the CFA. When the country in question has ratified the convention concerned, the Committee on Freedom of Association usually draws the Committee of Experts' attention to the conclusions it has drawn on points of law. The CEACR is asked to follow developments in the situation. Some of the issues of fact referred to the CFA are too specific to be examined by the CEACR. Others, however, relate to constant or widespread practices that permanently erode the application of the conventions on freedom of association. The

855. *See* Article 37 of the ILO Constitution; *see also* para. 147 *et seq. above*.
856. ILC (103rd session, 2014), *Report of the Committee of Experts on the Application of Conventions and Recommendations*, Report III (Part 1A), General Report, Geneva, ILO, 2014, para. 31.
857. *See* ILC (70th session, 1984), *Report of the Director-General*, Geneva, ILO, 1984, p. 41.
858. C.W. Jenks, *The International Protection of Trade Union Freedom*, London, Stevens, 1957, p. 196; and 'The international protection of trade union rights' in E. Luard (ed.), *The International Protection of Human Rights*, London, Thames and Hudson, 1967, pp. 236–237.
859. ILC, *op. cit.*, para. 32.

Committee of Experts' attention is systematically drawn to those cases, so that it can analyse the consequences for the application of ratified conventions.

II. The Credentials Committee

1059. The International Labour Conference is composed, as we have said,[860] of four representatives of each member country: two government delegates, one employers' delegate and one workers' delegate. The ILO Constitution stipulates[861] that the States undertake 'to nominate non-Government delegates and advisers chosen in agreement with the industrial organizations, if such organizations exist, which are most representative of employers or workpeople, as the case may be, in their respective countries'. The credentials of the delegates (and of their advisers) are subject to verification by the Conference, which can, by a two-thirds majority of the delegates present, refuse to admit a delegate (or adviser) it deems was not selected in accordance with the ILO Constitution.

1060. At each session, the Conference appoints a tripartite Credentials Committee consisting of one government delegate, one employers' delegate and one workers' delegate. The Committee examines the credentials of delegates and their advisers, and any objection relating thereto,[862] in accordance with a procedure spelled out in the Conference Standing Orders.[863] It considers whether the objection is receivable and well-founded and submits a report as a matter of urgency. If the Committee or one of its members advises that the Conference should refuse to admit a delegate or adviser, the President submits this proposal to the plenary. The Conference then decides whether or not the delegate or adviser has been nominated in conformity with the requirements of the Constitution; if not, it may refuse by a two-thirds majority of the delegates present to admit the delegate or adviser.

1061. The Committee has examined many cases concerning the delegates of employers' organizations, and many more concerning trade union delegates. It has had in particular to assess whether or not they were representative. The Permanent Court of International Justice was ultimately asked to rule on the exact scope of Article 3, paragraph 5, of the Constitution, which states that the countries undertake to appoint non-governmental delegates and advisers 'in agreement with the industrial organizations (…) which are most representative of employers or workpeople', in a case concerning whether or not the government of the Netherlands should select the workers' delegate from the trade union with the most members, or – as in this instance – with their agreement, from three other organizations that, together, had more members. The Court ruled that the obligation imposed on the government was one of means (seek an agreement with the most representative

860. *See* para. 13 *above*.
861. Article 3.
862. Article 5 of the ILC Standing Orders. The Credentials Committee may also consider complaints that a State Member has failed to comply with Article 13(2)(a) of the Constitution (payment of the travelling and subsistence expenses of their delegates and technical advisers).
863. Article 26.

organizations) and not of outcome (obtain their agreement). The Court felt that 'the aim of each government must, of course, be an agreement with all the most representative organizations', but that, 'however, is an ideal which it is extremely difficult to attain'. 'What is required of governments is that they should do their best to effect an agreement which, in the circumstances, may be regarded as the best for the purpose of ensuring the representation of the workers of the country.'[864] Those principles subsequently guided the Credentials Committee and other ILO bodies in similar cases.[865] Today, in practice, the States which, like Belgium, France and Italy, have several trade unions use a formula of alternate attendance that all the main trade union federations have agreed to.

III. Other Special Procedures

1062. We have already discussed the procedures for the follow-up of the Tripartite Declaration of Principles concerning Multinational Enterprises and Social Policy (1977) and the Declaration on Fundamental Principles and Rights at Work (1998).[866] In other instances, the Governing Body or the Labour Conference have asked the International Labour Office to undertake a study or an investigation, rather than use the complaints machinery. Such initiatives, which are based on Article 10 of the Constitution, have also already been discussed.[867] They concern essentially fundamental rights at work, freedom of association and collective bargaining, the elimination of forced labour and discrimination in employment and occupation. It was felt that this method, which focused on collecting and analysing information rather than on formulating conclusions and recommendations, was more likely in a given political situation to lead to a solution that was satisfactory to all. It hardly needs saying that the community of States has always been reluctant to give any coercive authority to international institutions, especially in areas not concerning economics. An organization like ILO is therefore better able to promote its values by appealing to ethics and reason and through dialogue than by having recourse to sanctions. This observation brings us to reconsider the scope of the supervisory mechanisms.

§3. Putting the Supervisory Mechanisms in Perspective

1063. For it to be credible, a legal supervisory system must ensure that the methods of evaluation are applicable and enforceable to everyone: this closes the door to any form of partiality. The CEACR has thus deemed that it must strictly limit itself to the provisions of the international instruments of concern to it and compliance with which it has to verify, without taking into consideration factors, such as the

864. *See* Advisory Opinion No. 1, dated 31 July 1992: *Official Bulletin*, 16.8.1922, Vol. VI, No. 7, pp. 291–298.
865. For further details, *see* Valticos, *Droit international du travail, op. cit.*, paras 244, 248, 251 and 255.
866. *See* paras 201, 208 *et seq. above*.
867. *See* para. 27 *above*.

economic and social conditions in a country, that are not mentioned in the texts. By the same token, many statements to the Conference Committee on the Application of Standards stress that, although economic and social disparities might have led to flexible wording of the standards, the same attitude could not be adopted in monitoring their application, at the risk of making subjective appraisals.[868]

1064. Of course, the Organization's supervisory bodies assess the extent to which each country implements the conventions in the light of that country's socio-economic context, because they seek to verify effective application. But they cannot take those factors into account to change the scope or attenuate the strength of the provisions which, unless otherwise stated, are uniform. Their role is to ascertain whether or not the texts are fully applied, subject to recourse to the International Court of Justice.

1065. Concerned to deal with all States equally and to favour no State, ILO's supervisory bodies are therefore inflexible when it comes to pinpointing anomalies between a country's law and practice and a convention that country has freely and sovereignly undertaken to apply. But this in no way signifies that only legal means can be used to eliminate such anomalies. It is true that some of the supervisory bodies, in particular the CEACR, are composed of independent persons, judges, university professors and other well-known legal scholars whose opinions carry weight. It is also true that these different bodies scrupulously ensure, in the exercise of their mandate, respect for the general principles of due process so that the governments concerned can trust the system. But their conclusions are not decisions; they are not binding.

1066. Moreover, the comments, which may be very critical, are worded so as to incite to action and foster dialogue, not to condemn. In this respect, tripartite bodies such as the Conference Committee on the Application of Standards can play a special role. They have their own relays (national associations of employers and workers, delegates from countries that are close to the State concerned, etc.) that can help further understanding and acceptance of the recommendations adopted.

1067. Generally speaking, it is through a combination of diplomacy and what are basically moral urgings that the supervisory bodies endeavour to ensure application of international labour standards when they give rise to difficulties. The Organization has several means of exhorting a State to comply fully with the standards. For example, it can publicize the conclusions of the supervisory bodies. It can also make the discussions public in an international forum (the ILO Governing Body, the Conference and its Committee on the Application of Standards), for all States quite naturally seek to avoid being cited before the international community, where they do not necessarily have only friends.[869]

868. *See* para. 152 *et seq. above.*
869. *See also* E. Weisband, 'Discursive Multilateralism: Global Benchmarks, Shame, and Learning in the ILO Labor, Standards Monitoring Regime', *International Studies Quarterly*, 2000, 44, pp. 643–666.

1068. The Organization may adopt more dissuasive measures. Express provision is made for this in Article 33 of the Constitution in respect of the complaints procedure for violations of a ratified convention.[870] There is nothing to prevent measures from also being taken within the framework of supervisory procedures. In cases in which there have been serious violations of freedom of association, for example, it has been suggested that the ILO duty station (if there is one) be moved out of the country concerned, that ILO refuse to organize meetings there or that it scratch part or all of the technical assistance it provides. In brief, nothing impedes theoretically the Organization to decide on sanctions not only of a diplomatic, but also of an economic nature.

1069. But ILO has always preferred dialogue to sanctions. The bodies monitoring the application of international labour standards study the degree to which national law and practice conform to ILO instruments. Once the study has been concluded, their comments, if they have any, do not take the form of court rulings: their aim is to conciliate, or rather mediate (in that they formulate specific recommendations with a view to settling the differences that have arisen). The mediation has its own rules, in that the recommendations are based on the standards contained in ILO instruments. What is more, the procedures followed are akin to court proceedings. Both these guarantees, and the care taken in selecting the independent public figures who participate in the supervisory mechanisms, are intended to give the governments concerned the assurance that their case will be examined dispassionately and impartially. In short, although they are based on the legal rules set forth in ILO conventions, the recommendations of the supervisory bodies do not try to penalize misconduct; rather they are aimed at helping a State give effect to an instrument. ILO bodies seek, and usually obtain, the cooperation of the government concerned, as is implicitly required by the supervisory procedures. The government, for its part, has an interest in cooperating since this allows it to respond to the criticisms directed against it and to explain as required what is actually delaying full application of the convention. Even in simple cases, the supervisory bodies are not content, in their conclusions, to ascertain the existence of anomalies in respect of a convention. Their comments are accompanied, whenever appropriate, by specific proposals for solving the problems encountered. ILO's technical cooperation programmes can also be useful in this respect, particularly when it comes to drafting highly technical legislative texts.

1070. In order to build up cooperation, even if no critical comments have been made in respect of the application of a convention, the Organization, as we shall see,[871] has embarked on various activities (seminars on standards, internships for national public servants, brochures and manuals, etc.) aimed at enhancing understanding of the scope, objectives and workings of the supervisory machinery. It also has many channels for fostering constructive dialogue. In this respect, ILO's regional and local duty stations play a useful role. Regional Offices have staff that is in charge specifically of advising the governments on standards-related issues.

870. *See* para. 1044 *above*.
871. *See* para. 1083 *below*.

1071. It goes without saying that the more complex and serious the problems, the more elaborate the mechanisms for fostering cooperation and finding solutions in keeping with the conventions. Formal and informal contacts are forged with the help of external duty stations or during the annual session of the International Labour Conference. The procedure of the CFA expressly provides that the Committee chairman can be asked to make contact with government representatives during the Conference, in order to draw their attention to the case of their country and to discuss with them the reasons for the delay in transmitting the observations requested by the Committee. The Committee on Freedom of Association and the Conference Committee on the Application of Standards can also invite a government representative (and, in the case of the former, the complainant) to come before it and explain a given situation. Here again, the purpose of the hearing is not to read a bill of indictment, but to exchange views in order to obtain tangible results. Deadlocks have often been resolved by having senior ILO officials hold interviews or conduct on-site missions. The ILO Director-General can appoint, more officially, a special representative who is an ILO official or an independent person and ask them to investigate the situation on the spot and to seek a solution to the problems raised with all the interested parties. The 'direct contacts' visits are not intended, as we have said, to try the case against the government, but rather to clarify the situation and to use dialogue to foster a favourable climate for a positive outcome. Nevertheless, this procedure has often been perceived as the first stage in a process of sanction rather than as an act of cooperation. It has therefore become a much less suitable means of attaining the goal sought. The Governing Body may send a tripartite delegation to help in the solution of the problem, as occurred recently with Qatar.[872]

1072. All ILO supervisory procedures are underpinned by the will to use conciliation to overcome obstacles to the application of standards and to find an amicable settlement. In this respect, the Fact-finding and Conciliation Commission, which is made up of independent public figures who can, in exceptional cases, be asked to look into a matter on the recommendation of the CFA or the Conference Credentials Committee, is most aptly named. It is expressly authorized to 'discuss situations referred to it for investigation with the Government concerned with a view to securing the adjustment of difficulties by agreement'.[873] Even the commissions of inquiry established pursuant to complaints about violations of a ratified convention (Article 26 of ILO's Constitution) do not just establish the facts: they, too, endeavour to find answers to the questions raised that are in conformity with ILO standards and acceptable to the country concerned. At the same time, when the Office knows that a complaint or a grievance under Article 24 of the Constitution is about to be or indeed has just been filed, it can, if it considers it viable, try to obtain the parties' agreement to settle the alleged anomalies through conciliation. In that case, it asks the Governing Body to suspend the formal procedure for a limited time.

---

872. ILO, GB Document GB.326/INS/8 (Rev).

873. ILO, *Sixth Report of the International Labour Organization to the United Nations* (Geneva, 1952). Appendix V, First Report of the Committee on Freedom of Association, pp. 172–173, para. 13.

1073. ILO has dealt with cases in which it played officially or informally an even clearer role of mediator. The point is less to ascertain whether the government concerned acted in compliance with international labour standards than it is to solve, in keeping with the standards and in a way that is acceptable to each of the parties concerned, especially complex and delicate problems. The threat of a public debate in the ILO Governing Body or General Conference has led a number of governments to seek, with the help of high ILO officials or independent experts, an agreed settlement to the problem. A few examples are mentioned below. They concern labour disputes that arose within a particular country or exceeded its limits. More informally still, high international civil servants advised multinational enterprises on the way to improve the working conditions of their staff. To be successful, the concilator needs in all cases to have an in-depth technical knowledge of the question at stake, a full capacity to listen to the parties concerned and to adopt a very informal way to proceed.

I. Labour Disputes that Exceed the Borders of One State

1074. A first case concerned the violation of some maritime conventions. In May 1978, France lodged a representation against Panama, alleging that ships that fly its flag do not apply the provisions of the Food and Catering (Ships' Crews) Convention, 1946 (No. 68), the Repatriation of Seaman Convention, 1926 (No. 23) and the Officers' Competency Certificates Convention, 1936 (No. 53). Consultations took place within the International Labour Office. The two governments involved agreed to use the direct contacts procedure. The Governing Body suspended the examination of the case and some senior ILO officials were sent to Panama. They found out that the country was ready to take practical measures to improve the actual control of the relevant labour legislation and proposed the technical support of the Organisation. The expert contributed towards the elaboration of legislative provisions concerning the employment conditions in the merchant navy. Following his advices, Panama adopted two ordinances on the matter as well as two other measures with a view to giving effect to the relevant conventions. The compulsory insurance system was extended to cover foreign seamen. Four hundreds and twelve labour inspectors were appointed who could justify experience of maritime work and an adequate knowledge of national and international labour standards.[874] The success of the mediation permitted to put an end to the complaint without any further action. It may be added that Panama has now ratified the Maritime Labour Convention 2006.

1075. The same occurred in a case concerning the expulsion of some 30,000 Tunisians and 15,000 Egyptians workers by the Libyan authorities, in the late 1980s. Reasons appeared to be both technical (the fall of the oil price cut significant incomes) and political (the links considered as too close of their countries with the

874. ILO Governing Body, documents GB.214/5/5, 18–21 November 1980, and GB.226/13/5, 31 May–2 June 1984.

Unites States). Egypt and Tunisia had no diplomatic relations with Libya. The Tunisian Government launched a procedure on the basis of Article 24 of the Constitution for the violation of the Protection of Wages Convention, 1949 (No. 95), the Discrimination (Employment and Occupation) Convention, 1958 (No. 111), and the Equality of Treatment (Social Security) Convention, 1962 (No. 118). With regard to Egypt whose relationships with Libya were especially bad, the national confederation of trade unions submitted a representation. Here again, the formal procedure was suspended to permit ILO officials to go on the spot, to bring the parties around a table and to discuss the various options they proposed. An agreement was reached on the payment of unpaid wages, compensation for losses incurred and the transfer of acquired social security rights. The Tunisian workers were compensated on the basis of evidence by financial transfer operated by the Libyan Social Security Authorities to their equivalent in Tunisia. The complaint was withdrawn and the diplomatic relations restored in 1987.[875] The situation was more difficult with regard to Egypt. Discussions took place between the respective national workers' organization. Similar compensation principles were accepted and put an end to the procedure.

1076. To respond to the numerous allegations of discrimination and bad treatment against the Arab workers, the ILO has also sent regular missions to Israel and the Occupied Arab Territories with a view to collecting data and information about their living and employment conditions.

II. Domestic Labour Disputes

1077. A typical case involved deciding what would happen to the assets of the former corporatist trade organization after Spain returned to democratic government. The Committee on Freedom of Association, which dealt with the case, did not seek to determine to which organization the assets should go and in what proportion, but rather to indicate the criteria on which they should be divided.[876] The same approach prevailed in another case concerning the transfer back of the trade union properties to the Argentinean workers' organizations which had split in the meantime when the military regime felt in 1983.[877]

1078. A still more famous case regards Poland where the report of the Commission of inquiry dealing with the dissolution of the trade union movement Solidarnosc and the arrest of trade union leaders was used as the basis for the

875. ILO Governing Body, document GB.240/14/25, May–June 1988.

876. *Official Bulletin*, 1979, Series B, No. 2, 194th Report of the Committee on Freedom of Association, Case No. 900 (Spain), paras 238–262; and 1980, Series B, No. 2, 202nd Report, paras 337–354; *see also* on this question *idem, The Trade Union Situation and Industrial Relations in Spain*, Geneva, 1985, pp. 43–45.

877. *Official Bulletin*, vol. LXVII, 1984, Series B, no. 3, 236th Report of the Committee on Freedom of Association, case No. 842, §16.

democratization of the regime.[878] It would be erroneous to believe however that all complaints were settled positively. There is no surprise to observe blatant failures. How could it be otherwise? Colombia or Myanmar (ex-Burma) for a long time, and still to a certain extent, China are well known examples.

III. Labour Problems in Major Enterprises

1079. The ILO is an intergovernmental institution; it deals with the relations between States. While the national delegations have been widened to employers' and workers' representatives, the Organization has no constitutional basis to deal with the internal problems of multinational enterprises.[879] It does not follow that international officials, when informally consulted, should refuse to provide information and advices on ways and means to solve problems that arise, if they do so in full transparency and cooperation with the constituents. A transnational corporation learned for instance that some subcontractors use children's hands in carpet manufacturing and wanted to stop immediately such practices that contradicted totally its corporate culture and might damage its image or provoke a boycott of its products. To take advantage of the ILO experience in such a case is natural as it is to consult the Organization in the elaboration of a clause prohibiting child labour to be inserted in its code of conduct. The ILO may in particular advise on the spelling of the provision and on the manner to supervise its application. Another company feared the launch of a hostile campaign at the initiative of a NGO. The firm sold canned fruits and vegetables cultivated by a multinational in various plantations where the trade unions rights were not respected. With the unofficial help of an international official, the supermarkets company introduced in the supply contract with the agro-industrial firm a social-clause requiring the observation of the freedom of association principles; the NGO was put in charge of controlling the provision.

1080. The informal assistance of high international civil servants to multinational enterprises should be distinguished from the activities of the Multinational Enterprises Helpdesk created by the Organization to provide advice to a variety of users, in particular company managers and workers, to foster the implementation of the Tripartite Declaration of Principles concerning Multinational Enterprises and Social Policy, 1977,[880] in company operations. Being far from the local conditions, this initiative has been criticized for the extremely general character of some of its opinions. More efficient appears the help that the ILO provide to major companies and international trade unions to reach agreement, as it has been the case on 13 May

878. Fr. Blanchard, 'Une page d'histoire de l'OIT: la Pologne', in J.C. Javillier et B. Gernigon (ed.), *Les normes internationales du travail. Un patrimoine pour l'avenir, Mélanges en l'honneur de Nicolas Valticos*, Geneva, ILO, 2004, pp. 83–88.
879. F. Maupain, 'L'OIT, la justice sociale et la mondialisation', *Collected Course of the Academy of International Law*, Vol. 278, 1999, pp. 301–314.
880. *See* paras 199 *et seq. above*.

2013 between two Workers' confederations and a number of multinational enterprises on fire and building safety in Bangladesh after the tragedy of Rana Plaza.[881] The ILO facilitation and coordination of consultations have also led to an agreement in excess of US$5 million to provide compensation for loss of income, medical and allied care as well as rehabilitation, to the victims of the fire at the Ali Enterprises garment factory in Baldia, Karachi, on 11 September 2012.[882] A Resolution, adopted by the ILC in 2016, ask the Organization to strengthen its capacity to give guidance to enterprises on the application of labour standards within their supply chains.

* * *

1081. These mechanisms appear complex, but that is without doubt because of the complexity of the situations they deal with as international bodies; otherwise the problems would have been solved without their intervention. New procedures were successively established to supplement those provided for in the ILO Constitution, in response to specific problems. The complexity is due in particular to the fact that a balance has been struck between the technical supervisory bodies (including the possibility of recourse to the International Court of Justice) and the representative bodies (in which the representatives of employers' and workers' organizations play a vital role) that remain necessary at the current stage of development of international society in order to ensure that the procedures are effective.

§4. Promotion and Cooperation

1082. The fact that the supervision of the application of ILO standards emphasizes rational dialogue and cooperation paves the way for broader action for the true integration of these instruments in the law and practice of the member countries.

1083. At the same time, the secretarial has for many years endeavoured to develop technical assistance that is well adapted to the States' individual needs.[883] This has taken the form of targeted missions by ILO officials in charge of standards to ILO duty stations, backed by their colleagues at headquarters. These on-site missions can be of two kinds. They can aim to provide technical advice for bringing the law and practice of a country into line with a ratified convention or, more simply, to integrate the values embodied in the standards into the reform of labour legislation. They may also consist in participation in colloquia, seminars and

881. *See* M. Anner and J. Blasi, 'Toward Joint Liability in Global Supply Chains: Addressing the root Causes of Labor Violations in International Subcontracting', *Comp. Labour Law & Pol. Journal* vol. 35(1), fall 2013, pp. 1–43; B. ter Haar, M. Keune 'One step forward or more window-dressing? A legal analysis of recent CSR initiatives in the garment industry in Bangladesh', *Intern. Journal Comp. Labour, Law Ind. Rel.*, Vol 30(1), March 2014, pp. 5–25; F. Laronze et R. Quénaudon, 'Réflexions juridiques après la tragédie du Rana Plaza', *Revue de droit du travail*, No. 7/8, July–August 2013, pp. 487–490.

882. http://www.ilo.org/global/about-the-ilo/newsroom/news/WCMS_521510/lang--en/index.htm.

883. *See* the Governing Body Document 298/LILS/4, Geneva. March 2007, paras 54–73.

workshops where the standards are explained in detail and where the difficulties and objections to their implementation are openly discussed. Events of this kind bring together labour administrators, employers, trade union leaders, even specialized judges. The opinions and recommendations can also concern the reporting and supervisory mechanisms themselves and the way to make sure they do not overburden national administrations. The ILO International Training Centre in Turin plays a significant role in providing support for these assistance and promotion activities.

1084. The 1998 Declaration on Fundamental Principles and Rights at Work recalls several fundamental values established by ILO and introduces a gradual method for their widespread application. The Organization has successfully launched several campaigns for the ratification of its basic conventions, in particular, right after its adoption in 1999, Convention No. 182 on the worst forms of child labour. The International Programme on the Elimination of Child Labour (IPEC), which is financed through voluntary contributions, was a major factor in the success of that campaign.

1085. Convention No. 144 of 1976 on tripartite consultations on international labour standards, which has been widely ratified, has also undoubtedly helped mobilize efforts in support of ILO's standard-setting activities. It requires the operation of procedures ensuring effective consultations between representatives of the government (who provide administrative support), of employers and of workers (on an equal footing). As we have said,[884] the consultations must be on:

(a) government replies to questionnaires concerning items on the agenda of the International Labour Conference and government comments on proposed texts to be discussed by the Conference;
(b) the proposals to be made to the competent authority or authorities in connection with the submission of Conventions and Recommendations pursuant to Article 19 of the Constitution of the International Labour Organization;
(c) the re-examination at appropriate intervals of non-ratified Conventions and of Recommendations to which effect has not yet been given, to consider what measures might be taken to promote their implementation and ratification as appropriate;
(d) questions arising out of reports to be made to the international Labour Office under Article 22 of the Constitution of the International Labour Organization;
(e) proposals for the denunciation of ratified Conventions.

Recommendation No. 152 supplementing the Convention broadens the scope of the consultations on legislative or other measures to give effect to international labour standards and to resolutions and conclusions adopted by the Organization's bodies, to its technical cooperation programmes and the promotion of better knowledge about its activities in general. The consultations must be held at least once

884. *See* para. 543 *above*.

year. Arrangements must be made for the financing 'of training programmes where necessary'.

1086. The Organization has attempted to simplify its standard-setting activities, the volume of which ended up placing too heavy a burden on the governments concerned and on its own secretariat. It has done this basically in two ways. On the one hand, it has staggered the deadlines for the reports the governments must submit under Article 22 of the Constitution.[885] On the other, it has reviewed its conventions and recommendations with a focus on those it considers being truly up to date, the others being set aside for revision or deemed clearly out of date.[886]

1087. The following conventions are considered to be up to date:[887]

Weekly Rest (Industry) Convention, 1921 (No. 14)
Forced Labour Convention, 1930 (No. 29)
Protocol of 2014 to the Forced Labour Convention, 1930 (No. 29)
Medical Examination of Young Persons (Industry) Convention, 1946 (No. 77)
Medical Examination of Young Persons (Non-industrial Occupations) Convention, 1946 (No. 78)
Labour Inspection Convention, 1947 (No. 81)
Protocol of 1995 to the Labour Inspection Convention, 1947
Freedom of Association and Protection of the Right to Organize Convention, 1948 (No. 87)
Protocol of 1990 to the Night Work (Women) Convention (revised), 1948
Labour Clauses (Public Contracts) Convention, 1949 (No. 94)
Protection of Wages Convention, 1949 (No. 95)
Migration for Employment Convention (Revised), 1949 (No. 97)
Right to Organize and Collective Bargaining Convention, 1949 (No. 98)
Equal Remuneration Convention, 1951 (No. 100)
Social Security (Minimum Standards) Convention, 1952 (No. 102)
Abolition of Forced Labour Convention, 1957 (No. 105)
Weekly Rest (Commerce and Offices) Convention, 1957 (No. 106)
Plantations Convention, 1958 (No. 110)
Protocol of 1982 to Convention No. 110 on plantations, 1958
Discrimination (Employment and Occupation) Convention, 1958 (No. 111)
Radiation Protection Convention, 1960 (No. 115)
Equality of Treatment (Social Security) Convention, 1962 (No. 118)
Hygiene (Commerce and Offices) Convention, 1964 (No. 120)
Employment Injury Benefits Convention, 1964 (No. 121)
Employment Policy Convention, 1964 (No. 122)

885. ILO, *Handbook of Procedures Relating to International Labour Conventions and Recommendations*, Rev. 2012 (Geneva), ILO, pp 20 *et seq.*

886. *See* the Governing Body Document GB.285/LILS/5, November 2002, para. 8 and ILC (90th session, 2002), *Policy Regarding the Revision of Standards. Follow-up Decisions by the Governing Body*, Committee on the Application of Standards, Document C.APP./D.4.

887. *See* ILO, *Up to date instruments list-2013*, www.ilo.org/normes.

Medical Examination of Young Persons (Underground Work) Convention, 1965 (No. 124)
Invalidity, Old-age and Survivors' Benefits Convention, 1967 (No. 128)
Labour Inspection (Agriculture) Convention, 1969 (No. 129)
Medical Care and Sickness Benefits Convention, 1969 (No. 130)
Minimum Wage Fixing Convention, 1970 (No. 131)
Workers' Representatives Convention, 1971 (No. 135)
Minimum Age Convention, 1973 (No. 138)
Occupational Cancer Convention, 1974 (No. 139)
Paid Educational Leave Convention, 1974 (No. 140)
Rural Workers' Organizations Convention, 1975 (No. 141)
Human Resources Development Convention, 1975 (No. 142)
Migrant Workers (Supplementary Provisions) Convention, 1975 (No. 143)
Tripartite Consultations on International Labour Standards Convention, 1976 (No. 144)
Continuity of Employment (Seafarers) Convention, 1976 (No. 145)[888]
Seafarers' Annual Leave with Pay Convention, 1976 (No. 146),
Merchant Shipping (Minimum Standards) Convention, 1976 (No. 147),
Protocol of 1996 to the Merchant Shipping (Minimum Standards) Convention, 1976 (No. 147)[891]
Working Environment (Air Pollution, Noise and Vibration) Convention, 1977 (No. 148)
Nursing Personnel Convention, 1977 (No. 149)
Labour Administration Convention, 1978 (No. 150)
Labour Relations (Public Service) Convention, 1978 (No. 151)
Occupational Safety and Health (Dock Work) Convention, 1979 (No. 152)
Collective Bargaining Convention, 1981 (No. 154)
Occupational Safety and Health Convention, 1981 (No. 155)
Protocol of 2002 to Convention No. 155 on occupational safety and health, 1981
Workers with Family Responsibilities Convention, 1981 (No. 156)
Maintenance of Social Security Rights Convention, 1982 (No. 157)
Vocational Rehabilitation and Employment (Disabled Persons) Convention, 1983 (No. 159)
Labour Statistics Convention, 1985 (No. 160)
Occupational Health Services Convention, 1985 (No. 161)
Asbestos Convention, 1986 (No. 162)
Seafarers' Welfare Convention, 1987 (No. 163),
Health Protection and Medical Care (Seafarers) Convention, 1987 (No. 164),
Social Security (Seafarers) Convention (Revised), 1987 (No. 165),
Repatriation of Seafarers Convention (Revised), 1987 (No. 166),
Safety and Health in Construction Convention, 1988 (No. 167)
Employment Promotion and Protection against Unemployment Convention, 1988 (No. 168)
Indigenous and Tribal Peoples Convention, 1989 (No. 169)

888. Instruments revised by the Maritime Labour Convention, 2006 (No. 186). The Convention has entered into force on 20 August 2013.

Chemicals Convention, 1990 (No. 170)
Night Work Convention, 1990 (No. 171)
Working Conditions (Hotels and Restaurants) Convention, 1991 (No. 172)
Protection of Workers' Claims (Employer's Insolvency) Convention, 1992 (No. 173)
Prevention of Major Industrial Accidents Convention, 1993 (No. 174)
Part-time Work Convention, 1994 (No. 175)
Safety and Health in Mines Convention, 1995 (No. 176)
Home Work Convention, 1996 (No. 177)
Labour Inspection (Seafarers) Convention, 1996 (No. 178)[873]
Recruitment and Placement of Seafarers Convention, 1996 (No. 179)
Seafarers' Hours of Work and the Manning of Ships Convention, 1996 (No. 180)[873]
Private Employment Agencies Convention, 1997 (No. 181)
Worst Forms of Child Labour Convention, 1999 (No. 182)
Maternity Protection Convention, 2000 (No. 183)
Safety and Health in Agriculture Convention, 2001 (No. 184)
Seafarers' Identity Documents Convention (revised), 2003 (No. 185)
Maritime Labour Convention, 2006 ('MLC' No. 186)
Promotional Framework for Occupational Safety and Health Convention, 2006 (No. 187)
Work in Fishing Convention, 2007 (No. 188)
Domestic Workers Convention, 2011 (No. 189).

1088. With regard to recommendations, the following are considered to be up to date:

Forced Labour (Indirect Compulsion) Recommendation, 1930 (No. 35)
Income Security Recommendation, 1944 (No. 67)
Medical Examination of Young Persons Recommendation, 1946 (No. 79)
Labour Inspection Recommendation, 1947 (No. 81)
Labour Inspection (Mining and Transport) Recommendation, 1947 (No. 82)
Labour Clauses (Public Contracts) Recommendation, 1949 (No. 84)
Protection of Wages Recommendation, 1949 (No. 85)
Migration for Employment Recommendation (Revised), 1949 (No. 86)
Equal Remuneration Recommendation, 1951 (No. 90)
Collective Agreements Recommendation, 1951 (No. 91)
Protection of Workers' Health Recommendation, 195 (No. 97)
Vocational Rehabilitation (Disabled) Recommendation, 1955 (No. 99)
Welfare Facilities Recommendation, 1956 (No. 102)
Weekly Rest (Commerce and Offices) Recommendation, 1957 (No. 103)
Indigenous and Tribal Populations Recommendation, 1957 (No. 104)
Plantations Recommendation, 1958 (No. 110)
Discrimination (Employment and Occupation) Recommendation, 1958 (No. 111)
Consultation (Industrial and National Levels) Recommendation, 1960 (No. 113)
Radiation Protection Recommendation, 1960 (No. 114)
Workers' Housing Recommendation, 1961 (No. 115)
Reduction of Hours of Work Recommendation, 1962 (No. 116)

Hygiene (Commerce and Offices) Recommendation, 1964 (No. 120)
Employment Injury Benefits Recommendation, 1964 (No. 121)
Employment Policy Recommendation, 1964 (No. 122)
Conditions of Employment of Young Persons (Underground Work) Recommendation, 1965 (No. 125)
Invalidity, Old-Age and Survivors' Benefits Recommendation, 1967 (No. 131)
Tenants and Share-croppers Recommendation, 1968 (No. 132)
Labour Inspection (Agriculture) Recommendation, 1969 (No. 133)
Medical Care and Sickness Benefits Recommendation, 1969 (No. 134)
Minimum Wage Fixing Recommendation, 1970 (No. 135)
Workers' Representatives Recommendation, 1971 (No. 143)
Minimum Age Recommendation, 1973 (No. 146)
Occupational Cancer Recommendation, 1974 (No.147)
Rural Workers' Organisations Recommendation, 1975 (No.149)
Migrant Workers Recommendation, 1975 (No. 151)
Tripartite Consultation (Activities of the International Labour Organisation) Recommendation, 1976 (No. 152)
Protection of Young Seafarers Recommendation, 1976 (No. 153)
Continuity of Employment (Seafarers) Recommendation, 1976 (No. 154)
Merchant Shipping (Improvement of Standards) Recommendation, 1976 (No. 155)
Working Environment (Air Pollution, Noise and Vibration) Recommendation, 1977 (No. 156)
Nursing Personnel Recommendation, 1977 (No. 157)
Labour Administration Recommendation, 1978 (No. 158)
Labour Relations (Public Service) Recommendation, 1978 (No. 159)
Occupational Safety and Health (Dock Work) Recommendation, 1979 (No. 160)
Collective Bargaining Recommendation, 1981 (No. 163)
Occupational Safety and Health Recommendation, 1981 (No. 164)
Workers with Family Responsibilities Recommendation, 1981 (No. 165)
Maintenance of Social Security Rights Recommendation, 1983 (No. 167)
Vocational Rehabilitation and Employment (Disabled Persons) Recommendation, 1983 (No. 168)
Employment Policy (Supplementary Provisions) Recommendation, 1984 (No. 169)
Labour Statistics Recommendation, 1985 (No. 170)
Occupational Health Services Recommendation, 1985 (No. 171)
Asbestos Recommendation, 1986 (No. 172)
Seafarers' Welfare Recommendation, 1987 (No. 173)
Repatriation of Seafarers Recommendation, 1987 (No. 174)
Safety and Health in Construction Recommendation, 1988 (No. 175)
Employment Promotion and Protection against Unemployment Recommendation, 1988 (No. 176)
Chemicals Recommendation, 1990 (No. 177)
Night Work Recommendation, 1990 (No. 178)
Working Conditions (Hotels and Restaurants) Recommendation, 1991 (No. 179)

Protection of Workers' Claims (Employer's Insolvency) Recommendation, 1992 (No. 180)
Prevention of Major Industrial Accidents Recommendation, 1993 (No. 181)
Part-Time Work Recommendation, 1994 (No. 182)
Safety and Health in Mines Recommendation, 1995 (No. 183)
Home Work Recommendation, 1996 (No. 184)
Labour Inspection (Seafarers) Recommendation, 1996 (No. 185)
Recruitment and Placement of Seafarers Recommendation, 1996 (No.186)
Seafarers' Wages, Hours of Work and the Manning of Ships Recommendation, 1996 (No. 187)
Private Employment Agencies Recommendation, 1997 (No. 188)
Job Creation in Small and Medium-Sized Enterprises Recommendation, 1998 (No. 189)
Worst Forms of Child Labour Recommendation, 1999 (No. 190)
Maternity Protection Recommendation, 2000 (No. 191)
Safety and Health in Agriculture Recommendation, 2001 (No. 192)
Promotion of Cooperatives Recommendation, 2002 (No. 193)
List of Occupational Diseases Recommendation, 2002 (No. 194)
Human Resources Development Recommendation, 2004 (No. 195)
Promotional Framework for Occupational Safety and Health Recommendation, 2006 (No. 197)
Employment Relationship Recommendation, 2006 (No. 198)
Work in Fishing Recommendation, 2007 (No. 199)
HIV and AIDS Recommendation, 2010 (No. 200)
Domestic Workers Recommendation, 2011 (No. 201)
Social Protection Floors Recommendation, 2012 (No. 202)
Forced Labour (Supplementary Measures) Recommendation, 2014 (No. 203).
Transition from the Informal to the Formal Economy Recommendation, 2015 (No. 204)

The ILC should adopt in 2017 a Recommendation on Employment and Decent Work for Peace and Resilience, revising the Employment (Transition from War to Peace) Recommendation, 1944 (No. 71).

1089. The ILO supervisory machinery may be improved. The bulk of the national reports and of the comments of the CEACR and other bodies is such that the whole system is close to implosion, or at least to blunt its effects. The complaints procedures are more contingent than the regular reporting mechanism. They imply to lodge allegations and free employers 'and workers 'organizations to do so. When it is not the case however, international confederations can take the initiative; representations and complaints normally point out also the most serious problems. Nicolas Valticos, an authority in the ILO standard-setting activities, had suggested to limit the control to this type of recourses. To focus on complaints procedures would certainly relieve the task of the international civil servants and experts as well as the obligations of the States, while keeping in principle a control a strict control on the abuses.

1090. Codes of conduct, labelling, certification and social initiatives adopted by the enterprises appear to be welcome in most cases.[889] They usefully permit to improve national law, or more often, to make its application more effective. They should aim at complementing rather than substituting or modifying ILO standards. The influence of the Organization on those activities is limited, but significant. It may increase. The ILO has engaged, together with other international institutions,[890] in new efforts to promote its values and standards through partnerships with the private sector, as recalled in the 2008 Declaration on Social Justice for a Fair Globalization.

1091. Should new standards be adopted, specifying the content of the Social Corporate Responsibility, indicating its compulsory character and providing for control procedures?[891] It would surely be desirable, but unlikely to be voted and implemented. It seems more realistic to organize a better coordination between public and private international standards, adopted by all kinds of institutions; their messy proliferation damages the efficiency of all. A good example of such a collaboration is the partnership agreed upon in September 2015 by the ILO and Japan Tobacco International to step up joint work to promote fundamental labour rights, including particularly protection against child labour, in the tobacco supply chain.[892]

1092. Furthermore we should again revisit the problematic of the social clause in trade codes and agreements.[893] It raises the question of the efficiency of the sanctions in international labour law as well as of the cost of the social legislation in economics. In spite of the ILO reluctance to deal with the theme, minimum labour standards have been more and more inserted in commercial legislation as well as in trade agreements. Those developments are unlikely to stop. The ILO could establish teams of social auditors, similar to the squad imagined by the OECD to fight tax fraud. There is here a new role for ILO: the quality of its experts and their first-hand knowledge of development in less industrialized countries make the Organization an ideal neutral third party to examine a dispute between two States on the clause in their cooperation treaty referring to some international labour standards. The agreement concludes in the garment industry between the United States and Cambodia is an extremely interesting precedent.[894]

---

889. *See* paras 227–231 *above*.
890. World Commission on the Social Dimension of Globalization, *A Fair Globalization. Creating Opportunities for All*, Geneva, ILO, 2004, paras 553–559; ILC (92nd Session, 2004), *A Fair Globalization. The Role of the ILO*, Report of the Director-General, Geneva, ILO, 2004, pp. 25–27.
891. F. Maupain, *The Future of the International Labour Organization in the Global Economy*, Oxford, Hart Publishing, 2014.
892. http://www.ilo.org/pardev/news/WCMS_409381/lang--en/index.htm. Another example is the Global Business Network for Social Protection Floors (GBN for SPFs) launched by the ILO in 2015.
893. *See* paras 35 *et seq.*
894. *See* para. 65 *above*. *See also* S. Polaski, *Harnessing Global Forces to Create Decent Work in* Cambodia, Geneva, ILO, 2009.

1093. The same could be written for the provisions contained in enterprises social initiatives. In both cases, its involvement would contribute to solve the difficulties linked with the creation of a strict and credible system of supervision

1094. Lastly, the supranational dimension of current socio-economic developments could breathe fresh life into the old idea of asking the Organization to maintain a list of international labour conciliators who would be available as needed and who would obviously have to have the requisite technical skills and moral qualities.

Chapter 2. Implementation Difficulties

1095. We have already noted that the conclusions of the ILO supervisory bodies are not binding. In brief, the ILO cannot send in the police to oblige a country to apply a convention it has ratified. Furthermore the Organization is reluctant to use the sanctions at its disposal in the case of an infringement of its standards. Beyond dialogue and conciliation, the supervisory system relies mainly upon diplomatic sanction and last recourse to the International Court of Justice.

1096. This being said, the Organization has furthered the implementation of international labour standards in many cases. These standards, needless to say, are frequently violated, some governments being more respectful of them in speech than in actual practice. Indeed, situations sometimes arise where no overall solution seems forthcoming. However, even in cases in which ILO is not able to reverse the situation, its action is beneficial. And these cases should not overshadow the others. A good example of the ILO's positive action is that on trade union rights. Through the activities of the Committee on Freedom of Association, many arbitrarily arrested trade unionists or employer representatives have been released or, if accused of activities unrelated to their representative functions, given a fair trial; workers who were dismissed in reprisal for their union activities have been reinstated; legislation incompatible with the principles of trade union freedoms has been amended; and, more generally, a dialogue has often been resumed between the government and the employers' and workers' associations, which are essential components of public life in all countries[895].

1097. The Organization owes these successes to a supervisory system that has been thoughtfully and carefully conceived and which has been built up gradually over the years. It owes them to the will, not only to make, in the light of ILO standards, an objective and technically accurate analysis of each situation, but also to formulate comments which call for dialogue and cooperation, instead of criticism and condemnation.

1098. Although there is no room, as we have said, for flexibility in the supervision of the application of standards which States have freely committed themselves to apply, this does not mean that the Organization necessarily needs to pass judgment in order to solve discrepancies. The supervisory bodies have borrowed from the judiciary process a scrupulous concern for due process of law. Yet it is through the combined efforts of diplomacy and essentially moral incitements that they try to secure the implementation of standards when problems of application arise.

895. R. Hernández Pulido, *Derechos humanos fundamentales y sindicales en tiempo de las dictaduras en el cono Sur. La labor de restitución de los derechos emprendida por el Comité de libertad sindical,* Santiago de Chile, OIT, 2014.

1099. The Organization is certainly not without means for urging a State to comply fully with standards.[896] Firstly, giving publicity to the conclusions of the supervisory bodies regarding States is one possible means. The States, very naturally, try to avoid being mentioned before the international community, especially before countries with which their relations are not the best. Secondly, these comments lead to public discussion within an international forum (within the Committee on the Application of Standards of the International Labour Conference, for example, where actual hearings of the governments concerned are initiated). Thirdly, there is the possibility of adopting more dissuasive measures, i.e. establishing a commission of inquiry, for which the ILO Constitution expressly provides. Other measures have been suggested with a view to 'mobilizing shame' against certain situations. However, the Organization has always preferred dialogue to sanctions, even if purely moral.

1100. Above all, the role of the supervisory bodies is not to pass judgment: they formulate recommendations based on ILO standards and address them to the governments concerned to allow them to overcome certain difficulties. The whole procedure is geared to this end, but the more complex or serious the problem, the more elaborate the methods that have been devised to bring about a constructive dialogue and arrive at solutions consistent with the conventions. In various cases, even informal missions and talks carried out by high-level officials of the Organization have helped to break a deadlock. It is with this vision in mind that the Institution has always resisted proposals for coercive action, such as recourse to tariff and trade sanctions.

1101. The achievements of ILO's supervisory machinery are more than significant.[897] Also revealing are the sentences where national courts used ratified or even non ratified conventions with a view to correcting or interpreting national provisions or to identify new general principles of law.[898] In the Council of Europe too,

896. *See* para. 1066 *et seq. above*.
897. For studies on the influence of the ILO standards, *see* S. Charnovitz 'The influence of international labour standards on the world trading regime: A historical review', *ILR*, Vol. 126(5), September–October 1987, pp. 565–584; M. Brassey: 'Something new, something borrowed ... : Comparative labour law in South Africa', in R. Blanpain and R. Weiss (eds.), *The Changing Face of Labour Law and Industrial Relations, Liber Amicorum Clyde W. Summers*, Baden-Baden, Nomos Verlagsgesselschaft, 1993, pp. 139–140; S. van Eck, 'Employment Agencies: International Norms and Developments in South Africa', *IJCLLIR*, vol. 28(1), 2012, pp. 29–44; S. Deery and R. Mitchell (eds.), *Labour Law and Industrial Relations in Asia, Eight Country Studies*, Melbourne, Longman Cheshire, 1993, p. 9; J. B. Acosta Estevez, *El Sistema Jurídico de la Organización Internacional del Trabajo y el Derecho Español*, Cedecs Editorial, Barcelona, 1997; N. Lyutov, 'The role of the ILO in the adoption of the New Russian Labour Code', *The International Journal of Comparative Labour Law and Industrial Relations*, Summer 2003, Vol. 19/2, pp. 163–177; S.L. Kang, *Human Rights and Labor Solidarity: Trade Unions in the Global Economy*, Philadelphia (PA), University of Pennsylvania Press, 2012; E. Gravel, I. Duplessis and B. Gernigon, *The Committee on Freedom of Association: Its Impact over 50 years* (Geneva) ILO, 2001; E. Gravel and Ch. Charbonneau-Jobin, *The Committee of Experts on the Application of Conventions and Recommendations: Its dynamic and impact* (Geneva) ILO, 2003.
898. *See* para. 139 *above*. *See also*, in the case of Canada, the Supreme Court's decision on the right to strike, issued on 30 January 2015 (*Saskatchewan Federation of Labour* v. *Saskatchewan*, 2015 SCC

the European Committee of Social Rights[899] and Court of Human Rights have referred to ILO standards and comments by the supervisory organs. In the *Demir and Baykara* v. *Turkey* case in particular, reference is not confined to observations by the Committee of Experts concerning Turkey specifically, but also extends to the whole body of principles drawn from earlier conclusions, including by the Freedom of Association Committee.[900] Generally speaking, a number of authors have underlined the influence of the international labour standards in the development of national or European law.[901]

1102. Nevertheless numerous problems still remain in the implementation of ILO conventions. Time and again, objections have been raised by delegates in the ILO Governing Body and at the annual Conference with regard to standard-setting activities as a whole (§1). Responses have already been given (§2). More in-depth difficulties have still to be overcome, however, before fully satisfactory results are achieved in terms of the application of all international labour standards. These difficulties must be analysed in an open and serene manner with a view to facilitating appropriate solutions (§3).

§1. The Problems Raised

1103. The collapse of the communist regimes in Central and Eastern Europe ended the long-standing opposition of the countries of the region, and particularly of the former Soviet Union, to ILO's supervisory machinery. Conflicting views expressed in the Governing Body or at the Conference nowadays merely reflect the differences of interest between employers' and workers' representatives, as recently illustrated by the controversy the right to strike.[902]

1104. The basic question raised in today's debates is the capacity for countries, even highly industrialized ones, to bear the financial cost of ILO standards in the face of present economic challenges.

---

4); C.T. Toselli, 'Aplicación de las normas de la OIT en los juicios del trabajo', *Revista venezolana de legislación y jurisprudencia*, 2013, pp. 271–289.

899. *See for example* decision of 7 December 2012, complaint No. 76/2012 of the Federation of employed pensioners of Greece.

900. *Demir and Baykara* v. *Turkey*, 12 November 2008, req. No. 34503/97, http://www.echr.coe.int/echr. *See* K.D. Ewing, J. Hendy, 'The dramatic implications of Demir and Baykara', *Industrial Law Journal*, March 2010, Vol. 39 (1), pp. 2–51.

901. *See* J. Thirkell, R. Scase and S. Vickerstaff (eds.), *Labour Relations and Political Change in Eastern Europe. A Comparative Perspective*, London, University College London, 1995, especially pp. 4, 35, 177; K. Lenaerts, 'Interlocking legal orders in the European Union and Comparative Law', *International and Comparative Labour Quarterly*, Vol. 52, No. 4, October 2003, pp. 873–906; M. Schmitt, 'L'influence des conventions de l'OIT sur les jurisprudences européennes. Approche comparée en matière de droit de négociation collective', *Revue de droit du travail*, No. 7/8, July–August 2013, pp. 513–525. *See* also the Court of Justice of the European Union in *KHS*, 22 November 2011, case No. 214/14, paras 3–4 and 41–42.

902. *See above* para. 282.

1105. It has been pointed out, quite correctly,[903] that the cost price of a product depends on numerous factors: the price of raw materials, existing markets, monetary fluctuations, investment policy, tax schemes, customs duties, manpower qualifications and managerial quality, to cite but a few. It is therefore dangerous to attempt to measure the cost of international labour standards, all the more so because they are very diverse and applied in countries which are very different from one another because of their size or industrial structure.

1106. The research conducted for a number of years calls for a number of additional comments. Firstly: the cost of standards, which protect the physical and psychological soundness of workers, seems quite modest in relation to the total amount of investment in machinery and equipment. In addition, the preventive measures taken against occupational diseases or accidents help to avoid expenses which are sometimes much higher, since employers and the nation as a whole pay a heavy price for diseases or accidents. Moreover, the question can be put quite differently if considered macro-economically, when all costs have to be assessed, not to mention the benefits of adequate labour and social protection in terms of labour force performance and productivity.[904] Secondly: it is useless and unsound to contest the need to adapt to developments in the economy and technological change. Adjustments are always necessary, particularly during a crisis; it is not advisable to delay them. Indeed, it is important to weigh their social effects carefully. Here again, international labour standards have an essential role to play: they should form, it has been said, a safety net for those whose employment or incomes are threatened, preserving their productive capacity; in other words, they should alleviate the social consequences during transitional periods and prevent the weak from becoming even weaker.

1107. That is not all. The positive economic effects of social programmes on the national budget must not be ignored. Such programmes also help ensure the social peace that is vital for the economic system to function smoothly. The ILO have, on several occasions, referred to the risks involved, in more general terms, in sacrificing the long term for the short term. In the difficult search for an acceptable trade-off between economic constraints (structural transformations, the struggle against disequilibrium) and social, or more simply, human imperatives (justice, equal opportunity, maintenance of a decent standard of living), standards for labour-management relations, in particular those for collective bargaining, are extremely

903. Valticos and von Potobsky, 'International Labour Law', in *International Encyclopaedia for Labour Law and Industrial Relations*, Deventer, Kluwer, 1995, paras 10–15; W. Sengenberger, *Globalisation and Social Progress: The Role and Impact of International Labour Standards*, Bonn, Friedrich-Ebert Stiftung, 2002, mainly p. 31 and *et seq.*; *see* also paras 1153–1154 *below*.

904. *See* for example OECD, International Trade and Core Labour Standards, Paris, 2000; W. Sengenberger and D. Campbell (eds.), Creating Economic Opportunities. The Role of Labour Standards in Industrial Restructuring (Geneva), International Institute for Labour Studies, 1994; D. Kucera, 'Core labour standards and foreign direct investment', *ILR*, 2002, Vol. 141, Nos. 1–2, pp. 31–69; S. Lee and McCann D. (eds.), *Regulating for Decent Work: New Directions in Labour Market Regulation*, Geneva, ILO, 2011; S. Deakin, J. Malmberg and P. Sarkar, 'How do labour laws affect unemployment and the labour share of national income? The experience of six OECD countries, 1970–2010', *ILR*, vol. 153(1), 2014, pp. 1–28.

useful. Regularly maintained relations between free employers' and workers' organizations and the public authorities have, in a new and effective way, on various occasions made it possible to avoid crises and economic disorder wreaking havoc and weighing heavily on employment security and incomes. The adherence and support of employers, workers and their respective associations have proven to be decisive factors in the implementation of a policy of austerity.

1108. The applicability of international labour standards to developing countries, where a large proportion of the population often lives in deplorable conditions, has to be given further consideration. The representatives of some of these countries have complained that ILO standards, adopted before their countries became independent, did not take sufficient account of their specific difficulties. Some have added that their financial situation hindered their full participation in the procedure of preparing standards; the shortage of personnel within their labour administrations prevented them from providing substantial replies to preparatory questionnaires, and the members of their delegations at the annual Conference were too few to allow for their active participation in all the committees where standards were discussed. Nonetheless, the recent trend in the number of ratifications continues to demonstrate a clear commitment, including from developing countries.[905]

1109. It has been suggested that the universal standards be replaced by regional rules. Rules adapted to each region may surely facilitate the implementation of universal standards, even make them richer. They should nevertheless come as a complement, not as an exception or an adjustments that would make them weaker. Some have gone so far in that direction as claiming that child labour is part of the inheritance of Southern African countries and have put forward theories of the relativism of human rights to denounce international standards urging their abolition[906] The idea however was not greeted with open arms, especially by those countries which might well have benefited from this type of flexibility. 'Sub-standard norms for sub-standard men' are unacceptable. The application of basic standards should not be held up since it endangered the fundamental equality of all working men and women everywhere.[907]

§2. RESPONSES GIVEN

1110. ILO considers that every national legal system integrates a number of factors of a political, economic, social or cultural nature; the historical dimension is also, in its view, of distinct importance. In other words, the Organization does not try to impose any type of legal system on a particular country. It only proposes minimum standards, basic principles that can be readily adapted to most if not all

905. *See* the list of the latest ratifications on the ILO site under www.ilo.org/dyn/normlex.
906. Tendai Charity Nhenga *Application of the international prohibition of child labour in an African context: Lesotho, Zimbabwe and South Africa,* Capetown University, PhD thesis, 2008.
907. On this matter, *see also* J.M. Thouvenin et d'A. Trebilcock (eds.), *Droit international social*, 2 vols, Brussels, Bruylant, 2013, pp. 72 *et seq.*, 87 *et seq.*

national systems. Its Constitution states clearly[908] that 'in framing any Convention or Recommendation of general application the Conference shall have due regard to those countries in which climatic conditions, the imperfect development of industrial organization, or other special circumstances make the industrial conditions substantially different and shall suggest the modifications, if any, which it considers may be required to meet the case of such countries'.

1111. The Organization has done much to respond to the specific concerns of developing countries. Numerous conventions have been revised. Other instruments have been subject to re-examination which has often resulted in new or complementary standards being adopted, even if, in the strictest sense, the earlier standards were not revised. The Organization has also taken steps to facilitate the participation of Member States in the establishment of standards, and to make the supervisory procedures and content of the conventions and recommendations well known. This, for example, is one of the primary tasks of ILO's decentralized legal experts who work in the Organization's worldwide network of duty stations. The ILO also conducts information meetings and special missions to this effect.

1112. To facilitate their application everywhere, even where the level of economic development makes implementation particularly difficult, international labour standards must be formulated in sufficiently flexible terms. The ILO's founders inscribed these principles in the Constitution. Their successors subsequently applied them, employing various devices.[909] In short, ILO instruments, especially the more recent ones, offer various options with regard to both content and scope: they allow for only certain parts of a convention to be ratified or the choice of several parts with differing obligations; they also allow States to exclude categories of workers or particular branches of economic activity from the application of the instrument. Several conventions expressly allow for the gradual application of the instrument and even permit specified temporary exceptions. Such provisions actually make it possible to start with the application of international labour conventions in the modern sector of a developing country's economy without waiting for its possible extension to more traditional sectors. Some conventions authorize the ratifying State to make exception to certain standards if national provisions exist which give a substantially equivalent protection. These so-called clauses of equivalence are useful when the requirements of a convention are of a very technical nature. The Work in Fishing Convention, 2007, No. 188, for example, authorizes a State which is not in a position to implement the provisions of its annex III (concerning the fishing vessel accommodation), after consultation, to adopt 'provisions in its law and regulations or other measures which are substantially equivalent'.[910] The Maritime Labour Convention, 2006, No. 186, contains a similar provision, but of a much larger scope, as it applies to all the mandatory

908. Article 19, para. 3.

909. *See* paras 672–673 *above*. For a systematic analysis, *see* GB, 244th Session (Geneva, November 1989) (Committee on Standing Orders and the Application of Conventions and Recommendations): *Follow-up to the report of the Governing Body Working Party on International Labour Standards*, doc. GB.244/SC/3/3.

910. Article 28, para 2.

standards included in its Code.[911] It would not be possible however to extend the device to too many cases as it lacks the necessary precision to permit due supervision. The Conventions may also be flexible as regards the methods of application, and allow countries to give effect to a convention by means other than national law and regulations, such as by custom, collective agreements, court decisions, arbitration awards or simple administrative instructions. Nevertheless, on the whole, States tend to make little use of the flexibility techniques offered to them.

1113. Other flexibility techniques are also used. The Conference has sometimes limited the standards contained in a convention to general principles, reserving the more precise and detailed provisions for a supplementary recommendation, the standards of which are not binding. It has adopted programmatic conventions in pursuance of a specific objective; the conventions call for the adoption of certain policies and the formulation of certain programmes, rather than containing precise legal obligations with which the countries concerned must comply. There is a limit to flexibility, however. Standards should not become devoid of all substance and should remain sufficiently stringent to stimulate action. Moreover, as the International Labour Conference has often recalled, there should be no flexibility in conventions dealing with fundamental human rights and freedom. On the other hand, promotional or programmatic conventions can have a direct and positive influence on development. For example, although an active vocational training and guidance policy by no means constitutes a miracle solution to unemployment, poverty or economic stagnation, a rational, dynamic and systematic policy to improve occupational skills, as envisaged in the Human Resources Development Convention (No. 142) and Recommendation (No. 150), 1975, can be an important factor in economic development. The absence of such a policy – or of the resources to implement it – may seriously and even permanently jeopardize future growth in the countries concerned.

1114. ILO's technical cooperation programmes can also facilitate the application of standards. There does exist, in fact, a clear complementarity between legal procedures, dissemination of information, and technical cooperation, whereby the latter plays a significant role in enabling countries to overcome some of the obstacles.[912]

1115. The Organization undertakes operational activities linked to human rights and international labour standards in order to promote broader understanding and acceptance as well as to encourage the ratification and observance of the standards. With this in mind, the sector concerned organizes regional and sub-regional seminars and symposia and participates in national meetings. It also provides advisory services and organizes special programmes to familiarize national civil servants with the obligations of Member States and the Organization's procedures relating to standards. For their part, the international labour standards specialists based in the

911. Article VI, para 3 and 4. *See* para 105 *above* and 1134 *below*.
912. *See* http://www.ilo.org/global/standards/applying-and-promoting-international-labour-standards/technical-assistance-and-training/lang – en/index.htm.

various duty stations endeavour to ensure that these standards are respected. Efforts are also made in the area of training, for instance, to ensure that such standards are integrated whenever necessary into ILO's technical cooperation activities. Special attention is given for example to the concerns of women workers and the principles of equality of opportunity and treatment between men and women. Increasingly, this is done by including measurable indicators at the design stage of the projects to facilitate subsequent monitoring and evaluation. Meetings and analyses of gender-specific data for project planning and implementation constitute another operational goal.

1116. If the link between operational activities and other means of action – research in particular – has always been underlined, this has not necessarily been the case with regard to the international labour standards. Indeed, since the very beginning of technical cooperation, this has been a subject of animated discussion and the debate has even gathered intensity in recent years. At the start, fears were expressed in the Governing Body that the Organization might lose control over the general policy forming the foundation of its operational activities and which could then be imposed from outside. It was also feared that ILO might abandon its traditional activities for the legal protection of the workers. Moreover, there was concern about ILO's ability to put the limited resources placed at its disposal to good use in the absence of any pre-established plans and given the possibility that programmes would be tailored to demands rather than the outcome of its own initiatives.[913] Even if such fears were subsequently allayed, ensuing developments demonstrated that technical cooperation tended to concentrate in areas where few conventions and recommendations existed, those that did being mostly of recent adoption and promotional in nature. In terms of resources, technical cooperation became the most important activity.[914] For these and other reasons – the complexity of the mechanisms governing technical cooperation and the qualifications of project staff – the interaction between ILO's two prime means of action was not always clear. The so-called Decent Work Agenda, adopted more recently by the Organization, has certainly permitted a better coordination of those activities.[915]

1117. The Office has introduced a series of measures to better inform and enlighten its technical cooperation staff and experts, as well as its partners (UNDP, other donors and beneficiary countries) as to the role of international labour standards. Steps have been also taken to improve the flow of information within the Office and to highlight its correlation with standards in documents relating to the preparation, execution and evaluation of technical cooperation projects. These measures have made it possible to ensure that the International Labour Standards Department is duly consulted in cases where difficulties jeopardize the application

913. *Minutes of the GB*: 113th Session (Brussels, Nov. 1950), pp. 39–40; *ibid.*, 114th Session (Geneva, March 1951), p. 107; *ibid.*, 117th Session (Geneva, Nov. 1951), pp. 69–70; *ibid.*, 127th Session (Rome, Nov. 1954), pp. 30–31. *See also* A. Alcock, *History of the International Labour Organization*, London, Macmillan, 1971, p. 219.

914. *See* A. Aboughanem, *Etude sur les relations entre les normes internationales du travail et la coopération technique*, Geneva ILO, 1985 (restricted distribution), pp. 23 and 110.

915. *See below* the last section of this chapter.

of certain fundamental standards relating to human rights, the protection of workers, or the application of ratified conventions. The Office's concern is to ensure that projects under its jurisdiction did not allow situations to develop which were contrary to its standards on human rights in particular.[916] The Organization has firmly stressed the need for greater global coherence drawing from new strategies developed in both areas. This called for genuine synergy, not conditionality whereby standards and technical cooperation would mutually support each other.[917]

1118. Such coordinated action goes beyond measures taken to prevent conflicts and eliminate contradictions, and even transcends the use of technical cooperation – especially regular budget – resources, to assist Member States in putting standards into practice and in establishing the economic and social base that would enable them to do so in the best way possible. This approach is intended to be comprehensive and positive. It is also in response to the wish expressed by the ILO's membership that the Organization refocus its activities on its mandate and not engage in activities – even if their funding is assured – that deviate from it. In short, ILO technical cooperation should aim at assisting countries to adopt policies which correspond to the ideals of social justice and respect for human beings contained within its Constitution. Seen from this perspective, the Organization's objectives of necessity converge, in that standards help create an environment which favours harmonious economic and social development, and one where a major obstacle – poverty – threatening the application of standards could be overcome. Indeed, most technical cooperation activities aim at creating such an enabling environment. This undertaking to achieve greater synergy implies that these efforts must be integrated coherently within Member States' policies. In turn, governments and the social partners (in addition to donor countries or institutions) must not only accept, but truly adhere to such an ideal. Hence, serious violations of fundamental standards might imply a change in the order of priorities among national objectives and could lead the ILO to reorient, accelerate, slow down or discontinue specific projects in order to facilitate a return to a situation more compatible with reciprocally accepted commitments, as it has been recently the case with regard to Myanmar.[918]

1119. The ILO Declaration on Fundamental Principles and Rights at Work and its Follow-up. adopted in 1998, had already enhanced the links between standard-setting activities and technical cooperation. It stresses the obligation of the Organization to assist its Members, in response to their established and expressed needs, in attaining the realization of those principles and rights at work and to make full use for that aim of its constitutional, operational and budgetary resources and support. The ILO should also encourage other international organizations to support these efforts by:

916. GB, 252nd Session (Geneva. Feb.-Mar. 1992), *International Labour Standards and Technical Cooperation*, doc. GB.252/15/1, paras 27 to 29.
917. *See* the ILO Declaration on Social Justice for a Fair Globalization adopted by the ILC in 2008.
918. International Labour Conference (102nd Session, Geneva, June 2013), *Provisional Record*, No. 17, Geneva, ILO, 2013.

(a) offering technical cooperation and advisory services to promote the ratification and implementation of the fundamental Conventions;
(b) (…) assisting those Members not yet in a position to ratify some or all of these Conventions in their efforts to respect, to promote and to realize the principles concerning fundamental rights which are the subject of those conventions; and
(c) (…) helping the Members in their efforts to create a climate for economic and social development.

1120. The Declaration has given strong impetus to technical cooperation programmes in the field of workers' rights. Amongst them, the International Programme for the Elimination of Child Labour (known as IPEC) should receive a special mention. It pursues several goals: (a) to contribute substantially in the long term to the elimination of child labour in a selected group of countries; (b) to enhance the ability of the Member States concerned to design and implement policies and programmes that effectively protect working children and combat child labour; and (c) to increase public awareness of the extent of child labour and its consequences and of obligations imposed under international law. The measures taken to date include removing child workers from factories and other hazardous workplaces; protecting them from the worst forms of exploitation; improving working conditions and alerting working children, their parents, the community and the public at large to the adverse effects of child labour and the need for its abolishment. They encourage trade union activities (particularly self-help groups), provide counselling and other support services for the protection and well-being of working children, advocate non-formal education, prevocational training and the reintegration of children into the formal schooling system wherever possible, and encourage the development of governmental and non-governmental institutions to combat child labour. Other major programmes concern the promotion of true social dialogue between national social partners.

§3. Ongoing Difficulties

1121. In public debate today on the future of labour, it becomes clear that social policies and their implementing legislation will have to adapt to more open and competitive markets, and to a way of organizing production that is at one and the same time more complex, segmented and dependent on new techniques. It is difficult indeed to question the need for adjusting the labour law provisions to the new systems of production information and communication. The problem is therefore not so much to know if, but how the remodelling takes place. Bringing social policies up to date re-ignites the debate on the optimal synthesis between the guarantees given to workers, job creation, and competitiveness, or in other words, between development and the values and rights that a given national community holds dear.

1122. The question applies to ILO standards as much as to national laws, if not more, and in a very acute manner with regard to developing countries. The international labour conventions are regularly criticized for their supposed lack of realism and of concrete influence on national law and practice. It has been underlined that the number of ratifications has markedly decreased since 1989, that the rhythm of adoption of new conventions has dramatically diminished and that the preparatory discussions has lead to more difficulties; at the same time several non binding recommendations have been adopted since 1998 without being the complement to a convention.[919] The main objections focus on the precarious forms of work, and especially on the growing informal sector of poor countries. We have seen that it is oversimplistic to just extend the scope of general labour and social security laws to specific categories of vulnerable workers as, in a majority of instances, they are then not effectively executed. It does not make any difference if social legislation is limited to a number of general principles, as regulation does not possess in those cases any real significance in terms of implementation.[920]

1123. In general terms, the enforcement of labour standards does not depend only on the will of national governments, but on a variety of actors and factors.[921] There is a need for a further reflection on the application of the ILO instruments especially with these types of work. It relates to the problematic of the actual application of national law, and consequently to the kind of normative policy that should be adopted: how to adjust labour standards to these forms of activities? Which protection to provide? The problems relate to the very existence of the labour standard and its wording, its supervision and the socio-economic milieu in which it is applied.

I. Difficulties Relating to the Existence of the Standard and its Wording

1124. The first thing is to determine the nature of the labour regulation in question. The legal process, which relies on constraint, is not the only option for implementing labour goals: other methods exist. They rely chiefly on rationality and persuasion, and comprise the conclusion of political undertakings, the adoption of economic measures, the launch of training initiatives and information campaigns and the preparation of 'technical' (as opposed to 'legal') standards and practical guidelines. They can all be put into use without turning to measures that are legal in nature; in this case the term 'soft law' is quite ambiguous. This in no way detracts from their usefulness as upheld, for example, by the EU countries in the coordination of their efforts to promote an European employment strategy.[922] Concern to keep the labour market from becoming too rigid has made the regulatory authorities more reluctant to favour the law as the solution to labour problems. We have underscored the advantages ILO has and still can obtain from these means of action.

1125. The possibility for confusion about the concept of law, in particular in terms of social rights, requires clarification at this point. The concept of law refers

919. G. W. von Potobsky, 'El devenir de las normas internacionales del trabajo', *Revista de Derecho Social – Latinoamérica* (Buenos Aires), No. 3 2007.
920. *See* paras 176–190 *above*.
921. *See also* D. McCann, S. Lee *et al.*, *Creative Labour Regulation. Indeterminacy and Protection in an Uncertain World,* Geneva, ILO, Basingstoke, Palgrave Macmillan, 2014, p. 27.
922. *See* articles 145–150 of the Treaty on the functioning of the EU.

first to a means of implementing a policy (in this case a social policy); it serves to require a certain kind of conduct under threat of sanction. This policy, and that conduct, can sometimes appear abhorrent (for example, if imposed by a brutal dictator); the binding strength of the legal rules expressing it is not necessarily affected as a result.

1126. Another concept is overlaid on this concept of law, one that gives the latter – rather than the power issuing it – a specific purpose: the pursuance of certain values (i.e. social justice) based on religious or moral precepts, or on the vision one has of society and the relationships between its members.[923]

1127. It seems eminently reasonable and even desirable to invoke principles, to set labour objectives when drawing up and implementing policy. However, the affirmation in this context of moral 'rights' that everyone should enjoy, does not automatically make those rights binding. Proclaiming, for instance, a right to employment without adopting an accompanying threat of sanction for failure to respect that right is tantamount to expressing a wish or a political message, something that it is obviously important to do but that has no legal value.

1128. Our remarks are, we repeat, in no way intended to undermine the usefulness of such declarations, their ability to convince, their trigger effect. In many cases, the socio-economic situation precludes the addition of the legal dimension that would ensure permanence and coercion. We have pointed out[924] that in recent years, a number of international labour recommendations has been adopted that do not complement a binding convention.

1129. Another point to remember: the conditions might at one point have existed for the adoption of the legal remedy, then disappeared. In that case the rule tends no longer to be applied, to fade into disuse, even if it is not formally abrogated. This situation arises when the principal players on the social scene – employers, workers, inspectors – no longer know that certain rules exist, or do not give them the minimum support needed for their practical implementation.

1130. This holds true for all labour standards, whether national or international. Before examining their effects in practice, their existence and legal nature have to be verified. Issues of wording arise for some of them; some, however, relate more to international law.

1131. The delegates to the International Labour Conference drafted the international labour conventions in terms whose specificity varies with the subject dealt with (technical or more political), the characteristics of the standard (more or less

923. *See for example* J.M. Bonvin, *L'Organisation internationale du Travail. Etude sur une agence productrice de normes*, Paris, PUF, 1998.

924. *See* para. 1122 *above*. *See* also Politakis G. P. Markow K., 'Les recommandations internationales du travail: instruments mal exploités ou maillon faible du système normatif', in J.-C. Javillier and B. Gernigon (eds.), *Les normes internationales du travail: un patrimoine pour l'avenir. Mélanges en l'honneur de Nicolas Valticos*, ILO, Geneva. 2004, pp. 497–525.

programmatic) and their objectives when they adopted the standard. The tendency is clearly marked in the drafting of more general texts. It stems from the desire to extend the application of the instruments to countries of differing levels of development. It can also be explained by the deep changes that have taken place in the world of work, especially as a result of the introduction of new production and communication techniques, and their rapid replacement. The example of occupational health is illustrative of this in many ways, including the recent adoption of Convention No. 187, 2006, concerning the promotional framework for occupational safety and health. We have seen[925] that the translation into legal terms of the modern concept of occupational health required more flexible wording of the standards. This adaptation also took place in the form of the flexibility clauses.[926]

1132. Indeed, texts that are written in general terms leave those interpreting them a power of appraisal that is not without risk. There is a very real danger of subjectivity from which no one is really entirely free. It is, for example, tempting to seek to justify employment discrimination that is momentarily politically correct, without considering what is shocking about that discrimination. Today still, some people try to justify differences in treatment in respect of women at work. The first danger, therefore, is that the scope of such provisions will be excessively limited, the distinguishing characteristics that are said to arise from the nature of things multiplied. But there is a second danger: the converse one of a radical reading of the texts, of eliminating the most natural distinctions. In the case of international instruments, where the supervisory mechanisms are weaker, criticism based on an extreme interpretation can prompt governments who want to reject the comments made to them to question the authority of the supervisory bodies and even to denounce the conventions concerned.

1133. It would be remiss not to mention the work done to elaborate the consolidated convention on maritime labour that the Labour Conference has adopted in 2006. We have seen that the MLC convention No. 186 contains a number of innovations. An instrument that groups standards relating to several fields of a specific sector is not unknown at ILO. One example is Convention No. 110 of 1958, on plantations. A more recent one is the Work in Fishing Convention (No. 188), 2007. However, the new instrument on maritime labour more thoroughly change the common practice of adopting a series of conventions on limited topics.[927]

1134. It has an original structure that distinguishes four parts.[928] The first, which is similar to a classic convention, deals with the essential rights; it also contains provisions on entry into force, implementation, the amendment procedure and other general matters. The other three parts are based on the instruments of the International Maritime Organization (IMO). The second, called 'regulations', reiterates the basic provisions of the conventions already adopted on maritime labour. They have

925. *See* paras 664–666 and 670–672 *above*.
926. *See* paras 1112 and 1113 *above*.
927. *See* Governing Body document GB.286/LILS/8, Geneva, March 2003.
928. *See* paras 858–859 *above*.

the same effects as the articles of the convention, the difference lying in a presentation that distinguishes between principles deemed to be essential and more technical rules. The third and fourth parts form a code, divided into specific 'mandatory standards' that are binding in nature and 'guidelines' that are not, on how to give effect to the rules. The way in which the convention can be updated is also original in its greater simplicity: the amendment procedure differs depending on whether the changes are to articles of the convention and regulations, on the one hand, or to the code, on the other. The scope of the consolidated instrument implies that very many changes will no doubt have to be made in the coming decades; a simplified procedure that is nevertheless consistent with the constitutional mechanism has seemed more appropriate.

1135. It would not be accurate to see too many similarities between this instrument and the national framework laws with their implementing regulations; here there is only one regulatory authority. The 'code' nevertheless has points in common, in any event from the terminological point of view, with certain "codes" appended to Anglo-Saxon statutes. This being said, the code is legally different from the first two parts of the instrument. In particular, the 'guidelines' are not binding; however, the States must, by virtue of the convention, give 'due consideration' to the implementation of their obligations.[929] It is this attitude that will be scrutinized by ILO's supervisory bodies. The Convention No. 187, 2006, concerning the promotional framework for occupational safety and health has more in common with a national framework legislation; we know that it is complemented by a Recommendation No. 197 of the same year.

1136. The combination of provisions[930] is aimed at ensuring universal application of the maritime labour standards set forth in the convention, even if a number of States fail to ratify: every ratifying State must establish a system of certificates and documents of compliance relating to conditions on board ship and a system for ensuring the convention is implemented. This is the responsibility not only of the flag State but also of the port State and of the State in which the seafarer resides.

II. Difficulties Relating to Supervision of Labour Standards

1137. The CEACR faces more and more difficulties in fulfilling its task. The percentage of reports due and sent by the governments has sharply decreased; many also are received after a major delay.[931] A reform of the system has been requested for a long time, but has not yet been agreed upon.[932]

1138. The implementation of international labour standards, and the national laws and regulations used to that end, also call for supervision by labour inspectors

929. Article VI and para. 858 *above.*
930. *See* para. 861 *above.*
931. Von Potobsky, *op. cit.*
932. GB Document 298/PV, 298th session, Geneva. March 2007, para. 241.

belonging to well trained, adequately staffed bodies of civil servants. Although the laws, no matter what kind, are never totally respected, in the field of labour the State's limit to impose an obligation is quickly reached. There are sectors in which work is hidden or clandestine and where, more often, cheating and fraud are rampant, where, in any event, it is difficult to monitor application of the law. For some people passing economic difficulties apparently justify all manner of infringements. If the discrepancies are too frequent, the legal value – and the usefulness – of the labour standards can give rise to doubt; their credibility can be laid open to question.

1139. In fact, the stumbling blocks laid in the path of the labour administrator often resemble an obstacle course. We know what they are. They have to do first with the excessive complexity and overextended scope of labour regulations, their particular character or, more simply, their inadaptability to certain sectors of activity. Even if the law is adapted – and the labour administration has a special responsibility in this respect when it comes to preparing laws and regulations – those concerned, employers and wage earners, can ignore it, especially in small businesses. In some cases, of course, they are also reluctant to comply because it would cost too much, or for other reasons. Labour inspection, for its part, suffers even in the most prosperous countries from the traditional weaknesses of insufficient resources, understaffing (and what staff there is must sometime also perform other functions), inadequate training and lack of transportation to reach far-flung workplaces. Already in 1947 the need to remedy this situation was mentioned in ILO Convention No. 81 on labour inspection.[933]

1140. These obstacles prompted consideration of the methods used to implement labour laws, specifically of the means of ensuring they are binding. The most traditional measure, which immediately comes to mind, is to penalize infringements. Many ILO conventions refer to this expressly. In many countries genuine criminal codes for labour and social security law have emerged. The law punishes either the employer alone, or the workers as well, and any other person (the constructor, the seller, the renter of an inadequate machine, etc.) infringing protective provisions, by means of a fine or imprisonment. The effects – in particular the preventive effects – of these penalties are not to be underestimated, but neither should they be exaggerated, because in practice judges are often reluctant to hand down severe penalties, in particular a harsh prison sentence, and the effectiveness of fines depends on their amount and on their regular adjustment to changes in the cost of living. In addition, the wheels of justice turn slowly, making the penalty even less effective.

1141. To remedy this situation, national legislators have conferred on the administrative authorities, sometimes on social security agencies, the power to collect fines. In fact, however, the labour inspectors themselves usually prefer – except in serious cases – to provide advice, to use persuasion, rather than to take steps that would result in a penalty.

933. *See* para. 540 *above*.

1142. Little by little, therefore, other procedures that are preventive rather than repressive in nature have emerged: they require prudence on the part of the employers and also of the workers (who, if truth be told, sometimes fail to take even the most basic precautions to prevent employment injuries and are little aware of the risks they take). These provisions figure for the most part in ILO Recommendation No. 31, a precursor (it dates from 1929) on the prevention of occupational accidents. They are to be found again in Recommendation No. 81 of 1947 on labour inspection, and since, more systematically, in recent instruments. They are in addition to, and do not replace, punitive measures and focus on information, training, education and advice. They are based on the very simple idea that employers and workers must be convinced of the usefulness of these standards, must understand their underlying rationale, must be made to feel the standards concern them. If the message is not put in a language that sparks their interest, if they do not feel concerned, the chances that they will comply drop sharply.[934]

1143. Today, many countries provide training to those who may be exposed or who may expose others to an occupational risk, information campaigns are launched in the press, using posters, brochures, lectures, instructions, etc. Other, more incitative measures have also emerged. For example, German law provides that social insurance contributions can rise and fall in proportion to the number of accidents in an enterprise. Italian law[935] makes some of the advantages granted to (above all small) enterprises dependent on compliance with the provisions set forth in the law or the collective agreement.

1144. The labour administration plays a crucial role in prevention, as do non-governmental institutions, especially in terms of occupational accidents and diseases. To consider the institution as inefficient and useless in a number of developing countries is clearly an over generalization that the practice refutes[936].Here, a special role is obviously played by employers' and workers' associations, which have become increasingly active down through the years. Their activities run the gamut from heightening management awareness and uncovering sources of risks, to participation, in a variety of modes (consultation, collective agreements, and so on) in the adoption of protective and preventive rules and, more broadly, a genuine health policy.

1145. What is more, in 1981 ILO Recommendation No. 164 on occupational safety and health established the practice of several European countries in particular of appointing worker safety delegates or setting up (workers' or joint) safety and health committees whose functions are primarily consultative. Going a step further,

934. *See* paras 545–547 *above.*
935. T. Treu, 'European unification and Italian labor relations', *Comparative Labor Law Journal*, Vol. 11, No. 4, summer 1990, p. 457.
936. *See* for example Lee, S., McCann, D. (eds.), *Regulating for Decent Work. New Directions in Labour Market Regulation,* Geneva, ILO, 2011, p. 23 and the contribution of R. Rocha C. Pires pp. 313–338.

countries such as Luxembourg and to some extent Belgium have made workers' delegates a part of the labour inspectorate. In several countries, the institutions in charge of fighting employment injuries include representatives of workers' and employers' organizations.

1146. That is not all. Multinationals that subcontract all or some of their production to countries where wages are low are increasingly concerned by the conduct of the companies they choose in respect of their staff. In addition to the ethical questions the situation poses, these large corporations are worried about their images and the threats of boycotts brandished at the instigation of unions or human rights organizations. Consumers would undoubtedly be shocked to learn that their clothes were manufactured or their fruit picked by children in abysmal conditions of health and safety, or by workers deprived of the basic right to organize and of collective bargaining. In a positive step forward, this has prompted a number of multinationals to oblige their subcontractors to accept a relatively detailed code of good conduct and to have its application monitored by genuine private inspectors hired by them. Thus, the private sector makes up for the absence of adequate protective legislation and for the shortcomings in national supervision.

1147. The new view of the implementation of labour standards has engendered other problems, such as that mentioned earlier of the means that could replace the law in labour regulation.[937] The law was long considered the surest means of giving effect to protective measures. We now know, and recent ILO instruments refer to the fact explicitly, that other procedures are better suited for dealing with a given subject in a way that is concordant with the characteristics and traditions of a national society.

1148. These new means supplement rather than replace the earlier ones. In areas such as occupational health, many countries have adopted framework laws and even constitutional provisions that contain general principles and basic standards. Very often, however, the texts alone are not enough; they must be supplemented with regulatory provisions. In addition, the labour administration frequently draws up technical 'standards' and practical guidelines that are not binding in and of themselves, but whose effects are nevertheless beyond contestation. Such standards can also be drawn up by specialized public institutions and social security agencies (which have an obvious interest in preventing diseases, accidents and the consequent costs). The same task falls to the employers, their associations, and trade unions in the negotiations they conduct at different levels. There is nothing new about this, but their role to that end has grown where industrial relations have been efficiently developed.

1149. In addition, intervention by the social partners guarantees greater equality in the application of labour standards. The powers given to the administration in authoritarian political systems can lead to abuse, to anomalies and to inspections

937. *See* para. 1124 *above*.

that change according to who is being inspected. The example of the former ultra-centralized regimes of Central and Eastern Europe are revelatory in this respect. Before the fall of the Berlin Wall, the implementation of an employment and labour policy in those countries comprised reams of regulations, rulings, administrative instructions, all of which had absolutely to be followed. The sheer number of prescriptions made their systematic supervision a matter of chance. In particular, the application of provisions protecting the workers left much to be desired in those countries, whose efforts were increasingly focused on greater productivity. Whatever the case may be, this accumulation of rules and the organization of those States gave the public authorities powers that were all the greater in that court independence and remedies against their decisions were limited and there was no true collective bargaining, in the traditional meaning of the word, between employers and trade unions.

1150. Limits to the government's powers, true independence of the courts and the social players, change the picture completely. The implementation of a labour policy, even of labour legislation, in a market economy implies, if not adhesion, at least the absence of determined opposition on the part of those to whom it applies. Acceptance replaces, to varying but very real degrees, constraint. In continental Europe, the rules of labour law are often drafted in consultation with employers and trade unions, even where there is no collective agreement. At the same time, the supervisor-public servant's discretionary power of interpretation disappears.

1151. The transition from a totalitarian to a *laissez-faire* system can also result in deregulation: 'less State' also means fewer State rules and, in some cases, the development of freely negotiated collective agreements. It must nevertheless be said that fewer laws does not mean less law since the courts continue to deal with all situations. What does happen is that jurisdiction moves from the administrator to the judge, in two ways. First, since the legal texts do not cover all circumstances, the judge has greater authority to assess a situation and decide. Second, in democratic systems the courts usually have the power to monitor the administration's acts. This is even one of their attributes.

III. Factors Relating to the Socio-economic Context

1152. The universal character of international labour standards makes it more complex to give effect to the obligations they contain: the usual legal difficulties relating to content, wording, supervision, etc., are compounded by other factors. The level of economic development in particular plays a key role in the process of integrating international labour law into the domestic legal order.

1153. There is obvious confusion in the discussions about the economic advantages and disadvantages of certain rules or types of labour regulations. The fact that the controversy concerns specialists from different fields – sociologists, political scientists, philosophers and many others in addition to lawyers and economists – only adds to the confusion. To clarify the issue, the first thing required is the capacity to evaluate the economic impact of those standards relatively accurately. A quantitative or qualitative method can be chosen, but most of those who have tried their hand at the evaluation have opted for the second.[938] Many claim that satisfactory employment and labour protection gives enterprises – and economies – a very real competitive edge. It stimulates staff motivation and increases productivity. This so-called 'high road' argument seems in many respects convincing, but it has not put an end to the debate. Many employers still believe that paying low salaries and limiting expenditure on working environment arrangements will help them cut costs. What is more, in Europe and Japan, where the phenomenon was until recently limited, a sharp increase has been observed in the recruitment of contingent workers, so as not to incur the financial risks of contracts without limit of time. Exact figures seem to be expected in an area where it is apparently impossible to be certain of anything. How, then, to define accurately the economic effect of provisions on job security? And yet, for want of facts and figures, the vague and often in many respects irrational fear subsists that a limited period of notice for terminating an employment contract can jeopardize company competitiveness.

1154. Reliable indicators are needed to evaluate the economic impact of implementing the values embodied in certain rules.[939] While the purely economic and the socio-economic effects should not be overlooked, a distinction must be made between them. We cannot place enough emphasis on the importance of defining and selecting the factors to be used in constructing the indicators. Also, clear distinctions must be made for the size of the enterprise and between the micro- and macroeconomic levels. Legislation on the prevention and compensation of occupational accidents, as we have seen,[940] obliges enterprises to cover certain costs, but it can also allow them to save more. The effects thereof on the national accounting would nevertheless appear on the whole to be even more positive. These indicators can be used as a basis on which to consider the application of certain values in different socio-economic contexts, separating that which is absolute (the protection of workers' lives) from that which is relative (worker comfort) in terms of values and their means of implementation.

---

938. *See also* paras 1105–1107 *above*. There is a wealth of literature on the subject, but it is well worth rereading, for example, R. Freeman and J.L. Medoff, *What do Unions do?*, New York, Basic books, 1984, or W. Sengenberger and D. Campbell (eds.), *Creating Economic Opportunities: The Role of Labour Standards in Industrial Restructuring*, Geneva, International Institute for Labour Studies, 1994.

939. *See* for instance D. Kucera, 'Core labour standards and foreign direct investment', *International Labour Review*, Vol. 141, Nos. 1–2, 2002, pp. 31–69; J. Berg and S. Cazes, *'The Doing Business Indicators: Measurement Issues and Political Implications,' ILO Economic and Market Paper*, 2007/6, http://www.ilo.org/public/english/employment/download/elm/elm07-6.pdf; Y. Kryvoi 'The World Bank and the ILO: Two Visions of Employment Relations', in R. Blanpain and C. Grant (eds), *Fixed-term Employment Contracts: Two Visions of Employment Regulation*, Brugge, Vanden Broele, 2009, pp. 47–58; ILO, *World of Work 2014: Developing with jobs*, Geneva, 2014; ILO, *Decent Work Indicators Concepts and definitions*, Geneva, 2012.

940. *See* paras 683–687 *above*.

1155. More generally, effective execution of labour standards depends on the institutional capacity of each State;[941] social security springs to mind. If the State is weak, the application of both national and international labour rules can but run into problems. In addition, the very technical character of some standards in fields such as working hours or social security only adds to the difficulties.

1156. The effectiveness of supervision also depends on the importance of the law, in a given society, as a means of settling disputes. American citizens turn more readily to the courts than those of East and South-East Asia, who see court action as a last resort when all efforts at conciliation have failed. Another factor is that disciplined conduct and respect for authority are more marked in some mentalities and periods than others, as evidenced by the well-known anecdote about German railway workers in the early 20th century who bought their platform tickets before joining a demonstration at a railway station platform. Times have certainly changed – where in today's world could one imagine workers acting like that? The religious convictions encourage observation of measures to protect others. When faith gives way to superstition, however, the effect can be perverse, such as in the case of the Thai workers in a knife factory who thought there was no point in wearing the requisite safety equipment once the workshop had been blessed by a Buddhist monk.

1157. The methods chosen to implement labour standards are also predicated on the historical and social context, the power of employers' and workers' associations, the experience of their leaders, and the respective place of the law and collective work agreements in the system of industrial relations. More fundamentally, how a rule is worded and given effect depends on the ideas, customs, skills, arts, etc., of a people or group, that are transferred, communicated or passed along, as in or to succeeding generations; in other words, on its culture.[942]

1158. All these factors show how difficult is the adjustment of the ILO law to present time. The State and the national social partners are no longer able to control entirely the rules of the social game. The globalization process has led to complex interactions between different levels of decisions – local, national, regional and transnational.[943] Another problem is that most of the international regulation has been linked to a particular production system, the one associated with large-scale mass production.[944]

---

941. *See* T. L. Caraway, 'Protective repression, international pressure and institutional design: explaining labor reform in Indonesia', *Studies in Comparative International Development*, fall 2004, Vol. 39 No. 3. pp 28–49.
942. This is how culture is defined in *Webster's New World Dictionary*, 3rd College Edition, Simon & Schuster Inc., 1994.
943. See also for example J. Malmberg, '*Enforcement of Labour Law*', in B. Hepple and B. Veneziani (eds.), *The Transformation of Labour Law in Europe: A Comparative Study of 15 Countries 1945–2009*, Oxford and Portland, Oregon, Hart Publishing, 2009, p. 287.
944. M. Piore, 'Rethinking International Labor Standard', in W. Milberg, *Labor and Globalization of Production. Causes and Consequences of Industrial Upgrading*, Basingstoke (Hampshire), Palgrave Macmillan, 2004, p. 263.

1159. The supranational relations have become more transnational than international in the sense that a number of sometimes extremely powerful groupings (multinational companies, global NGOs, regional entities) are added to the traditional relationship between nations. The example of the European Union illustrates the practical difficulties in the collaboration between the ILO and new actors whenever a clear institutional framework is missing.

1160. Difficulties have arisen when it came to determining the relationship between the rights and obligations under the ILO's Constitution and those under the European treaties. They centred principally on the respective competencies of the State Members of the EU and of its Commission in the following areas: drawing up of international labour standards (prior consultation of the State Members of the ILO and in particular of the most representative national organizations of employers and workers; consideration and adoption of international labour standards); obligation to submit Conventions and Recommendations, once adopted, to the competent authority; obligations regarding various aspects of the application of these instruments. As already mentioned, the Court of Justice of the European Communities considered, in an Opinion No. 2/91 of 31 March 1993, that the "conclusion" of ILO Conventions "falls within the joint competence of the State Members and the Community", but rejected the notion that the Community as such could ratify an ILO Convention[945]. The involvement of the EU in the procedure for the preparation and application of international labour standards might nevertheless detract from the dynamism of the ILO's standards-setting activities, to which traditionally the countries concerned have greatly contributed in terms of ratification of standards as in practice the EU gives the Member States the authorization to ratify ILO Conventions as evidenced by the European Council Decision n° 2007/431 of 7 June 2007 regarding the Maritime Labour Convention.

§4. The Search for New Solutions

I. Striking a Balance: the Decent Work Agenda

1161. The difficulties we have mentioned usually reflect resistance to implementing ILO standards for socio-economic reasons. Experience however demonstrates that these standards, because of the way they are elaborated, do in fact offer invaluable benchmarks to governments, judiciaries, enterprises, trade unions and other NGOs. If ratified, the ILO Conventions are compulsory; if not, they may still be considered as patterns by national authorities who wish to improve, complete or precise their national rules and regulations. Let us examine the notion of 'decent work' as used in the ILO terminology.

945. GB, 256th Session (Geneva, May 1993): Advisory Opinion of the Court of Justice of the European Communities on Ratification of the Chemicals Convention, 1990 (no. 170), doc. GB.256/SC/1/3. *See* paras 114 and 238 *above*.

1162. The concept of decent work, as used by the ILO, seeks to group under one umbrella all the elements of harmonious economic and social development, of which protective labour rules are an essential component.

> The goal is not just the creation of jobs, but the creation of jobs of acceptable quality. The quantity of employment cannot be divorced from its quality. All societies have a notion of decent work, but the quality of employment can mean many things. It could relate to different forms of work, and also to different conditions of work, as well as feelings of value and satisfaction. The need today is to devise social and economic systems which ensure basic security and employment while remaining capable of adaptation to rapidly changing circumstances in a highly competitive global market.[946]

From the standard-setting perspective, this approach aims to group all the conditions required to ensure that labour law is effectively applied.

1163. The word of decency with regard to the working conditions has been used in particular by George Orwell. He described his journey to northern England in 1936 and the unemployment and proletarian life he observed in the poor mining areas.[947] Reflecting on class and the challenge facing socialism, he advocated 'common decency' and fair share for all. The concept clearly implies that men and women at work practise solidarity, without trying to dominate each other. It thus evokes dialogue, suggests that the support of the social partners must be sought in the conception, drafting and implementation of labour laws, as they are best placed to assess all the consequences, including the financial ones. The notion also implies that human relations are not to be reduced to utilitarian ideologies, that they must comprise an ethical dimension. The two elements correspond to the decent behaviour analysed by Amartya Sen particularly in his book on *The Idea of Justice*.[948] Decent work is a call for action. Decent means adequate, not generous, acting in a fit and proper manner, while taking fully into account the interests of the enterprises and of the economy at large. The International Covenant on Economic, Social and Cultural Rights refers for example to a remuneration which provides workers with a decent living.[949]

1164. The Declaration on Social Justice for a Fair Globalization of 10 June 2008 considers legal norms as instruments for the elaboration and actual implementation of the desirable social policies rather than as values themselves. The text confirms a recent change in the approach of the Organization: only 'fundamental principles and rights at work' constitute one of its 'strategic objectives'. The international labour standards are means of achieving them all. Member States should review

---

946. ILC, Report of the Director General, *Decent Work*. 87th Session, ILO, Geneva, 1999 p. 4; ILO, *World of Work 2014: Developing with jobs*, Geneva, 2014.
947. *The Road to Wigan Pier*, London, Penguin, 1962 (original edition 1937).
948. London, Penguin Books, 2009.
949. Article 7. See paras 613 and 614 *above*.

their situation as regards the ratification of the ILO conventions, as well as the application of its conventions and recommendations, in their efforts to reach more social justice through the ILO priorities. Special emphasis however is put on the instruments classified as core labour standards, together with those regarded as most significant from the viewpoint of governance covering tripartism, employment policy and labour inspection.[950] While the importance put on the core labour standards, i.e. the one mentioned in the previous Declaration, brings no surprise, the priority given to tripartism, employment policy and labour inspection appear to be a further move that leads to controversies: why safety at work for example is not considered as an important element of governance? A high rate of work accidents is more and more recognized, even from managerial point of view, as a negative indicator of performance at the enterprise or national level. Furthermore, one may wonder whether a sophisticated hierarchy of international labour conventions does not deviate from the standards-setting provisions of the ILO Constitution that treats all standards equally.

1165. As a follow-up to the Declaration, the Annex indicates that the Organization has introduced a scheme of recurrent discussions by international labour, without duplicating the ILO's supervisory mechanisms. It will constitute one item on the agenda of the Conference aside from technical topics. Modalities have been agreed by the Governing Body. The cycle of recurrent discussions has started in 2010. The scheme offers the opportunity to streamline the agenda of the International Labour Conference. In addition to the regular examination of the Governments reports on ratified conventions,[951] the Committee of experts on the application of conventions and recommendations elaborates each year for the Conference a general survey[952] on the application of some ILO instruments by countries that has or has not ratified the relevant instruments. The subjects of the survey are now aligned with the strategic objective covered in the recurrent item of the year and their scope, adapted so that they become a source on law and practice for the discussion.[953]

1166. More generally, the Declaration of 2008 appears as a programmatic document that intends to rationalize the ILO activities in its different fields of competence and to mobilize its means and capacities. It focus on a better understanding of Members' needs, on the strengthening of technical cooperation, and expert advice, on the improvement of research capacity, empirical knowledge and understanding and, as already mentioned, on the development of new partnerships with economic actors and other non-state entities, such as multinational enterprises and trade unions operating at the global sector level. The Member States are invited to reschedule their social goals along those lines, including through bilateral, regional or multilateral arrangements. Other international and regional organizations with

950. The Annex to the Declaration mentions the Labour Inspection Convention, 1947 (No. 81), the Employment Policy Convention, 1964 (No. 122), the Labour Inspection (Agriculture) Convention, 1969 (No. 129), the Tripartite Consultation (International Labour Standards) Convention, 1976 (No. 144), 'and those standards identified on subsequently updated lists'.

951. The reports requested under Article 22 of the ILO Constitution.

952. Based on Article 19 of the Constitution. *See* para. 1030 *above*.

953. Document GB. 303/SG/DECL/2 303rd Session, paras 15–21.

mandates in closely related fields may have an important contribution to make to the implementation of the integrated approach. They should also be associated.

1167. The new Declaration has succeeded in involving more of the ILO in the global debate on economic development as exemplified by its participation in the G8 and G20 meetings. The Organization has regularly the opportunity to present its views on employment and social issues; they have been welcome and supported at that level.[954] The chance to influence the policies of the main global actors has thus been improved.

1168. The Declaration takes a further step to move development and employment issues towards the centre of the ILO concern and to give international labour standards a lower priority, with the exception of the fundamental principles and rights at work. The change involves a danger of further weakening the legal dimension of the Organization. The search for improved coherence and interaction between the various items discussed at the International Labour Conference, including the general surveys of the legal experts does not compensate the imbalance.

1169. The application of employment protection standards will not be improved by any weakening of their binding nature and by greater reliance on 'soft law'. Persuasion and conciliation will not work unless there is ultimately a sanction which can be invoked.[955] To deny the usefulness of sanctions would tempt many countries to backtrack on the commitments they entered into by ratifying conventions. Admittedly, non-binding mechanisms can usefully supplement legal procedures, but they cannot be substituted for those procedures unless the aim is to 'deregulate'. While aiming at adapting the ILO setting activities to the present time, the new Declaration also brings the risk to be interpreted in a way that reduces the strength and the impact of the ILO *corpus juris*. Actually the standard-setting may be made more fragile even on essential issues, as illustrated by the recent refusal of the employers group and a number of governments at the ILO Conference to continue to consider the right to strike as implicitly contained in the recognition of the trade union freedom. Fortunately, the right to take collective action has now been reconfirmed.[956]

II. Future Prospects

1170. The future of the international labour standards is viewed in some quarters with great pessimism, and the rapid spread of the informal sector in both industrialized and developing countries is mentioned to underline the decline of the ILO standard-setting activities. There is no doubt that a perfect and universal Social Justice, based on a totally equitable institutional framework, is out of reach. If identified, such a system would require for its implementation a sovereign World State

954. Document GB 306/WP/SDG/1 306th Session, Geneva, ILO, November 2009.
955. See also B. Hepple, *Labour Law and Global Trade*, Hart Publishing, Oxford and Portland, Oregon, 2005, p. 274
956. *See* para. 282 *above*.

that does not exist.[957] This does not mean that one can not search for tangible solutions which fit well with the present socio-economic environment, to have recourse whenever possible to those programmatic standards we would like to see more of and to encourage the social negotiators, who are closer with day to day realities, to assume greater responsibility, where they have not already done so, in the implementation of labour policies. Also if more substantive labour standards are preferred, new forms of security can be proposed which better adjust to the present instability of employment.

1171. The elements we have identified in the concept of decent work – in particular the use of non-binding instruments; the special focus on the fundamental rights; the emphasis on solidarity and on social dialogue – leads to reflect on some recent developments in social policies that may strengthen international labour standards. New actors have emerged; certain types of norms have been more largely been adopted; new links have appeared with competition law.

1172. Globalization has diminished the role of the State and of the actors of the social scene born with the industrial revolution, employers' and workers' organizations. It has induced the growing strength of new world players, first and foremost the multinationals. Some of them (albeit as yet only a few) no longer even have privileged ties with a specific country; their headquarters are located wherever their principal leaders are to be found at any given moment. They are sometimes accused, namely in the oil and mining industries, of escaping from any labour legislation. Regional groups, such as the European Union, Mercosur or NAFTA, constitute other new global players, NGOs have for their part used the new communication technologies to create transnational networks which can carry great weight. All of these players have better adapted to the opening of borders and trade liberalization than the more rigidly structured public authorities themselves. Certain groups have an acknowledged ability to make them heard in the media. This is the explanation for some of the difficulties facing international organizations, whose structures and modes of action continue to depend on inter-State relations.[958] The efforts of those organizations to bring representatives of the global civil society into the fold reflect their desire to adapt to this new reality.

1173. This brings us to underline the usefulness of classifying international labour standards in three categories,[959] in accordance with their fundamental aim and hence their priority, and the nature of the obligations they contain. The first group concerns fundamental labour rights; the second relates to the more technicalprovisions of labour and social security legislation; the third covers the programmatic rules in which employers' and workers' organizations usually have a key role.

957. A. Sen, *The Idea of Justice*, London, Penguin Books, 2009.

958. *See* also L. Baccaro and V. Mele, *Pathologies of Path-Dependency: The ILO's Standard-Setting Model and the Challenge of 'New Governance'* Paper presented at the Workshop 'The Idea of Labour Law', Cambridge University, 8-9, April 2010.

959. *See* J.-M. Servais 'Le droit international en mouvement: déploiement et approches nouvelles'. *Droit social*, May 1991, No. 5. p. 449 *et seq.*; compare W. Jenks, *Law, Freedom and Welfare*. London, Oceans Publications, 1963, p. 103.

The presence of the latter has been more marked in recent ILO instruments, a development that reflects the determination of delegates to the International Labour Conference to take fuller account of the difficulties of application mentioned above.

1174. The provisions in the first category can be either technical or programmatic in nature. The expression 'fundamental rights' covers a variety of concepts that are not easy to define, particularly in the case of social rights.[960] The trend among some academics, emphasizing that the defence of workers' rights is one aspect of the defence of human rights, can be seen as an attempt to strengthen social solidarity in countries where the accent is on voluntarism in the industrial relations[961]. Recent developments in the case-law of the European Court of Human Rights may be interpreted as an answer by those who wish to maintain worker protection, in response to those who promote greater flexibility in labour relations. [962] It should be added that the development of electronic exchanges has also led to greater interest in protecting privacy.

1175. What sets fundamental labour rights apart is the clear pre-eminence they have been given by ILO's managing bodies. They are based on basic principles concerning civil liberties and social rights. That they are fundamental is recognized by everyone, or almost everyone. One example is the United Nations Covenants on Civil and Political, and especially on Economic, Social and Cultural Rights. Others are the ILO Constitution, and several ILO conventions. These texts, which are succinctly worded, establish general principles that can be applied in a multitude of ways. This is why difficulties of interpretation sometimes arise (for which, as we have said,[963] a balance must be struck between laxness and radicalism) that recall those in respect of national constitutional provisions. In the Declaration on Fundamental Principles and Rights at Work and its Follow-up, adopted in 1998 by the

960. See on this topic: Ch. Kaufmann, *Globalization and Labour Rights: the Conflict between Core Labour Rights and International Economic Law*, Oxford, Hart Publishing, 2007; J. Fudge, 'The new discourse of labor rights: from social to fundamental rights?', *Comparative Labor Law & Policy Journal*, autumn 2007, Vol. 29 No. 1, p. 29–66; L. Gay, E. Mazuyer, D. Nazet-Allouche (eds.), *Les droits sociaux fondamentaux, entre droits nationaux et droit européen*. Brussels, Bruylant, 2006, p. 10; J. A. Sagardoy Bengoechea, 'Los derechos fundamentales y el contrato de trabajo', *Derecho del trabajo* (Barquisimeto, Venezuela) no. 1, January–December 2005, pp. 15–28; A. Lyon-Caen and p. Lokiec (eds.), *Droits fondamentaux et droit social*, Paris, Dalloz, 2004 J. Iliopoulso-Stangas, *La protection des droits sociaux fondamentaux dans les Etats Membres de l'Union européenne*, Bruxelles, Sakoulas-Bruylant-Nomos, 2000.

961. See P. Alston, *Labour Rights as Human Rights*, Oxford University Press, 2005; R. Goldschmidt and C.L. Strapazzon, 'La hermenéutica responsable y su papel en la protección y promoción del derecho fundamental al trabajo digno: el caso de la nueva redacción del inciso iii de la súmala 244 del tribunal superior del trabajo', *Revista general de derecho del trabajo y seguridad social*, no. 39, December 2014.

962. Filip Dorssemont, Klaus Lörcher and Isabelle Schömann (eds.), *The European Convention on Human Rights and the Employment Relation*, Oxford, Hart Publishing, 2013. Comp. C. Fenwick and T. Novitz (eds.), *Human Rights at Work: Perspectives on Law and Regulation*, Portland, Hart Publishing, 2010.

963. *See* para. 1132 *above*.

International Labour Conference, they deal with freedom of association and collective bargaining, the abolition of child and forced labour, and equality of opportunity and treatment in employment.[964]

1176. It must be stressed that the 1998 Declaration, has the potential to go beyond the purely interstate framework, even if it is essentially addressed to the Organization's Member States. It concentrates on all the previously mentioned fundamental social rights, which it lists without going into detail about the specific means of implementing them. Its binding value is limited, and the follow-up procedures clearly less demanding than the traditional ILO supervisory mechanisms. Although it is therefore intended first and foremost for the Member States, which are invited to adopt implementing measures, it can easily, precisely because it is generally worded, serve as a direct reference for the new global players. It has been integrated in the UN Global Compact. It has been used to define the rules to be followed together by ILO and the major international financial institutions in their activities at country level. It has been echoed in the social charters adopted by regional bodies (European Union, Council of Europe, NAFTA, and MERCOSUR, in particular); more often than not, those social charters are broadly based on ILO standards. Even more, it can be invoked by NGOs calling for the establishment of a list of basic principles to be respected in terms of social policy. It has served as an inspiration for multinational enterprises when they draft their codes of social conduct or define the criteria to be observed in their social reports or audits. Private initiatives thus supplement national law on these points or, what is more often the case, ensure enhanced respect for it.

1177. Fundamental labour standards enshrine essential public principles that, in the words of the 1998 Declaration, enable the workers themselves 'to claim freely and on the basis of equality of opportunity their fair share of the wealth which they have helped to generate and to achieve fully their human potential'. They are based on ideas of freedom and democracy. Inserting these standards into constitutional texts establishes their pre-eminence; reiterating them in legislative texts serves to couple them with sanctions in the event of a violation. Although the usefulness of other, non-legal measures of promoting application in certain socio-economic circumstances is not to be underestimated, the importance of legal means cannot and indeed does not appear to be contested.

1178. Most labour standards belong to the second category, which has a more specific technical content. They deal with conditions of employment in the broad senses, and of social security. They are the focus of most of the debate about the future of the legal protection of labour. The international – or national – lawmaker has to cope with sometimes contradictory objectives, with tension between the divergent concerns of employers and wage earners, and even other groups, and with the need to bring them into harmony with the general interest. Choices must be made. These are sometimes the outcome of more or less official negotiations and reciprocal concessions; at others, they are the result of delicate arbitration. At ILO,

964. *See* paras 203–210 *above*.

most of the debates on the flexibility of conventions centre on these standards. It is also the adoption of the new standards in this category that gives rise to the most objections. We have already pointed out that agreement is more easily reached on topics like occupational health and safety than on others (working hours in particular).[965]

1179. This kind of agreement on basic regulatory principles is usually missing today; as a result entire swaths of labour law are being called into question. Compromise seems all the more problematic in that trade union and even employers' confederations themselves are finding it more difficult than in the past to speak with one voice for all those they represent. The technical standards focus most of the debate on the best possible synthesis between economic objectives and labour protection.

1180. These difficulties do not impede technical standards too to serve as an inspiration for States that are unable to ratify a certain convention because of discordance with some of its provisions, for regional groupings that aim at the harmonization of their Members' social legislation or for enterprises that set up their social initiatives. One example is the ILO instruments on safety at work. Technical standards are used by private consultation firms, enterprise associations, trade unions, NGOs or governments when they issue management frameworks or other model codes for others to use as a basis in developing their operational initiatives, like the ISO model or the performance model that the UN has developed with the Global Compact. References to technical norms of the Organization have also been included in trade legislations or agreements that subordinate the economic advantages granted to other countries to compliance on their part with minimum workers' rights.[966]

1181. The lack of consensus on the technical norms explains the tendency to seek a solution in the third category of standards, which is less immediately binding, this final category covers standards that are programmatic in character and intended essentially to prompt action: they set goals to be attained by means of promotion activities and their implementation relies in particular on those non-legal modes of regulation mentioned earlier: defining political projects; economic measures; information, training campaigns; recourse to non-legal provisions, etc. In short, they reflect the determination to regulate by setting objectives, drawing from modern human resources management methods to do so. They are couched in general and flexible terms, and contain no obligation of result for an employer or any other person, but an obligation of means that is plated on the States themselves: to conduct certain activities, to draw up or implement certain projects, to encourage certain approaches, etc.

965. *See* paras 80–82 *above*.
966. *See above* paras 60–65, 213–217, 225–234.

1182. These standards are to be found first and foremost in the fields of employment,[967] vocational training and the fight against discrimination.[968] The standards in question seek to make the action of the public authorities in these fields more coherent and systematic. They create mechanisms and structures that are suited to the programmes chosen; in some cases they provide for concrete action on the labour market and the means of evaluating its effectiveness. In terms of employment, for example, some of the measures are directed more at the immediate future (such as to launch a project of relief work), while others are aimed at laying the groundwork for a strategy to combat unemployment (such as remodelling the vocational training

---

967. Thus, Articles 1 and 2 of Convention No. 122, 1964, on employment policy, state: 'Article 1

1. With a view to stimulating economic growth and development, raising levels of living, meeting manpower requirements and overcoming unemployment and underemployment, each Member shall declare and pursue, as a major goal, an active policy designed to promote full, productive and freely chosen employment.
2. The said policy shall aim at ensuring that –
   (a) there is work for all who are available for and seeking work;
   (b) such work is as productive as possible;
   (c) there is freedom of choice of employment and the fullest possible opportunity for each worker to qualify for, and to use his skills and endowments in, a job for which he is will suited, irrespective of race, colour, sex, religion, political opinion, national extraction of social origin.
3. The said policy shall take due account of the stage and level of economic development and the mutual relationships between employment objectives and other economic and social objectives, and shall be pursued by methods that are appropriate to national conditions and practices.

Article 2: Each Member shall, by such methods and to such extent as may be appropriate under national conditions –

(a) decide on and keep under review, within the framework of a co-ordinated economic and social policy, the measures to be adopted for attaining the objectives specified in Article 1;
(b) take such steps as may be needed, including when appropriate the establishment programmes, for the application of these measures.'

968. Articles 2 and 3 of Convention No. 111, 1958, on discrimination (employment and occupation), provide:

'Article 2: Each Member for which this Convention is in force undertakes so declare and pursue a national policy designed to promote, by methods appropriate to national conditions and practice, equality of opportunity and treatment in respect of employment and occupation, with a view to eliminating any discrimination in respect thereof.

Article 3: Each Member for which this Convention is in force undertakes, by methods appropriate to national conditions and practice –

(a) to seek the co-operation of employers' and workers' organizations and other appropriate bodies in promoting the acceptance and observance, of this policy;
(b) to enact such legislation and to promote such educational programmes as may be calculated to secure the acceptance and observance of the policy;
(c) to repeal any statutory provisions and modify any administrative instructions or practices which are inconsistent with the policy;
(d) to pursue the policy in respect of employment under the direct control of a national authority:
(e) to ensure observance of the policy in the activities of vocational guidance, vocational training and placement services under the direction of a national authority;
(f) to indicate in its annual reports on the application of the Convention the action taken in pursuance of the policy and the results secured by such action.'

system or, more simply, encouraging geographical or occupational mobility). In each case, the instrument stresses cooperation between employers' and workers' associations.

1183. Directly binding provisions can exist alongside programmatic standards in the same convention. There are numerous examples of this in legislation on equality of opportunity and treatment, in which rules on measures to promote equality can co-exist with provisions on the annulment of discriminatory acts in the field considered. What is more, programmatic standards and technical standards can deal with the same subject (for example, occupational health), as do framework laws and implementing regulations. The programmatic standards establish the basic principles, and the technical standards supplement them with specific provisions.

1184. The concept of programmatic standards also covers rules that directly facilitate communications between social groups and other institutions, in order to enable them to find a solution to the problems identified[969]; as have been said, they 'shape a process'. Many provisions on collective industrial relations are in this category.

1185. The supervision of the implementation of programmatic standards gives rise to specific problems in that it concerns the means used more than the results ultimately obtained. However, legislating by this means does not mean 'deregulating' or adopting a purely laissez-faire attitude, leaving individuals and the social partners entirely free to decide on their relations.[970] Quite the contrary, the contacts between the parties are inserted in a framework and objectives that are determined by legal rules, i.e. coupled with the threat of sanction in the event of violations. This being said, when they confer a role on trade unions, they presuppose the existence of a reasonable balance of power between employers and workers, in other words that the two can act on a more or less equal footing. The elaboration and use of a set of indicators assessing their actual application seems particularly appropriate.

1186. Standards of this kind give rise to little debate. They are usually well accepted. They provide invaluable opportunities for adapting labour protection to the economic imperatives of the day. More than the basic standards, they also serve rapidly to update the rules in the light of scientific and technological developments.

---

969. *See* on this B. Hepple (ed.), *The Making of Labour Law in Europe. A Comparative Study of 9 Countries up to 1945*, London, Mansell 1986, p. 10; J. Habermas, 'Law as medium and law as institution', in G. Treubner (ed.), *Dilemmas of Law in the Welfare State*, W. de Gruyter, Berlin, 1986; T. Treu 'Strikes in essential services in Italy: an extreme case of pluralistic regulation', *Comparative Labor Law Journal*, Vol. 15(4), summer 1994, p. 461 *et seq.*; C. Barnard, S. Deakin, 'Corporate governance, European governance and social rights', in B. Hepple (ed.), *Social and Labour Rights in a Global Context. International and Comparative Perspectives*, Cambridge University Press, 2002, pp. 122–150.

970. Comp. Wedderburn, 'The social charter in Britain. Labour law and Labour Courts', *The Modern Law Review*, 54(1), January 1991, pp. 3–4; J. de Munck, J. Lenoble and M. Molitor (ed.), *L'avenir de la concertation sociale en Europe*, Louvain, Centre de philosophie du droit (Université catholique de Louvain), 1995, tome I, p. 20 *et seq.*; A. Lyon-Caen, 'Droit du travail et procéduralisation', *ibid.*, tome I, p. 176 *et seq.*

They usually enable the parties directly concerned to help adapt their working conditions as closely as possible to daily reality; they ask them to strike the best possible balance between economic efficiency and worker guarantees. Although the players in the workplace must not be given exclusive responsibility for striking that balance, although some sense of the general interest must be maintained, there are many labour standards – both national and international – that could still be modernized in this way.

1187. This approach gives fresh impetus to the role of the State or more specifically to the public authorities at the national, regional and local levels. It is up to them to create, using these programmatic standards, the requisite institutional environment: to recognize the players, to promote their development and their access to information (by eliminating obstacles such as anti-trade-union practices), to recognize the mechanisms they establish (for example, by taking part in their foundation), by facilitating relations between them. In short, the State's role is less that of a 'tutor' than it is one of inspiration or mediator called on to foster a situation that favours dialogue. It imagines the communications structures that facilitate that dialogue;[971] it integrates those representative players into the bodies implementing social policies for vocational training, credit, social security, etc.; it extends the scope of their independent negotiations or systematically involves them in the preparation of labour policies and of the laws that translate the policies into lasting and, to some extent, binding measures. The responsibilities of the State thus defined take on a special dimension in respect of specific activities such as those of the informal economy or of SMEs, where social dialogue is harder to strike up. And yet, here too, there are examples of successful attempts to establish a favourable framework. The achievements obtained in the Emilia Romagna districts of Italy are an oft-studied example.[972] Even in the informal economy, success stories are not rare.[973] Strengthening the capacity of social negotiations should, if properly done, lead to a consolidation of the position of the State itself in a globalized context. The State must not promote only these new forms of participation, it must also ensure good coordination between the different levels.

1188. The programmatic standards thus have the advantage of affording an appropriate framework for the coordination of legal and non-legal means of implementing a social policy that, in the 21st century, reflects the same preoccupations as

---

971. *See also* A. Supiot (ed.), *Beyond Employment. Changes in Work and the Future of Labour Law in Europe*, Report to the European Commission, Oxford University Press, 2001, Chapter V in particular; F. Durán López, 'Globalización y relaciones de trabajo', *Civitas*, No. 32, Nov.–Dec. 1998, pp. 869–888. Comp. more generally P. Evans, 'The Eclipse of the State? Reflections on Stateness in an Era of Globalization' *World Politics*, Vol. 50(1), October 1997, pp. 62–87.

972. F. Pyke, G. Beccatini, W. Sengenberger (eds.), *Industrial districts and inter-firm cooperation in Italy*, Geneva, International Institute for Labour Studies, 1990; F. Cossentino, F. Pyke, W. Sengenberger, *Local and regional response to global pressure: the case of Italy and its industrial districts*, Geneva, International Institute for Labour Studies, 1996.

973. R. Agarwala, *Informal Labor, Formal Politics, and Dignified Discontent in India*, New York (NY), Cambridge University Press, 2013; ILC (91st session, 2003), *Working out of Poverty*, Geneva, ILO, 2003 p. 74; J.-M. Servais (ed.), 'Industrial Relations, democracy and social stability', *World Labour Report 1997–98* (Geneva), ILO, 1997, p. 175 *et seq.*

at ILO's inception: concern for the individual, understanding for the requirements of the economy and the desire to consolidate social unity, in each country and among all nations.

1189. A second path of modernizing international labour law is to introduce in the substantive legislation new forms of security that are compatible with a less stable employment situation. When self-employment and precarious forms of wage employment are growing, the protection of work can no longer be based, in the same manner, on the permanent labour relationship. The establishment of health care institutions and basic pension schemes should therefore be decided everywhere, independently of the type of employment. This should even constitute an absolute priority in the developing countries. In the industrialized ones, institutions serving as points of anchorage in a context of increased mobility (from one company, one working relationship or one activity to another) have to be invented or revived.

1190. 'Flexicurity' is an example. The term has come from the Netherlands and from a legislation that has tried to find a balance between work flexibility and the necessary protection of the employees: the Act of 1 January 1999, based on an informal agreement amongst the social partners, has stabilized the position of temporary workers.[974] The formula provides some security to the employees concerned, in the sense that they may after a time benefit fully from labour and social security law, while maintaining the required mobility. It seems well accepted by all parties involved.

1191. The concept, however, has taken a broader significance in the European public debate.[975] It addresses every social policy that aims at reaching the optimal balance between flexibility in the labour market and social protection. It differentiates Nordic countries (especially Denmark) from Southern European countries like Spain, France and Italy. In the first ones,[976] dismissal is relatively easy, but unemployment benefits pretty generous, financed by high taxation, employment policies are active and successful. The second ones have adopted a completely different type

974. G. Heerma van Voss, 'The "Tulip Model" and the New Legislation on Temporary Work in the Netherlands, *The International Journal of Comparative Labour Law and Industrial Relations*', 1999, no. 15(4), pp. 80–4; T. Jaspers, 'Flexiguridad:? es la respuesta acertada a la modernización del Derecho del Trabajo? Una perpectiva holandesa', in J.P. Landa Zapirain (ed.), *Estudios sobre la estrategia europea de flexiseguridad: una aproximación critica*, Albacete, Ed. Bomarzo, 2009, pp. 25–56; ILO, 'Combining flexibility and security for decent work', *Document GB.306/ESP/3/1*, Geneva, November 2009, §4.

975. European Industrial Relations Observatory on-line *EU Countries: Flexicurity and industrial relations*, 30 September 2008, http://www.eurofound.europa.eu/eiro/2008/09/index.htm. *See also* F. Hendrikx (ed), *Flexicurity and the Lisbon Agenda. A Cross-Disciplinary Reflection,* Mortzal, Intersentia, 2008; R. Blanpain, J.P. Landa and B. Langille (eds.), 'Employment Policies and Multilevel Governance', *Bulletin of Comparative Labour Relations*, The Netherlands, Kluwer, no. 71, 2009.

976. Those countries are also amongst the ones with the highest trade union rate: *see*, J.-M. Servais (ed.), *Industrial Relations Democracy and Social Stability, World Labour Report 1997–1998,* Geneva, ILO, 1997, pp. 26–27.

of policies; termination of the employment relationship still appears to be difficult, while active reintegration policies and unemployment benefits are limited; taxation and social deductions are also less high.[977]

1192. Certain categories of workers appear to be at the margin of a wage relationship. It may be difficult in many cases to decide whether persons such as home-based workers, sportsmen or women, artists, professional journalists, lorry or taxi drivers should be considered as employees or rather self-employed entrepreneurs. In some countries (Canada, France, Germany, the Netherlands, Sweden), the legislation extends the application of labour provisions to some of those workers. In others (Belgium, France, Germany, Portugal, South Africa, Spain, etc.), law goes further on and presumes either their subordination to an employer (or on the contrary their independence). Some legislations (Germany, Spain, United Kingdom) have elaborated an intermediary category, often called by its Italian name 'para-subordinazione'. It covers workers who are not legally employees of an employer, but depends economically of one or few contractors. They enjoy some but not all the rights granted to the wage employees.[978]

1193. One may also observe the use, in a number of other countries like France, of a shared, i.e. *in solidum* or subsidiary, liability of the principal enterprise in case of subcontracting and temporary supplying or loan of staff.[979] The technique has allowed strengthening the guarantees of the workers concerned that have precarious labour relations, but with more than one firm. While the purpose appears quite similar, North-American law has elaborated distinct figures, in particular the legal institutions of sole or joint employer.[980] Furthermore the responsibility of the leading enterprise could still be extended[981] as shown in Ruggie's principles which ask

977. B. Palier, 'Refonder la Protection Sociale: les Experiences européennes', *Esprit*, 2006, pp. 53–78; D. Anxo and H. Nickclasson, 'The Swedish model in turbulent times: Decline or renaissance?', *International Labour Review*, 2006, no. 145(4), pp. 379.

978. *See* para 727 *above. See* also Guy Davidov and Brian Langille (eds), *Boundaries and Frontiers of Labour Law*, International Institute for Labour Studies, Oxford and Portland, Oregon, 2006; D. Melann, *Regulating Flexible Work*, Oxford University Press, 2006; A. Bronstein, *Current Challenges of Labour Law*, Geneva, ILO/Palgrave, 2009; Leah Vosko, *Managing the Margins: Gender, Citizenship and International Regulation of Precarious Employment*, New York (NY), Oxford University Press, 2010. See also Guy Davidov, 'The goals of regulating work: between universalism and selectivity', *Labour Law Research Network*, December 2012.

979. European Industrial Relations Observatory on-line, *Temporary agency work and collective bargaining in the EU*, May, 28, 2009, http://www.eurofound.europa.eu/eiro/studies/tn0807019s; M.L. Morin 'Labour Law and New Forms of Corporate organization', *International Labour Review*, vol. 144(1), 2005.

980. P. Verge (with the collaboration of S. Dufour), *Configuration diversifiée de l'entreprise et droit du travail*, Saint Nicolas (Québec), P U Laval, 2003.

981. R.-Cl. Drouin, 'Responsabiliser l'entreprise transnationale: portrait d'une normativité du travail en évolution', in Verge, P. (ed.), *Droit international du travail. Perspectives canadiennes*, Cowansville, Ed. Yvon Blais, 2010; G. Davidov, 'Indirect Employment: Should lead companies be liable?', *Comp. Labor Law and Policy Journal*, vol. 37(1), fall 2015, pp. 5-36. For a much broader vision of the shared responsibility, *see* Y. Dahan, H. Lerner and F. Milman-Sivan, 'Shared responsibility and the International Labour Organization', *Michigan Journal of International Law*, summer 2013, vol. 34(4), pp. 675-743

firms, in the case of adverse human rights impacts, to cease or prevent their contribution to business relationships or even to use their leverage to mitigate any remaining impact.

1194. Our vision of labour law, including of its international dimension, should not focus only on employment and industrial law, but open to other legal disciplines, such as civil and commercial law. Competition law in particular has a significant influence on its development, in a direction that not always favours the employer, as it appears in the European social law. Some European directives request Member States to consider the principal firm, with a ruling position, in the case of a group of companies or of triangular relations of the types we have just mentioned. More generally the concept of enterprise and its different meanings in European Law has to be examined in depth. Economic law has also inspired the requirements of transparency and accessibility of the information imposed in the European directive No 96/71/CE of December 16 1096 on the posting of workers. Those developments bring no surprise as European Law aims at harmonizing the working conditions in the European Union, at avoiding any kind of social dumping, and at seeking for the optimum between economic freedoms and social (including trade-union) rights.

1195. International labour law should also find a source of inspiration in those positive developments.

Selected Bibliography

Aboughanem, A., *Étude sur les relations entre les normes internationales du travail et la coopération technique*, ILO, Geneva (limited distribution), 1985.

Acosta Estevez, J.B., *El Sistema Jurídico de la Organización Internacional del Trabajo y el Derecho Español*, Cedecs Editorial, Barcelona, 1997.

Agarwala, R., *Informal Labor, Formal Politics, and Dignified Discontent in India*, New York (NY), Cambridge University Press, 2013.

Agosti-Panaredo, J., Ebert, F. CH, LeClercq, D., "ILO Labor Standards and Trade Agreements: A Case of Consistency", *Comp. Labour Law & Pol. Journal*, vol. 36 (3), spring 2015, pp. 347-380.

Aguidioli Kenoukon, C.H., *Effectivité et efficacité des normes fondamentaleset prioritaires de l'OIT. Cas du Bénin et du Togo*, IILS, Geneva, 2007.

Alcock, A., *History of the International Labour Organization*, Macmillan, London, 1971.

Aliprantis, N., Papageorgiou, I. (eds), *Social Rights at the European, Regional and International Level. Challenges for the 21st Century*, Brussels, Bruylant, 2010.

Alston, P., 'Core Labour Standards' and the Transformation of the International Labour Rights Regime', *European Journal of International Law*, Vol. 1(3), 2004, pp. 457–521.

—— 'Facing up the Complexities of the ILO's Core Labour Standards Agenda', *European Journal of International Law*, Vol. 16(3), 2005, pp. 467–480.

—— (ed.), *Labour Rights as Human Rights*, Oxford University Press, 2005.

Alston, P. and Goodman, R., *International Human Rights*, Oxford University Press, 2013.

Andreoni, D., *Cost of Occupational Accidents and Diseases*, ILO, Geneva, 1986.

Anner, M. and J. Blasi, J., 'Toward Joint Liability in Global Supply Chains: Addressing the Root Causes of Labor Violations in International Subcontracting', *Comp. Labour Law & Pol. Journal*, Vol. 35(1), fall 2013, pp. 1–43.

Arese, C., *Derechos Humanos Laborales. Teoría y práctica de un Nuevo Derecho del Trabajo*, Buenos Aires, Editorial Rubinzal Culzoni, 2014.

Auby, J.B., *La globalisation, le droit et l'Etat*, 2nd edn., LGDJ, Paris, 2010.

Arellano Ortiz, P., Olivier, M., Vonk, G., 'Social Security and Migrant Workers. Selected Studies of Cross-Border Social Security Mechanisms', No. 84, *Bulletin of Comparative Labour Relations*, The Hague: Kluwer, 2013.

Baccaro, L. and Mele, V., 'Pathologies of Path-Dependency: The ILO's Standard-Setting Model and the Challenge of "New Governance"' Paper presented at the Workshop *The Idea of Labour Law*, Cambridge University, 8–9 April 2010.

Bales, K., 'International Labor Standards: Quality of Information and Measures of Progress in Combating Forced Labor', *Comparative Labor Law & Policy Journal*, Vol. 24(2), Winter 2003, pp. 321–363.

Selected Bibliography

Barbagelata, H.H. (ed.), *El derecho a la formación profesional y las normas internacionales*, CINTERFOR, Montevideo, 2000.

Barnard, C., Deakin, S., and Morris, G.S., *The Future of Labour Law. Liber Amicorum Bob Hepple QC*, Hart Publishing, London, 2004.

Bartolomei de la Cruz, H., Potobsky, G. von and Swepston, L, (eds.), *International Labor Organization: the International Standards System and Basic Human Rights*, Westview Press, Boulder, 1996.

Basu, K., Horn, H., Román, L. and Shapiro, J., *International Labour Standards*, Blackwell, Oxford, 2003.

Beaudonnet, X., La utilización del derecho internacional del trabajo por los tribunales nacionales, noticias de una evolución en marcha', *Revista del Derecho Laboral* (Montevideo), Vol. 53(28), June 2010, pp. 245–269.

—— (ed.), *International Labour Law and Domestic Law: A Training Manual for Judges, Lawyers and Legal Educators*, International Training Centre of the ILO, Turin, 2010.

Becker, U., Maydell von, B. and Nussberger, A., *Die Implementierung internationaler Sozialstandards*, Baden-Baden, Nomos, 2006.

Bellace, J., 'The ILO Declaration of Fundamental Principles and Rights at work', *International Journal of Comparative Labour Law and Industrial Relations*, Vol. 17(3), Autumn 2001, pp. 269–287.

—— 'Human Rights at Work: the Need for Definitional Coherence in the Global Governance System', *Comp. Labour Law & Pol. Journal*, Vol. 30(2), 2014, pp. 175–198.

—— 'The ILO and the Right to Strike', *ILR*, Vol. 153(1), 2014, pp. 29–70.

Berenstein, A., 'Development and Scope of Economic and Social Rights', *Labour and Society*, Vol. 7(3–4), Jul–Sep 1982, Oct–Dec 1982, pp. 291–307, 393–407.

—— *Les organisations ouvrières. Leur compétence et leur rôle dans la Société des Nations et notamment dans l'Organisation internationale du Travail*, Pédone, Paris, 1936.

Berg, J. and Cazes, S., *The Doing Business Indicators: Measurement Issues and Political Implications*, ILO Economic and Market Paper, 2007/6, http://www.ilo.org/public/english/employment/ download/elm/elm07-6.pdf.

Betten, L., *International Labour Law. Selected Issues*. Kluwer, The Hague, 1993.

Bezou, C., *La clause sociale, la négociation internationale et l'OIT*, ESKA, Paris, 2008.

Bhagwati, J. and Hudec, R., *Fair Trade and Harmonisation: Prerequisites for Free Trade?* Cambridge (Mass.), The MIT Press, 1996.

Blackett, A., Trebilcock, A. (eds.), *Research Handbook on Transnational Labour Law*, Cheltenham, E. Elgar, 2015.

Blanchard, F., *L'Organisation internationale du travail. De la guerre froide à un nouvel ordre mondial*. Seuil, Paris, 2004.

Blanpain, R., *Multinational Enterprises and the Social Challenges of the Century*. Kluwer, The Hague, 2001.

—— (ed.), *Confronting Globalization: The Quest for a Social Agenda*. Kluwer, The Hague, 2005.

Blanpain, R. *et al.*, The *Global Workplace. International and Comparative Employment Law. Cases and Materials*, Cambridge University Press, 2007.

Bogg, A., 'Viking and Laval: The International Labour Law Perspective', in Freedman, M., Prassl, J. (eds.), *Viking, Laval and Beyond*, Oxford, Hart Publishing, 2014, pp. 41-74.

Boisson de Chazournes, L., Mazuyer, E. (eds.), *Le Pacte mondial des Nations-Unies 10 ans après*, Brusseles, Bruylant, 2011.

Boiral, O., 'The Certification of Corporate Conduct: Issues and prospects', *ILR*, Vol. 142(3), Geneva, 2003, pp. 317–340.

Boivin, I. and Odero, A., 'The Committee of Experts on the Application of Conventions and Recommendations: Progress Achieved in National Labour Legislation', *ILR*, Vol. 145(3), 2006, pp. 207–220.

Bonvin, J.M., *L'Organisation internationale du Travail. Etude sur une agence productrice de normes*, PUF, Paris, 1998.

Borelli, S., Vieille, P. (eds.), *Quality of Employment in Europe: Legal and Normative Perspectives*, Brussels, Peter Lang, 2012.

Borenfreund, G,Bacarie, I, *Le droit social, l'égalité et les discriminations*, Paris, Dalloz, 2013

Bosse, Cl., 'The ILO Recommendation 198, the Employment Relationship Recommendation', in Pennings, F. and Bosse, Cl. *The Protection of Working Relationship*, The Hague, Kluwer, 2011, pp. 15-28.

Bronstein, A., *Collective Bargaining and Sex Discrimination in European Labour Law*. A Report on the Proceedings of the VIIth European Congress of Labour Law and Social Security (Stockholm, 4–6 September 2002). Collective Bargaining, Discrimination, R. Blanpain (ed.), Social Security and European Integration, Kluwer, The Hague, 2003.

—— *Derecho internacional del trabajo*, Buenos Aires, Astrea, 2013.

Brossey, M., 'Something new, something borrowed … : Comparative labour law in South Africa'. *The Changing Face of Labour Law and Industrial Relations*, R. Blanpain and M. Weiss (eds.), *Liber Amicorum Clyde W. Summers*, Baden Baden, Nomos Verlagsgesellschaft, 1993.

Bruun, N. and Jacobs, A., 'Das ILO-Übereinkommen 94 am Morgen nach Rüffert', *Arbeit und Recht*, December 2008, pp. 417–423.

Burkett, W.B., Craig, J.D.R. and Gallagher, J., 'Canada and the ILO: Freedom of Association since 1982', *Canadian Journal of Labour and Employment Law*, 2003, Vol. 10, p. 231.

Cabin, M. A., 'Labor Rights in the Peru Agreement: Can Vague Principles Yield Concrete Change?', *Columbia Law Review*, Vol. 109, 2009, pp. 1047–1093.

Camós, Victoria I. and Rojo Torrecilla, E., 'La convención internacional sobre la protección de los derechos de los trabajadores migrantes y de sus familias', *Revista Migraciones*, no. 16, 2004, pp. 7–40.

Candland, C., 'Core Labour Standards under the Administration of George W. Bush', *ILR*, Vol. 148(1–2), 2009, pp. 169–181.

Charbonneau, A., *Marché international du travail maritime. Un cadre juridique en formation*, Aix-en-Provence, Presses universitaires d'Aix-Marseille, 2009.

—— 'Bienestar de los Marinos: el procedimiento para la interposición de quejas en tierra', *Revista del Ministerio de Trabajo e Inmigración*, Derecho social Internacional y Comunitario, no. 82, 2009, pp. 357–381.

—— 'L'originalité du secteur maritime: interventions judiciaires, règlements alternatifs des conflits et action syndicale', in H. Muir Watt (ed.), *Justice et mondialisation du droit du travail*, Paris, Dalloz, 2010.

——'La référence aux principes et droits fondamentaux au travail dans les convention de l'OIT. L'article 3 de la Convention du travail maritime de 2006 (MLC, 2006)', *Droit prospectif*, 2011 -3, pp. 1361–1387.

Charbonneau, A., Chaumette, P. and Proutière-Maulion, G., 'De Maritieme Arbeidconventie van de IAO van 2006 en Conventie nr 188 over de arbeid in de visserij', *Arbeidsrechtelijke Annotaties*, 2009, no. 2, pp. 22–49.

Ciudad Reynaud, A., *Labour Standards and the Integration Process in the Americas*, Geneva, ILO, 2001.

Compa, L., 'The Wagner Model and International Freedom of Association Standards', in D. Roux (ed.), *Autonomie collective et droit du travail: Mélanges en l'honneur du professeur Pierre Verge*, Quebec, Les Presses de l'Université de Laval, 2014, pp. 427-464.

Compa, L. and Brooks, T., *NAFTA and the NAALC: Twenty Years of North American Trade-Labour Linkage*, Alphen aan den Rijn, Wolters Kluwer Law & Business, 2015

Compa, L. and Vogt, J.S., 'Labor Rights in the Generalized System of Preferences: a 20-year Review', *Comparative Labor Law and Policy Journal*, Vol. 22, Nos. 2/3, 2001, pp. 199–238.

Compa, L. and Diamond, S.F. (eds.), *Human Rights, Labor Rights and International Trade*, University of Pennsylvania Press, Philadelphia, 2003.

Charnovitz, S., *Trade Law and Global Governance*, Cameron May, London, 2002.

Chaumette, P. (ed.), *Seafarers: An International Labour Market in Prespective - Gens de Mer : un Marché International du Travail,* Gomylex, Bilbao, 2016.

Craig, J. and Lynk, S.M., *Globalization and the Future of Labour Law,* Cambridge University Press, 2006.

Creighton, B., McCrystal, Sh., 'Who is a "worker" in international law?', *Comp. Labour Law & Pol. Journal*, vol. 37(3), spring 2016, pp. 691–725.

Dahan, Y., Lerner, H., Milman-Sivan, F., 'Shared responsibility and the International Labour Organization', *Michigan Journal of International Law*, summer 2013, vol. 34(4), pp. 675–743.

--------, (eds.), *Global Justice and International Labour Rights*, Cambridge University Press, 2016.

Daoudi, M.S. and Dajani, M.S., *Economic Sanctions: Ideals and Experience*, Routledge and Kegan Poul, London, 1983.

Davidov, G., 'Comment on Alan Hyde: The Perils of Economic Justifications for International Labor Standards', *Law and Ethics of Human Rights*, vol. 3 (2), 2009, article 3.

—— 'The Goals of Regulating Work: between Universalism and Selectivity', *Labour Law Research Network*, December 2012.

Daugareilh, I. (ed.), *Mondialisation, travail et droits fondamentaux*, Bruylant, Brussels, LGDJ, Paris, 2005.

—— 'La dimension sociale des principes fondateurs de l'OCDE à l'intention des entreprises multinationales', *Revue générale de droit international public*, 2008, no. 3, pp. 567–599.

—— (ed.), *Responsabilité social de l'entreprise et globalisation*, Brusseles, Bruylant, 2010.

Deakin, S., Malmberg, J. and Sarkar, P., 'How do labour laws affect unemployment and the labour share of national income? The experience of six OECD countries, 1970–2010', *ILR*, vol. 153(1), 2014, pp. 1–28.

Deery, S. and Mitchell, R. (eds.), *Labour Law and Industrial Relations in Asia: Eight Country Studies*, Longman Cheshine, Melbourne, 1993.

Deneve, C. *Internationaal Arbeidsrecht*, Brugge, Die Keure, 2010.

De Schutter, O., *Trade in the Service of Sustainable Development: Linking Trade to Labour Rights and Environmental Standards*, Oxford, Hart Publishing, 2015.

Doherty, M., 'Emergency Exit? Collective Bargaining, the ILO and Irish Law', ELLJ, Vol. 4(3), 2013, pp. 171–195.

Doumbé-Billé (eds.), *Nouveaux droits de l'homme et internationalisation du droit*, Brussels, Bruylant, 2012.

Doumbia-Henry, C. and Gravel, E., 'Free trade agreements and labour rights: recent developments', *ILR*, Vol. 145(3), 2006, pp. 185–206.

Dubin, L., *La protection des normes sociales dans les échanges internationaux*, Aix-en Provence, Presses universitaires d'Aix-Marseille, 2003.

Dumas, M., 'Three Misunderstanding about Consumocratic Labor Law', *Comp. Labour Law & Pol. Journal*, Vol. 35(1), fall 2013, pp. 67-91.

Duplessis, I., 'La déclaration de l'OIT relative aux droits fondamentaux au travail. Une nouvelle forme de régulation efficace?' *Relations industrielles/Industrial Relations*, Vol. 59(1), 2004, pp. 52–72.

Dupuy, R.J. (ed.), *Mélanges en l'honneur de Nicolas Valticos. Droit et justice*, Pedone, Paris, 1999.

Dutoit, D. (ed.), *Exploited, Undervalued and Essential: Domestic Workers and the Realization of their Rights*, Pretoria University Press, 2013.

Elliott, K.A. and Freeman, R.B., *Can Labor Standards Improve under Globalization?* Institute for International Economics, Washington DC, 2003.

Elsheikh Mahgoub, K., *The International Law on the Right of the Child to Survival and Development*, Cambridge, Intersentia, 2015.

Etherington, B., 'The B.C. Health Services and Support-Decision – The Constitutionalization of a Right to bargain collectively in Canada: where did it come from and where it lead?', *Comparative Labour Law and Policy Journal*, Vol. 30(4), summer 2009, pp. 740–741.

Evju, S. (ed.), *Regulating Transnational Labour in Europe: The Quandaries of Multilevel Governance,* Department of Private Law, University of Oslo. Publications Series No. 196, 2014.

European Centre for the Development of Vocational Training, *Social Dialogue and Lifelong Learning: Supporting Industrial Changes*. Results from a peer learning activity, Working paper No. 2, Thessaloniki, Cedefop, December 2008.

Ewing, K.D., 'Myth and Reality of the Right to Strike as a 'Fundamental Labour Right', *IJCLLIR*, Vol. 29(2), June 2013, pp. 145–165.

Ewing, K.D. and Hendy, J., 'The dramatic implications of Demir and Baykara', *Industrial Law Journal*, Vol. 39(1), March 2010, pp. 2–51.

Fenwick, C. and Novitz, T. (eds.), *Human Rights at Work: Perspectives on Law and Regulation*. Oxford, Hart Publishing, 2010.

Selected Bibliography

Filali Meknassi, R., *L'effectivité du droit du travail et l'aspiration au travail décent dans les pays en développement. Une grille d'analyse*, IILS (working paper), Geneva, 2007.

Fiorentino A. *et al.*, "La Jurisprudence Sociale et le Droit International: Complémentarité ou Hostilité?", *Revue de droit comparé du travail et de la sécurité sociale*, 2016/1, pp.93 and ff.

Flanagan, R.J. and Gould IV W.B. (eds.), *International Labour Standards: Globalization, trade and public policy*. Stanford University Press, 2003.

Follows, J., *Antecedents of the International Labour Organization*. Clarendon Press, Oxford, 1951.

Foreign Trade Information System, www.sice.oas.org.

Fotinopoulou Bazurko, O., 'La indemnización por daños y el accidente de trabajo marítimo', *Revista General de Derecho del Trabajo y Seguridad Social,* No. 31, July 2012.

Freedman, M. and Prassl, J. (eds.), *Viking, Laval and Beyond*, Oxford, Hart Publishing, 2014.

Fudge, J., 'Constitutional Rights, Collective Bargaining and the Supreme Court of Canada: Retreat and Reversal in the Frase Case', *Industrial Law Journal*, 2012, Vol. 41 (1), pp. 1–29.

Fuss, H., *L'OIT.* 'Ses nouveaux objectifs', *Revue des sciences économiques*, September 1948, pp. 111–124.

Gamonal, S., 'Labour Obligations in the US-Chile Free Agreement: the Illusion of Soft Law', *IJCLLIR*, Vol. 27(4), 2011, pp. 407–417.

Garcia – Muñoz Alhambra, M.A., ter Haar, B. Kun, A., 'Soft on the Inside, Hard on the Outside: An Analysis of the Legal Nature of the New Forms of International Labour Law', *IJCLLIR*, Vol. 27(4), 2011, pp. 337–363.

Gil y Gil, J.L. (ed.), *Migraciones internacionales e impacto de la crisis económica*, Lisboa, Ed. Juruá, 2013.

—— *Las reformas laborales frente a la crisis a la luz de los estándares de la OIT. Un análisis crítico desde la perspectiva internacional, nacional y comparada*, Lisboa, Ed. Juruá, 2014.

Ghébali, V-Y. and Kolb, R. (ed.), *Organisation internationale et guerre mondiale. Le cas de la Société des Nations et de l'Organisation internationale du travail pendant la seconde guerre mondiale*, Brussels, Bruylant, 2013.

Goldschmidt, R. and Strapazzon, C.L., 'La hermenéutica responsable y su papel en la protección y promoción del derecho fundamental al trabajo digno: el caso de la nueva redacción del inciso iii de la súmala 244 del tribunal superior del trabajo', *Revista general de derecho del trabajo y seguridad social*, No. 39, December 2014.

Gravel, E., Duplessis, I. and Gernigon, B., *The Committee on Freedom of Association: Its Impact over 50 years*. ILO, Geneva, 2001.

Gravel, E. and Charbonneau-Jobin, C., *The Committee of Experts on the Application of Conventions and Recommendations: Its Dynamic and Impact*, Geneva, ILO, 2003.

Gravel, E. and Delpech, Q., 'International Labour Standards: Recent Developments in Complementarity between the International and National Supervisory Systems', *ILR*, Vol. 147(4), 2008, pp. 403–415.

—— 'The Comments of the ILO's Supervisory Bodies: Usefulness in the Context of the Sanction-based Dimension of Labour Provisions in US Free Trade Agreements', ILO Research Paper No.4, Geneva, ILO, March 2013.

Greber, P.Y., *Droit international et européen de la sécurité sociale: ONU, OIT et Conseil de l'Europe*. Bâle, Helbing Lichtenhahn, 2011.

Gross, J.A. and Compa, L., *Human Rights in Labour and Employment Relations: International and Domestic Perspectives*. Cornell University Press, 2009.

Guyon Ch., *L'influence des normes supranationales sur le droit français du travail*, Paris, LexisNexis, 2015.

Haas, E.B., *Beyond the Nation-State. Functionalism and International Organization*. Stanford University Press, 1964.

—— *Human Rights and International Action: the Case of Freedom of Association*. Stanford University Press, 1970.

Hefner, L.R., 'Understanding Change in International Organizations: Globalization and Innovation in the ILO', *Van der Bilt Law Review*, 2006, Vol. 59(3), pp. 649–728.

Hendricks, F. (ed.), *Active Ageing and Labour Law. Contributions in Honour of Roger Blanpain*. Cambridge, Intersentia, 2012.

Hennion, S., Le Barbier-Le Bris, M., Del Sol, M., *Droit social européen et international*. PUF, Paris, 2010.

Hepple, B., *Labour Laws and Global Trade*. Hart Publishing, London, 2005.

—— *Rights at work: Global, European and British Perspectives*. London, Sweet and Maxwell, 2005.

—— and Veneziani, B. (eds.), *The transformation of Labour Law in Europe: A Comparative study of 15 Countries 1945–2009*. Oxford and Portland, Oregon, Hart Publishing, 2009.

——, Le Roux R. and Sciarra S. (eds.), *Laws against Strikes: The South African Experience in an International and Comparative Perspective*, Milan, Franco Angeli, 2015.

Hernández Pulido, R., *Derechos humanos fundamentales y sindicales en tiempo de las dictaduras en el cono Sur. La labor de restitución de los derechos emprendida por el Comité de libertad sindical,* Santiago de Chile, OIT, 2014.

Herzfeld Olsson, P., 'The ILO Acquits and EU Labour Law', in M. Rönnmar, *Labour Law, Fundamental Rights and Social Europe*. Oxford, Hart Publishing, 2011.

Hiessl, Ch., 'Employer-Centred Benefits and Atypical Workforce', *IJCLLIR*, Vol. 30 (1), March 2014, pp. 67–85.

Hoehtker, D. and Kott, S. (eds.), *À la rencontre de l'Europe au travail. Récits de voyages d'Albert Thomas (1920-1932)*, Paris, Editions de la Sorbonne, 2015.

Horsey, H. *Ending Forced Labour in Myanmar: Engaging a Pariah Regime*. London and New York: Routledge, 2011.

Humblet, M. and Silva, R., *Standards for the XXIst Century: Social Security*. Geneva, ILO, 2002.

Hyman, R., Dufresne, A., 'Transnational Collective Bargaining', special issue, *Comparative Journal of Industrial Relations,* Vol. 18(2), June 2012.

Selected Bibliography

ILC, *Strengthening the ILO's capacity to assist its Members' efforts to reach its objectives in the context of globalization (general discussion)*, Report of the Conference's Committee, Provisional Record No. 23, 96th Session, ILO, Geneva, 2007.

—— Report of the Director General, *Decent Work*. 87th Session, ILO, Geneva, 1999.

—— Report of the Director General, *Reducing the Decent Work Deficit: A global challenge*, 89th Session, ILO, Geneva, 2001.

—— Report of the Director General, *Working out of Poverty*, 91st Session, ILO, Geneva, 2003.

—— Report of the Director-General on the World Commission on the Social Dimension of Globalization, *A Fair Globalization: The role of the ILO*, 92nd Session, ILO, Geneva, 2004.

—— *Conditions of Work in the Fishing Sector: A comprehensive standard (a Convention supplemented by a Recommendation) on work in the fishing sector*, 92nd Session, Report V(1), ILO, Geneva, 2003.

—— *Dock Work: Social repercussions of new methods of cargo handling*, Report III (Part 1B), 90th Session, ILO, Geneva, 2002.

—— *Equality in Employment Occupation*, Report III (Part 4B), 83rd Session, ILO, Geneva, 1996.

—— *ILO Standards-related Activities in the Area of Occupational Safety and Health*, Report VI, 91st Session, ILO, Geneva, 2003.

—— *Labour Inspection*, Report III (Part 1B), 95th Session, ILO, Geneva, 2006.

—— *Protection of Wages. Standards and safeguards relating to the payment of labour remuneration*, Report III (Part 1B), 91st Session, ILO, Geneva, 2003.

—— *Hours of work, From fixed to flexibility?* 93rd Session, Report III (1B), ILO, Geneva, 2005.

—— *Eradication of forced labour*, 96th Session, Report III (1B), ILO, Geneva, 2007.

—— *Social Security for Social Justice and a Fair Globalization* (Report VI), Geneva, 100th Session, ILO, 2011.

—— *Social Security and the Rule of Law*. Report of the Committee of Experts on the Application of Conventions and Recommendations, Report III (Part 1B) 100th Session, 2011, ILO, Geneva, 2011.

—— (100th session, 2011), *Labour administration and labour inspection*, Report V, Geneva, ILO, 2011.

—— (101st Session, 2012), *Giving globalization a human face*, General Survey on the fundamental Conventions concerning rights at work in light of the ILO Declaration on Social Justice for a Fair Globalization, 2008, Report III (Part 1B), Geneva, ILO, 2012.

—— (102nd Session, 2013), *Towards the ILO Centenary: Realities, Renewal and Tripartite Commitment,* Report of the Director-General, Report 1(A), Geneva, ILO, 2013.

—— (102nd session, 2013), *Report of the Committee of Experts for the application of Conventions and Recommendations*, General report, Geneva, ILO, 2013.

—— (103rd session, 2014), *Minimum wage systems*, report III (Part 1B), Geneva, ILO, 2014. .

—— (103rd session, 2014), *Report of the Committee of Experts on the Application of Conventions and Recommendations*, Report III (Part 1A), General Report, Geneva, ILO, 2014.

—— (103rd Session, 2014), *Fair migration: Setting an ILO agenda*, Geneva, ILO, 2014.

—— *Transitioning from the informal to the formal economy*, report V (1), Geneva, ILO, 2014.

—— (104th session, 2015), *Giving a Voice to Rural Workers*, report III (Part 1 B), Geneva, ILO, 2015.

—— www.ilo.org.

—— *Freedom of Association: Digest of decisions and principles of the Freedom of Association Committee of the Governing Body of the ILO*, 5th (revised) edition, Geneva, 2006.

—— *Fundamental Rights at Work and International Labour Standards*, Geneva, 2003.

—— *Marking progress against child labour.Global estimates and trends 2000-2012*, Geneva, ILO, 2013.

—— *Investing in Child Labour: An economic study on the cost and benefits of eliminating child labour*, Geneva, 2004.

—— *The International Labour Code 1919–1951*, set of 2 volumes. Geneva, 1952.

—— *International Labour Standards: A global approach*, Geneva, 2001.

—— *International Labour Organisation: the first decade*, Geneva, 1931.

—— *Overview of global developments and Office activities concerning codes of conduct, social labelling and other private sector initiatives addressing labour issues*, GB.273/WP/SDL/1 (November 1998).

—— *The Committee on the Application of Standards ot the International Labour Conference. A dynamic and impact built of dialogue and supervision*, Geneva, 2011.

—— *Forced Labour and Human Trakkicking: Casebook of Court Decisions*, Geneva, 2009.

—— *Better jobs for better economy*, World of work report 2012, Geneva, 2012, pp. 37-57.

—— *World of Work Report 2009. The Global Crisis and beyond*, Geneva, 2009

—— *Extending the scope of application of labour laws to informal economy*, Digest of comments of the ILO's supervisory bodies related to the informal economy, Geneva, 2010.

—— *Decent Work Indicators Concepts and definitions*, Geneva, 2012.

—— World Bank, *Inventory of Policy Responses to the Financial and Economic Crisis*, Washington, World Bank, Geneva, ILO, 2012.

—— *World of Work 2014: Developing with jobs*, Geneva, 2014.

—— *World Social Protection Report 2014/15: Building economic recovery, inclusive development and social justice*, Geneva, 2014.

—— *Profits and Poverty: The Economics of Forced Labour*, Geneva, 2014.

ISSA, *Coping with the Crisis: Managing Social Security in Uncertain Times*, Geneva, 2012.

Ivanov, S.A., 'Sur les études comparatives en droit du travail', *Revue internationale de droit comparé*, No. 2, April–June 1985.

Selected Bibliography

Jansen, M. and Lee, E., *Commerce et emploi. Un défi pour la recherche en matière de politiques*. Geneva, BIT/OMT, 2007.

Javillier, J.C. and Gernigon, B. (eds.), Politakis G.P. (coordinator), *Les normes internationales du travail. Un patrimoine pour l'avenir. Mélanges en l'honneur de Nicolas Valticos*. ILO, Geneva, 2004.

Javillier, J.C., 'Pour une contribution des universitaires à la dynamique des normes internationales du travail', *Changing Industrial Relations and Modernization of Labour Law, Liber Amicorum in Honour of Professor Marco Biagi*, R. Blanpain and M. Weiss (eds.), Kluwer, The Hague, 2003.

—— 'Pragmatism and Daring in International Labour Law: Reflections of a labour lawyer'. *ILR*, Vol. 133(4), Geneva, 1994, pp. 485–500.

—— (ed.), *Governance, international law and corporate social responsibility*, IILS, Geneva, 2007.

Jenks C.W., *Law, Freedom and Welfare*. Oceana Publications, London, 1963.

—— 'The International Protection of Trade Union Rights', *The International Protection of Human Rights*, E. Luard (ed.), Thames and Hudson, London, 1967.

—— 'The Significance for International Law of the Tripartite Character of the International Labour Organization'. *Transactions of the Grotius Society*, Eastern Press, London, Vol. 22, 1937.

—— 'La compétence de l'Organisation internationale du Travail. Examen de quatre avis consultatifs rendus par la Cour permanente de Justice internationale', *Revue drt. int. et lég. comp.*, 1937, No. 1, pp. 156–183; No. 3, pp. 586–623.

—— *The International Protection of Trade Union Freedom*. Stevens, London, 1957.

—— 'The Application of International Labour Conventions by Means of Collective Agreements', *Zeitschrift für ausländisches öffentliches Recht und Völkerrecht (Heidelberg)*, Vol. 19, August 1958, pp. 197–224.

—— 'Influences économiques et sociales sur le développement du droit international', *RCADI*, 1973, Vol. 1, pp. 463–468.

—— *Human Rights, Social Justice and Peace: The Broader Significance of the ILO Experience*, Norwegian Nobel Institute, Symposium of the International Protection of Human Rights (25–27 September 1967).

Kahn-Nisser, S., 'External Governance, Convention Ratification and Monitoring: The EU, the ILO and Labour Standards in EU Accession Countries', *European Journal of Industrial Relations*, vol. 20(4), 2014, pp. 383–398.

Kang, S.L., *Human Rights and Labor Solidarity: Trade Unions in the Global Economy*. Philadelphia (PA), University of Pennsylvania Press, 2012

Kaufmann, Ch., *Globalization and Labour Rights: the Conflict between Core Labour Rights and International Economic Law*. Oxford, Hart Publishing, 2007.

Kellerson, H., 'The ILO Declaration of 1998 on Fundamental Principles and Rights: A challenge for the future', *ILR*, Vol. 137(2), Geneva, 1998, pp. 223–235.

Kern, M., Sottas, C., 'The abolition of forced or compulsory labour', *Fundamental Rights at Work and International Labours Standards*, ILO, Geneva, 2003, pp. 33–55.

—— 'Freedom of Workers: The abolition of forced or compulsory labour', *International Labour Standards: A Global Approach*. ILO, Geneva, 2001, pp. 53–74.

Korda, M, *The Role of International Social Security Standards*. Cambridge, Intersentia, 2013.

Kott, S., Droux, J. (eds.), *Globalizing Social Rights: The International Labour Organization and beyond*. Geneva, ILO, Basingstoke, Palgrave Macmillan, 2012.

Kryvoi, Y., 'The World Bank and the ILO: Two Visions of Employment Relations' in R. Blanpain and C. Grant (eds.), *Fixed-term Employment Contracts: Two Visions of Employment Regulation*, Brugge, Vanden Broele, 2009, pp. 47–58.

Kucera, D., 'Core Labour Standards and Foreign Direct Investment', *ILR*, Vol. 141, (1–2), Geneva, 2002, pp. 31–69.

La Hovary, C., *Les droits fondamentaux au travail. Origines, statut et impact en droit international*. Geneva, The Graduate Institute of International and Development Studies, 2009.

—— 'The informal economy and the ILO: A legal perspective', *IJCLLIR*, vol. 30 (4), December 2014, pp. 341–412.

—— 'A Challenging Ménage à Trois? Tripartism in the International Labour Organization', *International Organizations Law Review*, 12, 2015, pp. 204–236.

Landau, E.C. and Beigbeider, Y., *From ILO Standards to EU Law*: *The Case of Equality between Men and Women at Work*. Leiden, Martinus Nijhoff, 2008.

Langille B. 'Core labour rights – the true story (reply to Alston)', *European Journal of International Law*, Vol. 16(3), 2005, pp. 409–437.

—— 'Can We Rely on the ILO'? *Canadian Journal of Labour and Employment Law*, 2007, Vol. 13, p. 363.

—— 'Imagining Post Geneva Consensus: Labor Law for Post Washington Consensus Development', *Comparative Labor Law and Policy Journal*, Vol. 31(3), Spring 2010, pp. 323–552, followed by the comments of A. Trebilcock, pp. 553–570.

Langille, B., Davidoff, D.(eds.), *Boundaries and Frontiers of Labour Law*. Oxford, Hart Publishing, 2006.

Laronze, F., Quénaudon, R., 'Réflexions juridiques après la tragédie du Rana Plaza', *Revue de droit du travail*, no. 7/8, July-August 2013, pp. 487–480.

Lavallée, C., *La protection internationale des droits de l'enfant: entre déalisme et pragmatisme*, Brussels, Bruylant, 2015.

Lee, E., 'Globalization and Labour Standards: A review of issues', *ILR*, Vol. 136(2), Geneva, 1997, pp. 173–189.

Lee, Sangheon, McCann, D. and Messenger, J.C., *Working Time around the World*, London/New York, Routledge, 2007.

Lee, Sangheon, McCann, D. (eds.), *Regulating for Decent Work. New Directions in Labour Market Regulation*. Geneva, ILO, 2011.

Lennox, C. and Short, D. (eds.), *Handbook of Indigenous Peoples' Rights*, Abingdon, Routledge, 2015.

Lespinet-Moret, I., Viet, V. (eds.), *L'Organisation internationale du Travail. Origine. Développement. Avenir*. Rennes, Presses Universitaires de Rennes, 2011.

Liukkunen, U., Chen Yifeng, Blanpain, R. (eds.) 'China and ILO Fundamental Principles and Rights at Work', *Bulletin of Comparative Labour Relations*, No. 86, 2014, The Hague, Kluwer, 2013

Locke, R., *The Promise and Limits of Private Power: Promoting Labor Standards in the Global Economy*. Ithaca (NY), Cornell University Press, 2013.

Lokiec, P. and Robin-Olivier, S. *et al.* 'Liberalisation du commerce et justice sociale. Lectures croisées d'une étude menée conjointement par le BIT et l'OMC', *Revue de droit du travail*, No. 10, October 2007, pp. 608–615.

Lopez Morales, G., Silva, R. and Egorov, A., 'Social Security', *International Labour Standards: A global approach*. ILO, Geneva, 2001, pp. 441–484.

Louis, M., *L'Organisation internationale du travail et le travail décent. Un agenda pour le multilatéralisme*. Paris, L'Harmathan, 2011.

—— *Qu'est-ce qu'une bonne représentation? L'Organisation internationale du travail de 1919 à nos jours*, Paris, Dalloz, 2016.

Lyon-Caen, G. and A., *Droit social international et européen*. Dalloz (Précis), Paris, 8th edn, 1997.

Lyutov, N., 'The Role of the ILO in the Adoption of the New Russian Labour Code', *International Journal of Comparative Labour Law and Industrial Relations*, Vol. 19(2), 2003, pp. 163–177.

Mahaim, E., 'L'Association internationale pour la protection légale des travailleurs. Son histoire. Son but. Son œuvre', *Revue économique internationale*. Brussels, October 1904.

—— *Le droit international ouvrier*. Librairie de la Société du Recueil Sirey, Paris 1913.

—— 'L'Organisation permanente du Travail', *RCADI*, Brussels, 1924, Vol. III, pp. 69–221.

Malmberg, J., 'Enforcement of Labour Law, in Hepple B., Veneziani, B. (eds), *The Transformation of Labour Law in Europe: A Comparative Study of 15 Countries 1945–2009*. Oxford and Portland, Oregon, Hart Publishing, 2009, pp. 263–287.

Mamic, I., *Implementing Codes of Conduct: How Businesses Manage Social Performance in Global Supply Chains*. ILO, Geneva, 2004.

Marchand, D., 'Heurs et malheurs de la succession d'États aux conventions internationales du travail', *Droit social*, February 2001, pp. 153–166.

Maupain, F., 'Une révolution tranquille dans le droit des traités. L'abrogation des conventions internationales du travail obsolètes', *Annuaire français de droit international*, Vol. 42, 1996, pp. 629–635.

—— *L'interprétation des conventions internationales du travail. Mélanges en l'honneur de Nicolas Valticos*, R.-J. Dupuy (ed.), Droit et justice, Pedone, Paris, 1999, pp. 567–583.

—— *The Future of the International Labour Organization in the Global Economy*. Oxford, Hart Publishing, 2013.

Maul, D.R., *Human Rights, Development and Decolonization. The International Labour Organization, 1940–70*, London, Palgrave Macmillan, 2012.

Maydell von, B., *et al.*, *Enabling Social Europe*. Berlin, Springer, 2006.

Mayer, J., 'International Labour Standards and Technical Co-operation: the Case of special public works programmes', *ILR*, Vol. 128(2), Geneva, 1989, pp. 155–175.

—— 'The Employment Policy Convention: Scope, assessment and prospects', *ILR*, Vol. 130(3), Geneva, 1991, pp. 339–358.

Mazuyer, E., 'Labor regulation in the North American Free Trade Area: a study on the North American Agreement on Labor Cooperation', *Comparative Labor Law and Policy Journal*, 2001, Vol. 22 pp. 239–259.

—— (ed.), *Regards croisés sur la responsabilité sociale de l'entreprise*. Paris, La documentation française, 2010.

McCann, D. S. Lee et al., *Creative Labour Regulation. Indeterminacy and Protection in an Uncertain World.* Geneva, ILO, Basingstoke, Palgrave MacMillan, 2014.

McCune Lindsay, S., *The Problem of American Cooperation: The Origins of the International Labor Organization*, J.T. Shotwell (ed.), Vol. 1, Columbia University Press, New York, 1934.

McHugh, P.G., *Aboriginal Title. The Modern Jurisprudence of Tribal Land Rights.* Oxford University Press, 2011.

Meyer-Bich, P., Friboulet, J.J. and Davoine, E. (eds), *L'effectivité des normes sociales internationale dans l'activité économique*. Brussels, Bruylant, Paris, LGDJ, Zurich, Schultess, 2008.

Messenger, J.C Ghosheh, N., *Work Sharing during the Great Recession New Developments and Beyond*. Geneva, ILO, 2013.

Miné, M., *Droit des discriminations dans l'emploi et le travail,* Brussels, Larcier, 2016.

Miné, M. *et alii*, *Le droit social international et européen en pratique*. 2nd edn, Eyrolles, Paris, 2013.

Missé, H., *Le droit international du travail en Afrique. Le cas du Cameroun.* L'Harmattan, Paris, 1987.

Moira McConnell, M., Devlin, D., Doumbia-Henry, Cl., The Maritime Labour Convention, *A Legal Primer to an Emerging International Regime*, Biggleswade (United Kingdom), Brill, 2011.

Moisard, N., 'L'usage des conventions de l'OIT par la Cour européenne des droits de l'homme', *Droit social*, no 4, april 2014, pp. 365 *et seq.*

Moreau M.A., *Normes sociales, droit du travail et mondialisation. Confrontations et mutations*. Dalloz, Paris, 2006.

—— 'Travail forcé, RSE et sous-traitance dans l'industrie textile en Asie. Réflexion sur l'action de l'OIT', *Droit social*, No. 5, May 2014, pp. 413–422.

Moreau, M.-A., Rodière, P., Watt, HM (eds.), *Justice et mondialisation en droit du travail (du rôle du juge aux conflits alternatifs)*. Dalloz, Paris, 2010.

Morgenstern, F., 'Déclaration de principes tripartite de l'OIT sur les entreprises multinationales et la politique sociale. Nouveaux problèmes, nouvelles méthodes', *Journal du Droit international*, Clunet, 1983, No. 1, pp. 61–75.

Morse, D.A., *The Origin and Evolution of the ILO and its Role in the World Community*. Cornell University, Ithaca, 1969.

Muckenberger, U., 'Hybrid Global Labour Law' in R. Blanpain and F. Hendricks (eds.), *Labour Law between Change and Tradition. In Honour A. Jacobs*. The Hague, Kluwer, 2011.

Murray, J., *Transnational Labour Regulation: the ILO and EC compared*. Kluwer, The Hagve, 2002.

Nagel, S.G. and Thalamy, Ch., *Le droit international de la sécurité sociale*, Paris, PUF (Que sais-je?), 1993.

Necker, J., *De l'importance des opinions religieuses*. C. Plomteux, Liège, 1788.

Nesi, G., Nogler, L. and Pertile, M. (eds.), *Child Labour in a Globalized World: A Legal Analysis of ILO Action*. Aldershot, Ashgate, 2008.

Selected Bibliography

Nielsen, H.K., 'The concept of discrimination in ILO Convention No. 111', *International and Comparative Law Quarterly*, Vol. 43, No. 4, Oct. 1994, pp. 840–843.

Nikolaeva-Dimitrova, D., Blanpain, R. (eds.), *Seafarers'Rights in the Globalized Maritime Industry*, Bulletin of Comparative Labour Relations (Kluwer), no 75, 2010.

Novitz, T., *International and European Protection of the Right to Strike*, Oxford University Press, 2003.

OECD, www.oecd.org.

——, *International Trade and Core Labour Standards*, Paris, 2000.

—, *Ageing and Employment Policies/Vieillissement et politiques de l'emploi. Live Longer, Work Longer,* Paris, 2006.

——, 'Activating the Unemployed: What countries do?', Chapter 5, *Employment Outlook* 2007, Paris, 2007, pp. 207-241

Oechslin, J.J., *Les employeurs et les normes internationales du travail. Mélanges en l'honneur de Nicolas Valticos*, R.J. Dupuy (eds.), Droit et justice, Pedone, Paris, 1999, pp. 585–593.

Oechslin J.J. and Retournard J.F., 'International Employers' Organizations', *International Encyclopaedia for Labour Law and Industrial Relations*, R. Blanpain (ed.) (Deventer), Kluwer, 1991.

Oeltz, M., 'The ILO's Domestic Workers Convention and Recommendation: A Window of Opportunity for Social Justice', *ILR*, Vol. 143(1), 2014, pp. 143 *et seq.*

Olney, S. and Cholewinski, R., 'Migrant Workers and the Right to Non-Discrimination and Equality', in C. Castello and M. Freedland (eds.), *Migrants at work*, Oxford University Press, 2014, pp. 259–281.

Ojeda Avilés, A., *Derecho transnacional del Trabajo*. Valencia, Tirant Lo Blanch, 2013.

Orbie, J., Tortell, L. (ed.), *The European Union and the Social Dimension of Globalization: How the EU Influences the World.* London, Routledge, 2008.

— 'The New GSP+ Beneficiaries: Ticking the Box or Truly Consistent with ILO Findings', *European Foreign Affairs Review*, Vol. 14, 2009, pp. 663-681.

Pärli, K. *et al.*, *Arbeitsrecht im internationalen Kontext*, Zurich, Dike Verlag, 2016.

Pennings, F., *Between Soft and Hard Law: The Impact of International Social Security Standards on National Social Security*, The Hague, Kluwer, 2006.

Perrin G., 'Histoire du droit international de la sécurité sociale', *La sécurité sociale. Son histoire à travers les textes*, A. Barjot (ed.), Association pour l'étude de l'Histoire de la sécurité sociale, Paris, vol. V, 1993.

Pertek, J., *Coopération entre juges nationaux et Cour de justice de l'UE. Le renvoi préjudiciel*, Brussels, Bruylant, 2013.

Perulli, A., 'Fundamental Social Rights, Market Regulation and EU External Action', *IJCLLIR*, Vol. 30(1), 2014, pp. 27–47.

Philip, C., *Normes internationales du travail: universalisme ou régionalisme?* Brussels, Bruylant, 1978.

Piniella, F., Silos, J. M., Bernal, F. 'Who will give effect to the ILO's Maritime Labour Convention?', *ILR*, 2006, pp. 59–83.

Piore, M. 'Rethinking International Labor Standards' in Milberg, W. (ed.), *Labor and the Globalization of Production: Causes and Consequences of Industrial Upgrading*. Palgrave, Baskingstoke, 2004, pp. 249–264.

Plant, R., *Linking International Labour Standards with Employment and Development Concerns: Some Conceptual and Policy Issues*. Conditions of Work and Employment Programme. ILO, Geneva, 1993.

Politakis, G.P., 'The ILO and the Protection of Wages', *Labour Education*, No. 128, ILO, Geneva, 2002, pp. 1–7.

—— (ed.), *Protecting Labour Rights as Human Rights:Present and Future of International Supervision*. ILO, Geneva, 2007.

Politakis, G.P. and Markow K., 'Les recommandations internationales du travail:instruments mal exploités ou maillon faible du système normatif', in Javillier J.-C. and Gernigon B. (eds.), Politakis G.P. (coordinator). *Les normes internationales du travail. Un patrimoine pour l'avenir. Mélanges en l'honneur de Nicolas Valticos*. ILO, Geneva, 2004, pp. 497–525.

Pougoué, G., *Droit du travail et de la prévoyance sociale au Cameroun*, Rescue Afrique PUC, Paris/Yaoundé, Vol. 1, 1988.

Quénaudon, R. de, Sachs-Durand, C., 'Les principes directeurs de l'OCDE, quelle efficacité?', *Revue de droit du travail*, No. 11, november 2010, pp. 655–656.

Revue de droit comparé du travail et de la sécurité sociale, *La mise en œuvre de la Convention du travail maritime de l'OIT. Espoirs et défis*, special issue, No. 2013/2.

Ricca, S., *Introduction to Public Employment Services: A Workers' Education Manual*, ILO, Geneva, 1994.

Ritualo, A.R., Castro, C.L. and Gormly, S., 'Measuring Child Labor: Implications for policy and program design', *Comparative Labor Law & Policy Journal*, Vol. 24(2), Winter 2003, pp. 401–433.

Robin-Olivier, S., 'Politique sociale de l'Union européenne. Chronique 2013', *RTDeur*., April-June 2013.

Rodgers, G., Lee, E., Swepston, L. and and Van Daele, J., *The ILO and the Quest for Social Justice, 1919–2009*. Geneva, ILO, 2009.

Rodriguez-Piñero, M., 'The control system of the ILO international conventions and the role of the committee of expert', in N. Aliprantis and I. Papageorgiou (eds.), *Social Rights at European, Regional and International Level*. Brussels, Bruylant, 2010.

Rogowski, R., *Reflexive Labour Law in World Society*, Cheltenham, Edward Elgar, 2014.

Roman, D., 'Les droits sociaux entre "injusticiabilité" et "conditionalité." Elements pour une comparaison', *Revue internationale de droit comparé*, 2002 (2), pp. 284–314.

Rossi, A., Luinstra, A. and Pickles, J. (eds.), *Towards Better Work: Understanding Labour in Apparel Global Value Chains*, Basingstoke, Palgrave Macmillan, 2014.

Routh, S. and Borghi, V., *Workers and the Global Informal, Economy*, London and New York: Routledge, 2016.

Royle, T., 'The ILO's shift to promotional principles and the privatization of labour rights: an analysis of labour standards, voluntary self-regulation and social clauses', *International Journal of Comp. Labour Law & Industrial Relations*, Vol. 26(3), 2010, pp. 249–271.

Rubin, N., Kalula, E. and Hepple, B. (eds.), *Code of International Labour Law. Law, Practice and Jurisprudence*. Cambridge University Press, 2 vols, 2005.

Sauze, D., 'Résurgence du contrat à durée déterminée en France depuis les années 1980: une analyse à partir de la mise en perspective de la détermination de la durée des relations de travail aux 19ème et 20ème siècles', in J.-M. Dupuis, C. El Mouden, F. Gravel, I. Lebon, G. Maurau, N. Ogier, Politiques sociales et croissance, Vol. 2, 2002, Paris, L'Harmattan, pp. 107–122.

Scelle, G., *L'Organisation internationale du Travail et le BIT*. Rivière, Paris, 1930.

Schiek, D., Lawson A. (eds.), *European Union non-discrimination law and intersectionality: investigating the triangle of racial, gender and disability discrimination*. Ashgate, Farnham, 2011.

Schmitt, M., 'L'influence des conventions de l'OIT sur les jurisprudences européennes. Approche comparée en matière de négociation collective', *Revue de droit du travail*, No. 7/8, July-August 2013. pp. 513–525.

Seifert, A., 'The Still Complex Relationship between the ILO and the EU: the Example of the Anti-Discrimination Law', *Intl. J. Comp. Lab. L. & Indus. Rel.*, Vol. 29(1), March 2013, pp. 39–63.

Sen A., 'Work and Rights', *ILR*, Vol. 139(2), Geneva, 2000, pp. 119–128.

—— *Development as Freedom*. Oxford University Press, 1999.

—— *The Idea of Justice*, London, Penguin Books, Harvard University Press, 2009.

Senarclens, P. de (ed.), *Maîtriser la mondialisation. La régulation sociale internationale*. Presses de Sciences Po, Paris, 2000.

Secunda, P.M. 'An Analysis of the Treatment of Employee Pension and Wage Claims in Insolvency and Under Guarantee Schemes in OECD Countries: Comparative Law Lessons for Detroit and the United States', *Fordham Urban Law Journal*, Vol. 41, 2014 (forthcoming).

Sengenberger, W., *Globalization and Social Progress: the Role and Impact of International Labour Standards*. Friedrich-Ebert Stiftung, Bonn, 2002.

Sengenberger, W. and Campbell, D. (eds.), *International Labour Standards and Economic Interdependence*. Institut international d'études sociales, Geneva, 1994.

—— *Creating Economic Opportunities: the Role of Labour Standards in Industrial Restructuring*, International Institute for Labour Studies, Geneva, 1994.

Servais, J.M., 'Social Clause in Trade Agreements: Wishful thinking or an instrument of social progress'? *ILR*, Vol. 128, No. 4, Geneva, 1989, pp. 423–432.

—— 'The Informal Sector. Any future for labour law?' *International Journal of Comparative Labour Law and Industrial Relations*, Vol. 8(4) (Winter), 1992, pp. 299–318.

—— 'Les aspects sociaux de la libéralisation du commerce international ou la clause sociale revisitée', *Bulletin de droit comparé du travail et de la sécurité sociale*, Bordeaux, 1996, pp. 212–229.

—— *The International Labour Organization*, International Encyclopaedia of Laws, R. Blanpain (dir. de publication), Kluwer, Deventer, 3rd edn, 2011.

—— 'Labour and employment agencies: Public or private management', *Labour Law at the Crossroads: Changing Employment Relationships. Studies in honour of Benjamin Aaron*, J. Bellace et M. Rood (eds.), Kluwer, Deventer, 1997, pp. 165–181.

—— *Droits en synergie sur le travail. Éléments de droits international et comparé du travail.* Brussels, Bruylant, 1997.

—— 'Le couple travail-emploi et son évolution dans les activités de l'OIT, avec une référence spécifique au travail indépendant', *Le travail en perspectives.* A. Supiot (ed.), LGDJ, Paris, 1998.

—— 'Labour and Cross-Border Cooperation among Unions', *Transnational cooperation among Labor Unions.* M.E. Gordon and L. Turner (eds.), ILR Press, Ithaca (N.Y.), 2000, pp. 44–59.

—— 'Labour Conflicts, Courts and Social Policy. Reflections based on ILO deliberations on Decent Work', *Labour Law, Human Rights and Social Justice*, R. Blanpain (ed.), Liber Amicorum Professor Ruth Ben Israel, Kluwer, The Hague, 2001, pp. 77–88.

—— 'Universal Labour Standards and National Cultures', *Comp. Labour Law & Pol. Journal*, Vol. 26(1), fall 2004, pp. 35–54.

—— Normes internationales du travail et responsabilité sociale des entreprises», dans Ph. Auvergnon (dir. de publ.): *Quelle responsabilité sociale pour l'entreprise? Approches juridiques nationales et comparatives*, Bordeaux, Université Montesquieu-Bordeaux IV, (Comptrasec), 2005, pp. 37-58.

—— 'ILO Law and the Right to Strike', *The Canadian Labour and Employment Law Journal*, Vol. 15(2), 2010, pp. 147–163.

—— 'L'incontournable besoin d'une agence de régulation sociale', *Revue de droit du travail*, No. 10, October 2012, pp. 530-533.

—— *International Social Security Law* in W. van Eeckhoutte (ed.), *International Encyclopaedia for Social Security Law*. The Hague, Kluwer, 2013.

Shelton, D. (ed.), *Commitment and Compliance. The Role of Non-Binding Norms in the International legal System.* Oxford University Press, 2000.

Sheppard, C. 'Mapping anti-discrimination law onto inequality at work: Expanding the meaning of equality in international labour law', *ILR*, Vol. 151(1-2), 2012.

Shotwell, J.T. (ed.), *The Origins of the International Labor Organization*, Columbia University Press, New York (2 vols), 1934.

Spyroupoulos G., 'Encadrement social de la mondialisation de l'économie. Bilan et perspectives d'avenir de l'action normative au niveau international dans le domaine du travail', *Droit social*, No. 6, 1996, pp. 551–561.

Standing, G. 'The ILO: An Agency for Globalization'? *Development and Change*, Vol. 39(3), 2008, pp. 355–384.

Supiot, A. *L'esprit de Philadelphie. La justice sociale face au marché total.* Paris, Le Seuil, 2010.

—— (ed.), *La solidarité. Enquête sur un principe juridique*, Paris, Odile Jacob, 2015.

—— 'The position of social security in the system of international labor standards'. *Comparative Labor Law & Policy Journal*, Vol. 27(2), 2006, pp. 113–121.

—— 'Towards an international social order? Preliminary observations on the "new regulations" in work, employment and social protection', in P. Auer and Chr. Daniel, *The Future of Work, Employment and Social Protection.* Geneva, ILO, 2002, pp. 115–138.

Selected Bibliography

Swepston, L., 'Supervision of ILO Standards', *International Journal of Comparative Labour Law and Industrial Relations*, Vol. 13(4), Winter 1997, pp. 327–344.

—— 'International Labour Law', *Comparative Labour Law and Industrial Relations in Industrialized Market Economies*, R. Blanpain, C. Engels (eds.), 10th (revised) edition. Kluwer, The Hague, 2010, pp. 141 *et seq.*

Tajgman, D., *Employment Relations and Labour Law in the Dar-es-Salaam Informal Sector*, Working paper DP INF./WP.5, ILO, Geneva, 1996.

ter Haar, B., Keune, M., 'One step forward or more window-dressing? A legal analysis of recent CSR initiatives in the garment industry in Bangladesh', *Intern. Journal Comp. Labour Law Ind. Rel.*, Vol. 30(1), March 2014, pp. 5-25.

Teyssié, B., (ed.), *La norme transnationale et les relations de travail*, Paris, Ed. Panthéon-Assas, 2014.

Thirkell, J., Scase, R. and Vickerstaff, S. (eds.), *Labour Relations and Political Change in Eastern Europe: A Comparative Perspective*. University College, London, 1995.

Tikriti, A.K., *Tripartism and the International Labour Organization. A Study of the Legal Concept: Its Origins, Function and Evolution in the Law of Nations*. Stockholm, Almqvist and Wiksell International, 1982.

Thomas, C., 'Information Sources and Measures of International Labor Standards on Employment Discrimination', *Comparative Labor Law & Policy Journal*, Vol. 24(2), Winter 2003, pp. 365–400.

Thouvenin, J.M., Trebilcock, A. (eds.), *Droit international social,* 2 volumes, Brusseles, Bruylant, 2013.

Tockman V. 'The informal economy, insecurity and social cohesion in Latin America', *ILR*, Vol. 146(1–2), 2007.

Toselli, C.T., 'Aplicación de las normas de la OIT en los juicios del trabajo', *Revista venezolana de legislación y jurisprudencia*, No. 2013, pp. 271–289.

Troclet, L.E., *Législation sociale internationale*, Librairie Encyclopédique, Brussels, 1952.

United States Trade Representative. www.ustr.gov.

Valticos N., 'Social conditions, equitable competition and trade', *World interdependence and economic co-operation among developing countries, North-South Dialogue* (Geneva, Centre d'études pratiques de la négociation internationale), Autumn 1981, pp. 49–60.

—— 'Contrat – Convention – Traité – Loi? Les conventions internationales du travail', *Revue des sciences morales et politiques*, 1996, pp. 403–413.

—— 'Un système de contrôle international: la mise en œuvre des conventions internationales du travail', *RCADI*, The Hague, Vol. I, 1968, pp. 315–407.

—— 'Les méthodes de la protection internationale de la liberté syndicale', *RCADI* (Leiden), A.W. Sijthoff, 1976, Vol. I, pp. 77–138.

—— 'L'inspection internationale dans le droit international du travail', *L'inspection internationale*. Bruylant, Brussels, 1976.

—— *Droit international du travail*. Dalloz, Paris, 2nd edition, 1983.

Valticos N. and von Potobsky G.W., *International Labour Law. International Encyclopaedia for Labour Law and Industrial Relations*, R. Blanpain (ed.), Kluwer, The Hague, 1995 (2nd Edition).

Van Daele, J., Rodríguez García, M., Van Goethem, G., van der Linden, M. (eds), *ILO Histories. Essays on the International Labour Organization and Its Impact on the World during the Twentieth Century*. Peter Lang, Berne, 2010

Vandamme, F., 'Les normes internationales du travail de l'Organisation internationale du Travail: musée ou phares de la politique sociale internationale'? *Journal des tribunaux du travail*, Brussels, No. 624, 20 September, 1995, pp. 329–334.

van Eck, S., 'Employment Agencies: International Norms and Developments in South Africa', *IJCLLIR*, Vol. 28(1), 2012, pp. 29-44.

——'Revisiting Agency Work in Namibia and South Africa: Any lessons from the Decent Work Agenda and the Flexicurity Approach?', *IJCLLIR*, vol. 30(1), march 2014, pp. 49-66.

van Langendonck, J., *Verfassung, Theorie und Praxis des Sozialstaats, Festschrift für Hans F. Zacher zum 70. Geburtstag* (F. Ruland, B.von Maydell, Papier ed., C. F. Müller Verlag, Heidelberg, 1998), pp. 477–488.

Vannes, V., *Le droit de grève. Principe de proportionnalité. Droit international, européen et national*. Brussels, Larcier, 2013.

Verdier, J.M., 'Débat sur le droit de grève à la Conférence internationale du Travail', *Droit social*, No. 12, December 1994, pp. 968–971.

—— 'La déclaration de l'Organisation internationale du travail de juin 1998: Complémentarité de la promotion et du contrôle du respect des droits fondamentaux au travail, In *De tous les horizons. Mélanges Xavier Blanc-Jouvan*. Société de législation comparée, Paris, 2005, pp. 403–412.

Verge, P. (ed.), *Droit international du travail. Perspectives canadiennes*, Cowansville, Ed. Yvon Blais, 2010.

Verge, P., Trudeau, G. and Vallée, G., *Le droit du travail par ses sources*. Editions Themis, Montréal, 2006.

Villanueva, F., 'La définition du niveau de négociation collective au pérou: un processus singulier d'appropriation des décisions du Comitéde la liberté syndicale de l'OIT par le Tribunal constitutionnel', *Revue de droit comparé du travail et de la sécurité sociale*, 2016/1, pp. 70–83.

Villasmil Prieto, H. and Torres De León, V., *Estudio de Derecho internacional del trabajo. En homenaje al Prof. Dr.Rolando Murgas Torrazza*. Panama, Academia panameña de derecho del trabajo, 2012.

Vogel-Polsky, B., *Du tripartisme à l'Organisation internationale du Travail*. Ed. de l'Institut de sociologie de l'Université Libre de Bruxelles, Brussels, 1966.

von Potobsky, G.W.., 'Eficacia jurídica de los convenios de la OIT en el plano nacional', In Javillier, J.-C. and Gernigon, B. (eds.), *Les normes internationales du travail: un patrimoine pour l'avenir. Mélanges en l'honneur de Nicolas Valticos*. ILO, Geneva, 2004, pp. 287–305.

—— 'El devenir de las normas internacionales del trabajo', *Revista de Derecho Social – Latinoamérica* (Buenos Aires), No. 3 – 2007.

—— 'On-the-spot Visit: An Important Cog in the ILO's Supervisory Machinery', *ILR*, Vol. 120(5), Geneva, 1981, pp. 581–596.

von Potobsky, G.W., and Bartolomei de la Cruz, H.G., *La Organización Internacional del Trabajo*. Ed. Astrea, Buenos Aires, 1990.

Vosko, L., *Managing the Margins:Gender, Citizenship and International Regulation of Precarious Employment*. New York (NY), Oxford University Press, 2010.

Weisband, E., 'Discursive Multilateralism, Global Benchmarks, Shame and Learning in the ILO Labor Standards Monitoring Regime', *International Studies Quarterly*, Vol. 44, 2000, pp. 643–666.

Weiss, Th. G., Carayannis, T., Emmerij, L. *et al.*, *UN Voices: the Struggle for Development and Social Justice*. Bloomington, Indiana University Press, 2005.

Wells, D., 'Best Practices in the Regulation of International Labor Standards: Lessons from Cambodia Textile Agreement', *Comp. Labor Law & Policy Journal*, Vol. 27(3), 2006, pp. 357-376.

Winterton, J., 'Building Social Dialogue over Training and Learning: European and National Developments', *European Journal of Industrial Relations*, Vol. 13(3), 2007, pp. 281-300.

Wisskirchen, A., 'Die normensetzende und normenüberwachende Tätigkeit der Internationalen Arbeitsorganisation (IAO)', *Zeitschrift für Arbeitsrecht*, Vol. 34(4), Oct.–Dec. 2003, pp. 691–733.

—— 'The standard-setting and monitoring activity of the ILO: Legal questions and practical experience', *ILR*, Vol. 144(3), 2005, pp. 253–289.

Wisskirchen, A. and Hess C., *Employers' Handbook on ILO Standards-Related Activities*. ILO, Geneva, 2002.

Wolf, F., 'L'interdépendance des conventions internationales du travail', *RCADI*, 1967-II, pp. 117–217.

Wood J., 'International Labour Organization Conventions – Labour Code or Treaties?', *International and Comparative Law Quaterly*, Vol. 40(3), July 1991, pp. 649–657.

Yemin E., *Legislative Powers in the United Nations and Specialized Agencies*. A.W. Sijthoff, Leiden, 1969.

Yépez del Castillo I., *Les syndicats à l'heure de la précarisation de l'emploi*. Academia-L'Harmattan, Louvain-la-Neuve, 1993.

Index

The numbers given refer to paragraphs

Index

Index

Index

Index

www.ingramcontent.com/pod-product-compliance
Lightning Source LLC
Chambersburg PA
CBHW071413230926
51846CB00001B/73
9789041189097